A Useable Past

~~~

Volume 3: Class Conflict and Co-operation in 19th and 20th Century Britain.
Education for Association: Re-Membering for a New Moral World

A Useable Past

A History of Association, Co-operation, and un-Statist
Socialism in 19th and Early 20th Century Britain.
In 3 volumes.

~~~

Volume 3: Class Conflict and Co-operation
in 19th and 20th Century Britain.
Education for Association: Re-Membering for a
New Moral World

Stephen Yeo

Historian, University of Sussex, 1966–1989;
Principal of Ruskin College, Oxford, 1989–1997;
Chair of the Co-operative College and then the
Co-operative Heritage Trust, 1999–2015

EER
Edward Everett Root, Publishers, Brighton, 2025

EER
Edward Everett Root, Publishers, Co. Ltd.
3rd Floor, 15 West Street, Brighton, Sussex, BN1 2RE, England

www.eerpublishing.com
edwardeverettroot@yahoo.co.uk

First published in Great Britain in 2024

© Stephen Yeo, 2024

This edition © Edward Everett Root Publishers 2025

ISBN 9781915115720 paperback
ISBN 9781911204619 hardback
ISBN 9781911204848 eBook

Stephen Yeo has asserted his right to be identified as the author of this Work in accordance with the Copyright, Designs and Patents Act 1988 as the owner of this Work.

All rights reserved. No part of this publication may be reproduced, stored in a retrieval system or transmitted in any form or by any means, electronic, mechanical, photocopying, recording or otherwise, without the prior permission of the copyright owner.

Front-cover image by John Cooke; used with permission

Design and typesetting by Pageset Ltd, High Wycombe, Buckinghamshire

The three volumes in this set are

Volume 1. *Victorian Agitator*
George Jacob Holyoake:
Co-operation as this 'New Order of Life'

Volume 2. *A New Life*
The Religion of Socialism in Britain 1883–1896:
Alternatives to State Socialism

Volume 3. *Class Conflict and Co-operation*
in 19th and 20th Century Britain.
Education for Association: Re-Membering for a New Moral World

For any of the c. one billion members in any of the c. three million co-operatives world-wide who continue to affiliate to the International Co-operative Alliance (ICA) and continue to be inspired by the Rochdale Pioneers of the 1840s, to 'arrange the powers of production, distribution, government and education' for ourselves.

And for John Spiers, publisher extraordinary, who, disagreeing and agreeing with my ideas and commitments ever since my – and his – first tutorial at the University of Sussex in 1967, still works to make them widely available.

Contents

Preface and acknowledgements   1

1. Rival clusters of potential: a way of seeing competition *versus* co-operation   10

2. State, class, and associational forms in Britain: conflict and struggle from *c.* 1850   20

3. Working-class association, private capital, welfare, and the State in the late nineteenth and twentieth centuries   53

4. Who was J. T. W. Mitchell?   90

5. Towards a co-operative university   157

6. Co-operation, mutuality, and the democratic deficit – or re-membering democracy   180

7. Theorising co-operative studies: obstacles and opportunities for twenty-first century co-operative and mutual enterprises   232

8. Towards co-operative politics: using early to generate late socialism   278

NOTES AND REFERENCES   307

INDEX   378

Preface

This is the third and final volume of *A Useable Past*, assembled from a lifetime of taking part in, writing, and imagining the history, the presence, and the future possibilities of the co-operative movement in Britain and across the world. It will be clear to readers of Volumes 1 (2017) and 2 (2018) that I see co-operation and mutuality as the fundamentals of associational socialisms in our own deeply troubled, grossly unequal, less than democratic, and far from peaceful global times.

I say socialisms in the plural because, as with capitalisms and as with states of society and societies of states in general, to think of socialism as incorrigibly plural could help to generate micro-interventions from below. Bodies – federal forms of organisation as complex systems – composed of such live cells could enable the macro (revolutionary) changes which are now needed if we are to give human life on Earth a chance of survival in anything like democratic ways.

General theories about singular, 'scientific' understandings of 'society' and its -isms ('keys to all mythologies', as George Eliot expressed it) could help. Of course. But so can 'branch reports': accounts of actually existing movements or presences with futurity (kinetic energy) alive in them; prefigurative associational forms; and accounts of transformed places and times – including their defeats, inevitable within limited human life-spans. In William Morris's *A Dream of John Ball* (1888), men fight and lose the battle, and the thing that they fought for comes about in spite of their defeat, and when it comes turns out not to be what they meant, and other men have to fight for what they meant under another name.

The narrator ('Guest') in Morris's masterpiece *News from Nowhere* (1890) – the 1892 Kelmscott edition of which is again in print – begins by losing his temper. Returning home after a disputatious branch meeting of the Socialist League, he had forgotten the points that he had longed to make to fellow members. There had been 'six persons present and consequently six sections of the party represented, four of which had strong but divergent Anarchist opinions'. He muses 'discontentedly and unhappily' before going to bed – to be visited by his 'vision not a dream' of a socialist society in microcosm. 'If I could but see a day of it,' he says to himself, 'if I could but see it …'. *News from Nowhere* tells how he does see it, in vivid detail and with key objections argued through.

*

For most of my writing life, my bent has been towards interventions of a shorter kind than monographs. For example, pamphlets, articles, and essays, not always produced for mainstream academic publications. Books have been edited by friends, practitioners, and scholars of co-operation and mutuality. With advancing age, I have increasingly wanted to gather together such interventions, in case they can be of future use.

Hence this third volume of *A USEABLE PAST*, which, like the second volume, consists of previously published pieces, now lightly revised and re-edited, and arranged here in a sequence of eight chapters. There is overlap, repetition, and anachronism within and between these chapters, for example in quotations and references. But coherence too, I hope. Catherine Robinson my editor, Gillian Lonergan my indexer, and Timothy Ashplant my friend have identified many of these: delete, delete! But I decided to retain some of this untidiness, knowing that readers will seek out those chapters that chime with or challenge their own work or enthusiasms, rather than reading from page 1 to The End.

The run of the argument in this volume begins in Chapter 1 with a *way of seeing* co-operative and mutual association as labour's own capital, necessarily opposed both to, and by, capitalist and statist formations. In Chapter 2 I then use this way of seeing to attempt an overview of the class *conflict* and conscious *struggle* between state, class, and 'associational' forms in Britain from c. 1850 onwards. Chapter 3 highlights the conflict between Friendly Societies and private industrial insurance companies over the form that National Insurance was to take in 1911, as an early step towards the Welfare State of thirty years later. In Chapter 4, I look closely at the life and aspirations of J. T. W. Mitchell, the working-class 'business genius', as Beatrice Webb described him, who was responsible for leading the Co-operative Wholesale Society in its formative days. Chapter 5 changes register and moves to the recent past, when the Co-operative College, under the leadership of Cilla Ross, was putting on the agenda an idea whose time will surely come – the idea of a Co-operative University. Chapters 6 and 7 develop a keynote address and seminar which Ian MacPherson invited me to give at an international conference hosted by the Institute for Co-operative Studies at the University of British Columbia in 2003. The Institute aimed 'to encourage the development of Co-operative Studies as an interdisciplinary, international field of enquiry'. My spoken talk and published paper form the basis of these two chapters. Chapter 6 suggests the contribution which co-operation and mutuality, both as ideas and as actually existing co-ops and mutual associations, could make to 're-membering', and thereby reducing, the West's yawning democratic deficit. Chapter 7 begins the task of theorising Co-operative Studies by identifying some obstacles and opportunities for 21st-century Co-operative and Mutual Enterprises (CMEs). Finally, Chapter 8 goes back to 'early', mostly Owenite, associational socialisms to suggest ways in which they might contribute to 'late' (too late?) associational socialism in our own times (apocalyptic, like their own).

*

Chapter 1 first appeared in Stephen Yeo (ed.) *New Views of Co-operation* (London and New York: Routledge, 1988), pp. 1-9;

Chapter 2 in Philip Corrigan (ed.) *Capitalism, State Formation and Marxist Theory: Historical Investigations* (London and New York: Quartet, 1980), pp. 111-14;

and Chapter 3 in M. Rustin and N. Parry (eds.) *Social Work and the State* (London: Arnold, 1979), pp. 48-71.

Chapter 4 was first published as *Who was J. T. W. Mitchell?* (New Century House, Manchester: CWS Membership Services, 1995), pp. 1-93.

Chapter 5 first appeared in Tom Woodin (ed.) *Co-operation, Learning and Co-operative Values: Contemporary Issues in Education* (London: Routledge, 2015) pp. 131-146;

Chapters 6 and 7 in Ian MacPherson and Erin Mclaughlin

(eds.) *Integrating Diversities within a Complex Heritage: Essays in the Field of Co-operative Studies* (University of Victoria, Canada: New Rochdale Press, British Columbia Institute for Co-operative Studies, 2008), pp. 223-276 and 345-389;

and Chapter 8 in the *Journal of Co-operative Studies*, Vol. 42:3 number 127 (2009), pp. 22-35.

*

I would like to have kept up with recent books, articles, and doctoral theses from many different countries and universities on the subjects that this volume explores. In the last few years there has been a renewed scholarly interest in the socialisms of the 1890s and the early years of the present century. In relation to gender, the work of women scholars and students who created the feminist revolution in social history has been very strong; mine, like the social movements on which I have focused here, is comparatively deficient in this regard. I must also own up to the insularity, the Britishness, of my own work. The breadth and depth of past and current organisations and theories of co-operation and mutuality from African, Asian, North American, and South American countries are well documented by other scholars and practitioners. I have left it too late for an ageing body and brain to re-tool. In a word, I am out of date as far as recent scholarship is concerned.

Insularity was strikingly not true of the work that Ian MacPherson drew together in the book from which Chapters 6 and 7 have been developed. *Integrating Diversities within a Complex Heritage; Essays in the Field of Co-operative Studies* (British Columbia Institute for Co-operative Studies, New Rochdale Press, 2008) was global in its reach and grasp, as were all the many publications of the BCICS. Daniel Cote,

Roger Spear, Mirta Vuotto, Gabor G. Szabo, Madhave Madane, Rita Rhodes, Leslie Brown, Viola Winstanley, Brett Fairbairn, the staff of the Centre for Co-operative Studies at the University of Cork, Panu Kalmi, Jean-Francois Draperi, and Ian MacPherson himself have all worked within a global framework.

But, but ... owing to tensions at the highest managerial level between creative, developmental 'Centres', disciplinary and cross-disciplinary Departments, and top (down) money-led University Management during the last twenty years, scores of radical university units in 'the West' have simply been closed down or 'rationalised'. It is now difficult or impossible to buy many of the publications of the BCICS, including *Integrating Diversities,* or even to read them online. The Institute itself was under attack well before Ian MacPherson's death in 2013. I can trace only a handful of libraries which hold *Integrating Diversities,* mostly in Canada and not even including copyright libraries in Britain.

I have worked in the belief that there is something absolute about the value of fully co-operative and mutual presences sustained by working people in and against capitalisms and their state formations all over the world, and informed by a sense of class not as sociological classification, but as material, future possibility: what J. S. Mill called 'futurity'. Such absolutes cannot be re-membered or honoured enough, inside or outside the academy.

Acknowledgements

I owe thanks to many people for enabling me to persist with my own associational preoccupations for so long.

First to Eileen Janes-Yeo for years of joint working, writing, teaching and bringing up Jake and Ben together. We shared generations of students and friends at the

University of Sussex. Some of these students and colleagues came together in a tribute to Professor John F. C. Harrison in *New Views of Co-operation* (Routledge, 1988). Thanks are due to Andy Durr, Robin Thornes, Peter Gurney, Mick Reed, Keith Harding, Alistair Thomson, Gill Scott, Sally Mullen, Lawrence Magnanie, and Neil Killingback – each of them with subsequent, creative trajectories of their own. I also particularly thank Robin Thornes, Stephen Humphries, and Philip Gardener among successive generations of research students from whom we learned in the MA course that we taught: *'Keywords and Concepts in Social History, Social History in Keywords and Concepts'*. In the jointly edited *Popular Culture and Class Conflict 1590–1914: Explorations in the History of Labour and Leisure* (1981), dedicated to Asa Briggs, many of the chapters, by Keith Wrightson, Arnold Rattenbury, Vic Gammon, Anthony Delves, Alun Howkins, Penelope Summerfield, and Timothy Ashplant – and the conference and ideas from which the book was drawn – owed much to the (then) radical new Sussex curriculum which liberated so many people to think about knowledge and its juxtapositions in new ways.

I owe a great deal to the friendship, inspiration, and encouragement of fellow travellers. Prominent among these is Ken Worpole, *animateur* and co-instigator of the Federation of Worker Writers and Community Publishers (FWWCP), in which Brighton's QueenSpark Books was an early participant; also Ruskin College students, particularly Sean Gibson and John Bell; co-operators in and beyond the Co-operative College in Manchester when it was led by Mervyn Wilson and Cilla Ross; the Midcounties Co-operative Society which grew out of Oxford, Swindon and Gloucester Co-operative Society, led by Bob Burlton and his successors; Co-operative Futures, led by Peter Couchman and Jo White from the year 2000 onwards; Co-ops UK, led by Pauline Green and Ed Mayo; the Co-operative Group when it was led by Sir Graham Melmoth; the Centre for Civil Society at the London School of Economics and its Mutuality Network, led by Helmut Anheier and Nicholas Deakin; historians and other thinkers in the Society for Co-operative Studies and its Journal; Gillian Lonergan, legendary Librarian for the Co-operative College and National Co-operative Archive in Holyoake House Manchester (and indexer supreme); and my first fellow Trustees of the Co-operative Heritage Trust and Pioneers Museum in Rochdale, re-energised in the early years of the present century in beautifully restored and extended form, thanks to funding from the National Lottery Heritage Trust, and the Co-operative Group.

Over many years Rob Colls, Robin Murray, Pat Conaty, and Philip Corrigan persistently refused to let me leave my work on associational socialism unfinished. It still is: but what friends to have had! Finally, without Ursula Howard's daily encouragement, solidarity, energy, and love in every sphere of life, I would have given up writing prose and poetry years ago.

Co-operative Studies are, of course, peopled and practised as well as published. Within living memory, a window in the central store of the Liverpool Co-operative Society displayed two sets of decorative tiles. One proclaimed 'Liberty, Equality, Fraternity'; the other said 'Boot Repairs'. An early saying within the Royal Arsenal Co-operative Society Education Department affirmed 'We are eating our way into the future'. During the nearly thirty years that Ursula and I have lived five minutes' walk from the Eynsham Village Store, an Oxfordshire branch of Midcounties Co-operative, there have been dedicated teams, particularly Cheryl, Kay, Sarah, and now Mary, who have had a smile, and more, for every shopper. Such co-operators keep the shelves stacked, ask after our welfare, ask everyone for their Member's Card (to make sure we get the dividend), ask 'Have you done your Members' Survey yet?', and explain to customers how to join the Society if they have not already done so. Such 'associates' keep the tills going as well as keeping the visions alive – pandemic or no pandemic.

Thank you!

1. Rival clusters of potential: a way of seeing competition *versus* co-operation

Association (as, for instance, in co-operatives and in the co-operative movement itself) may be regarded as labour's own capital. It may be seen as what, in the end, constitutes labour's power: what labour has to work with and to work for – free association.

Indeed, as more and more people are deprived of ownership and control over the dominant means of producing and exchanging in modern societies, association may even become all that labour has left. For those who 'only have their labour force to depend on', 'social combinations' have been a unique opportunity for struggle on their own behalf, and therefore also a particular site for struggle against them on behalf of superior interests.[1] Class conflict within and against co-operatives is a major theme in all the chapters of this book. 'Every-one who had nothing brought it together and it made a lot'; 'the mighty power of the million pence;'[2] 'make yourselves powerful by your united strength if you cannot be powerful by your separate strength'.[3] Getting together, union, combination, co-operation, association ... all may be seen as part of the power inherent in (human) labour power, potentially usable for itself, for labour, as well as being a matter for deliberate organisation on capital's behalf in the era of large-scale industry.

Co-operators in Britain have known about this for two hundred years. In a speech at the Co-operative Union Congress of 1894, Catherine Webb spoke of 'association' alongside 'machinery' as the 'modern methods of production' needing to be applied to women's domestic work. The vision of the main body of the movement has been that through associations for exchange (co-operative societies/stores) members would use what they produced and produce what they used, making capital into a hired servant of theirs,rather than their continuing as hired servants of capital. In their living critique of competition, which they saw as a cancer on the body politic, they favoured the language of 'association'.[4] Among their journals of the 1820s was one called *The Associate*. The subtitle of *The Co-operative News* from 1886 onwards was *and Journal of Associated Industry*. The CWS magazine, *The Millgate Monthly*, founded in 1905, was to be 'A Popular Magazine devoted to Association, Education, Literature and General Amusement'. 'Is it not true to say', asked T. W. Mercer in 1920, 'that whereas members of the Labour Party are collectivists, co-operators are associationists.'[5] Their favourite slogan was 'each for all and all for each'.

> The Co-operative ideal may be expressed thus: – by means of mutual association to eliminate the present competitive industrial system, and to substitute mutual Co-operation for the common good as the basis of all human society ... by the principle of service for service, the instinct of self-interest is made to promote the common good.[6]

CWS own-brand seeds were called 'One and All'. Through co-operative membership, members would unite capital and labour, and producers and consumers, in a single (their own) body: members one of another. Or, as expressed by the first two principles agreed at a co-operative conference in Rochdale in 1855 (recorded by George Jacob Holyoake in his *Self-help by the People: The History of the Rochdale Pioneers*),

> I. That human society is a body consisting of many members, the real interests of which are identical.
> II. That true workmen should be fellow workers.

'This is the simple difference between competitive and co-operative production and trading', explained a piece (probably written by Dr John Watts) in the CWS *Almanac and Diary* for 1881: 'under competition everyone strives to benefit himself alone, whilst under co-operation everyone works for the common good'. The whole was the precondition of the health of the part: as Brighton co-operators expressed it in the late 1820s, members should 'never eat or drink ... wear or consume any article the profit of which goes to enrich any single individual, if such an article can be procured of any society where the whole receive the equal benefit'. The Co-operative Wholesale Society was a direct continuation of this commitment to 'equal benefit' well into the twentieth century. *The Wheatsheaf* (the CWS journal launched in 1896) explained its name to readers in July 1900:

> The essential part performed in our life by wheat symbolises the importance of Co-operative principles. The inability of the grain to stand upright unless bound up with its fellows illustrates the power of association.

Pulling capital back into their own hands – money, machines, knowledge, organisation – has been the project for which working-class co-operators have sought adequate language, adequate activity, adequate associational forms. Language, as always, was indicative. Key words like 'profit' and 'consumers' went into inverted commas because in a co-operative context they meant something different. 'Profits as understood by the ordinary economist have no existence in the co-operative movement'; 'the real reason why the control of industry, as regards the owning and managing of factories, should be in the hands of the "consumers" is because they are ultimately *the whole community*, and they work for the interest of all'[7] (my emphasis). The phrase for the Pioneers' 'world-making' project was a more active one than 'nationalizing the means'. It was 'arranging the powers', 'powers of production, distribution, education and government'.[8] This project involved finding forms of association which did without masters, an independence which stuck in the gullet of many would-be patrons of the co-operative movement all through the second half of the nineteenth century: 'the working class', as Holyoake explained, in their defence, in his *History of the Rochdale Pioneers*, 'are not considered to be very rich in the quality of self-trust, or mutual trust. The business habit is not thought to be their forte. The art of creating a large concern, and governing all its complications, is not usually supposed to belong to them.' Working-class co-operators experienced relations of production as integrated with the forces thereof, but also as imbricated in wider social or less-than-social relations. They therefore sought to transform them, as a whole, from competition to Co-operation through deliberate, conscious construction, towards a commonwealth or 'close community'.[9] 'Association', in Holyoake's view, was 'a moral art as well as a new form of economy'.[10]

'They had the power of organisation and understood the requirements of their fellow men.'[11] In the co-operative movement in the nineteenth century and early twentieth century in Britain, it sometimes seemed so simple. They had the power of association. Legal rights might be a problem. Much of what they did was, in the first instance, illegal. The Rochdale Pioneers had a long struggle with Tidd Pratt, the responsible Registrar under the Industrial and Provident Society Acts, over the illegality of setting aside funds for educational purposes.[12] But legislation seemed, as it came, to confirm their capacities rather than to deny them. It thus appeared transparent, rational, and progressive, that large-scale co-operation was the future form, and competition the past. 'The members have now a great lever within their reach', 'the complete emancipation of the workers of this country is assured'.[13] A truly social economy would, because it could, replace the existing political one. This social economy would recuperate some of the characteristics of an older, moral economy. It was already available: 'the alternative society does exist': it took the form of flour mills, for instance, as well as ideas.[14] In the phrase of an Owenite author of a series of 'Letters on Associated Labour' in 1834, they had resolved 'to constitute the society for which we work'.[15] And because of the inventiveness of their resolution, expressed in clock towers as well as on bits of paper, in jubilee teapots as well as in mid-town buildings which dwarfed town halls, in Congresses and 'Parliaments of Labour', as well as in packets of biscuits, its potential was attacked. The attacks came as conflicts from within – as they are bound to do in a movement of any size – as well as in the form of struggle by hostile interests from outside.

For at least three hundred years in Britain there has been manifest conflict over associational form, private ('economic') conflict as well as public ('political') conflict. The question for capital and for labour has been: how can dominant forms of association – factories, schools, entertainments, as well as 'voluntary associations' like sects, co-ops, unions –

how can such forms be contrived so that they work in *our* interests more than *theirs*? This may sound like a crude way of putting it. In practice, however, it has rarely been a matter of either/or – either capital's or labour's interests – but of both, to differing degrees, and within the same associations. The most interesting associations, such as unions and co-operative societies, have been sites of (class) conflict rather than unambiguous instruments of either side. It has also only rarely been a matter of explicit intention, conspiracy, or conscious struggle, on either side. But there have been two tendencies in conflict, two opposed clusters of potential. And one of the interesting things about co-operators which will become evident in this book has been the extent to which they articulated them as such.

The chapters that follow will point towards working-class potential – potential for the material development of labour as a class for itself, able to construct (or so many people thought) a whole 'society' – embodied in a wide and linked array of associational forms, and strong by the turn of the nineteenth and twentieth centuries. This potential was even located in the most 'basic' area of all: that of material production. One estimate has it that co-operative production was at its strongest in relation to the rest of the economy *circa* 1905.[16] Certainly the movement was very large by then, with a million members nation-wide, and with the Co-operative Wholesale Society constituting one of the largest businesses in the world. It was early in the twentieth century that W. H. Lever, for instance, became most concerned about the CWS's soap works at Irlam, Silvertown, and Dunston-on-Tyne. He took legal action against the refusal of co-operative societies to stock Sunlight Soap, in the Taff Vale of the co-operative movement.[17] Concern at labour's potential power, by private capital and by government and State servants, continues into twenty-first-century Britain. 'Socialism' continues as bogey, more powerfully than as belief.

Having indicated potential-for-labour, however, and writing during the first quarter of the twenty-first century, it is also necessary to emphasise the dissipation of labour's potential, at least at a national level, its non-realisation, even destruction. In a prolonged and general crisis which is still with us, but which was at its most acute between about 1870 and 1930, capital undertook a broadly successful vaccination programme against labour's associational presence. This programme has not been easy to discern, let alone to interpret. It was carried out by would-be friends (for instance in the Labour Party) as well as by obvious enemies, by class warriors (from above) as well as by gentler folk who dislike the language of class, preferring, for instance, the language of 'community'. Bodies and antibodies fought over visions as well as over practical facts, dreams as well as numbers: reinterpreting impulses so that they returned unrecognisable to those whose energy they had once been essential. Thomas Rigby, co-operator, author of Bury Co-operative Society's Jubilee History in 1905, had a vision of 'the general transference of the spirit of association from a political into an industrial form'. For him there was a time to 'look forward to ... when all distinctions, except those of merit and high attainment in the cause of progress, shall be abolished'.[18] This was in line with J. T. W. Mitchell's commitment to human equality as Chairman of the CWS from 1878 to 1895.[19] It was also in line with the revolutionary side of Samuel Smiles's vision, in his book on *Character* (1871), that 'all men might become what some men are'.[20] It was in line with 'one of the remarkable facts about the Wholesale Societies, that the men to whom is entrusted the executive control of this vast organisation are all workers who have risen from the ranks of

Co-operation, having won the respect and confidence of the Movement by years of service'.[21] But it was not in line with a more characteristic twentieth-century utterance on 'the spirit of association' in a book with that title published in 1913, in which the author purported to praise co-operatives, trade unions, and friendly societies but in which the project was in fact to police them:

> The attitude of mind which conceives that any one person can do a given job as well as another, has often accounted for a pitiable misconception of the facts of daily life. There will be differences in capacity so long as this world revolves upon its axis.[22]

Giving such differences psychological, theological, biological, educational, material, managerial ... (facts of life) bases, and then using them to determine (limit and contain) mutuality, has been a large part of what has been done to the co-operative movement in our time. Defeat has not been total, but its processes are probably as important to draw attention to as the many partial, preliminary victories achieved. An articulated working-class movement which was cheap enough to be generally available but high in class dividend; which was geographically and socially accessible but also patient of universalisation; and which was independent but also engaged with allies and against enemies – such a formation has not, so far, come into being in modern Britain. It was immanent during the late nineteenth and early twentieth centuries, for instance in the co-operative movement, but blocked. The processes of blockage may be a fruitful way of looking at British social history from labour's point of view.

A sense of federal, open-ended aspiration and activity at a personal and an associational level; identification of *class* with creativity and confidence rather than with subordination, with a future rather than with a past, with capacity rather than with apathy; serious inventiveness about the cultural and political and social components of 'democracy' if ever that new order of society was to be universalised; determination to go through civil society to the State, through private spaces into the reconstruction of the public sphere; recognition of human differences as reasons for co-operation rather than justification for competition ... all these ran away, earthed like an electric charge. Large possibilities – involving labour doing away with masters, and doing its own, associated production and allocation of would-be dominant forms and spaces – have been channelled into underground wells, waiting for creative politics to divine them again.

This is to anticipate. Defeat remains as a direction, not a finished result. To the extent that defeat has occurred, moreover, it need not be blamed upon earlier working-class initiatives. These can only be diminished (or inflated) by being seen as the causes, in a simple sense, of later happenings. The fact that the world did not go their way should not be allowed to conceal what Holyoake called the 'world-making' project of co-operators: results need not be allowed to erase struggles, nor need defeat be equated with failure. Other chapters in this book will attempt to seize what is perhaps the social historian's main opportunity, namely to get behind effects into processes or struggles. 'We have to develop modes of analysis which, instead of reducing works to finished products, and activities to fixed positions, are capable of discerning, in good faith, the finite but significant openness of many actual initiatives and contributions.'[23] 'The whole in Co-operation is better than a part, but it would be unwise not to accomplish in part what we desire and stand so much in need of, because we cannot at once realise it perfectly.'[24] One of the two main opposed tendencies or clusters of potential in modern Britain, namely private capital (often referred to within the co-operative movement as 'competition'), could only have developed and can only continue to develop through subordinating the other. The other tendency, namely private labour (often signified, during the nineteenth century, by words like 'co-operation' or 'mutuality'), could have developed and can only develop towards universalising the most generous possibilities disclosed within capitalism through superseding private capital, thus shaping a whole 'associated mode' of production.[25] The two clusters of potential are locked hopefully (or tragically) together.

How did the struggle go? In what did the struggle consist? Who, in less abstract terms than 'capital' and 'labour', 'competition' and 'co-operation', were some of the protagonists? What did they believe and dare and do? This book makes some preliminary attempts to find out.

2. State, class, and associational forms in Britain: conflict and struggle from c. 1850

Won't people say then
It could never have worked?
The heaviest laden
Will wish they had shirked.

What will remind them
Of all the killed?
Wounds still unhealed
Those will remind them.

Bertolt Brecht, from *In Times of Extreme Persecution*

Needs and forms

Producing, distributing, and using basic goods such as food, soap, or clothes; learning in general about a universe, as well as learning in particular for a life; entertaining and being entertained; getting and embellishing shelter and places of assembly; finding ways of dealing with old age, infancy, sickness, and periods of less (or no) productive work: these are all material human needs. In any actually existing human society, the manners of meeting, or exploiting, such needs are deeply connected with each other. So they are resistant to arrangement, by historians and others, in neat hierarchies with fixed 'economic' bases. Such needs have been met in differing forms of association distinguishable from 'society' at most times and in most places in human history.

Near to our own time and place, as soon as a brief list is made ('workshops, factories, farms, allotments, schools, families, chain stores, co-ops, corner shops, pubs, clubs, music-halls, cinemas, television, friendly societies, private insurance companies, welfare states, council estates, trading estates, garden suburbs, mutual building societies, permanent building societies, promoter building societies'), the varieties of product and social relations involved in meeting or exploiting such needs cry out: What kind? For whom? How much? How patterned? By whom? In what relations with each other? How can they best be 'read'?[1]

For example, 'co-operative factories of the labourers themselves', the Co-operative Wholesale Society (1863), and local retailing Co-ops have been ways of producing, distributing, and using basic goods such as food, soap, or clothes, as have Unilever and Marks and Spencer. However, they are obviously not the *same* ways. The various methods have not remained static throughout their history, nor has the relative presence of any or either of them been constant. A society in which one was dominant and the other recessive would not be the same as one in which the roles were reversed. The same could be said of mutual insurance (for fraternity, through friendly societies), private insurance (for profit, through companies), or National Insurance (for 'social security', through the State), each of them ways of dealing with old age, infancy, sickness, and other contingencies. Similar distinctions could be made within each of the needs and forms listed.

Struggle and history

Ways of life (whose?) in societies like our own clash, coexist, compete, are killed, survive, change ... as different ways of associating and producing for meeting and exploiting such needs are developed. From a conservative point of view, uninterested in change or in history except as a ratification and celebration of the present, attempts are always being made to collapse 'ways of life' into a single 'society' or 'system'. And then the way is open to say that the means by which we meet, define, multiply, or divide needs constitute a single 'culture' — 'our' way of life, *the* system, *the* economy.

The function of so doing is to remove from view ownership, power, struggle, interests. It is to conceal alternative, latent potentials and achievements, in the interests of existing, manifest facts and ideologies. Above all, it is to devalue memory and its collectivisation in history. Competition and struggle involve loss and defeat as well as growth: presents involve running over unrealised but partly surviving pasts and temporarily blocked futures. As so often, a poet puts it most succinctly — William Carlos Williams, in 'The Descent':

> The descent beckons
>   as the ascent beckoned.
>   Memory is a kind
> of accomplishment,
>   a sort of renewal
>   even
> an initiation, since the spaces it opens are new places
>   inhabited by hordes
>   heretofore unrealized,
> of new kinds —
>   since their movements
>   are toward new objectives

(even though formerly they were abandoned).

No defeat is made up entirely of defeat — since
the world it opens is always a place
   formerly
      unsuspected. A
world lost,
   a world unsuspected,
      beckons to new places
and no whiteness (lost) is so white as the memory
of whiteness.

Needs involve *things* or useable products, and they entail (as we are human) more or less *social* relations. But neither 'society' nor forms of association constituting 'it', neither any particular whole set of social relations nor sub-sets, can be read off from needs such as the ones listed in the first paragraph of this chapter, or from useable products ('satisfying the needs of the stomach or the imagination') involved with those needs.

If they could, it would be possible to abnegate struggle and say, 'If you are going to have basic goods x y or z (say, cheap soap or mass insurance), you must have form a b or c (say, Unilever or the Prudential).' It would be possible to say that things *are*, in their very nature, commodities, rather than that they become so with the development of particular dominant social relations and forms. In this way a terrifying closure between possibility and what *is* would have been effected, and it is precisely this closure that a careful study of history can prevent.[2]

Still less should history be read as if it were the story of even higher Stages in Progress towards meeting Need and supplying useable products. If it is so read, it becomes possible to hold social relations constant and to say, 'If we are to have adequate food supplies or other "wealth", then we must have the existing retailing industry or "economy", with all the costs and prices entailed.' Such attempts, by capital, for capital, to underwrite existing social relations are always being made. They involve, quite explicitly now, making the whole social relation into a contract: something *given* to 'society' by the individual/family (such as restraint, economic or political, or like work or 'labour') in return for something else (such as privacy, or leisure, or life). Such public social relations are not, it is widely admitted, the best that are humanly or materially possible. But, say the suppliers of basic goods x y and z, they are all that we can have if the world is to be made safer for forms a b and c. A whole history is involved here: a history which sees earlier relations and forms only in so far as they feed into later ones, as forerunners rather than as hopeful, rational, and available resources for a better future. In the end, history itself can be dispensed with. After all, as suggested by a pioneer of a particular form, that of mass production of cars, designed to 'take out' as many earlier forms as possible in order to exploit in a specific way the human need to travel, more or less all history is 'bunk' (Henry Ford).

Class and change

To change social relations from labour's point of view requires a somewhat finer perspective. To change social relations, for labour rather than for capital, means to realise them in one of the other forms that they make materially possible at any one time, as opposed to 'understanding' them or 'explaining' them from the point of view of what they predominantly are. This means operating through the facts and with a particular conception of class. 'Nothing', as a British pioneer of mass production remarked, 'could be more dangerous'.[3]

Contrary, perhaps, to expectations, a class perspective is neither mechanical nor structural. It is not the view which says 'change the basic needs/products, and all the rest will follow'. Only in the crudest capitalist, and hence mechanical Marxist, view of humanity could some forms of production which are seen as the only truly necessary or material ones be held to explain all others or to provide the forms to which all others can be reduced. Nor is it the view which says 'Uncover for me the laws and structures of which events are mere illustrations, and through that disclosure we, the conscious ones, will direct the only possible change'. Only in the most élite capitalist — and hence structural Marxist — view of the division of labour between thinking and doing could such a search for the single, scientific fulcrum claim such priority among so many thinkers wishing to be on labour's side.

No such magic will ever (or has ever) worked, even for capital. Those were not the spectacles worn by capitalists creating *their* world, nor will they be the spectacles worn by socialists if ever we are to create ours. Social relations are what they say: social *relations*, not one-way traffics from basics to secondaries; and *social* relations, productive, specific and thus determined, but not puppets unable to pull their own strings. We have to look to particular humans and classes of humans, to their/our choices, past and present, to their/our ways of producing useable things (including ideas), to their/our acquired positions and powers in relation to other humans across very wide and increasingly inclusive areas of social activity. If we are to help to change needs and forms through struggle in a place and over time, we have to find ways of seeing them such as class ways, which make them vulnerable to our associated, co-operative interventions and creativity.

This, in the end, is the only justification, for labour, of the historical category, *class*. Incidentally, it is how and why the category first came into active use, for capital in the 'middle-class' politics of the first half of the nineteenth century.[4] But I am aware that I am using 'class', when I write 'for labour' or 'for capital' in what increasingly seems to be an idiosyncratic way. I shall now define my terms.

Class may be the best tool we have for pinpointing the limits and possibilities of associated, collectively conscious activity and production in and beyond capitalist modes. As a historical category it has been and can be used to point to the necessity, opportunity, and difficulty of association – first, then, for capital, now for labour. Its test of usefulness in action is whether it points to the real constraints and potentials, for capital and for labour, through time and place, better than other categories; and whether it shows, more helpfully than other categories, what can, as well as what cannot, be done. It is, however, not talismanic. It can neither explain, without the detail of the story, what has happened; nor can it predict, leaving aside the heat and chance of the struggle, what will happen. But it can, if it can do anything, *enable* the history and the struggle, for labour. As a means of understanding social relations which constitute it, 'class' can be used to change those relations.

With the development of capitalism there is also the unavoidable-by-capital (unless it resorts to slavery, fascism, neo-liberal or some other increasingly technically possible closed mutant)[5] development of the material possibility, for labour, of making things in ways which can transcend capital's dominant mode. Capitalism has built-in and of-its-essence limitations to the forms that it can adopt, to the distribution or sociology of the articulation of needs within it, and to who can share its highest promises and possibilities. 'The capitalist mode of production, by its very nature, excludes all rational improvement beyond a certain point.' Its development is bounded by its own dynamics: private, or at least minority-controlled / owned accumulation; private or at least privately disposable surplus; competition; the subordination of labour through forms of wage payment; and the maintenance of labour power as a commodity and the labour process as an 'economic' activity within the constraints of 'the self-valorization of capital ... by means of the "free" purchase and consumption of labour power'. Capitalism's very essence and dynamic is that some people (indeed, a whole class) cannot be what others are, and all cannot be what some have become. Times of desire, imitations, aspiration towards 'producing fully developed human beings' are dangerous to it: more so than its own economic crises. Inequality is its core, and it is this that it must protect against Christianity, 'religion', or any serious variety of humanism. It must, in the end, destroy or provide permanent ideological channels for the insistent, nagging comparisons that humans make between each other's situations. The facts and human conceptions of class will make it hard, but not necessarily impossible, for this protection to be permanently achieved.[6]

Labour's potential and limitations are necessarily harder to spell out. But they explain my interest in class struggle and associational form in the UK, particularly from the mid-nineteenth century onwards. It should be possible to imagine and even to describe the material possibilities for labour, not in idealist or historicist ways, but as visibly possible, partly achieved, partly destroyed, outlines. And not just in a negative way as a reaction to capital either; not just as the opposite of everything that capital stands for. Ways of producing, which change through time and through struggle and in specific locations, are ways which are in some sense linked, even if only in contradiction, or through the unity of opposites. They are also ways which are amenable to our agency, our wills, associations, and forms, to the ways in which we act in relation to the facts and concepts of class, using past struggles as capital for ourselves. This is not to deny constraints and determinations. But such constraints are not transcendent: they are contextual, particular to social formations, places, and times, and vulnerable to (because they are made up from) associated creativity.

So, where are we now?

We (most readers of this book) are now in a period of capitalism which, over the two hundred years, has seen momentous domestic (social) and international (geographic) extensions of the capitalist mode of production, and portentous extensions of human attempts to grasp its history, its beginning, and its ending. These human efforts have included large associations of working people trying to change or move beyond social relations as they found them (including such consequences as unventilated workshops, adulterated food, pauper funerals, or rented slums), as well as heroically grand theory and attempts at 'general overturn'. All these kinds of extension have been located in the UK — wider social and geographical penetration by capitalism, *and* Marx-Engels writing with significant reference to Britain from 1842 through to the early 1890s, *and* what an Austrian observer during the late 1880s called 'the theatre of a gigantic development of associated life which gives to her [England's] labour, her education, her social intercourse, nay to the entire development of her culture, a pronounced direction, a decisive stamp'.[7]

For Marx, the material outlines of a social economy[8] were visible in Britain while he was writing. More strongly than that, we can now see that such outlines were part of the determinants of his work; components of the tensions which gave it life and growth without which it could not have been the same. Marx did not make the mistake (however he presented a finished book like *Capital,* Vol. I) of believing that what he was thinking/writing had primacy over what he was thinking/writing about; nor were Manchester working people, agitators for factory reform, Chartists, Co-operators, First Internationalists, Communards ... mere examples of what he or Engels already knew.[9] By 1854 and in capitalism 'the working millions of Great Britain' had 'first laid down the real basis of a new society'. Capitalism had 'called into life the material means of ennobling labour itself'.[10] Capitalism, like any other mode of production which has not effected total closure, included and includes more-than-capitalist *humans* as well as factors of production (like labour or capital) and classes: it also changed and changes through alterable forms (for example, factories, credit, stock companies) over time. If it is important for cognition (understanding the world) not to collapse capitalist relations into human relationships, it is also important, for revolution (changing the world), not to collapse human relationships into capitalist relations. By 1867 The Scientific Socialist in his great work of Science called on 'us' (the readers of *Capital,* Vol. I) to *'imagine,* [my italics] for a change, an association of free men, working with the means of production held in common, and expending their many different forms of labour power in full self-awareness, as one single social labour force'.[11]

Marx could see spaces between predominant modes of production and society: spaces for other forms and relations to have 'influence' — their own limited, determined 'specific gravity'.[12] 'When the development of the material forces of production and of the corresponding forms of social production has reached a certain stage', new modes, 'as forms of transition from the capitalist mode of production to the associated one' may 'naturally grow'. According to *Capital*, Vol. III, this was actually happening in Britain, negatively in capital's own forms, positively in working-class social products such as the co-operative movements. It had always been, in Marx's view, the singular opportunity of the 'labouring classes' to emancipate themselves and hence 'man'. Once the 'productive powers of modern industry' had, 'thanks to the sweat of their brows and brains', reached the 'inexhaustible' stage even of the early 1850s, they no longer lacked the strength and 'real basis' for such a task. What they 'wanted' then were adequate forms for 'the organization of their common strength', and on a national rather than merely local or episodic scale. So Marx was on the look-out for initiatives with potential in this direction, like the anti-Parliament of 1854.[13] Hence his excitement when looking back, from 1864 to 1848, at the 'great facts' of working-class achievement in Britain during those years and the possibilities for transition that they constituted.[14] The greatest of these facts was 'the co-operative movement, especially the co-operative factories raised by the unassisted efforts of a few bold "hands". The value of these great social experiments cannot be overrated.' They had shown 'by deed instead of by argument' that existing social forms and relations were *not* essential to 'production on a large scale and in accord with the behests of modern science', and that 'associated labour plying its toil with a willing hand, a ready mind and a joyous heart' could make 'hired labour' as archaic as slave or serf labour.[15] Such were the real goals of emancipation, for which political organisation was vital, but to which it must be subordinate.[16]

Marx knew the difference between first victories and whole campaigns — what student of the rise of capitalism could not? In the very act of announcing his great facts in 1864 — in the very next paragraph — he began the analysis of their active containment and their false friends. He was never slow to denounce deformations, of Co-operation or of anything else.[17] But the first victories in broad daylight of the political economy of labour ('social production controlled by social foresight'[18]) over and against that of capital had, in his view, been won in 1847 with the Ten Hours Act. They were 'the product of a protracted and more or less concealed civil war between the capitalist class and the working class'. 'What a great change from that time!'[19] In such partial, preliminary victories — 'modest Magna Carta's' — which quickly turned into defeats and each one of which aspired to seem total and permanent, it was not only *what* was fought for, but *when* and *where*. Who held the initiative? This is a different question from who is in formal, or even real, control. Whether a reform was 'bourgeois', 'reformist', or not, depended not only on the substance but on the form. Each initiative had to be 'read' and related to politically. In what context? England, Britain, or France? Successfully counter-attacked or not? This was the case with suffrage reform, which could be revolutionary, as much as with factory legislation.[20]

By the late 1880s it had become transparently evident in rotten-ripe Britain how much of the initiative even in narrowly defined 'economic' production and even in self-imprisoning rationalisation and modernisation of industry — leaving aside 'social production' — was owed to labour. It was irritatingly clear to Engels, particularly, how otiose British capital*ists* had begun to look by the end of his life.[21] 'If we could but see a day of it ...', as William Morris yearned in *News from Nowhere*. To understand our own century (let alone the moods of late-nineteenth-century socialists in Britain such as Engels or Morris), we have to see, against all the narrowing of vision, privatisations, mass killings, world wars, social sciences, State National Socialisms, minutest divisions within and between intellectual and manual labour which have characterised it, that such a day was indeed no dream but had a real basis. It could have been Somewhere, not far from Here. Indeed, the narrowing of vision, mass killing, world wars, social sciences, etc. are inexplicable without this real possibility.

This, presumably, is what contradiction is about. Even in the very act of 'really' subordinating labour, with all the technical development of the forces of production that that implied, the possibilities of a division of labour which was a division of work not of humans — a state of complex rather than merely simple co-operation — were being created. Even as head was separated most visibly from hand and from humanity itself, the possibility of 'educated' labour and a withering away of older reasons for the division of labour were coming into being.[22] Even as a determined, structured, monstrous 'system' was growing up — evidenced in Empire as well as in entertainment, linked through capitalist uses of communication — and even as the eye was being battered by more and more appearances in commodity form, human efforts to comprehend and resist were (are) being made, and it was becoming materially possible to supersede such a system in a way never before possible in human history. Hence the image of the sorcerer in the Communist Manifesto: 'modern bourgeois society ... no longer able to control the powers of the nether world whom he has called up by his spells'.

This reading (or emphasis within a reading) of Marx which cannot be singular does not suggest a voluntarist, or any other naughty-ist, perspective, leading one to say: 'It's all easy. Just look at things differently and go out and make socialism.' It is a reading which calls for the politics of detail: building, federating, linking, articulating on the basis of what is there (here) for labour. This is just as hard a task as *theoretical* practice, although practitioners in that mode make it look incomparably difficult, as priests do salvation. But at least it is scientific, unlike the utopian alchemy which tries to turn epistemological breaks into social ones, immaculately.[23] And there are resources, outside ourselves and outside books like mine! 'Already', as Brecht told his Danish working-class actors in his Speech on the Art of Observation,

> Many of you are studying the laws of men's life together,
>   already
> Your class is determined to master its problems and thereby
> The problems of
> All mankind. And that is where you
> The workers' actors, as you learn and teach,
> Can play your part creatively in all the struggles
> Of men of your time, thereby
> Helping, with the seriousness of study and the cheerfulness
>   of knowledge
> To turn the struggle into common experience and
>   Justice into a passion.

The reading of Marx in the context suggested here might even explain why all this has been (and remains) so difficult. Of course labour is really, rather than just formally, subordinate; of course the working class is an *under*-class. But because it is an under-*class,* it also has a possible future. The fact that this has not yet become the present has been attributed by modern Marxists, sometimes moralistically, to the inadequacies of workers. Their 'level' of consciousness has not been high enough; they have been 'reformist', 'apathetic', 'corporate', etc. So they need more of the 'level' of consciousness of modern Marxists, instead of those Marxists (us) needing to develop more creative ways of seeing forms of struggle, with and for labour, and as the labourers (albeit mental) that we are. As Marx and Engels wrote four years before Marx's death:

> For almost forty years, we have stressed the class struggle as the most immediate driving power in history, and, in particular, the class struggle between the bourgeoisie and the proletariat as the great lever of the modern social upheaval; therefore it is impossible for us to ally ourselves with people who want to eliminate this class struggle from the movement. When the International was formed, we expressly formulated the battlecry: the emancipation of the working class must be the work of the working class itself. We cannot ally ourselves, therefore, with people who openly declare that the workers are too uneducated to free themselves and must first be liberated from above by philanthropic big bourgeois and petty bourgeois.[24]

Of course it *can* help to expound the logic of a system of commodity production at the level of Marx's most elevated abstractions. Such a way of seeing capitalism as a whole is essential for getting behind its myriad and all-present results, into the labour processes and class struggles which compose and decompose it. Indeed, that is what Marxism pre-eminently is: a way of getting behind results in capitalism and entering into process and struggle. Of course there *is* the nightmare of clinging to the known and old, a 'world-historical necromancy', pulling us back at critical moments 'just when they [we] appear to be engaged in the revolutionary transformation of themselves [ourselves] and their [our] material surroundings, in the creation of something which does not yet exist'.[25] But there is also a more positive inheritance: known or unknown, we cannot escape it. 'It must be kept in mind that the new forces of production and relations of production do not develop out of nothing, nor drop from the sky, nor from the womb of the self-positing Idea but from within and in antithesis to the existing development of production and the inherited traditional relations of property.'[26] There were (are) spaces away from the State, but not entirely behind its back, perhaps pre-eminently in the UK, for thought and activity with and for working-class associations directed towards a new state of affairs, rather than the old State modernised and rationalised and captured — as it will need to be across the world now as well as in the UK — by State Socialist rulers. The reversals of our own times, carrying middle-class liberalism with it as much as working-class socialism and threatening to carry Marxism too, and the resources that we may have for dealing with it, cannot be grasped without some exploration of labour's (and hence humanity's) stored capital, for itself, for our selves. We need to know, among other things, how far labour was travelling down a possible road for itself through the second half of nineteenth-century Britain — the most bourgeois society, we are told, that the world has ever known — in order to get some helpful bearings on where we are now.[27]

'English Associations of Working Men'

At this point some detail would help. 'Reading' associational forms, as they constitute class struggle, requires episodic analysis and narrative concentration — i.e. history — of a kind which can only be pointed to in an overview like this. Trade unions, co-operative societies, friendly societies, building societies, educational associations, etc. — by no means all male — each have their own complicated, particular histories gathering permanent institutional momentum rapidly from the mid-nineteenth century onwards. In what follows I am going to use, argue with, and trespass beyond existing research on some of these particular histories, in order to see their subjects as a whole. The hope is that their history can then be written more creatively, for labour.

One justification for this order of business is that my assertions will not be one-sided. They will be not-only-but-also points, seeking a dialectical, rather than functional, way of seeing associational form and change. Functional ways of seeing the second half of the nineteenth century have themselves functioned to excise, for capital, whole areas of class struggle from twentieth-century British history.

If associational life, in this case from c. 1850 to 1900 and onwards, simply functioned (in cahoots with imperialism) to 'incorporate' 'labour aristocrats' and to divide them willingly and comfortably from other workers; if such life never constituted any threat of potentially displacing growth within 'the system'; if it was subject anyway to universal, brass 'laws' of bureaucratisation ... then what is my problem, where was the struggle?[28] Associations such as the Co-ops, in this perspective, gave way through relative affluence and human attributes like 'apathy' to business modes and consumerism; surrounded by the law of value, their chances of success were slight from the very beginning. Then, lo and behold, there came the technology of the modern 'mass entertainment' industry, available at exactly the right time — the mid-1890s,[29] to serve 'demand', alongside a freshly benevolent 'welfare state'. *Tit-Bits,* Empire Music-Halls, cinema chains, and National Insurance Benefits were 'what people really wanted'. The whole project of a person like J. T. W. Mitchell — or John Stuart Mill for that matter — was a huge, if noble, mistake, based upon false ideas of 'what people are really like'.[30] Human Nature has hitherto been hidden, owing to lack of Progress; however, it has now been revealed in Modern Societies for the whole world to see.

Against such a parody, not-only-but-also's fight to do justice to great facts. Not only were there forms of working-class association which constituted evidence of different, possible futures for labour, but also, admittedly, such evidence was heavily overlaid even *within* the forms themselves. That is one of the good reasons, alongside the many bad ones, why these forms have not been recognised by historians. There was material evidence of different futures in the sense that, for example, the giant Affiliated Orders of Friendly Societies tried, in practice and with some success, to unite the contradictory imperatives for working-class association of economies and equities of scale with local autonomy and accessibility to control from below.[31] Indeed the *affiliated* form, characteristic of many working-class associations from Trades Councils, to the TUC, to the pre-1918 Labour Party, to the Miners' Federation, has been, at its best, an attempt through federation to displace the *from below/from above* dichotomy. There would be Congresses, not to pass down leadership from above, and not to advertise to 'the general public', but to associate opinion.[32] Co-ops also tried in practice to unite production and consumption, to make the working class their own employers, and to educate for a Co-operative Commonwealth and against Competition. One can choose whether to affect surprise at their 'failure', or build on the fact that the attempt was (still is) made at all. All forms of working-class association characteristic of the second half of the nineteenth century in the UK, including Working Men's Clubs, explicitly fought for unities and mutualities, against divisions and 'structural differentiation'.

In addition such evidence *was* overlaid within the forms themselves. That is to say, there was struggle, with class implications, *within* such forms as trade unions, clubs, and building societies, as well as between them and unambiguously capitalist forms.[33] For example, the incipient giants of the Permanent Building Society movement clearly had a vested interest in suppressing more mutual and accessible Promoter forms, as they also did in discouraging, in the early days, Municipal mortgage schemes.[34] Not only did the State nurture such internal tensions within the forms themselves through a process of artificial selection and legislative encouragement of some forms (and therefore discouragement of others), but it also made it possible for a whole branch of social production (for example, building societies or the Labour Party) as it were to go over to capital's side. A whole branch could start to act explicitly and mainly for capital, which is not to say that there would be no room in it for further struggle for labour. A whole branch could start to act itself as a chartered, licensed, 'registered', 'official', 'legitimate' monopolist, preventing and policing for capital the possibility of more challenging forms of association developing in that branch. Thus the Labour Party has occupied much of the space available for politics-for-labour since the first decade of the twentieth century.[35] Clubs have occupied a lot of the space for formal sociability-for-labour, Co-ops the space for co-operation, and so on ... such huge 'legitimate' presences have recently been cracking, although fresh forms of struggle for labour, against them and within them, have not yet clearly emerged.

Associations of collective self-help — indeed, continuous, formal movements /associations of all kinds — were, to varying degrees, confined to an upper stratum of working people. Given the constraints on time, money, and spare cultural resources of any kind in most nineteenth- and early-twentieth-century working lives, there was no way except through charity, or 'vice-presidential' or public subsidy, that participation in such associations could have been available on a majority scale.[36] Given the deformation and scarcity of direct charity, and the constraints that followed vice-presidential domination (which was what the 1880s revolt, for example in the London Working Men's Clubs, was about), *some* form of public (State) financial aid was a real temptation, even a necessity, for associations with universalising ambitions. Creative ingenuity over forms of membership, forms of payment, the goods that were offered, and organisational modes was necessary in order to achieve *any* kind of economic autonomy combined with wide availability (members unlimited) among working-class associations. Some branches of social production were more open to such ingenuity than others. It was easier to think of going through groceries into the Co-operative Commonwealth ('eating their way into the future', as a Royal Arsenal Co-operator put it), or through the bar takings into the wider goals of Clubland, than it was to find an equivalent vehicle for the goals of, for example, relatively autonomous *class* education. Even Co-operation needed a State-defined tax position (won in 1880), and clubs needed a State-defined licensing position (continually attacked from the 1890s through to 1908); education, however, was recalcitrant to privacy on any scale for capital, let alone for labour. Sheer scale was one way out in some branches; checking off almost unnoticed sums from very large numbers has been a way into mass 'free' trade unionism, for example, or mass Labour electoral politics.[37]

In this inherently limited, difficult situation for labour, with quite specific determinations operating, the degree of 'success' or 'failure' imputed depends on how one looks at it contextually, as opposed to moralistically. It also all depends upon politics. It depends upon whether committed activists wish to take a creative part in the construction of associated enterprise for labour, or to be a party to its emasculation. There is a continual (and in the end political) choice to be made, from within such enterprises today, whether to emphasise what is being achieved (however small) and could be achieved (however visionary), or to stress what has not been, is not being, or cannot be achieved.

Given the constraints, I find the amount of involvement in associations of working people during the second half of the nineteenth century in the UK more remarkable than the degree of confinement. In the same way, given the economic, systematic determinants in capitalism of the stratification and uneven development of the working class, I find the extent to which class associations kicked against these obstacles more interesting than the extent to which they 'functioned' to reinforce them or 'reflect' them.[38] I also find that, to a significant extent, the degree of confinement was not willingly accepted. There was a search for devices to overcome it, a search which had to risk sacrificing class content (for labour) to universalising ambitions and expansion in a necessarily recalcitrant (since mainly for-capital) context.[39] This search may even be interpreted as the search, on behalf of an embryonic mode of production, to overthrow an existing 'ready-made foundation' and 'create for itself a new basis appropriate to its own mode of production'.[40] There is a history to complaints about 'apathy'. In the Reading Co-op, for example, in the years before 1914 at least, such complaints were a register of active aspiration towards something else, in a situation (to us) of extraordinary participation and vision, rather than the moralising ratification of permanent rule by the few which such complaints have since become.

It is also important not to measure actually existing class formations against Platonic working-classness. There are good class-struggle reasons why the working class cannot become an 'it', perfect and entire, until the moment(s) of abolition of class as such, sometimes called The Revolution.[41] Until then, ruling-class struggle necessarily prevents more than partial class formation. The facts that English Associations of Working Men were not pan-class, that they degenerated early on, that the society that their visionaries believed in did not come about, have been attributed, in a moralistic manner, to their intentions. They have become a reformist 'gap' in labour-movement development between 1848 and the 1890s. They have then been seen as 'giving way' to higher forms, rather than as having been destroyed in a grinding series of twentieth-century counter attacks. In this way, the struggles within them and against them have been removed from view.

Thus, at a strategic moment of possible state-supported generalisation of some of the mutual achievements of Friendly Societies in 1911, the private industrial insurance industry influenced the State in its own favour in an explicit struggle between rival class forms.[42] Thus, because of a period of impressive Co-operative consolidation in Britain between the wars, organised private retailing capital tried, through the Royal Commission on Income Tax (1920) and the Raeburn Committee (1932), to get Co-ops, registered under Industrial and Provident Society legislation, assimilated to private capitalist forms, registered under the Companies Acts. If one asks, 'So how did the Co-ops become the businesses that they are now, with their mimetic responses to capitalist competition?', one of the explanations, admittedly, is internal: their own self-appointed Dr Beechings, oligarchic degeneration, and the inadequacy of attempts from inside to organise for any rival vision. But another answer, the history of which remains to be written, is *through the law*. Thus, between c. 1890 and 1908 – a period notable for a multiplicity of Club forms and some remaining energy of vision and desire (at least compared with that of today) – there was an active struggle through the State and over forms of Licensing between Working Men's Clubs and private licensed victuallers allied with temperance enthusiasts.[43] Such struggles were no less determining in relation to labour's potential during the twentieth century than the better-known offensive on trade unionism that was under way at the same time.[44]

Across the whole range of associational forms there has been an active process of artificial selection and incorporation, in its legal sense. This process long preceded the intense period of counter-attack by capital from the late nineteenth century onwards. I am not suggesting a period of autonomy followed by one of regulation. Very early on, almost simultaneously with their autochthonous creation, associations for the working class were licensed by the State in some forms rather than others, and lionised — in such a way as to try to breed lambs — by social reformers of many varieties. Even to expound the Acts of Parliament involved would exceed the space available for a single chapter. Again, *timing* was important, with legislation sometimes running along behind, trying to baptise already born bastards. But, in many branches of cultural/social production, an attempt to discriminate between 'chartered', 'legitimate', 'official', 'licensed', 'registered' forms and 'illegitimate', 'sham', 'bogus', 'unofficial' forms can be traced. Often, the association itself in its 'legitimate' form (for example, affiliated clubs) would be incorporated as the main policeman against less desirable forms in the same branch. Often, too, the overt reasons for such legislative selection would be entirely rational: for example, fire hazard in the case of the smaller music-halls in London in the 1880s, and cinemas in the Cinematograph Act of 1910. But the consequence was the same. As in the sphere of material production, more conventionally understood, there has been a reduction of space and resources available for less lionised forms. Big trees help to determine the undergrowth in any forest.

Characteristic means of growth for nineteenth-century working-class associations — schism, secession, federation, horizontal alliance, local innovation — became more difficult. They gave way to twentieth-century means such as take-over and 'ecumenical' merger. The rising technical or organic composition of capital in material production has its direct — and of course linked — counterpart in social production. This is not to say that space for partial or total challenge to dominant forms ever gets blocked completely: indeed, through the contradictions of any particular branch at one time, or across the whole 'system', they may suddenly open up in ways for which it is vital to be prepared. Nor is this rising public or bureaucratic or State composition of social (or associational) capital a 'natural' growth, or even an 'iron' law: it is constituted by, unintelligible without, and unchangeable except through, class struggle, whether 'privately' competitive ('economic') or publicly coercive ('political'). Indeed, this is what class struggle *means*.

Not only has there been this process of attempted subordination: there has also been autonomous life. Resistance to registration was often noticed.[45] Indeed the legislation, direct competition, and boycotts etc. faced by working-class associations cannot be explained as an on-going story except by reference to vigorous independence. 'Independent' has been a keyword in Raymond Williams' sense: with labour and capital attaching it to opposed projects. Class struggle is not only labour against capital, with capital in its fixed, achieved, 'capital*ism*' positions. It is also constituted by the struggles of capitalists against positions already won by labour. Indeed, such struggle against labour is an essential component of any explanation of nineteenth- and twentieth-century economic history, from factories onwards, let alone social and political history. The situation of the late twentieth-century British economy, indeed, cannot be explained without reference to the recalcitrance of labour. The British sickness is sometimes labour's obstinate health.

The relatively autonomous life of associations of working people needs separate and lengthy descriptions elsewhere. Here I can only urge that the pompous language surrounding the smallest happenings in their associational life, particularly during the second half of the nineteenth century, should be listened to *as* aspiration, drawing attention to details, rather than dismissed as quaint rhetorical decoration. Society, as in the authentic liberalism of the period more generally, was not seen as end-stopped, with existing institutions defining its goals. And Co-operators, for example, had not yet vested the goals of co-operation entirely in the health of their own organisation: 'the Co-op'.[46] To the extent that society was seen as 'system' (which it was from above, more than from below), it was seen as an open one. It was tolerant of educated progress, growth, and improvement, capable of changing the world, and thereby being changed, Given such confidence, there was much organisational fertility and inventiveness. Beatrice and Sydney Webb, who were great classifiers and collectors of associational forms, recognised, in forms such as the trade unionism of the miners and cotton workers, creative, highly skilled production of new social forms and relations. For some time indeed, and in many branches, associations of working people held the initiative. They were the most dynamic, progressive, and fertile forms of undertaking in their branch. Hence they pioneered and precipitated, in more specifically capitalist forms, the rationalisation and modernisation of their branch of production, to the extent that such modernisation occurred in the UK. Co-operation is only the most obvious example, being a pioneer in the introduction of new retailing forms (for example, self-service systems and sliced bread) as well as in specifically co-operative practices right up until the 1950s.

The aspiration was for autonomy, independence, and freedom from external control or subordination. An anthology of anti-Statist speeches and writings could be compiled from among organised working people, particularly between 1850 and 1890. Such sentiments have so far not been recognised as 'political', still less as 'socialist', in any sense, even when they explain that it is *State* socialism to which they object. They have been seen as 'liberal', 'corporate', 'reformist', or, with a dash of added snobbery, 'petty-bourgeois'. Pre-1850 working-class anti-Statism has had less trouble in making its way as part of our conscious socialist inheritance, partly because there was a large element of programmatic State reform in it, notably the six points of the People's Charter. After Thatcherism, working-class anti-Statism has become private, and sometimes genuinely reactionary, and needs digging out of a range of familial concerns concealed under blankets like 'privatisation' and 'apathy'. But such were the growths of Statism, and discontinuously large capitalist and 'socialist' States, from the early twentieth century onwards (with much longer roots of course[47]), and such was the extent to which socialism itself (even Marxism) came to mirror this Statism from the early twentieth century onwards, that working-class creativity in its specifically anti-Statist forms during earlier periods has mainly been seen as reactionary. It was indeed a reaction: to things like the defeat of Chartism, Chadwickian centralisation, incipient forms of machine politics from the 1870s onwards, sinister 'Liberal' populist imperialists such as Joseph Chamberlain, and to State 'welfare' initiatives which looked as though they might de-skill working-class social production entirely. And in the end, the liberal England of which it was a part did not die — as in Dangerfield's classic *The Strange Death of Liberal England;* it was murdered, albeit more slowly, humanely, and with more resistance than elsewhere. But the fact that 'the power is there, latent to be awakened one day', as William J. Braithwaite noted after a major episode in the subordination of Friendly Societies, is the achievement of the anti-Statism of the second half of the nineteenth century. It survives as part of our own socialist resources and inheritance, although much colonised by Right-wing populists in recent years. There has been accumulation by labour for itself, as well as by capital. Does some sleeping capital remain for labour, waiting to be roused through bold leadership, accurate history, accurate politics? In George J. Holyoake's phrase, through a revival of 'the moral art of association'?

In the day-to-day practice of working-class association, co-operative (as opposed to competitive) practices very different from the 'spirit of capitalism' were evident. They were not always articulated as such, but they were there and they could be listed at length. In a sense, however, they are not the point. The potential scandal, to capital, of these associations was not that they constituted another, essentially proletarian, way of life, whole and entire, waiting to break through from under the ground, and of which there could be no intimations before immortality, 'after the revolution'. Rather the opposite: the problem for capital was how seriously labour could take, and in part appropriate, some 'bourgeois values'. They had their own disciplines and rationalities, controlled by their own associations. These were not in substance always very different from 'middle-class values'. Indeed, to have allowed rational values, of the kind necessary to build and sustain 'social production controlled by social foresight' in *any* state of affairs, to be called 'middle class' is a bourgeois trick which Marxists, labour historians, or anyone else should never have allowed to be played. There is a sense in which imitation of 'its' values, growing from relatively autonomous working-class bases, is more dangerous to capital than rejection in the name of 'not working within the system'.

Initiative in labour's hands was not confined to the 'voluntary sector' either. By the end of the nineteenth century there was a basis for working-class penetration and innovation within elected bodies such as School Boards, Boards of Guardians, and local Councils. Such bodies had access to public finance and the capacity to control key areas of the production of social policy, to some extent independently of a State 'system' which indeed had to be systematised ('regulated') in order to bring them to heel. Believers in a national, professional, and central 'system' tried, both in their histories and in their politics, to cut their way through 'muddle' and 'primitive' untidinesses around them in order to find an efficient 'way out'. The case of the School Boards struggle, culminating in their abolition in 1902, is only the most obvious example. Indeed, the evident possibilities for labour within elected bodies — Labour 'captured' West Ham in 1898 — alongside parallel potentials with which they could conceivably have linked up, for example in the trade-union and co-operative movements, may explain the timing of an intensified period of counter-attack on labour's forms between c. 1890 and c. 1930, the full story of which remains to be written.[48]

Imagine and remember

The task, as always, is to make space between what has been and is, and what could be: using what has been, now, as a resource for making a different future.

The task is to imagine what would have been involved during subsequent generations in a successful generalisation of the partial, preliminary achievements of working-class associations during their first half century of achievement, while remembering that the exciting thing, in the British case, is that we have a material medium for our imagination and memory in the historical thoughts and practices of large numbers of working people. (In any case, British or otherwise, once those historical thoughts and practices are considered irrelevant, something other than socialism-for-labour is being attempted.) Before explaining what *did* happen, which would involve the detailed history of each branch of social production, and before being able to think materially about what could happen, for labour, in the future, we have to be able to see, in a more than Utopian manner, what could have happened. To make possible the exercise of the collective memory (i.e. history) and to liberate the exercise of the collective hope (i.e. politics), we need the play of the imagination, 'grasping', as Karl Liebknecht advised, 'for the impossible'.[49]

This means going backwards, in a more detailed way than I have been able to do here, rooting out the not-only-but-also points already made concerning the period c. 1850–90, then tracing the period of intensified counter-attack by capital, through the State, c. 1890–1930, and then on into the apotheosis of 'the market' in our own time. It is important to emphasise that I am not suggesting that, left to themselves (which, anyway, they had not been), 'English Associations of Working Men' would have constructed the Co-operative Commonwealth. I am saying that, in form as well as in substance, such associations represented enough of an actually existing alternative potential for 'the State', private capital, and working people to have been deeply involved in prolonged struggle over their shape and future presence.

Such struggle — best seen in class terms — was, and perhaps (see the obvious case of trade unions) still is, open and able to go either way.

To make general the achievements of working-class associations, and to transform them in such a way as to make this possible, would have involved — and did involve for capital doing the transformation predominantly in its direction during the twentieth century — going through public, political relations of production which it is convenient to call 'the State'. For capital this meant, for example, cabinet discussions about the dangers of autochthonous working-class education in the post-1917 crisis, followed by artificial selection of the Workers' Educational Association as a Responsible Body in 1924, the equivalent of Friendly Societies as Approved Societies in 1911. There were, of course, real financial difficulties in the previous twenty-year history of autochthonous efforts which made such intervention appear partly as a genuine rescue and achievement for labour. Again, for 'the Combine' of private Industrial Insurance Companies in 1911, going through the public area of social relations meant getting Lloyd George to define in their precise interests what the status of 'Approved Societies' (including the Friendly Societies) under National Insurance Legislation would be. With W. H. Lever it meant taking 22 Co-operative societies to court in 1910 in an attempt, which failed, to make them legally bound to stock his soap, rather than to challenge his empire through exclusive dealing. I will tell this story in another essay.[50] The fight was on, the battleground was public, and there was (and can be) no escape from that, no exit to the diminishing territory 'behind society's back'.

Indeed, the working class, to fulfil its maximum potential and reach its goal (sometimes called Socialism, perhaps better called a social or associated mode of production), needs the public branch of production of social relations — the State — more, earlier, and in different forms from its predecessors, the carriers of capitalism. There are material differences between the forms as well as the substances of a bourgeois (as compared with a proletarian) revolution. For labour, the forms are the substance. There can be no promising of the one without the other, as in capitalism (some substance without the forms), or State Socialism (some forms without the substance). This is partly for the elementary reason that there are more labourers than owners, and the 'socialist' project cannot be achieved until every worker (every human) is his or her own boss, in some associated complex-co-operative (as opposed to competitive) sense. This is what capitalism promises but cannot, without total transformation or revolution, deliver. 'All previous historical movements', the Communist Manifesto suggested, 'were movements of minorities, or in the interests of minorities. The proletarian movement is the self-conscious, independent movement of the immense majority, in the interest of the immense majority. The proletariat, the lowest stratum of our present society, cannot stir, cannot raise itself up, without the whole superincumbent strata of official society being sprung into the air.' Capitalism must involve formal, real, and then systematic subordination and division into two (historically active) classes, whereas socialism or an associated mode must involve systematic, universal mutuality, fraternity, equality. Society cannot be rescued for the working class behind its back or from its 'economic base' alone or in any other twisted posture, whereas it can and must for the bourgeoisie. For them, *coups d'état,* followed by night-watchmen states, 'holding the ring', are entirely adequate forms of revolution and post-revolutionary politics. The State can even be left in other hands, in the hands of those predominantly or partly representing an earlier mode (or even a later mode, as in the case of social democracy), for long stretches of time, while, back at the 'economic' ranch, material production is developed entirely adequately for capital. Such a separation of the economic from the political is impossible for the working class, if it is to realise its own potential: for the proletariat to rule by dictatorship is a contradiction in terms. If the proletariat is ruling by dictatorship, someone else is ruling and pretending to be the proletariat.

But this is where imagination is tempted towards evasion-by-words, or immaterial incantation. I am already slipping into such incantation. Alongside its realism, there is some of this evasion in the Communist Manifesto too. For example: 'In place of the old bourgeois society, with its classes and class antagonisms, we shall have an association, in which the free development of each is the condition for the free development of all.' ... 'When, in the course of development, class distinctions have disappeared, and all production has been concentrated in the hands of a vast association of the whole nation, the public power will lose its political character.'

Yes, we shall have such an association ... if we can avoid 'the common ruin of the contending classes'. But that development, must be, like the generation of new means of production and exchange in feudal society, 'a movement going on before our own eyes'.[51] In which case what does it, what can it, look like?

Systematic and universal mutuality, fraternity, equality, 'a vast association of the whole nation', will have to consist of myriads of actual activities, links, and administrations in the public sphere. To abolish the political in a complex society will mean so many horizontal lines and bonds that the vertical is entirely constituted by those lines and bonds. Some of these must be visible before all of them can be actual. They cannot all be drawn at a stroke. Thus, the question for labour is not *whether* to employ the State, or how to talk in general about states of affairs replacing states, but *in what* (changing) *forms?* What is (would be and is) involved for labour is finding the forms (economic, social, cultural, political) which can resolve, rather than abolish, a set of contradictions. By this I mean providing forms within which necessary contradictions have space to move.

These contradictions need to be specified in the most material way possible. Elsewhere, I have tried to summarise them as the contradiction between low cost to labour and high-class dividend; the contradiction between accessibility and effectiveness (or capacity for universalisation), and the contradiction between autonomy and engagement, with allies and against enemies.[52] Labour's project cannot be achieved without uniting such opposites in an active tension, hard enough mentally and even harder to sustain in social practice, through long stretches of time, in a given place. For labour, there can be no real distinction between the problem of agency, or constituting an associated mode, and the problems of realising and living within and maintaining that mode itself. If the associated mode is to be actually and materially for labour, rather than, say, for a new administrative, technical cadre, all of its problems have to be solved to the extent that they are humanly soluble, away from and as a necessary preliminary for — indeed constituent of — the *coup de grace*, the capture, which is also the dis-integration of 'the State', taking away its definite article. For this we shall need all the resources, historical and otherwise, that we can muster.

3. Working-class association, private capital, welfare, and the State in the late nineteenth and twentieth centuries

> Spade deep in order to gain some idea of the under-soil throughout.
>
> > S. Reynolds and Bob and Tom Woolley, *Seems So! A Working-class View of Politics* (London: Macmillan, 1911) p. xv

> We all of us in England still fancy, at least, that we believe in the blessings of freedom, yet, to quote an expression which has become proverbial, 'today we are all of us socialists'. The confusion reaches much deeper than a mere opposition between the beliefs of different classes. Let each man, according to the advice of the preachers, look within. He will find that inconsistent social theories are battling in his own mind for victory.
>
> > A.V. Dicey, *Lectures on the Relation between Law and Public Opinion in England during the Nineteenth Century* (2nd edn., London: Macmillan, 1914, p. 273)

> I do not believe the Friendly Society people knew what they were doing. They all had a very good lunch (with wine) and got very convivial. ... No further effort was ever made to secure real self-government. The power, however, is there, latent to be awakened one day.
>
> W. J. Braithwaite (1911), in *Lloyd George's Ambulance Wagon: being the memoirs of William J. Braithwaite, 1911–1912* (London: Methuen, 1957, p. 212)

I

George Bernard Shaw would have been the best person to write this chapter. H. G. Wells tried imaginative discussion of our themes in his novel *The New Machiavelli* (1911), but drama would be the best form in which to embody the anxious personal and social struggles which characterised the 'social politics' of the late nineteenth and early twentieth centuries.

Persons became symbols, carrying the weight of opposed social directions with labels like 'collectivism' or 'individualism'. Such 'isms' now appear blurred and inaccurate, but to participants in the struggles they felt distinct. They confronted each other across royal commissions such as the strategic Royal Commission on the Poor Laws 1905–09. They manipulated each other and laughed at each other at breakfast tables such as Lloyd George's, or at dinner tables such as the Webbs' – the joke being richer for participants' recent reading of *The New Machiavelli*, with its acid caricature of the Webbs as 'the Baileys'.[1]

The struggles were accompanied by the feeling that a new epoch was being made, by ambiguous forces called 'the people', 'the Coming Race', 'the masses', or 'bureaucrats'.[2] There was an expectation that political power and minimum living standards would in some sense be diffused or generalised. But on whose terms? It was not yet determined that 'the vote' and 'the benefit' would be the predominant forms of mass consumption of 'politics' and 'welfare'. Nor that passive, individuated, alienated, centralised *consumption* rather than active, associated, accessible, controlled *production* by and for the majority would colour these areas of social life so strongly during the twentieth century.

Drama could also best convey the inconsistencies referred to by A. V. Dicey in the quotation above, dated 1914, and the sense of defeated but not destroyed power and possibility, the unfinished business in the back of W. J. Braithwaite's mind in 1911. Which 'social theories' were to live with, and which were to suppress others? Which were progressive – the ones that won, or parts of the ones that lost? Which would have carried, perhaps could still carry, a different, more ambitiously democratic day?

Reactions to social politics during the years 1908–1914 were certainly as theatrical and shrill as reactions had been to franchise politics in the equally climactic years 1866–67. A. V. Dicey took part in both. In 1867 he was quite sanguine.[3] By 1914 his concern about the statist, unconstitutional directions taken by Liberal social policy, expressed in his new long introduction to his *Lectures,* was as 'extreme' as Carlyle's concern about suffrage reform had been in his 'Shooting Niagara' (1867). Acts such as the Education (Provision of Meals) Act 1906, the Trades Disputes Act (1906), the National Insurance Act (1911), those fixing minimum rates of wages in particular trades, the Finance (1909–10) Act, and the Mental Deficiency Act (1913) together constituted, for Dicey, a revolution. They constituted 'socialism', but not 'democracy'.

How are we to understand his sense of outrage? What can it tell us about what was going on? Was it merely the 'reaction' of a quaint Liberal Unionist who could seriously suggest that old-age pensioners (after the Pensions Act of 1908) should be disenfranchised? They were, thought Dicey, in receipt of 'a new form of outdoor relief for the poor'.

It is tempting to pass by on the other side of such resistance to an Act which modern welfare historians claim 'enormously eased the financial burden of old age'.[4] After all, old-age pensions were part of a series of measures usually seen as 'the foundations of the welfare state'. They get written about as milestones in books with titles like *England's Road to Social Security*,[5] and are seen as part of a whole period from the Education Act of 1870 to the National Health Service Act in 1948, during which benevolent social reform was added to political reform.

Perhaps, however, we should stop and look. To see, for instance, that Section 3, sub-section I(b) of the Pensions Act (1908) did indeed state that a person is not entitled to a pension if, before he becomes so entitled, 'he has habitually failed to work according to his ability, opportunity and need, for the maintenance or benefit of himself and those legally dependent upon him'. Or to see the scales of pensionability. One of the Charity Organization Society's criticisms of the Act was that the sums involved were so small. They started at 70 years of age with 5s. a week (the cost of a cabinet minister's cigar, Ben Tillett pointed out at the 1908 Trades Union Congress) if the recipient's means did not exceed about 8s. a week. The 'enormous easement' of the financial burdens of old age then went gradually down, to a pension of 1s. a week if income did not exceed about 12s. a week, and then to nothing. Readers who wish to penetrate behind the systematic exaggeration of the material benefits conferred by Liberal social legislation in these years, or who wish to see behind the celebratory newspaper coverage of the first Pension Day, should assess such sums of money in terms of any contemporary surveys of the lives of the poor, for example Mrs Pember Reeves's *Round About a Pound a Week* (1913).

As concerned as Dicey, but from a different point of view and class position, were the Friendly Societies. Although their offices still exist in inner-city areas – and their names on pub-signs – it is safe to say that what went on within is unknown to most social workers, socialists, and even social historians. They were enormous, but not universal, mutual associations of working men, the theory of whose practice was collective self-help. In their most developed forms they practised and believed in federal, associated self-government and in the connections between social goods like recreation, drink, helping others, hospital care, proper funerals, and the maintenance of an adequate quality of life when sick, old, or unemployed. They were autonomous working-class products in which the State and respectable opinion showed an obsessive and shaping interest throughout the nineteenth century.[6] Their 'failure' to become universal, and the 'failure' of their most advanced forms to fulfil their highest ambitions must not be attributed to their intentions or lack of intentions, and thus be moralised rather than explained. It has, rather, to be considered in the context of the material constraints of majority working-class life – the absolute deprivation of spare time, money, and cultural resources for all but a minority stratum of workers.

There was competition within and between different forms of Friendly Society: those that assimilated the principles and organisational modes of private businesses, with their wage-worker/consumer mode, as opposed to those with greater commitment to mutuality and associated production of insurance through mutual social relations. 'The State' materially aided the former types as well as the latter, through legal recognition under Industrial and Provident Society legislation. There was a continual effort to 'license' and 'register' both into acceptable forms. Business forms were also encouraged into being through the effects of competition from private capitalist firms active in the same field, registered under the Companies Acts. As with retailing, from the 1860s onwards private capitalist forms of insurance were preparing to reap where working-class forms had sown. Through the second half of the nineteenth century, however, the vast Affiliated Orders – the Ancient Order of Foresters (1899, 666,000 members) and the Manchester Unity of Oddfellows (1899, 713,000 members) – had greatly expanded. Considering their size, they have not been greatly studied since the pioneer work of P. H. J. H. Gosden.[7] Their history may be read – against current orthodoxies – as attempts (albeit cribbed, cabined, and confined) to universalise the whole range of Friendly Society benefits – mutuality as well as insurance – but on Friendly Society, for-labour terms, rather than on private company, for-capital terms. Their internal history, as well as the history of their relations with other forms like the Collecting Societies, may then be read as a terrain upon which active and explicit struggle took place – as active and explicit as in China since 1948 – over whether 'economics' was to triumph over 'politics', rationalisation over *democratic centralism*, 'actuarial science' over fraternal social relations, State subordination over public subsidy. Through the second half of the nineteenth century the Affiliated Orders and parallel smaller associations struggled on in times that were increasingly difficult ones for their original commitments.

For example, they were keen on combining the contradictory goods of democratic branch autonomy with centralised scale and administrative/financial back-up. They were keen on 'irrationally' diffused office holding. 'From each according to his ability' meant *resistance* to the actuarial common sense of contributions graded according to age. They were *affiliated* orders: affiliation and federation being quintessentially working-class or mass democratic or seventeenth-century nonconformist ('congregational') devices, as opposed to the vertically organised commercial, political, and cultural machines that are favoured by private capital and which penetrated working-class forms during the twentieth century.

How, then, are we to understand their worries? Because their politics – which must be seen as such, however unfamiliar the term – were anti-State, and because 'progressive' politics during the twentieth century (including Marxist/socialist politics) have been statist, Friendly Society fears and resistance to welfare changes have been made to appear archaic. They have been understood as mere institutional conservatism, labour-aristocratic self-interest – as 'reactionary', by commentators such as Dicey.

When they are allowed to speak, and still less when their own associations are examined in the detail that cannot be provided here, matters cannot now seem so simple. Their own time witnessed many explicit statist critiques of working-class forms, together with proposals for their replacement by national compulsion, for instance by H. S. Tremenheere in the 1870s and 1880s.[8] Our own time has been too full of bloated states masquerading as socialisms for us to pass by on the other side of any such large-scale working-class creativity. The Grand High Chief Ranger of the Foresters (Bro. Radley) described the offer of government subsidy for pensions in 1891 as:

> a mess of pottage which does not exist in reality. ... Care must be taken that the rising generations are not enticed by bribes drawn from the pockets of those who esteem their freedom or

forced by legislative compulsion to exchange the stimulating atmosphere of independence and work for an enervating system of mechanical obedience to State management and control – the certain sequel to State subsidy.[9]

In a clever speech in Birmingham Town Hall in 1894, Joseph Chamberlain tried to allay such fears. After all, he urged, 'the nation and the Friendly Societies have a common interest and a common object, and our effort should be to bring them into cooperation'. 'It is evident that a great deal too much has been made of this question of State interference which is not so important as many of my critics suppose. ... The honest man does not fear the policeman, and it is only the thief that thinks each bush an officer.' One of his critics – evidently with thieving tendencies – was J. Lister Stead, assistant secretary of the Foresters. Chamberlain's pension scheme, thought Stead, 'is considered a very alluring bait to obtain the support of Friendly Societies; but concealed under the bait, to use an angler's illustration, is an insidious hook, which would drag us out of the free waters of self-dependence, and land us on the enervating bank of State control. ... It may be depended upon as a solid truth that the State will not grant us special privileges without wanting to have a finger in our pie.[10] The history of the succeeding fifteen years, let alone the next one hundred, might well suggest that such 'reactionaries' were at least half right, and their 'progressive' foes were three-quarters sinister.

II

For people with an interest in changing any situation, it can be liberating to try to understand its place in *time* and in *struggle*. This is particularly so in a situation such as 'the welfare state' which can seem so hugely present, progressive, for the good of all and for always. It is particularly difficult for my generation (born in 1939) to get behind welfare's baroque facade. We have been the direct beneficiaries of one of its most creative periods, from 1941 to 1948. We literally have it in our bones. Fairer shares for all *were* fought for and achieved during this time under the pressure of war and its associated radical populism. There *was* a (temporary) thrust towards universal public provision of (some) minimum rights, even towards universalising the best of some social goods away from the market place, as in the National Health Service. Late, but large, steps have been taken in our time. In 1948 not only was 'one person, one vote' achieved in the Representation of the People Act, but the Poor Law was repealed in the National Assistance Act.

Never particularly popular among working people, the welfare state has produced, and been produced by, national experts in 'social administration' (that is, running the way we live), who then explain it to further professionals (including social workers), who try to distribute its benefits to consumers or clients.

The 'welfare state' was a term first used late in the 1930s and not generally current until the mid-1940s. It was not, any more than 'democracy', a known destination deliberately reached through routes carefully chosen by far-sighted reformers or politicians. Improvisation in response to immediately felt pressures was Lloyd George's method during the passage of the National Insurance Act in 1911. But it has also been the way with much welfare legislation. Nevertheless, with hindsight we can pick out broad directions of development between the 1870s and the 1940s.[11]

First, elected *ad hoc* bodies (such as school boards, or boards of guardians), with access to public finance and potentially beyond the control of central government or even of local middle-class leadership, were finally abolished when the guardians' functions were taken over by Public Assistance Committees of county boroughs/councils, in 1929. The Local Government Act of that year was part of an aggressive central tightening of control over relatively autonomous local, and sometimes working-class, practices following the defeat of the General Strike.

Second, national 'services', whether of local government (block grants, 1929) or of unemployment relief (Unemployment Assistance Board, 1934) or of hospitals (Public Health Act, 1936), became visible as rationalising edges cutting through overlapping local responsibilities. There were, and still are, resistances – formidable and partly successful in the case of the UAB. But such services were eventually to be centrally financed and controlled, often by appointment rather than election. The absorption of the Local Government Board (1871), alongside the Insurance Commission (1911), into the Ministry of Health in 1919 was another step towards the rationalisation of welfare.

Third, this period was also characterised by the adoption of the contributory 'insurance' principle as the main mode of British welfare provision, with the triad of State, employer, and worker each paying notionally fair (but regressive) contributions towards 'benefits'. Richard Titmuss saw the 1911 National Insurance Act as 'the birth of the "insurance principle" as a public institution in Britain'.[12] There always remained a stratum to be dealt with away from contributions, through the Poor Law and its successors down to the modern 'SS' (social security). Pensions had been financed out of taxation in 1908 but moved towards insurance in 1925. The same triad of State, employer, and worker at the same time became, with the same degree of dignified 'fairness', parties to the mainstream conduct of industrial relations, in an almost 'constitutional' manner.

Fourth, there was also a decisive switch during this period away from working-class associations – the 'English Associations of Working Men' which were so celebrated by serious liberals from about 1850 to 1900 – as creative *producers* of welfare, with the real subordination of Friendly Societies as 'Approved Societies' in 1911. Then there was a switch away from such associations even as *distributors* of welfare, with the 1937 'Black-Coated Workers' Pensions Act and the 1948 National Health Insurance measures pushing even Approved Societies off the stage. By then an ironic element of incorporation had been achieved. A working-class association – the Co-operative Insurance Society – having found a place in the sun to grow as an Approved Society after 1911 – came to act as a major lobbyist against one of the recommendations of the Beveridge Report: the nationalisation of the industrial insurance industry.

Fifth, administrative changes in welfare often concealed – or were undertaken in order to ensure – underlying continuities of attitude. Arrangements for 'Deposit Contributors' in 1911 recalled the ideas behind the New Poor Law of 1834. The Poor Law Act of 1930 restated poor-law principles for the guidance of public assistance committees just after the abolition of the guardians; and poor-law attitudes have survived through every decade since 1948, as anyone in receipt of social-security benefits will know.

But large, contextual, philosophical changes also defined the period. On the one hand, after 1934 it was no longer possible to insist – even in theory – that relief could be given only to able-bodied persons in an institution, or to maintain formal deterrent tests. Universal rights and dignities did not inform the realities of welfare provision, but they had increasingly to be taken into account as ideas and as material possibilities. On the other hand, competitive business nationalism became pervasive as the main context for welfare reform. Between the 1880s and the 1920s a general ruling recognition broke through: namely that a discontinuously large amount of State activity/expenditure was, first, possible; and then that it was, however much disliked in the back of the mind, an essential concomitant of national efficiency, health, security, prosperity ... vis à vis 'competitors', whether the competition came from domestic working-class forces and potentials, or from other national economies/empires. War was the most obvious spur, but not the only one, to this development.

Rather than chronicling the major acts of people or acts of parliament in order to give flesh to these trends – they are now accessible in many brief histories[13] – it may be more helpful to raise the eyes away from the separate trees towards the whole wood, before lowering them again to a single tree. The important thing to notice about the whole wood is precisely its accumulated size: 20 acts of parliament on unemployment between 1920 and the Unemployment Act of 1934; 15 million claims for various kinds of benefit in England and Wales in one 'normal' year (1956) – approximately one for every three inhabitants; discontinuous public-spending proportions which have become part of the daily rhetoric of politics, for and against. All these acts and consolidated acts were important as a total phenomenon, almost regardless of their specific content. Such a volume of centrally made 'machinery' – as with machinery in its more conventional realm of material production – necessarily limits and shapes (even 'determines') the freedom of manoeuvre of subsequent actors wishing to compete on the same stage, whatever their social or ideological position. It accumulates capital for capital in a process sometimes known as 'stabilisation', and constrains the accumulation of labour's own future capital. The other side of the reactionary label for all this State activity, as 'demoralisation' of the individual and family, is that it is indeed de-skilling of the working class in spheres other than the 'economic'.

Once there, such a large and rising national State, bureaucratic, or public composition of 'capital' in this 'social policy' sphere has material consequences comparable to those of the more familiar rising technical or organic composition of 'economic' capital. As the simplest form, it has to be taken account of: it has to be gone through rather than ignored, in order to come out on the other side. The 'welfare state' is, as it were, a State: it will not and cannot wither, without positive and creative activity which has to risk, all the time, the danger of incorporation if ever, in Beveridge's vision, 'human society may become a friendly society'. W. H. Beveridge's contradictory, inconsistent central belief, against all his statist contributions, was that 'the making of a good society depends not on the state but on the citizens, acting individually or in free association with one another'. He had a dream, a deeply troubled one by the 1940s, of how society as a friendly society might be 'an affiliated order of branches, some large and many small, each with its own life in freedom, each linked to the rest by common purpose and by bonds to serve that purpose. So the night's insane dream of power over other men, without limit and without mercy, shall fade. So mankind in brotherhood shall bring back the day.'[14]

III

Less well known opponents of the statist tendency of Liberal pre-1914 social legislation, writing in a study by and of Devon fishermen – but one which had much wider implications

– maintained in 1911: 'The alternative lies, not between knowing a few people and knowing all to an equal degree, but between scratching the surface of the whole of a field, and digging a portion of it spade-deep in order to gain some idea of the under-soil throughout.'[15] The same could not be said of the Acts and attitudes to which they reacted in their work entitled *Seems So! A Working-Class View of Politics*. Rather than attempting a wide survey therefore, the focus of the rest of this chapter will shift to a single Act or part of an Act: the health-related sections of the National Insurance Act, 1911.

Lloyd George chose to call it 'health' rather than 'sickness' because, as a recent historian has put it, 'in the rapidly expanding area where politics and advertising overlap' it sounded better.[16] The measure brought beneficiary-contributed health insurance to five-sixths of the families of the nation. It imposed by law novel duties on some 15 million individuals workers, employers, officials, doctors. It was presented with new razzmatazz as 'the Great Insurance Act', in *Tit-Bits*[17] and elsewhere. And it was *experienced* as something discontinuous, however subsequent historians may try to insist on continuities. Everyone reacted to it, in a manner reminiscent of 1866–67. 'It was, I believe,' wrote an insurance civil servant, Sir Henry Bunbury, 'the first time that civil servants had to explain novel and complex matters to the unlettered masses in plain and simple English'.[18] Stephen Reynolds replied on behalf of highly 'lettered' Devon fishermen who resiled from the language of 'masses', 'It is no use offering them freedom from destitution if, as a condition, they must knuckle under to a scheme of industrial conscription like the Webb Minority Report; or offering them national insurance if the result is to make the master more powerfully a master, and the man more impotently a workman than ever.'[19]

In other words, there is some digging to do, to gain some idea of the under-soil throughout. The digging is to reveal that what is large or small, recessive or dominant in our social relations today – for example, the relative and shifting weight of private (for profit) as against mutual (for fraternity) as against State or 'social'[20] (for what?) insurance in the welfare field – is an *achieved* result. It is the consequence of bypassing, suppressing, or concealing alternatives, through struggle. Such struggle may best be understood (from the point of view of achieving change as well as understanding) in terms of class. This is not to say that it may best be understood as a straight fight between proletarians in the red corner and bosses in the blue. Class is an historical and theoretical category which may help us precisely to see behind such crude simplicities, and to explain their non-appearance. It may help us to apprehend Dicey's 'inconsistencies', mentioned above. Each latent alternative in the welfare field, as well as the temporarily manifest present, has its own mix of distinct material possibilities and constraints and is carried by its own mix of social relations or class forces.

W. J. Braithwaite was the civil servant at the heart of the struggles over the National Insurance Bill 1911. He was a liberal and a Liberal, liked to see himself as a 'socialist' but was staunchly anti-Fabian. His father had been a Friendly Society stalwart. He moved from the Inland Revenue to being Lloyd George's principal Treasury assistant on insurance, and was then unceremoniously pushed back to Inland Revenue, after the defeat of his hopes for the Act, and those of the mutual Friendly Societies.

In contrast to many people who have talked about the withering away of the State, Braithwaite fought for practicable plans towards such an end, near to the centres of power. He wanted the whole national insurance machine to be constructed on mutual, local, autonomous, self-governing lines in such a way that it 'could be run from a third floor office in the Strand' with minimal government interference. He wanted to exclude private firms from administering the Act as 'Approved Societies', unless they allowed consumers to be *members* in a Friendly Society sense. He also wanted to exclude Friendly Societies whose only relationship to their 'members' was through collectors, by inserting clauses in the Act which would require, first, that there should be democratic 'local management committees' for each 250 members of an Approved Society who lived more than three miles from the nearest branch office. This became Clause 18 of the Bill introduced on 4 May 1911. Secondly, he wanted to insist that Approved Societies should be precluded from distributing any of their funds except by way of benefits, and that they should make provisions in their constitutions for the election of all their committees, representatives, and officers by members (Clause 21).

We are fortunate in having a ringside seat from which to observe what happened. Braithwaite's memoirs of these years were published, partly in diary form, as *Lloyd George's Ambulance Wagon*. Bentley Gilbert has also produced an outstandingly honest modern account, based upon these and other personal, State, and printed papers.[21] At stake were large human needs and the social relations through which they were predominantly to be met in the twentieth-century United Kingdom: such basics as the need to provide a decent funeral for one's own dead, or the need to be able to live with dignity when old, sick, left alone, or out of work. Just as with other human needs during precisely the same years, such as the need to eat and be clothed, or to wash with a helpful substance such as soap; or the need to entertain and be entertained, or to drink stimulating/refreshing liquids, or to acquire shelter, there was open conflict between large combines of private capital as forms for stimulating or exploiting such needs through competition and for profit, and working-class forms for meeting them in ways that showed the immanent possibility of alternative, co-operative, associated, social relations. This conflict was class conflict in the fullest sense, whether obvious, even though as yet little known, as between the Prudential and the Ancient Order of Foresters, Unilever and the Co-ops, big brewers and Working Men's Clubs, or more subtle, as in the conflicts *within* mutual or potentially mutual forms themselves, for example Building Societies or Friendly Societies. More and more of these conflicts, as in the case of national insurance, were necessarily taking place early in the twentieth century in and through the public area of social/political relations known as 'the State'.

The industrial insurance industry was a very powerful, concentrated, and, after 1901, well organised branch of capital. The Prudential was the nation's largest holder of railway stock, the largest private owner of ground rents and freehold properties, the biggest source of local government borrowing, and the largest holder of Bank of England stocks. In 1901 the 24 largest companies formed an association, known as the 'Combine'. They had voices such as the *Insurance Mail*, and lobbyists such as a young solicitor named Kingsley Wood, later to become powerful in Conservative and National politics as an active antagonist of labour's forms on behalf of private property. But their most powerful weapon was their army of agents. Seventy thousand collecting agents were employed (20,000 of them by the Prudential) to collect 40 million funeral policies (20 million with the Prudential). These men sold benefits door to door – 1½ pence a week drew a £10 death benefit – and thus had direct access to most working-class homes. They were also the owners of commodities, their 'books', which gave them semi-self-employed livelihoods that they could not afford to lose. As canvassers they were the fear and envy of other machines that were beginning to operate with the door-to-door, 'consumer' mode (rather than with the branch-meeting, membership, processional, or 'mutual' mode) such as the orthodox political parties. These agents may not have liked their companies. There is some evidence that they did not,[22] but they had a direct interest in seeing their business grow.

When the companies were under pressure, the agents were presented as 'philosophers', guides and friends of the people, as social workers not salesmen. The 'man from the Pru' was said to be 'looked upon as a member of the family, consulted on many matters quite apart from his business'.[23] The whole operation was paradigmatic of the kind of private social relations that twentieth-century private capital has favoured, and diametrically opposite to the most developed labour aristocratic and liberal public visions of the second half of the nineteenth century.

The industry made a lot of money: each month the Prudential's investment portfolio grew by an additional half-million pounds. In that sense, and in that sense alone, it was 'efficient'. To read the semi-automatic description of Friendly Societies by modern historians as 'inefficient' or 'out of date' leaves one aghast at the biased measure being used. Scarcely one third of the total amount collected in private industrial insurance contributions was ever paid in benefits. Efficiency lies in the (class) eye of the beholder. The Independent Labour Party had long targeted the Prudential in particular, before the formation of the Combine, as a sweated employer. Throughout the period there were signs of pressure from 'modern office methods' on clerks and agents, and of resistance to such pressure.[24] Indeed, the insurance industry has been in the van of modern private capital's power and concentrated presence. Liberals like Braithwaite and even Lloyd George always assumed that eventually it would be displaced from its perch by an assertion through nationalisation of public social responsibility.

When the Combine got wind of the possible democratic shapes of a major State innovation – national insurance – a formidable campaign was launched. Up until then, it was the most aggressive parliamentary lobby mounted by capital. The fascinating details cannot be rehearsed here. Through the summer of 1910 and into the late autumn of 1911 the Combine managed to secure, first, the dropping of widows' and orphans' pensions from the plan. These were not to be reintroduced until 1925. They were thought to threaten the death-benefit business by the Friendly Societies as much as by the industry. Then they got Clauses 18 and 21 removed from the Bill, thus allowing themselves as Approved Societies to register the insured, conduct the day-to-day business of health insurance, examine claims, help to determine benefits, and so on. Then, alongside the British Medical Association, they encouraged the doctors to resist the control of Approved Societies and to assert their professional status. At one stage of the battle, Braithwaite recalled Kingsley Wood leaning over to him and whispering, 'we have got Lloyd George there (putting his thumb on the desk) and shall get our own terms'. They thus became the most important administrative agency of National Health insurance. In Gilbert's words (since it is to his researches that all of the above is owed):

> The insurance companies sought not to keep government insurance out of their field of operation, but rather to take over the government programme and run it themselves. Their enemy was not the state, but the originally designated operators

of the national insurance plan, the British Friendly Societies. It was private, not government competition they sought to destroy. ... During the passage of the National Insurance Act, the Societies were pushed aside by the insurance industry. While destroying the position of the old Friendly Societies, the insurance men reconstructed the entire Act. The measure had contemplated a simple extension of the fraternal Friendly Society principle to those elements of the population hitherto not covered. It became instead a form of national compulsory savings, administered awkwardly and expensively by private insurance firms, most of which saw the programme only as an avenue to the extension of their private business. ... The result was to destroy the fraternal aspects of even the strongest friendly societies and to turn them into semi-official agencies whose only reason for existence was the administration of health insurance.[25]

Braithwaite was sent back to the Inland Revenue after the Bill, thus mauled, became law. Robert Morant, the favourite civil servant of the Webbs, who had master-minded the destruction of the school boards in 1902, took over. The Webbs breathed a sigh of relief. They had been unhappy with the Act, even in its final form. To be fair to them, this was partly because of its real subordination of independent working-class forms. For these they, and particularly Beatrice, always had great respect. Their work on the history and typology of trade union forms, particularly in their masterpiece *Industrial Democracy* (1897), remains unrivalled. The fears of the Friendly Societies about pensions may be put in a rational context by quoting the Webbs, writing in 1911, on the implications of the Act:

And when we consider the question of self-government, we can hardly recognize as independence the condition of the

'Approved Friendly Societies' under the chancellor of the exchequer's scheme of 1911 – a condition in which the hitherto autonomous society has to accept a government scheme of benefits in lieu of its own, performs none of the work of collection, exercises no control over the accumulating funds, has no responsibility for their investment, is compelled every three years to vary its benefits as it may, on valuation, peremptorily be required to do, and is even subject to governmental regulation and control in respect of the formation of branches, and the appointment and payment of the medical men on whose skill and honourable dealing the whole efficiency, and indeed, the actuarial solvency, of the organization depends. In fact the 'Approved Friendly Societies' in this scheme become merely canvassing agents and benefit-paying cashiers to the great new government department which will control the taxation on employers and wage-earners of some five-and-twenty million pounds annually and which will manage the investment of a fund presently running into a hundred millions.[26]

What price Joseph Chamberlain's bland reassurances in 1894 now? By 1926 a minority report of the Royal Commission on Health Insurance found the lack of control of Approved Societies by their members scandalous. There were other reasons for the Webbs' dissatisfaction, smacking of the 'inconsistencies' warring within individuals' attitudes noticed by Dicey. Adequate *control* was also lacking, for them, in the scheme, as well as autonomy. Indeed, they admired the Friendly Societies partly because of the moral control exercised by branches over members. 'A most unscientific state aid', commented Beatrice in her diaries. 'The unconditionality of all payments under insurance schemes constitutes a grave defect. The state gets nothing for its money in the way of conduct, it may even encourage malingerers.' In its draft stages she thought the Bill was 'communist'.[27] However, Sydney minded the Act less, and reassurance came. 'Years afterwards I was told', wrote Braithwaite, 'that Webb had said that things would be "alright after all" as Morant was appointed to administer the Act.'[28]

IV

The word 'administer' conceals a much more creative process: 'not a classical ... a gothic building', as Lucy Masterman put it.[29] Unlike the other Liberal reforms of this period, this one could not slot into a pre-existing government department. A vast new machine had to be brought into being. The Act became law on 16 December 1911; collections began to be made on 15 July 1912, and it was not until 15 January 1913 that medical benefits began to take effect. For those involved, like Morant or C. F. G. Masterman, it was touch-and-go whether the Act would ever get off the ground. They genuinely feared that contributors might not pay. In an aggressive campaign which Braithwaite found 'entirely undemocratic', the *Daily Mail* was agitating that they should not.

Some features of this process of 'administration' need to be highlighted before further reactions to it can make sense. First, as with pensions, the material consequences for beneficiaries must not be exaggerated or predated. 'Security' did not 'happen' with each step along 'England's Road' to it. The health provisions were more comprehensive than pensions had been in 1908. They applied to all workers earning less than £160 per annum. In return for 4*d*. a week from the worker, 3*d*. from the employer, and 2*d*. from the Treasury ('9*d*. for 4*d*.' was Lloyd George's advertising slogan), beneficiaries were to get sickness benefit of 10*s*. a week for 13 weeks, 5*s*. for the next 13 weeks, plus free medical services and some other grants. All in all, E. P. Hennock has suggested, for the younger worker in good health 'this was not very much more than he would have obtained previously from a well-run [Friendly] Society'.[30] The description in the socialist press was 'the great insurance fraud'. There was also restriction, maternity grants being the only benefit not dependent on the sickness or liability of the wage-earner rather than others in the family.

Second, the material consequences were exaggerated, and systematically so. In the process it became clear that this was because they were not just financial, but had to do with novel social relations. The Act was complicated, necessitating four dense pages of even *Tit-Bits* ('we have been able to secure an early copy of the bill ...') in a special supplement of 23 May 1911. In this supplement it was referred to as the 'Great' National Insurance Bill. Like something else alleged to be 'Great' which began three years later, it was important to explain 'how it will affect nearly 15 million workers'. It had to be *sold,* it was a form of conscription or national mobilisation. 'No More Doctors' Bills', ran the *Tit-Bits* headline. 'No More Medicine Accounts!! Wages When Out-O'-Work!! Baby Grants Paid to Mothers!!' Meanwhile Lloyd George was busy appearing on plates, tiles, china bits of all kinds, as well as in the national and provincial press, which were the then means of bringing politicians into the nation's front rooms. Lecturers were recruited to expound the Act up and down the land. More than a million people attended the presentations. Columns of the local press were syndicated. In March 1912 the joint committee in charge of operations ordered the printing of 25 million circulars, explaining the Act in the simplest possible terms. Market-research and opinion-testing techniques were used, while the *Daily Mail* was screaming 'It [the Act] Must Not Happen'. 'In the early days of 1912', recalled R. W. Harris, the author of the mass circular, with biblical solemnity, 'it was decreed that there should be delivered by post at every home, cottage and tenement in the land, a paper which should tell every inhabitant of these islands what his position was under the new scheme. It was the first such wholesale delivery that had ever been undertaken. It fell to my lot to draw up this leaflet. I put it through a series of ten proofs and tried twenty copies of each on all sorts of people, including maidservants.'[31]

Third, in the hurry, corners were cut. These were corners with large constitutional consequences for a 'democracy' which in certain quarters took itself seriously as such. Lloyd George can be watched cutting them, as he told warring Friendly Society and insurance representatives in October 1911 at a secret meeting that 'at the present moment we are making law'.[32] So where was parliament, where the courts?

The best witnesses to such incisions in dignified, liberal democratic theory were honest and worried contemporary liberals. Even those doing the cutting themselves, such as C. F. G. Masterman, confessed: 'We were asked to complete a ... difficult scheme in six months. ... Half the clauses were highly technical; many contradicted each other, *some rendered necessary action obviously illegal*' [my emphasis].[33] What was sauce for the State gander was not for the voluntary associational goose – remember that these were years of considerable preoccupation with the *ultra vires* actions of working-class forms such as trade unions. A correspondent in *Clarion* made an explicit connection between the Bill and the Osborne Judgement, calling it 'the second move of the employing classes to smash the trade unions'.[34] Sir Ernest Gowers served a thoughtful apprenticeship for *Plain Words* while serving on the Insurance Commission. He recognised the dangers of illegality on the State's part which 'officials' had to be careful not to abet. He was particularly concerned about the interpretative role of the modern official and the consequent 'need of the official to adhere scrupulously to the words of an Act at a time when he finds it more and more difficult to be helpful otherwise than by departure from them'. He placed all his hopes for the protection of the citizens from officialdom not in the courts, where redress was too expensive for the ordinary person, but in local committees of taxpayers and contributors who could, he thought, act as juries and mediators. He and C. F. G. Masterman invested great hope in the less than autonomous local committees that accompanied pre-1914 Liberal social legislation, such as the insurance committees.[35] A. V. Dicey was more shrill. He thought that the National Insurance Act had introduced a large dose of the French *droit administratif* into the British polity. Government and its officials had acquired judicial authority: parliament and the courts had had their powers momentously impaired by the power of the Insurance Commissioners for Part I of the Act (Health) and by insurance officers and courts of referees in the case of Part II (Unemployment), without anyone realising what had happened. 'The power to make regulations is probably the widest power of subordinate legislation ever conferred by parliament upon any body of officials.'[36]

This perception of the quality of what was going on explained Dicey's whole tone in the introduction to his *Lectures on the Relation between Law and Public Opinion* (1914). He wanted to make it clear that there was a difference in ideals between 'an English socialist' and 'an English democrat' – 'in the attitude they respectively take up towards scientific experts. The socialist's ideal is a State ruled by officials or experts who are socialists. The democrat's ideal is a State governed by the people in conformity with the broad common sense he attributes to ordinary citizens.'[37] This concern was not his alone. Braithwaite was obviously bitter after his defeat, but in more than a personal way. About Morant he wrote, in 1912:

> Officially he was my very opposite in every way – distrustful, suspicious, a bureaucrat who really and truly thought bureaucracy a good thing in itself and for itself, who really believed that officials could and should do things for people; whereas I was so constituted that I regarded the humble efforts of small people to do their best for themselves and their neighbours as productive and praiseworthy and the frantic struggle of bureaucrats and bureaucracies for power, position and privilege and the right to control other people as demoralizing and disgusting.[38]

V

'Disgusting' is a strong word. But it may be an important one to hear if we are to avoid seeing the history of these years in terms of unimpeachably 'good things', such as adding 'welfare' and 'social security' to an achieved 'democracy', or 'founding' sociology, or 'professionalising' case work, or reconciling 'old' and 'new' liberalism in calm treatises like L. T. Hobhouse's classic *Liberalism* (1911).

'Disgusting' may help us to listen for uglier sounds – such as those picked up by Gareth Stedman Jones in his *Outcast London* (1971), when he pointed to the surgical, authoritarian, labour-camp (in those days 'colony') prescriptions behind late-nineteenth-century 'progressive', 'limited socialist' ways of dealing with 'the social problem'. It may help to place national insurance – and ourselves in relation to it – and indeed welfare legislation throughout this period if, in the rest of this chapter, we follow the scent laid by Braithwaite's strong language.

Ben Keeling (1886–1916) was, according to H. G. Wells, 'as complete and expressive a specimen of the educated youth of the first decade of this century as perhaps we are likely to get'. His mind was full of inconsistent social theories, battling for victory. Fortunately we can trace through his letters the dominant directions that it was taking.[39] After a conventional élite education culminating at Cambridge, he became a Fabian, a 'socialist', a social worker, a would-be 'sociologist', at a time when all these categories were cohering in one sense rather than another. By the time of the 1911 National Insurance Act, Keeling had begun to define himself as a Liberal. He was a rank-and-file Webbian – if such a thing is possible – naming one of his children Bernard Sydney after his two heroes. By about 1908 he had 'seen enough of "democratic" politics to sicken me of them for life', by which he meant his flirtations with working-class and socialist associations such as Social Democratic Federation open-air meetings and branches of the Independent Labour Party in south London.

His importance lies in the fact that he was self-conscious about characteristic twentieth-century replacements for such 'democratic politics'. He articulated these replacements, because he came to believe in them, shockingly well and in a manner which may make sense of words like 'disgusting'. In 1908 he explained to a correspondent how shocked some of his friends 'used to be when I explained how obvious it is that one must always sacrifice individuals, whatever their general position or relation to one self, to the general good'. He had children, but left their mother alone to look after them because, after all, there was social reform to be achieved. 'My whole philosophy of the business of life centres round the State', he wrote, even though 'on the whole it is a damned interesting thing to breed about the earth'. 'I have noticed several times that my entire disregard of any individual feelings when I am aiming at what I conceive to be a social end strikes many people as simply horrible.'[40]

Through his work and opinions as chief administrator of the Leeds Labour Exchange (the product of the Trade Boards Act of 1909, and of Beveridge's earliest influential intervention), Keeling can serve as an essential reminder that statism of an authentically disgusting kind constituted material relations between the 'new class' and workers, rather than mere study reveries or multi-volume histories. Furthermore, such statism seized some of the spaces for anti-capitalism, even socialism, and occupied them. When in Leeds in 1910, Keeling joined the Leeds Club,

> the exclusive snobbish club of the place – for the purpose of observing the habits of employers more closely. The only way of defeating a man is to be able to beat him at his own game. We have got to be better capitalists than the capitalists are. When we – that is, the administrative classes – have more will, more relentlessness, more austerity, more organizing ability, more class consciousness than they have, we shall crumple them in our hands. ... From day to day my dream shall be of a new model army, of vigilant administrators supplanting property inch by inch, steadily and slowly – with a jovial carouse to loosen the muscles now and again. And to hell with the snufflers and pimps alike. They shall go in pairs one of each to a hurdle after the precedent set by Henry VIII.[41]

The State won his mind, and 'social reforms' like child health, school care committees, re-employment, industrial regulation, and juvenile labour became his daily bread and the vehicle for his ambitions. Like many intellectuals at the time, he reached for a science and a practice which could put them together. Kirkman Gray felt 'the want of a word which will express the relation of the State and individual corresponding to that which is indicated between the town community and individual in the word *citizen*'.[42]

Eugenics appealed to Keeling, as did the army and 'turning the whole mass of unskilled boy workers into a corps'.[43] 'If only the State can make itself sufficiently loved – if only people feel that they owe a considerable part at least of the good things of life to it, that will be the real beginning of the end of *aberglaube*.'[44] Trade unions were, for Keeling, good, and working men in general were admirable. But there was a danger that they might 'fail to see the crying need for a strong State'.[45] In the context of this kind of thought Keeling found national insurance acceptable enough for him to get closer to Liberalism at that time. But he regretted that there had to be any *contributory* element in it at all. Contributions might weaken a general sense of debt and subordination to the State, a sense which Keeling observed to be much weaker in England than, say, in Australia or Germany. By 1913 he cared

> less and less about the shibboleths of socialism, and I think I like the socialist element in the Labour movement (except for a very few intellectuals) less than other parts of it. All we want is an infinite willingness to use the State or the municipality ... for any practical ends in the direction of increasing the security, wealth and civilization of the masses. ... Probably a much greater increase of conscious socialism would not really help practical socialist methods. It would tend to throw up dogmatists to the front – and they are a pernicious race on the whole.[46]

Such language and opinions smell worse than they did in the context of their own time, because they come through to us now with the stench of their twentieth-century extrapolations in Stalinism and fascism in our nostrils. Against them, what can be set by way of contemporary argument and opposition, as a different colour on the canvas upon which twentieth-century social policy in Britian was to be drawn? After all, Keeling would still not feel in Britain and in the mid-2020s that *aberglaube* of a potentially dangerous kind had been eliminated. And that may be seen as an activist achievement because it has been more nearly eliminated in other capitalisms and in other socialisms. Furthermore, Braithwaite's sense of 'power ... there latent, to be awakened one day' still does not read as wholly ridiculous. Why not?

The resistance of Braithwaite's own brand of liberalism, so near to the centres of power in Britain at times, must provide part of the answer. But that too was tainted, and limited, and should not be allowed to make its exit as the hero of this chapter. Braithwaite thought within eugenic categories. He too, like any sound 1834, New Poor Law man, was terrified of 'preferential' treatment of the inefficient.[47] And his reaction to working-class people when they presented themselves as critics of his whole universe was patronising in the extreme. In June 1911 there was a Social Democratic Party deputation to Lloyd George on national insurance. In Braithwaite's diary it became:

> One of the most amusing deputations from the SDF, the theoretical workmen. One of them, Mr Knee, ought really to have come out of a picture book. A little man with a large forehead and specs, going bald, very glib with the catch words of socialism, palpably genuine and honest, entirely unpractical, and unrepresentative of the British working man, asking the most impossible things, in a manner which at once became inconsistent under the Chancellor's cross examination, boldly sticking to his guns, and showing himself really a very decent

little fellow; I could see that the Chancellor was very much amused at him, and at the same time quite liked and admired the little fellow. As a practical man of course, he could not go with him and had to show his proposals up to the press ... but *he* did it very kindly, and there was a good deal of good-natured chaff, and the whole thing was a great success from everybody's point of view.[48]

Fortunately Fred Knee, this 'very decent little fellow', thanks to the work of David Englander and the Society for the Study of Labour History, can now speak for himself.[49]

He and others in the organised labour and socialist movements spoke where they could at the time. The Social Democratic Party (formerly Federation) had 'always advocated a universal system of free national insurance'.[50] They strongly opposed the contributory element. They were, on the whole, antagonistic to, or uninterested in, the Friendly Societies. 'With the rival demands of the doctors and friendly societies we have no concern, save for the hope their quarrel gives us that the Bill may be doomed not to pass at all, or not to work if passed.'[51] The Parliamentary Labour Party and Independent Labour Party were less definite. There were disagreements, for example between Philip Snowden and Keir Hardie, which Lloyd George could exploit. Parliamentary Labour opposition was weak, 'they don't seem to know really what they want'.[52] They were bought off in October 1911 by a Lloyd George promise to introduce a Bill for the payment of MPs, and by a favourable actuary's report (for which Lloyd George paid) on the effect of the Bill on trade-union finances.[53]

Such organisational self-interest at the highest levels of the labour movement constituted something less than rising to the occasion. Hopefully it is clear by now that the occasion was of some moment, both to working people and to twentieth-century socialism. An attempt was being made to take socialism's germs away from working-class hosts and to vaccinate the body politic, seen as 'corporate', with them in harmless, even health-giving, forms. There was an attempt, partly successful, to de-class the idea of socialism, or to nationalise it; to suggest loudly and often that it was a 'good thing' as an idea, even a *necessary* idea, but not attached to working-class interests or associations. One measure of the success of this imperialism has been the extent to which modern British socialists – particularly Fabians and Marxists – have come to regard working-class creativity and its fate (expressed in the situation of enormous associations like Friendly Societies or Co-operative Societies between, say, 1850 and 2000) as irrelevant for the socialist project.

Nor is this view of the portent of early twentieth-century welfare history mere historian's hindsight. The signals were there at the time. They were there, for example, in Chamberlain's 1894 Birmingham speech, quoted earlier. The setting of this speech was a perceived 'danger to social order', fears of 'a speedy and possibly a dangerous reaction' if a response other than the Poor Law was not made to old age 'in the bitter competition to which everyone is subjected'. It was *because* 'I regard it as a serious thing that there should be growing up, as I believe there is among the working classes, a sentiment that they are being treated with injustice and neglect' that Chamberlain felt that the Friendly Societies and 'the nation' must be brought 'into co-operation'. He was most surprised to be regarded as 'an intruder on their private domain and a poacher on their preserves', although Friendly Society figures were not the only people to see in Joseph Chamberlain a would-be populist 'despot'.[54]

Thinkers like Durkheim or, closer to the home of this chapter, A. V. Dicey, were very frank about the merits of national socialism over against articulate working-class interest. 'We must assume, we must indeed hope', Dicey whistled in the 1914 dark, 'that the socialists of England will accept the profoundly true dictum of Gabrielle Tarde that "a socialist party can, but a working man's party cannot, be in the great current of progress". For a party of socialists may aim at the benefit of a whole State, a labour party seeks the benefit of a class.'[55] There was a chorus of thought and action at this time to *make* people think, in spite of recalcitrant experience, that '"the government" is no entity outside of ourselves', and to regard 'the State as a vast benefit society of which the whole body of citizens are necessarily members'.[56] As L. T. Hobhouse told his readers in his strategic restatement of *Liberalism* in the year of national insurance: 'The British nation is not a mysterious entity over and above the forty odd millions of living souls who dwell together under a common law. Its life is their life, its well-being or ill-fortune their well-being or ill-fortune.'[57] What better material expression of this than a national, compulsory, accumulating (as opposed to dividing-out) insurance scheme?

A significant but small area of working-class thought, action, and association for which 'syndicalism' is a convenient label sensed the high stakes being played for from a class point of view. In his early work on syndicalism, Bob Holton began to uncover the meanings and extent of an active reassertion of socialism as *working-class* industrial and political activity from below which characterised the years before 1914, and which focused explicitly, among other things, on responding to the statist implications of Liberal welfare reforms. Hilaire Belloc's *The Servile State* (1912) is the best-known articulation of a much wider cultural movement. For Belloc, National Insurance (particularly the employment sections of the Act) had been designed 'to capture organized labour and to cut its claws'.[58] The socialist paper with the largest circulation agreed.[59]

Harder to catch, but probably of more subsequent staying power in preventing Keeling's dreams becoming mainstream realities of twentieth-century British social history, was a much wider working-class 'mentality'. This was a term used in Reynolds' and Woolley's *Seems So! A Working-Class View of Politics* (1911), whose views on national insurance have already been quoted. Their work makes it possible to hypothesise a collective, primarily defensive refusal to be incorporated, by important strands of twentieth-century working-class opinion in the United Kingdom.

Since the creative, public, associational voluntary life of so many English working people during the second half of the nineteenth century – for example in Friendly Societies – has been subordinated, rendered less ambitious, or assimilated to rational capitalist or bureaucratic models during the twentieth century, there has arguably been a turning away, a privatisation, a refusal to be attached in any deeply felt way to 'the State' or to most other benevolent-seeming associations. There has been a closing of the door, with a 'not today thank you', and many decisions, for example, to go fishing or dig the allotment, alone. State 'benefits' and 'consumer' goods have been taken, but not always and not often with enthusiasm or gratitude. There has been a certain resigned submission to being defined, from the outside, as 'apathetic', or as 'masses' for a 'mass market', but a refusal to accept such definitions as self-definitions. There has been a turning inwards towards, for example, the family as a defence, and towards doing-it-yourself. Areas of private, crabbed, deformed autonomy have been carved out, for such creative self-production and introspection as can be channelled through private zones such as the home, the allotment, dog ownership, and so on.[60]

When an adequate twentieth-century social history is written from labour's point of view, it will have to pay close attention to meanings, for working people as well as for capital, of these zones, including, of course, the often lamented 'failure' of those 'most in need' to 'take up' welfare benefits. It is to the other side, or other sides, of 'apathy', 'privatisation', 'mass consumption', and so on that we shall have to turn for 'a working-class view of politics' in the spaces left by the social policies of the enlarged twentieth-century State.

The previous paragraph is speculative, but it rests on a text of the times which answered the likes of Keeling point by point: Stephen Reynolds' and Bob and Tom Woolley's book published in 1911, *Seems So! A Working-Class View of Politics*. This remarkable work was written by two Devon fishermen and Reynolds, a 'settler'/novelist/writer/anthropologist of great acumen. It was a local study, but with universal ambition.

> States of mind, changes and trends of opinion, among large masses of people are notoriously difficult to ascertain – to catch on the wing, as it were, and to fasten down in plain statements – additionally so among working people whose only form of publicity is talk. The whole of the evidence can never be gathered together and against that which can be brought, contrary examples are nearly always obtainable. Opinion is fluid. Feeling is mostly subconscious. To try and arrest either is like scooping up water in a net. One *feels* the change: the change in direction and speed; and one *feels* the change in feeling [my italics].[61]

Aware of the difficulties, Reynolds and the Woolley brothers got much nearer to articulation than their modesty implies. In attacking Fabian and New Liberal attitudes and acts of parliament (national insurance as making 'the master more powerfully a master and the man more impotently a workman than ever'[62]) through the words and thoughts of working people, they made clear how central struggle – class conflict as well as struggle – was and is in the social history of welfare and social policy. Different conceptions of the world were at stake, different views of what ought to be. A full reading of the text would benefit social workers, socialists, and social historians alike. All that can be said here, by way of ending this chapter with it, is that it is a text partly written by working people which is, first, fully aware of the opacity of the world they are writing about. Next, the text is also fully and explicitly aware of the cultural imperialism which buries that world – including modern socialisms. The text is also fully aware of the growing gap between private and public expression, and the obtuse angle between 'political', 'party' organisation and 'mass' political opinion. 'Evidently there's a link broken somewhere between politics and people.'[63] 'Class antagonism is a very powerful force, growing rather than diminishing, acting in all sorts of unsuspected ways, cropping up in all sorts of unexpected places. Let things go wrong, make a false step, and in a moment it flashes out. … It was there, beneath, all the time.'[64] Social policy, social reform, is explicitly seen in *Seems So! A Working-Class View of Politics* as reformation of one class by another. Resistance to 'inspection' and to 'progressive' intellectuals is articulated in rare detail. 'It is possible to honour the socialists on account of their good intentions, but at the same time the worst tyranny to beware of is that of intellectuals ordering other people's lives. They are so well intentioned, so merely logical, so cruel.'[65] All this from one man who was 'an enthusiastic Tariff Reformer, another a Free Trader, and the third a political dark horse whose way of voting nobody knows'.[66]

We wants more money and they gives us more laws. ... An' when we ask for more rivets [money] they pass laws how us shall behave, so's our want of rivets shan't show, an' how to keep our health, so's us shall work better to their profit. What we wants is proper pay, the rivets to work out our own life according to our own ideas, not their's. But they is trying to make it heaven on the cheap. T'isn't to be done, I tell 'ee, an' so they'll find. ... [N]ew Acts, with new penalties attached, come tumbling upon his [the working man's] head from on high. After being left to fend for himself – with a success much greater in reality than in appearance – he suddenly finds himself regarded as incapable of taking care of himself in any respect whatever. He sees, dimly perhaps, that his democratic leaders flatter him and hold him in contempt at the same time. He is treated like a child badly brought up by its parents, a child very wronged and very naughty. If he could, and if he would, express his own private opinion with a frankness which he has found to be inexpedient, and with a particularity for which elections afford no scope, his well-wishers would be more than surprised. 'Why', they would ask, 'should he still be so ungrateful and resentful? See what we have done for him. See what we have given him.'[67]

Assembling the CWS jigsaw (a photograph by Stephen Yeo)

4. Who was J. T. W. Mitchell?

for H. E. Y. 1894–1957

I

To the extent that they can be discovered, I find the personal details strangely compelling. I will relate some of them here. But, to get to my main answer straight away, John Thomas Whitehead Mitchell (1828–1895) – 'Mitchell', as he was familiarly called 'and will ever best be known'[1] – is an outstanding figure in the history of the nineteenth- and twentieth-century working-class project.[2]

Mitchell was the Chairman of the Co-operative Wholesale Society from 1874 to 1895, re-elected Quarter by Quarter all through that period. By the late 1880s the turnover of the CWS exceeded £6 million a year, its 'warehouse at Manchester is a small town', and it was administering funds worth nearly £1 million in shares, loan capital, and reserves. By 1897 there were 8,407 people employed by the Society, working in the distributive departments and in the bank, as well as in the productive works and services.[3]

I shall argue that he was, in essence, a late-nineteenth-century Owenite, with strong early-nineteenth-century plebeian-radical connections. By this I mean that he believed in singular, complete solutions to society's problems. He did not call himself a socialist, although he used the word 'socialistic' about co-operation, and we will find him talking 'rather on the lines of a commune' in 1890.[4] While acknowledging Robert Owen as 'if not the actual founder of associated effort as understood today, at least the inspirer of the thoughts and aims of those who at one period or another have become the leaders of the Co-operative Movement', Mitchell knew his history and, therefore, had his doubts. 'So far as I can gather, he did not believe so much in co-operation; he thought the tribe of merchants could do business for them as well as they could do it for themselves.' 'Choosing to do their own business instead of allowing other people to do it for them' was one of Mitchell's favourite ways of describing his project. It sounded innocent, part of an Englishman's birthright. But he knew how radical a project it was, and how many vested interests it was already disturbing.[5] Mitchell's most famous maxim, *Never despise the store!*, was a rebuke to Robert Owen who, of course, did just that.[6]

Mitchell was a thinker. But he was wary of 'theory' and 'theorists'. In terms of conventional nineteenth-century political categories, he was a Radical or Advanced Liberal. He very occasionally referred to himself as a 'collectivist', but this was not a favoured label and not, as he pointed out in 1894, 'not by Act of Parliament'.[7] He was certainly strongly anti-individualist, even anti-individual, espousing only 'an individuality for the good of all'. 'Co-operation ought to be based on the principle of united interest with the societies and not individuals. Some persons taught that the individual should be the basis.'[8] Mitchell's was a quite specifically un-bourgeois life, making it ironic (no, offensive) that he and his movement have been used so much by labour historians as indices of the embourgeoisement of the working class. Full of talent which Beatrice Webb, for one, saw as business genius, Mitchell's was not an ordinary 'career'. It remains an extraordinary fact about the man, the movement, and the peculiarities of the English that the Chairman of 'the most varied if not the largest business enterprise in the world at that time' received something like £150 a year in fees and at his death was worth £350/17/8.[9] And this at a time when (to use a Mitchell phrase) in 'the Barnum wickedness of the competitive world'[10] conspicuous consumption by capitalists on the one hand and self-regarding professional management as a separate social group (class?) on the other were busy establishing themselves. 'Perhaps no man in Europe presided over so large a business, and certainly no man ever presided over so vast a concern who took such slender remuneration for so doing.'[11] The bedroom in which he died in John Street, Rochdale, was 'humble in the extreme'. It contained some of the old furniture owned by his mother when he was a boy; 'reports and balance sheets took the place of ordinary literature' – although Mitchell liked books; and there were portraits of a few friends, his copy of the Bible and his hymn book, and 'that was all'.[12]

II

Mitchell's funeral in Rochdale on Wednesday 20 March 1895 was a very public affair.[13] It was conducted by the Co-operative Wholesale Society, 'the deceased gentleman having no near relatives upon whom the duty could be supposed to fall'. Very few among the many wreaths at Milton Congregational Chapel, where Mitchell had been a Deacon, bore the names of individuals. It was not as though he did not love and was not loved. 'He stood that truest of all tests, that of closest intimacy and companionship. Our departed friend at least was not like the stage-trappings of the theatre, best seen at a distance; on the other hand, the nearer you got to him the more you liked him and the more thoroughly you understood the man and appreciated the all-pervading motives of his life.'[14]

One of the two people in the world closest to him was Abraham Howard, 'his close friend till his dying day'. 'They were like Damon and Phintias – their mutual confidence and esteem being only equalled by the strength of their attachment.'[15] The other very close friend was Thomas Butterworth.[16] At one time, Butterworth had been in disgrace in Rochdale: in prison for stealing from a Co-op. When he was released in about 1872, Mitchell held out his hand in friendship. They became inseparable. Butterworth inherited some property, 'yet because of Mitchell's kindness he became his willing serving man'. He lived nearby and would send his servant in to clean for Mitchell, and he himself ran messages, packed suitcases, and so on, 'the neighbours frequently remarking that if Mr. Mitchell died, Mr. Butterworth would have to accompany him, as he could not exist alone'. In the event, they died within a few days of each other, Butterworth not lasting long enough even to attend Mitchell's funeral.

So the first carriage in the procession to Rochdale Cemetery, in late March 1895, contained Mr Meather, Butterworth's executor – Butterworth was to have been Mitchell's – and 'some who had been near to him in his domestic life': Miss Wilby of Ossett, Yorks, and Miss Miller. This was followed by a carriage containing four cousins. And they were the only private mourners, in a procession which stretched without a break from Milton, down Smith Street, over Wellington Bridge and along South Parade to a point opposite the magnificent Town Hall, arguably itself a middle-class, civic response to Co-operation. Within Milton Chapel 'perfect order and decency' prevailed, and 'the greatest order was maintained throughout'. Careful arrangements had been made, and 'these were strictly adhered to'.[17] The Minister and six Deacons entered at exactly one o'clock. One pew immediately behind the clock in the south gallery remained unoccupied; 'heavy black drapings marked it out as the place of him who will sit there no more'. The main area of the Chapel was reserved for delegates from Co-operative Societies, the space at the rear under the gallery for representatives of local bodies (I take this distinction between delegates and representatives direct from the local press); the aisle to the right of the entrance was for teachers and scholars at the Sunday School where Mitchell had been active from scholar to superintendent for fifty years, week in and week out. The aisle to the left was reserved for members of the Milton congregation.

On the previous night the coffin had been taken from 15 John Street, 'a dark and sullen abode'. Mitchell had never lived more than a few hundred yards from there, though in five or six different rooms or houses. For more than twenty years he lived absolutely by himself.

The Sunday School movement had been his break. 'But for the help of the Sunday School, it is doubtful whether we should have known anything about him.'[18] He would not talk about the circumstances of his birth, even with close friends. At his funeral the Minister said that in his prayers at Sunday School 'the word "Father" seemed ever on his lips' and that he, Mitchell, was a father to the school with 'forbearance carried almost to a fault, if he had a fault in School work'.[19]

He was the illegitimate son of 'a man in good position but of ungoverned character'.[20] 'His forefathers (had) for generations been engaged in hat manufacture', a trade which became extinct in Rochdale during the early 1850s.[21] His mother was poor. She kept him out of the factories for as long as she could, until he was 10 or 11, when he went to work as a piecer for 18 pence a week. Other children started work at the age of 7 or 8. Relating this experience to profit-sharing versions of co-operation later on, Mitchell said: 'Whatever profit might have been handed to me I do not see that I could have done more'.[22] His mother kept John and herself partly by taking in lodgers, partly by running a beerhouse. She sent him to learn reading and writing at a school in Bailie Street. This was on Sundays and was run by a clerk in a foundry. Then John moved to another Sunday class. One day in 1846 two men (one of whom attended his funeral in 1895) were canvassing households around Hope Street for the Providence Chapel Sunday School. In the Mitchell house they found the boy reading and his mother making the dinner. 'They seemed to live on the most affectionate terms.' They asked John to join. His mother agreed. The next Sunday one of the men, Mr Pagan, called for him and joined Mitchell to his own (Mr Pagan's) class.

> Here Mitchell for the first time in his life discovered that he really had no opinions, either religious or political. A new life seemed to burst upon him ... Up to that time he said his mother had been his only friend.[23]

Becoming teetotal, which he did at that time, must have been a big decision: it meant breaking with one of his mother's only visible means of support.

Associational life in one of the largest of all nineteenth-century voluntary associations, Sunday Schools, was now added to Mitchell's daily working hours, which were from 6 in the morning until 7.30 at night. He used the library at Providence Sunday School. He joined their Juvenile Temperance Society, which led him into the Rochdale

Temperance Society, of which he became a committee member. He also became a member of the local Rechabite tent, which became the 'Love and Truth' division of the Sons of Temperance. He remained a member and official until he died. The sub-committee of the Temperance Society held meetings in Mitchell's room at the top of his mother's house. Then, in about 1850, Mitchell personally experienced secession – a characteristic event in the associational culture of the day. There was disagreement at Providence about the appointment of a new pastor. A number of members split to form the new Milton Congregational Church in Bailie Street. Mitchell went with them. By 1854 he was a Milton Sunday School teacher.

Mr Pagan did more than recruit and teach his young client. He owned a flannel mill and offered Mitchell a situation in the warehouse at 16/- a week. The firm changed hands several times. Mitchell stayed for 18 years, until 1867, and was promoted from wool sorter to manager of the wool department. In the Minute Books of the General Committee of Rochdale Equitable Pioneers Society (REPS) in May 1868, he referred to himself as 'Manager', living in John Street. By June 1871, his self-description was 'Manufacturer', having set himself up in trade as a flannel dealer. He did this on his own account for some years until he gradually let it go, as his work in the Co-operative Movement became too demanding.

Mitchell was clearly a man with a talent for organisational work, on the look-out for the chance to do business. This was his life-time affair. His contacts in the flannel trade later led to his appointment as liquidator of the Lancashire and Yorkshire Productive Society, a co-operative concern at Littleborough which hit hard times. From 1878 until the end of his life, he nursed that company round, thus prompting attacks on his probity, to which I shall return. No one else had hope for that

Society. But for much of his working life, even while at the CWS, Mitchell worked every morning between 7.30 and 9.30 to try to make it viable. Finally, he managed to free it from creditors and prepare it for takeover by the CWS. Mitchell had established a London agency to run his own business, getting cotton goods made by the Rochdale Manufacturing Society dyed and finished at Middleton which he then sold through this agency. He used his home as a warehouse, adding an adjoining cottage as the business grew. It is not clear exactly what the relations were between Mitchell's private trading at this time and the local societies with which he was connected. The failure of his London agent came as a blow, for Mitchell had held him in high regard. 'From this time he allowed his business quietly to slip away from him as he was giving all his time and attention to the Wholesale business.'[24] There is no doubt that the man later to be nicknamed 'Baron Wholesale'[25] had it in him to become boss of a very different kind of business empire.

III

However, he did not. He added Rochdale Co-operation to his Sunday School, Congregational, Temperance, and other reforming associations. He joined the Pioneers in 1853. Through the Rochdale Equitable Pioneers Society he was elected to the Board of the Co-operative Wholesale Society in 1869 and, in June 1874, became its Chairman. He held this position for the rest of his life. I will return to the details of his Rochdale Co-operative work, which are key elements in understanding what an associationist life, for labour, meant.

But first I will step aside from his story to look at it in the light of other people's views: that somewhat dim light in which Mitchell has been bathed ever since his death. For

Mitchell himself wrote practically nothing. There are his public speeches and activities, at Congress for instance – although it is interesting to note that he wrote no papers for Congress in all the years of his attendance from 1869 to 1895. Nor did he write articles in the CWS *Annuals* which were such an emblem of the Movement, often given as gifts of honour. We can watch him at work in his most characteristic setting, at the Quarterly Meetings of the CWS and its various committees, recorded in the Minutes or in the *Co-operative News*, or listen to him at the endless foundation-stone ceremonies, tea parties, and industrial exhibitions that he attended for local Co-operative Societies. From such material it is possible to piece together his ideas, though less easy to trace where they came from. I will attempt to do this in subsequent sections of this chapter.

Mitchell has been the object of an immense weight of opinion about him, however, as well as all this public material. His is not a name widely known outside the Co-operative Movement. Within the Movement, his after-life – his historical aura – has not been positive. As I went about my research, damnation and faint praise slipped out of the sides of the mouths of many people in the Movement. The mention of his name seemed to evoke a lingering bad odour. This was coupled with incredulity that I should be interested in finding out about Mitchell at all. We have all seemed to know what he was about: namely taking co-operation ('idealism') out of the Co-op and lining his own pocket, or maybe just his stomach, in the process.

The history of the Co-operative Movement during the second half of the nineteenth century (climaxing in the 1880s) has commonly been seen as a contest between goodies and baddies. The goodies were 'idealists', Christian Socialists, believers in producer co-operation. The baddies were materialists, shopkeepers, working men around the Co-operative Wholesale Society, believers in 'consumer co-operation'. Arguments between them centred on the rights of workers within producer co-ops: rights to shared control, and also economic rights, variously called the 'bonus to labour', 'co-partnership', or 'profit sharing'. Mitchell was against such economic rights, in so far as they were to be realised at the points of production, i.e. at the level of the firm rather than at the level of the Co-operative, or wider society. He was, it is commonly suggested, on the wrong side – and worse: on the big side; and the big side won. By the early twentieth century, the CWS position had, broadly speaking, won out within the mainstream Co-operative Movement. Mitchell, therefore, so that story tells, was party to – and symbolic of – the long corruption of the co-operative ideal in the hands of the working-class Co-operative Movement. This has been summed up by historians as 'from community building to shopkeeping': a long descent from Owenism.[26]

Yet perhaps this historical inheritance, carefully unravelled, can tell us about more than Mitchell. Inside his own Movement and during his own life time, there was smoke which I find more interesting than the small fire behind it. Immediately after his death, there were difficulties surrounding some of his private or public effects, following the death of his beloved executor, Butterworth. The problem, as it appears in the General Committee Minutes of the CWS, was to get insignia – silver trowels, medals, a silver watch and a gold one too – out of Mitchell's house and into CWS keeping. There does seem to have been some conflict about this.[27] What is interesting about it, perhaps – and very much in line with the feel of his funeral – is that the Society had no hesitation in regarding gifts made to Mitchell as its own, rather than private gifts to him and his heirs.

Who was J. T. W. Mitchell? Answer: Chairman of the Co-operative Wholesale Society. More than Chairman: the CWS incarnate[28] or – this was a very common epithet – its spouse, or father; and was there ever a more loving husband or father that ever looked after his progeny better?[29] The relationship undoubtedly involved a particular quality of commitment. It is interesting that the most available metaphor derived from marriage. The fact that Mitchell appeared to live happily alone was a puzzle too. As the Minister of Milton Chapel said at his funeral: 'In the days of his fatal illness, it did seem a little sad that in a domestic sense he was so lonely. Doubtless family ties would have cheered and enriched his life. But no one was more bright and cheery than he.'[30]

As I hope to show, people have had category problems with Mitchell. Why, after all, make him married – assimilating him to familial forms that involve commitment, for sure, but of a different order from Mitchell's public work – when he had no wife, no daughter or son, no known father, and when he spent his spirit trying to include the whole world rather than a single partner, whether for business or emotional support, in his Society? It is as if the only way to offer themselves explanation and consolation for Mitchell's apparently happy and fulfilled nature in such an odd life was to invent a married state for him, to contain him in a framework of social normality – to bring him in from the margins and cut him down to size. For the family metaphor does serve as a subtraction from inclusive enterprise which was (still is) unfamiliar, not least its degree of commitment to giant working-class enterprise in its creativity about non-bourgeois forms of association. Whatever else the Co-operative Wholesale Society was, it was not a typical late-nineteenth-century private firm.[31]

Why, too, make him corrupt – that lingering bad odour – unless that is the only available way of understanding (and subtracting from) a large, dynamic association *different* from the dominant, capitalist ones around it, with different ambitions, different ways of working, a different 'ethic'?

Allegations of corruption have been crude: financial corruption ('he's only in it for the money') and the corruption of ideals. Even though the smoke has not drifted far enough outside the Movement for many people to be aware of it, it may be worth looking directly into the fire. A dozen years before his death there had been disquiet, some of it directed specifically at Mitchell, over 'fees and fares' paid to CWS directors. This turned into 'agitation' in the early summer of 1884.[32] Mitchell was on a delegation to the United States at the time. His co-directors became anxious when the delegation came back later than anticipated. They were in trouble.

To the twenty-first century eye, accustomed to private excess, the sums spent on directors' expenses seem modest. It is the disquiet about them, rather than their amounts, which is most revealing. It is evidence of a belief in equality, healthy Jacobinism which can be picked up almost anywhere in the nineteenth- and early-twentieth-century socialist and labour-movement press and which still exists today, for instance in CIU (Club and Institute Union) working men's clubs. Money is bound to be a problem for working-class, democratic associations in a capitalist society. When who gets it and how they get it are not noticed, democratic forms decay, or become purely commercial. Matters of principle are involved. If money matters are not seen as matters of principle, working-class organisations inevitably degenerate.

Details are important. The form of payment for Directors of the CWS during the late 1870s was a fee of 2/6d per meeting.[33] There was also a *per diem* fee of 12/- for work performed away from Manchester, for example official visits to Ipswich or the USA.[34] When Mitchell attended the laying of a foundation stone for the Ipswich Society, he was away for two nights and was paid 36/-, this transaction being a distinct item of business passing through a General Committee meeting – in effect the Board of one of the largest companies in the world – on 23 January 1885. The local Society would probably also have offered him something, 'just such an acknowledgment as they chose to give. Be it ever so small, there was never a murmur as to its inadequacy for the service, even when it was barely sufficient to cover his travelling expenses, and not always even that.'[35] The total spent on directors' expenses in 1883 was £3,800. In 1879, the CWS was spending 4d. in the £ on management costs. This amounted to 1.75 per cent in a trading concern with a capital of £400,000 and with £600,000 worth of annual business. 'He (Mitchell) did not think there was a business of the same magnitude in the Kingdom that was managed so economically.'[36]

What mattered within the Movement, however, were the forms of accountability. The fees and fares issue came up in part because it was felt during 1885 that the General Committee had exceeded their powers in passing a resolution on 30 December 1884 in which they had authorised the payment of fares on the same basis as in 1874, without calling a General Meeting. At a Quarterly Meeting in September 1879, the delegate from Eccles asked whether it had been necessary for the whole General Committee to travel up to London for the laying of the foundation stone of the new CWS building in Leman Street. This was a good question: trips to London are at a premium, still, in movements among less well-off people. Chairman Mitchell took the point but said yes, in his judgment it was necessary, in order to demonstrate the success of 'true cooperation' in a city in which the Co-op had long had difficulty and in which spurious 'civil service' forms of co-operative trading had a head start. Visibility was advisable, he thought, particularly in a year in which a Select Committee was investigating such forms of ersatz co-operation. These matters were widely aired in meetings and in elaborate press reports. When asked in 1881 why the cost of reporting meetings in the *Co-operative News* had increased dramatically, Mitchell replied that the Committee had been accused of concealment because of the brevity of earlier reports. So now they employed Henry Pitman, formerly editor of *The Co-operator*, and carried five-page reports of their meetings in a form of public Minutes. We are dealing with a global business which, when Mitchell was on his deathbed, sent a Committee Member over to Rochdale to obtain guidance from their Chairman and then discussed the member's cab fare at Board level.[37]

During the mid-1880s an Investigating Committee was set up to examine 'fees and fares'. It is clear that Mitchell would have preferred to deal with the matter differently, answering written enquiries from Societies as they came in.[38] He was quite capable of exhibiting a Statist 'trust me' mentality against the associationist forms in which otherwise he was so imbricated. But he did not try to block the investigation. In November 1884 the Committee listed 12 directors and the amounts they had received in excess of their allowance, and suggested that in future a lump sum of £2,000 be allotted to the directors to be divided up as they saw fit. This idea was rejected. At one General Committee meeting, it got to the point of a motion being passed saying that fees paid to Mitchell on 3 March 1884 had been correct.[39] A reply to the Investigating Committee on behalf of the directors was printed and issued to shareholders.[40] Then an accountant submitted a report showing that Mr Mitchell had, in fact, been overpaid £1/13/-d on his March 1884 journey to Newtown. It was resolved (with Mitchell staying in the chair) that this amount be refunded by him. The

General Committee accepted that they should have appealed to a General Meeting to fix fresh payments to deputations. A special General Meeting was held on 24 January 1885. A leader was published in the *Co-operative News* on 31 January 1885 saying that the directors had indeed failed, in so far as they had not been seen to be fair. New scales were fixed.[41] At the end of the affair, the General Committee resolved that all papers to do with the Investigating Committee be turned over to them. 'Fees and fares' remained as a bite which could always be scratched. Mitchell was still referring to them in 1892. In his Presidential speech to Congress that year, he recalled the Rochdale Pioneers. 'At that time the Committee worked for naught. There was no bother in those days about fees and fares. (Laughter).'[42] 'This book I hold in my hand is one of the first copies of the rules of the Equitable Pioneers, and the name upon the corner is that of Samuel Ogden, Rochdale, No. 1 ... But I find at the finish of the rules it says that: "If the auditor does not attend to his duties he is to be fined 2s.6d., and if the delinquent be a salesman or cashier, he is to be fined 1s. A president being late, he was fined 3d., and if he did not come at all, he had to pay 6d." (A voice, "Grand old days").'[43]

Some of the internal politics of all this can still be discerned, although some of them are bound to be missed by an outsider like me. Mitchell was clearly under attack from particular delegates to the General Committee and to the Quarterly Meetings. These Quarterly Meetings were remarkable occasions. If only we could have a film of one of them, it would be the single most revealing document about Mitchell and the CWS. Up to 600 delegates gathered to discuss, formally to run, this vast working-class enterprise. What a way, W. H. Lever might have remarked, to run a fruit stall, let alone a business empire! They were occasions as remarkable as the cotton and coal 'parliaments' of the same period and the same culture which so impressed the Webbs in *Industrial Democracy* (1897). Working-class congress in nineteenth- and twentieth-century Britain was a major cultural form. At the CWS, grand initiatives jostled with minutiae, principles with personal animosities. Mitchell chaired them all. It was obviously his particular craft.

It is unsurprising that he received criticism as well as accolades. Trouble seemed to come mostly from the Manchester Equitable Society and the Heckmondwike Society, via Delegates Pigstone, Redfern, and Crabtree. Fees and fares were only one expression of it. In 1879, the issue of whether the CWS should join the Manchester Chamber of Commerce came up.[44] Crabtree and Pigstone were in favour, Mitchell against. Mitchell's view was that if they had been a mere joint-stock company, it would have been correct for them to join. But they were not. The Wholesale was not in the business of protecting the interests of private traders, unlike the Chamber, where there were many who had no sympathy for Co-operation. Pigstone (President of Manchester and Salford Equitable Cooperative Society) wanted the CWS to 'take its place in the commercial councils of this great community'. Mitchell wanted it to go on 'acting by itself'. Pigstone heard Mitchell's speech on the subject with 'great pain'. He accused him of stirring class feeling where none should be. At the Quarterly Meeting Mitchell only just won, losing 112 to 82 votes in Manchester but winning 170 to 112 through the aggregation of votes from Newcastle and London. The CWS had a democratic device whereby they conferred on identical agendas in different centres and then aggregated the votes.

It was James Crabtree (1831–1917) who got under Mitchell's skin more than anyone else, including his opponents the

Christian Socialists, Thomas Hughes, E. O. Greening, and E. V. Neale.[45] Crabtree had preceded Mitchell as Chairman of the CWS from 1870 to 1874. He had been the main mover in the foundation of the Heckmondwike Society. Crabtree was cautious. He was doubtful about innovations like Co-operative banking, CWS manufacturing, Mitchell's bold ambitions in the merchant shipping world, and extensions such as the opening of a CWS branch in Bristol. He was not the stuff of which entrepreneurs are made, individual or collective. He had resigned from the CWS Board when he became connected with the Heckmondwike Manufacturing Company Ltd, formed in 1873 to take over an old firm of carpet, blanket, and rug makers whose business had failed. Perhaps it was this decision, combined with his 'slowly, slowly' temperament, which led him to attack Mitchell so much over the latter's out-of-hours association with the Lancashire and Yorkshire Productive Society. When Mitchell applied to the CWS for a loan in order to cover an overdraft from this undertaking, Crabtree objected. He had a point. The discussion was about whether it was right for Mitchell, in his position, to be applying for loans on behalf of other societies. Mitchell felt that his integrity was being questioned. At a Quarterly Meeting he came near to losing his temper:

> He had told Mr. Crabtree before he made that statement that there was no personal interest whatever of any kind; then why should Mr. Crabtree continue to make prejudicial statements? (Mr. Crabtree: No). It must be so; it could not have any other effect, and it was impossible for them to have the same regard for their Chairman after these statements as they had before, because they would think he was appropriating their money when he was doing nothing of the kind, and he trusted he never should as long as he lived.[46]

Crabtree defended his conduct in a letter.[47] It was plain that he was not only resentful: there was a real issue at stake. It was a matter, he suggested, of the office not the man. 'We shall not always have Mr. Mitchell in the chair – we may have somebody else in.' Mitchell appealed for trust and confidence.[48] He was having an attack of that characteristic Statist disease of confusing himself with his office – *le mouvement c'est moi*. A few years before, in the *Co-operative News* in 1875, E. V. Neale had accused the entire CWS enterprise of 'Caesarism'.[49] Crabtree and Mitchell went on niggling, clearly at odds with each other. Following what Crabtree regarded as a 'savage attack' on him, he wrote to the *Co-operative News* saying that Mitchell 'has yet to learn to differ in opinion without differing in feeling, and thus making it a personal matter. It is in this sense I fear his vindictive spirit is calculated to injure innocent persons.'[50] In his memoir of Mitchell in the CWS *Annual* for 1896, William Maxwell, President of the Scottish CWS, defended his deceased friend against feelings that were obviously still alive: 'a pure-minded man ... sometimes suspected and doubted by men who were profiting by his unselfish labours'. It is interesting that at the time of his funeral in 1895, rumours about Mitchell being a wealthy man were circulating in Rochdale. Various figures were put about as to the exact sum, from £5,000 to £80,000. 'Now as a matter of fact', commented the *Rochdale Observer*, 'Mr. Mitchell died a poor man.'[51]

Mitchell's relations with the Lancashire and Yorkshire Productive Society were particularly controversial. In 1896 Maxwell provided detailed accounts of them. When Mitchell accepted the job of liquidator, the position was hopeless: 'he simply smiled at those who said it was a forlorn hope'. All of the share capital and half the loan capital was gone. Some of the Co-operative Societies holding capital struck it out of their assets, believing it lost. Mitchell began by raising 'special loans' on his own responsibility. These came to £4,000, which, with the overdraft from the CWS Bank, enabled him to keep the Littleborough works going. By August 1894 he was able to pay out the original private and sick burial societies' loans, at 5 per cent compound interest. These amounted to £4,350, leaving a debit balance at that date of £850. Mitchell succeeded in writing up the share capital to its original amount, from £2,640 to £6,600. He never received 'one penny for expenses or remuneration'. When he was voted £20 for expenses in April 1880, he did not take it. It was placed to his credit in the Society's books as loan capital. 'After that time he would not allow the subject of remuneration to be considered at the Society's meetings.' While acting as liquidator, he sold about 16 per cent of the product outside the Co-operative Movement. 'The highest wages were paid to the workers.'[52] After his death the loan standing in his name, amounting, with interest, to £41, was paid to his executors. Maxwell's verdict was: 'Comment on such work is useless. It speaks of a hero, a commercial giant – in fact it is unique in the commerce of the land.'[53]

William Maxwell was no slouch. He was a prime mover in the construction of the Shieldhall estate of SCWS productive works. His praise of Mitchell was intimate. But Crabtree's feelings can be understood. They were expressed during years when Mitchell was playing for high stakes, in a competitive casino which he did not find intimidating. He wanted to win, to be 'thoroughly and completely successful'. Such ambition may explain quite a lot of the attitudes of others towards him, both the working-class, Manchester, and Heckmondwike colleagues close to him within the Wholesale Society and the middle-class, 'Christian Socialist' idealists at a slightly greater distance, for whom independent plebeian ambition – and the palpable competence that went with it in this case – were problematic. As Holyoake wrote on page 1 of his *History of the Rochdale Equitable Pioneers*, defending the working class which was his class too, 'the business habit is not thought to be their forte. The art of creating a large concern, and governing all its complications, is not usually thought to belong to them.' The History was intended as a sustained correction of this view. So too was Mitchell's life.

Mitchell must sometimes have felt that he hardly needed attacks from within the Movement: his agenda in the contest with competition was formidable. For instance, during the years immediately following the case of the Littleborough loan, the question of the CWS owning their own fleet of merchant ships was raised. During the second quarter of 1883, Mitchell needed to explain a loss in the CWS shipping department.[54] This was at a time when he was also keen to expand it, against the caution of a minority of delegates to the Quarterly Meetings. In March 1884 he finally got the go-ahead to buy up to three new boats.[55] But not without drawing on his deepest resources of belief and entrepreneurial courage.

The Society was running boats between Hamburg and Goole. They were transporting butter. The CWS had wanted a reduction in transport costs. The private lines had refused, so the CWS started running its own boats. 'Immediately after doing that', Mitchell explained to delegates, 'they came into collision with other shipping interests of long-standing and greater power, *so far as money could give them power*' (my emphasis). Their opponents reduced their rates from 48/4d. to 30/- a ton, in order to drive the Wholesale off the seas. Instead, the CWS used its size to take the income loss and to let its customers in Co-operative societies have the benefit of lower prices. Whereupon the private traders also reduced their prices on a range of goods, including butter. 'As a gentle hint' said Mitchell, who clearly enjoyed the cut and thrust, 'and to show them that they were quite up to the competition mark, the Wholesale then reduced the (shipping) rates, which affected their competitors. ("Hear, Laughter").' The latter then approached the Society to ask if they could negotiate agreed rates.

Mitchell's buoyancy stemmed from his belief that Co-operators' power of association gave them an edge against private interests. Small and local were not beautiful, so far as he was concerned. His theory was that mobilisation of common hopes and purposes – in huge aggregations – was itself as material as money. Such mobilisation, indeed, constituted labour's capital, enabling members of Co-operative societies to put 'capital', as capitalists called it, in its proper place, which was as a hired servant of labour.

> I may tell you this, that there are people on the Eastern side of England who are very large people, and they have said that they will break us down, if it takes them ten years to do it. (A voice, "They can't"). If the co-operators have the pluck of Englishmen, they will say, as they have always said, they may fight for fifty years and they will not break us down. (Cheers) You have overcome as gigantic monopolies as these. It is only a class of monopoly, but it is monopoly of wealth, and you have as large wealth and as large power *within yourselves* [my emphasis] to break down that monopoly as ever you have had before. You are stronger now than you were formerly. You broke down hedges, banks, and gates, and though there are iron bars, you will break those down too, I hope. (Cheers)[56]

This was drawing on an old, eighteenth-century taproot of co-operation: countering the monopolists with the people's potentially monopolistic power, enclosing everywhere – the land in general – against petty landlords of corners of the human field. Such tyrants needed cutting down to size. This was the project for which Mitchell needed all the power he could muster, inside himself as well as in the Wholesale. The associational culture in which he had grown up had endowed him and, he thought, all other Co-operators, with a formidable amount of 'power within yourselves'. It was what Max Weber in an earlier context called an 'ethic'.

Before getting closer to this ethic and the political philosophy that went with it, I want to give further voice to some of those who reflected on Mitchell and his project from a greater class distance than the colleagues already quoted. I want to juxtapose some Christian Socialist and Fabian reactions to Mitchell with some more, rather different, contemporary observations of him from within the Movement. This may all seem rather indirect. But it is my contention that the class matrix in which Mitchell's project has been set, before and after his death, has been, in the first place, the main cause of the long concealment of that project. But, at the same time, that matrix has its own importance beyond J. T. W. Mitchell. It needs to be understood if the wider history and practice of co-operation is to be advanced.

Selfish, interested only in the dividend; business men not operators; materialists not idealists; in need of leading out (educating) into progress; incorrect, in the sense that a child's answer in an exercise book gets marked with a cross rather than a tick: theoretically mistaken; interested in consumption, not production; shopkeepers not community builders; facts and figures, figures and facts, not visions and dreams; incorporated, full of 'middle-class values'; at best reformist, at worst capitalist; certainly not revolutionary. To anyone who knows the literature on working-class association since 1850 in general or on the Co-operative Movement since 1844 in particular, this will be familiar ground. Its most direct expression in relation to Mitchell has been Backstrom's assertion that 'in most ways he reflected the attitudes of the bourgeoisie'.[57]

It is tones of voice that are important. From 1874 to 1902 Ben Jones (1847–1942) was general manager of all departments of the London Branch of the CWS except tea, coffee, and cocoa. His father had been a dyer's labourer, his mother a power-loom weaver. In 1894, he wrote a huge book, *Co-operative Production*, published by Oxford University Press. He regarded Mitchell as a father: 'personally, he treated me as if I were a son, and I shall always look back to him with feelings of admiration as a co-operator, and also with feelings of filial affection'.[58] His book is a key source for CWS theory, and massive testimony to the fact that there was such a thing. He picked up the tones of voice that I am referring to when, for example, he quoted Christian Socialist reaction to the break-up of their producer co-operatives ('workshops') in the mid-1850s:

> It has been found very necessary to have some proof that men have foresight and self-denial before they should be encouraged to associate. Working men in general are not fit for association. They come into it with the idea that it is to fill their pockets and lighten their work at once, and that every man is to be his own master.[59]

The second half of the nineteenth century saw a great deal of this. The welcome to co-operation and to working-class association more generally during this period was a loud and public one, but it was highly qualified. It was one of those embraces that make breathing difficult. It was, in fact, part of a fight, a fight against particular notions (independent, private, working-class notions) and particular potentials inherent in large-scale working-class association. The welcome aimed at preventing, as much as enabling, things to happen. To quote Thomas Brassey in 1873:

> It has seemed to be a belief in co-operative stores, and not altogether avoided in cooperative works, that anyone, without previous knowledge, might be a manager. It would be strange if a man whose life had been spent in manual labour could successfully and instantaneously become a buyer and trade in commodities of which he has hitherto only been a consumer, and much more strange to find one totally unaccustomed to mercantile life who could successfully carry on a large manufacturing concern.[60]

Even at Congress, or especially at Congress until the early 1890s, Bishops, Lords, and other would-be patrons were given to utterances of this kind. When I read them I always wish I could see who in the audience was frowning, and who nodding. Here is Lord Reay in 1882:

> English co-operators have never boasted that they were going to renovate English society ... Co-operation has been the best friend of capital and is, therefore, the strongest ally of the middle class.[61]

By the end of this chapter I hope I will have shown – at least with reference to Mitchell – what partial truth, partial rubbish (but equally important either way) the sheer quantity of this kind of wishful thinking was.[62]

On occasion, the gloves came off. By the early 1890s, the 'idealists' were in retreat within the main organisational centres of the Movement. In January 1892, Judge Hughes, the Christian Socialist, wrote to Holyoake thus:

If I had my way it would have been a much keener attack on that stronghold which the devil has managed to plump down in our midst and which may yet set the good time back for a generation. I had written this time last year to decline the usual gift of the Wholesale Annual, but didn't send it and the book back on Neale's advice. Still I am not sure that the time has not come for taking off the gloves with Mitchell and his tail, who have no faith in co-operation (or anything else) that "goes down deeper than their dinner".[63]

No wonder that at the height of arguments with these people Mitchell felt that the Wholesale was being 'slandered' and that he had to defend it, as at the 1887 and 1891 Congresses, as being as 'high' a form of co-operation as existed 'anywhere on earth'.

Beatrice Webb's gloves were of the choicest kid. On the face of it, she was admiring. Indeed, she regarded the CWS and its Board as 'above corruption'. She admired Mitchell greatly, to the point of 'genius'. She was anxious to praise the CWS in terms familiar to her, namely the political economy of W. S. Jevons. However, as always, her diaries said much more than her theories might allow. During 1889 she was studying the Co-operative Movement. She spent some time in Manchester getting to know the CWS.

> Mitchell, Chairman of the CWS, is one of the leading personalities in the Cooperative Movement ... a sort of embodiment of the working man customer, intent on getting the whole profit of production, out of the hands of the manufacturer and trader, for the consumer ... As the representative of the Wholesale, he is inspired by one idea – the enlargement and increased power of the organisation of which he is the head. He supports himself on the part proceeds of a small woollen business, and draws

perhaps 30s. a week from the Wholesale to which he devotes his whole energies. With few wants (for he is an old bachelor), he lives in a small lodging, eats copiously of heavy food and drinks freely of tea: no spirits and no tobacco. Corpulent, with a slow bumptious pronunciation of long phrases, melting now and again into a boyish bonhomie ... He is a good fellow, and in his inflated way a patriotic citizen ... His Board of Directors are entirely subordinate to him: they are corpulent, heavy eaters, but for the most part they are neither more nor less than simple tradesmen ... Three or four times I have dined with the Central Board. A higgledy-piggledy dinner; good materials served up coarsely, and shovelled down by the partakers in a way that is not appetizing.[64]

In June 1889, Beatrice attended the Ipswich Co-operative Congress. She was welcomed warmly at the door of the White Horse Inn by Mitchell and others of 'my old friends of the Wholesale'. She experienced the scene inside as 'a happy hunting ground for the social investigator'. Then she moved to the Pickwick Inn and observed how 'at the Co-operative Congress there is an absolute equality: all live together on the freest of terms'. 'It is Sunday evening and we are all assembled in the long coffee room.' Professor Marshall, who had tried to discourage Beatrice from writing a book on Co-operation on the grounds that it was not fit work for a woman, had been elected to give the inaugural address that year:

He looks every inch a professor. A small slight man with bushy moustache and long hair, nervous movements, sensitive and unhealthily pallid complexion, and preternaturally keen and apprehending eyes, the professor has the youthfulness of physical delicacy ... Tonight his desire to gain information outweighs his nervous fear of a sleepless night, and he is listening with mingled interest and impatience to the modicum of facts dealt out in the inflated and involved phrases of Mitchell.

Mitchell, 'raising his sonorous voice and thundering on the table with his fat fist', told Marshall of his beliefs:

having delivered himself of his usual tea party peroration and finding none to dispute his points ... (he) relapsed into the enjoyment of highly sugared tea and much-buttered toast; his huge corpulent form, shiny bald head, clean shaven face, exhibiting a full, good-tempered mouth, largely developed jaw and determined chin, so completely affirmed the force of his argument in favour of organised consumption, that it seemed useless to draw from him further verbal expressions of it.[65]

So Mitchell's body was his argument! By such criteria, neoclassical economics must have been thin indeed. We are dealing here with more than a few private remarks. We are dealing with a kind of acceptance which is, at the same instant, a profound – fastidious, physical, and ugly – rejection. We are also dealing with attitudes which have a long history and a wide sociology. We are dealing, in fact, with the discourse within which the history of the Co-operative Movement has been set.

The tones of voice registered here pre-date the alleged shift from community building to shopkeeping for which the Rochdale phase of Co-operation has been held responsible. From the earliest days of the organised Co-operative Movement in the late 1820s and early 1830s, there was this feeling in some quarters that organised selfishness, with particular reference to stomachs, was destroying the idealism of 'true co-operation'. During this early period, however, the arguments seem to have been about strategy, rather than the class prejudice so evident in the writings of Hughes and Webb.[66]

People on a level with Mitchell left images of him very different from the ones that we were left with in the Pickwick Inn, Ipswich. George Jacob Holyoake (1817–1906), a working-class Owenite by origin (like John Watts), was capable of ideological disagreement with Mitchell, but not the kind of physical prejudice quoted above which in ethnic settings would be recognised as racist stereotyping. Holyoake did not like what he saw as the 'grim fanaticism' of temperance advocates. He attacked them at the Co-operative Congress of 1878 in those terms, but hurried to make an exception of Mitchell, who 'thinks every advocate is as pleasant as himself' and 'whose face is as radiant as a jubilee';[67] 'I was in the presence of one of the courtliest, nicest and most-to-be-respected gentlemen';[68] 'his kindly and intelligent face at once making him attractive to all who came in contact with him'; 'although it cannot be said he was a musician, he was passionately fond of singing ... (this) often found expression in his bursting into some of the hymns he knew so well'; 'one of the brightest and happiest men on earth'; 'although his home was almost destitute of domestic comfort ... his brightness never forsook him ... his racy anecdote, beaming countenance and hearty handshake spoke of contentment and happiness'; 'his general demeanour tolerant in the extreme ... never evasive, always courteous and frequently humorous', 'his genial wisdom', 'his presence was hailed with gladness everywhere', 'his beautiful life';[69] 'transparent character', 'the kindling eye, the beaming smile, the rich, cordial tone of his voice', 'a more perfectly transparent and unsuspicious nature could not be found', 'a nameless charm of manner', 'the outshining of a sincere, childlike and generous soul', 'you young people will never forget ... the bright look that seemed to light up the School' (referring to the Sunday School);[70] 'blameless and Christlike'; 'an indispensable presence', 'perennial smile and amiability of character'.[71]

Mitchell's quickness (in the old sense of that word) on the platform and as a chairman also struck people close to him. The impression, which comes across from the close quarters of the Movement itself, is not that of the overstuffed receptacle, but rather that of the animated producer, of enthusiasm, what the French would call an *animateur*. 'Contagious' was Maxwell's description of him:

> His energy is unflagging, and the vigour of his mind enables him to accomplish the most arduous tasks ... he is a ready speaker, grasps ideas promptly, and has the somewhat rare power of expressing his opinions with clearness ... His wit loves to play not wound, and he is generous and 'religious of his word'.[72]

One of Robert Halstead's first memories of the Co-operative Movement in the Lancashire town where he came from was of seeing and hearing Mitchell on the platform, and of his 'vigorous speaking and quick energetic movements ... on the platform of our local Co-operative hall. I was too young at that time to realise what he had on his mind to get so excited about.[73] A correspondent of the *Daily Chronicle* was of the opinion that 'to see Mr. Mitchell at his best you must have been privileged to gain entrance to one of the Quarterly Meetings of the Wholesale in Manchester'. His 'vigour, enthusiasm, shrewdness and wholehearted devotion ... were simply elemental in character.'

> Punctual to the moment, the large, clean-shaven, ruddy-faced man in the chair would strike the gong and call the meeting,

usually as large as the House of Commons on a crowded night, to order. There was no opening speech, nothing in the way of palaver. But if the winds arose and the storms came, the Chairman was ready, sometimes with the softest of answers, oftener with a joke or a story that put the hard-headed Northerners into the best of humour, and on occasion with a decisive word which made one wonder what would happen if the giant really put his foot down. He was the purest embodiment of democracy at the helm conceivable and the co-operators enjoyed and appreciated the way he handled them. The openness and simplicity of it all were transparent. But it was a great exhibition of character, and a most signal instance on the delegates' part of the self-imposed discipline of democracy.[74]

William Maxwell was with Mitchell when he was 'heckled' by the Commissioners of the Royal Commission on Labour, when he appeared as a witness for the CWS in 1892. Once again, the imagery is rather different from that used by Beatrice Webb. Maxwell uses language which evokes innocence and enthusiasm, rather than bellying 'corpulence':

> He surprised some of the gentlemen by the enthusiastic descriptions he gave of the power of co-operation. He gambolled with millions of money in share and loan capital. He jauntily talked of fleets of co-operative steamers. He wrote down buildings and machinery by thousands of pounds annually, till some of his hearers called for proofs of his statements. Balance sheets were handed round immediately.[75]

All this presence, it was widely agreed, was achieved without self-regard. 'Disinterested ways';[76] 'without a trace of self-seeking' (Hirst Hollowell); 'than whom no more unselfish man ever existed'; 'he couldn't be corrupted' (Maxwell); 'I believe if ever there was an unselfish man it was Mr. Mitchell';[77] 'an attitude of simplicity, honest, original and at all times unspoilt by any craving for social distinction or titular decorations'; 'I can hear him saying at all times, "I'm only John Mitchell, doing my best for my fellow men", a sort of reincarnation of Abou Ben Adhem'.[78] And so on.

Contradictory reactions to Mitchell and his work can never be fashioned into a single truth. Instead, they can be assembled, and then used to tell us what they can about real material conflicts. They lead us into the long conflict, the class struggle, between reformers from above on the one hand and working-class associationists on the other.[79] Dominant, inherited views of Mitchell have been the result of the former attempting to diminish the latter. The Webb example is quintessential. There was much more than heavily buttered toast and well-sugared tea between Beatrice Webb and John Mitchell. The Webb *oeuvre* on Co-operation – beyond Beatrice's diaries[80] – did a number of things to Mitchell's project: four in fact, and all of them in the interests of their own, rather different, concerns.

First, the Webb work on co-operation suggested that the project was admirable but ham-fisted and untheoretical, led by 'neither more nor less than simple tradesmen', with 'good materials served up coarsely'. Secondly, the Webb work suggested that Mitchell and the CWS were unconsciously, as it were spontaneously, Jevonian: that is to say that they unwittingly subscribed to a *political economy*. This is wrong already: Mitchell and the CWS worked more within a moral economy, tending towards a social-economy tradition. The Webbs thought that the political economy which the Mitchell/CWS practice underwrote showed how 'it was in recognised "utility", or specific demand, that lay the dominating and determining factor of exchange value'. 'The Co-operative Movement of Great Britain ... perhaps because it was genuinely of working class origin, achieved without intending.'[81] Thirdly, the Webb view suggested that the CWS had shown that productive co-operation was an unscientific Shangri-La, and that 'Consumers' Co-operation' was the only way forward. There was, in their view, to be a division of labour between people as citizens, people as producers, and people as consumers. The Co-operative Movement was to be corralled into the consumer section. As I hope to show, Mitchell's ambition was, on the contrary, to shepherd all these functions into one Co-operative Movement in order to bring consumers and producers, governors and governed, face to face in a single association. Fourthly, and perhaps most important of all, Beatrice offered herself – and to a degree was accepted by inside CWS interpreters such as Percy Redfern – as the theorist articulating the CWS/Mitchell side of the late-nineteenth-century struggle over co-operation. In doing so, she tried to unload her version of 'the' State on to the co-operative movement. In her book on *The Co-operative Movement* (first edition 1891, going into four editions before 1899 and three reprints before 1910), Beatrice argued that the trade-union and co-operative movements, though bringing valuable 'moral reform', needed to be supplemented by socialist legislation.

This was fine, provided that it is recognised as more Beatrice's project than Mitchell's. The State was to be staffed by collectivist experts, trained via institutions such as the London School of Economics. Its construction was to constitute a break, a new civilisation. Working-class associations were fine, even heroic. No one has chronicled them in more loving, typological detail than the Webbs. But there was to be a next stage beyond them, in which the initiative would shift to 'social scientists'. These were not the Owenite and working-class critics of political economy who coined the phrase 'social science' earlier in the nineteenth century. They were to be a new cadre of professionals with, no doubt, similar reactions to places like the Pickwick Inn and with gatherings characteristically rather different from the 'absolute equality, all live together on the freest of terms' which Beatrice observed at Co-operative Congress. Working-class associations would have their place, but many of their inventions and much of their culture – for that is what it was – would come to look 'primitive' from a professional point of view, just like the Quarterly Meetings of the CWS from 1874 to 1895. To the extent that it contributed to the aborting of an emergent critique of the State from Labour's point of view, this may have been the Webbs' most crippling legacy to the autonomy and potential originality of the Co-operative Movement's contribution to working-class socialism in our time. For Mitchell and his ilk, working people doing it for themselves – the old 'who does what?' question of craft unionism – were all-important. To change who did what: that was the project. As I hope to show by getting back behind the Webbs, Mitchell was an egalitarian with gigantic ambition. But the ambition was for his own association, its ethic and all its federated forms, not for any actually existing State.

I will complete this section with two instances to bear in mind while reading the rest of this chapter. The first is Robert Owen writing in the *New Moral World* in 1837. 'The working classes never did direct any permanently successful operations ... Whenever the working classes have attempted any complicated, important measure that required unity, patience, and perseverance to bring it to a successful issue they have failed in every instance as soon as they have taken the direction of it.'[82]

The second instance is a Rochdale Pioneer making a presentation to Edward Vansittart Neale in May 1891. At this event, Abraham Greenwood cast his mind back forty years, to a day in 1851 when Christian Socialists were visiting the Rochdale Flour Mill. The image that stuck in his mind and which he recalled, to laughter, was that of the gentlemen taking their coats off and turning them inside out, lest they got dirty.[83]

And two final encores. Judge Hughes: 'No faith in co-operation or anything else that goes down deeper than their dinner'. Lord Reay: 'English co-operators never boasted that they were going to renovate English society'. We shall see.

IV

Not long before he died, Mitchell addressed a meeting at an exhibition of Co-operative products in Manchester. He said:

> Our Movement was no longer a theory, it was a great fact, the best outcome of civilisation, and an embodiment of Christianity in trade. The political economists of the last century made selfish individualism the basis of commerce and taught that men should compete with one another for their own good. Cooperation taught that men should work together for the good of the whole community, that wealth should not be confined to a few, but distributed for the benefit of the entire population. The present condition of things in the social and industrial world was a scandal to so-called civilisation. A few were living in palaces, clothed in silk and velvet, and thousands of men, women and children were half starved and in rags. Co-operation would bring to the masses of the people the comforts which heaven designed them to enjoy in this world.[84]

In 1879, he told a public meeting at Congress that his ambition was no less than 'to create a new order of things', 'to change the world'.⁸⁵ This was his language in front of the Royal Commission on Labour during the early 1890s too. He wanted 'a new state of things'. In 1874, the year that his work became Manchester/CWS-centred rather than Rochdale-centred, he went to the annual gathering of the Accrington and Church Industrial Co-operative Society. He used the occasion to look closely at their yearly statement and to get excited about the communal prospect that it opened up for the whole of Accrington. Over the preceding fifteen years, he observed, they had created a profit exceeding £100,000. Properly invested within the Society, he thought, that might have employed 500 of their members, 'receiving amongst themselves the profits of their own industry'.

> He was anxious that the lever which the working classes now had in their hands should be employed not to make other men rich, whilst they (the workers) labour and toil and sweat for a bare existence, but to secure for them a perpetual redemption from all acts of slavery and tyranny ... Capital was not the enemy of the working man: it was his friend. He wished them to use it for their own elevation and the good of their children. He asked why should not they conduct productive societies as well as distributive and thus secure to themselves the profits made in those manufacturing concerns. There was no reason why twenty years hence, Accrington should not be one gigantic productive concern, and that the profits should be divided amongst the whole inhabitants of the town.⁸⁶

'Perpetual redemption from all acts of slavery and tyranny'; a city as a gigantic productive concern with profits equally divided among everyone; the scandal of misery in a world where the comforts which heaven 'designed them to enjoy' were materially available to all, given proper social arrangements ... this was a Radical/Owenite stance. And in Mitchell's case, as in that of Dr John Watts, the same set of feelings was evident; I would call them their 'if only ...' mentality. There was no reason why not, and in twenty years' time too, if only... if only they retained the surplus of their labour for themselves; 'and if everybody will carry out our principle, I believe most emphatically that we shall reconcile the interests of capital, labour and consumption in a manner the world has never seen before'.[87] 'If the trade of this country could be carried on solely by co-operation, in fifty years' time the Society could buy up the whole of the land in England.' 'That was no exaggerated theory, but practical fact.'[88] 'Let them look forward to that time. He did not believe it to be a Utopian idea. He believed it to be a practical idea of trade that they should secure to themselves the great benefits both of import, manufacturing, merchanting and banking.'[89]

V

Mitchell's vision may, for convenience, be divided into four parts. The first will centre on the movement, the second on class, the third on system, and the final one on politics.

The movement and the ethic of association

'Our movement was no longer a theory. It was a great fact.'

Before looking at Mitchell through other people's eyes, we left him in Rochdale. He had joined the Sunday School, Congregational, Temperance, and Equitable Pioneers movements. He joined the Rochdale Equitable Pioneers in 1853. His grandfather had been a member of the 'Co-operative shop' at no. 15 Toad Lane, which failed 'on account of its giving credit to members', and had lost money in that failure.[90] At Mitchell's funeral a wreath arrived from Mr George Healy JP of Windermere, the only survivor of the original 28 Pioneers. By 1855, Mitchell was a Committee Member. He was elected Secretary in 1857.[91] By October 1868, he was Treasurer of the REPS Education Department of which the Minute Book for 1867–8 records him attending 117 out of a possible 155 meetings (and being late on four occasions).

Mitchell became an early member of the Co-operative Manufacturing Society at Mitchell Hey, from the mid-1850s through to the 1860s, and Chairman of the Directors there for a number of years. Initially, the 1,400 shareholders from the Rochdale Society tried profit sharing with the 300 workers in this cotton mill. But jealousy and friction entered in.[92] After a long and bitter controversy, and by a majority of 3 to 1, the bonus was abolished in 1862. 'There is reason to believe', wrote 'Prospero' during the 1920s, that Mitchell himself proposed the majority motion at that time, 'on practical grounds ... he had not formulated any theory'. There is evidence of religious or at least denominational dimensions to the controversy, with Secularists, Unitarians, and Churchmen supporting the bonus and Methodists and Congregationalists forming a 'united party' against it.[93]

Mitchell's 'positions' on key issues in the Movement were not positions in the sense that political people use the word: they were experiences in context, the results of his life experience as well as his political convictions. When discussing bonus to labour, he would recall his experience as a child factory worker, and wonder what difference a bonus scheme would have made. For him, the application of formulae which enabled Societies to achieve continuity – the reiterated contrast made by Mitchell between the first half of the nineteenth century and the second half – would have made the difference in lived family experience between poverty and comfort. During the middle years of the century he was also closely associated with the Rochdale Corn Mill Society; acted as the representative of the Pioneers at meetings of the Lancashire and Yorkshire Railway Company; and was particularly involved with the Education Committee of the Pioneers' Society. This was the only aspect of the REPS's work with which he remained 'intimately connected' long after concentrating his energies on the CWS.[94]

For 21 years Mitchell was also Honorary Secretary of the Science and Art Classes in Rochdale, a national (South Kensington Department) source of funds to which the Co-op in Rochdale was affiliated. So he knew the Co-operative Movement, just as he knew the Sunday School movement for which he would leave Congress early when it was meeting in distant places (as in Plymouth in 1886), in order to be in his place in Milton Chapel punctually on Sunday morning. The movement was not an adjunct to him, 'my club' in a different class discourse, or a sector of his life as in 'the voluntary sector'. It was his culture, the medium in which he grew. On the evidence of items published in the *Co-operative News*, the details of his whereabouts in the months of January to mid-February 1886 looked like this: Jan 15, Central Board Meeting, N-W Section, Manchester; Jan 20, Festival, Doncaster; Jan 23, Soiree, Eccles; Jan 27, Annual Festival, Lincoln; Feb 1, meeting of Manchester Ship Canal Co., Manchester; Feb 6, General Board Meeting of Co-operative Newspaper Society, Manchester and Annual Tea Party, Staithwaite; Feb 9, Coming-of-Age celebrations, Aspatria; Feb 13, Soiree, Rawtenstall.

According to the CWS Minute Books for 1883–84, there were sub-Committees responsible to the General Committee on Finance, Grocery, Drapery, Shipping, and Production. On each of these the GC had five members, and Mitchell served ex-officio, as the Chairman, on each of them, so that in January 1884 his meetings were as follows: Grocery Jan 8th-10th, Drapery Jan 9th, Shipping same day, Production Jan 10th, Property Jan 7th, Finance Jan 8th. He also attended the Newcastle Committee on Jan 3rd and the London one on Jan 5th. This was a way of life: not leisure, not work, but a culture. Through such means, Mitchell – in a key phrase of Maxwell's – 'governed himself'. He knew that these associational forms – means of production of labour's own labour power, if labour was ever to own its power – would have to be his class's specific resource if ever they were to be able to achieve their project as interpreted by Mitchell, against all odds.

He stood for 'rationality' in the Weberian sense, but for a specifically working-class (but universal not subaltern) rationality. Regularity, clearly articulated ends, deliberately chosen means, ruthless exclusion of tempting sideshows (for example, independent producer co-operatives), redemption through federation not vertical integration (as a good Congregationalist) in one big association: all these describe Mitchell's project. He was, of course, Protestant, not to say Puritan. He shared the old preference for kinds of romance other than fiction, in his case facts and figures. 'Talk of figures being "dry"! – why they were more interesting and wonderful than any novel.'[95] He was uninterested in personal accumulation and, therefore, like Weber's capitalists, good at social accumulation. He eschewed domesticity and drink. At one point he referred to Co-operators as 'peculiar people'.[96] It is tempting to see his project – Deacon of Milton Chapel – as another representation for labour of that fecund upside-down side of the seventeenth-century bourgeois revolution which Christopher Hill has made part of our history. Mitchell thought he was dealing not with his own dinner, but with 'the most Christian principle in the world. It was a divine principle.'[97]

The confidence of this conviction might explain why middle-class improvers were compelled either to miss Mitchell's project altogether, or to despise and attack it. By then they could not afford, as it were, to do anything else. It was not a matter solely of Mitchell, but also of the historical context. In the developed conditions of labour associating within British capitalism in the late-nineteenth and early-twentieth centuries, but also reaching out beyond it, Mitchell's could be an *inclusive* rationality, aiming for the universal. No wonder there had to be a Royal Commission on *Labour* during the early 1890s, and no wonder it was the setting in which Mitchell was goaded into stating his views at their best. He was much nicer to the Christian Socialists than they were to him. He was an eirenic character, operating with the confidence and in the class context *which could afford to include*. People noticed how he met sectarianism with a smile.[98] By the end of the nineteenth century, rationality and improvement from above could not afford even to appear to be inclusive. By then, there had to be limits to mutuality. Setting such limits was what private competition and public legislation was largely about during this period. There was a great deal of interest at this time, and has been ever since, vested in the *enclosure* of what threatened to become public, namely large numbers of working people associating democratically in order to change the world. Exclusivity was essential. Otherwise Samuel Smiles's (revolutionary?) dictum in *Self Help* (1859) that 'what some men are, all might without difficulty become'[99] might be taken too seriously. Serious liberalism, which Holyoake called 'deliberate liberalism', had to be rolled back.

This is what the discourse in and against the Co-operative Movement by its patrons in Mitchell's day was about. A space had to be reserved for masters, for Authority, against a Movement which, for all its faults and failings, was experimenting with new spaces, new ways of governing large-scale attempts 'to arrange the powers of production, distribution, education, and government'.[100] Hence the terms upon which, for instance, General Booth could advocate co-operation as central to the solution of the social problem in *In Darkest England and the Way Out* (1890). One of his most important experiments was to be a Co-operative Farm. 'I should propose to renew the experiment of Mr. E. T. Craig, which he found worked so successfully at Ralahine.'[101] At the same time, Booth had definite views on democracy within production:

> Management signifies government, and government implies authority, and authority is the last thing which co-operators of the Utopian order are willing to recognise as an essential element to the success of their schemes. The co-operative institution which is governed on parliamentary principles, with unlimited right of debate and right of obstruction, will never be able to compete successfully with institutions which are directed by a single brain wielding the united resources of a disciplined and obedient army of workers. Hence, to make co-operation a success, you must super-add to the principle of consent the principle of authority.[102]

'Institutions ... directed by a single brain wielding the united resources of a disciplined and obedient army of workers' – this is more redolent of the power-crazed enemies of Dr Who and other space avengers than of associational culture during the second half of the nineteenth century. Nor did Mitchell have a claque of Time Lords to back him up at CWS Quarterlies. Self-reliance was not about hierarchies of dependence:

Congregationalists hired and fired their own ministers. Leaders within this associational culture often pondered these matters. When naming one of the engines 'Equality' – the other one was called 'Fraternity' – in the new CWS Flour Mills at Dunston-on-Tyne in 1891,[103] Thomas Burt MP told how Ruskin had thought that the French revolutionaries had made one big mistake. They had left 'Paternity' out of their triad of principles, 'as the representative of authority'. Burt was not sure about this, but he did think that 'forward movement' needed authority in order to be orderly as well as progressive, and that Maxwell and Mitchell and the Wholesale Movement had it.

> I do not mean that we are to be governed by despotism, but until the time comes when every man can govern himself – and we know that time will come bye and bye – it is necessary that there should be authority somewhere ... My friends, the presidents of the Co-operative Wholesale Societies, Mr. Mitchell, Mr. Maxwell, and others, can report real progress.

The system that produced Mitchell, and which he was trying to multiply, was more egalitarian than Ruskin's. Admittedly, it would be hard to be less so. It was concerned with 'arranging powers' towards the time when every person could, in and through association, govern himself. (One huge caveat must be entered here, although it will have become apparent to today's readers already: the language, though not the entire project, as we shall see, was expressed in male terms.)

In Mitchell's time, the thrust towards universality was strong: the working class was to become its own employer. The Movement would move through education, biscuits, newspapers, merchant ships, etc. into the National Debt, the railways, and everything else. It constituted a Society, or set of Societies, which were capable of becoming society itself. Such Societies constituted a world, a way of life, and, through Cooperative insurance and the funeral service, a way of death too. There was much to gain from it for many thousands of working people who lived and died differently because it was there. When he was giving his testimony to the Royal Commission on Labour, Mitchell listed some of the advantages as steadier work, steadier wages, greater continuity of work, full and friendly dealing with trade unions, and a minimum of disputes.[104] Beyond that, bespoke production for use, for an organised, articulate market (the local Societies) was an implicit, but actual, critique of the commodity form itself. Beyond that, a *Daily Chronicle* correspondent suggested on Mitchell's death that,

> To him, the Wholesale Society and the Co-operative Movement was not merely 'a state within a state', but the very kernel of the state itself. For did it not embody the active habitual working of the principle by which states live and grow? Public service, and the welfare of 'the body politic' – a favourite phrase of his – as the condition of individual progress, this was Mr. Mitchell's civic gospel and cooperative faith.[105]

'The active habitual working of the principle by which states live and grow', a *'civic gospel and co-operative faith'*: the correspondent may have been nearer the mark than Judge Hughes' observation that 'no faith in co-operation (or anything else) goes down deeper than their dinner'.

The class, and equality among human beings

Mitchell was very class-conscious. He was in no doubt that 'as long as there were two classes in the community – capitalists and labourers – trade unions would be necessary'.[106] He wanted the Unions to bank with the Wholesale, so that they 'might make a beginning in co-operative industry'. He was proud of his class, insistent on class and the dignity of labour: 'in co-operation', he told Congress at Newcastle in 1880, 'they dignified labour'. It is not hard to imagine the feelings of the delegate from Rochdale when he attended the first of the new series of Co-operative Congresses in the West End of London in 1869, at the Society of Arts. It was a 'society function': all those gentlemen's coats the right way out, no flour please; and Ladies too, no beerhouse keepers. At this time the CWS, such as it was, held meetings in its back-street warehouse, 'the delegates finding rough seats on boards laid across barrels'.[107] Twenty years later, when Mitchell and three other Rochdale Pioneers assumed the Presidency of Congress, for the first time dispensing with outsiders (the custom was to have a different President on each day), the feeling of proud takeover was palpable; as the *Rochdale Observer* recorded: 'Co-operation has got beyond the need of patronage'.[108]

Mitchell's performance in front of the Royal Commission on Labour, also in 1892, was poised and rooted. He took the Commissioners right through the nineteenth-century history of the Co-operative Movement, supplying appendices listing the 260 societies already there in 1830. 'The ideas of the earlier co-operators', he suggested, 'were rather on the lines of a commune in which there should be no individual profit, but that all members of the community should work in the interests of all.' The CWS's present 'complete system' was only a materialisation of such ideas. Mitchell was in no mood to give the credit for these historic initiatives in 'associated effort' to anyone – including Robert Owen – but working-class people. The CWS was, he said, 'primarily working class'. He then produced a table of the 1,459 Co-operative Societies that were in this association of 'federal production'.

These 'are entirely working class societies. According to a Return obtained by the Cooperative Union a few years ago, there were only about 2 per cent of members in receipt of £150 per annum. Though, in some town societies, there might be, perhaps, 5 per cent, the lack of any such members in the country societies leaves the average as before stated.'[109]

Mitchell wanted to 'prevent the accumulation of wealth in any particular channel'. There was to be 'a universal distribution of wealth'. 'What we wanted to accomplish by co-operation was absolute equality in the distribution of wealth, though that hardly seemed possible.'[110] The CWS system was to be one of free flow, because it did not, in Mitchell's view, constitute a particular, privileged channel, but rather 'the people' (only once have I found him calling them 'the masses', and then it was 'the masses of the people'). Its social position was such that 'all the advantages shall flow in the direction of the body politic', rather than in the direction of a privileged group.

Thus redistribution of wealth would happen – but not by law. Active agency by the State-as-subject would turn the people into objects rather than the subjects of the social sentence that they should properly be. The project was, in good part, *about agency*. How changes happened from working people's point of view was a big part of what changes were. The federal aggregate of Wholesale and local Societies was to be the agent, through all the 'qualities that constitute a good man': self-government through thrift, industry, and sobriety.

The project was gigantic. Sharing a platform with Tom Mann in Bristol in 1893, Mitchell expressed it thus:

> We want to put the profits of trade into the pockets of the people, not a section of them but the entire community. Until the people get hold of trade profits they will never be able to

undertake the productive business of the world. Mr. Carnegie of America said that a thousand pounds in the hands of one person would do more good to the community than a thousand persons owning a pound apiece. That was absolutely untrue. It would be better still if the £700,000,000 of the British Debt were owned by the 40,000,000 of British people, than to belong to a small section of the community. Cooperators want to use the best means to get the entire wealth of this country, land and everything else, into the possession of the entire body politic.[111]

Cultural equality, through education, co-operative occasion, and so on, was important to Mitchell. A high proportion of his speeches reported in the *Co-operative News* can be read as protestant addresses, urging working people to feel equal in situations of great hierarchy, a bit like Adam Michnik's exhortations to Solidarity members in Poland to feel free even though they knew their wider situation was one of great repression. The Co-operative Movement in the second half of the nineteenth century in Britain may be seen as a sustained critique of internalised subalternity among working people: credit, for instance, was a power relation to be avoided where possible. 'Why', asked Mitchell at the annual meeting of the Oldham Equitable Co-operative Society on 15 January 1876, 'why should the children of any of those whom he saw before him have an inferior education to the Queen upon the throne? (Hear, hear).'

> Let them have confidence in themselves and in each other; let them promote the diffusion of that knowledge and the boon of that education which would drive away superstition and extinguish suspicion and jealousy, and they would have that bond of united interest which no power on earth could break

asunder – they could free themselves from the toil and misery which oppressed them; they could make for themselves a heaven upon earth.[112]

Yet Mitchell was not a romantic: for him, self-realisation lay in being a servant to the cause of 'heaven upon earth' to which, in his own eyes, he remained loyal all his life. There was nothing demeaning in that. An insistence on fundamental sameness among humans was very important to Mitchell's thought. To understand this, we need to know much more about the Congregationalism which was so important to him, and important in the formation of many male working-class associationists, for instance in the Brotherhood and Pleasant Sunday Afternoon movements, during the late nineteenth and early twentieth centuries. His thought was probably at least as much a theology as was that of the post-Frederick Denison Maurice Christian Socialists. 'God made all men alike', he said in a speech which was really a sermon on the first day of the Carlisle Congress of 1887. He would insist upon a commonality which was so strong that it would contain rather than be contained by divisions of labour. The notion of a 'common bond' was repeated. 'They wanted all co-operators to be bound in one common bond, to live, to work together, having one common interest, because it was only that common interest which would secure that kind of union which would be effective in binding the body politic for the purpose of promoting a great and glorious cause.'[113]

System, complete co-operation, and no new capitalists

For Mitchell, humanity was realised in association as much as in production as narrowly understood. His idea of human fulfilment was not individual, and not tied to creativity at the points of material production, and less intrinsically gendered than some socialisms – in the conditions of his day – in so far as *membership* rather than *going-to-work* was to be the channel through which the value of labour was to be (universally) shared. The hero, as it were, was not the male factory worker or, for that matter, the creative artist. Membership was unlimited. In his project, there was a notion of what we might call socialisation-for-labour which could, he hoped, include differentiation at work. Service to a system – a system of 'complete co-operation' – within which, because it was complete, there would be no class interests, was to include and override divisions of labour at work. This system, he thought, was already in place: all it had to do was to grow. Complete loyalty could thus be called for. There are echoes here of both Owenite and Soviet Communist mentalities: it is at this point that the line between theoretical commitment to the communitarian idea in Mitchell's head and organisational (CWS) self-interest (Co-operation in One Country), not to say pigheadedness, is at its thinnest.

When asked in front of the Royal Commission on Labour why the CWS did not follow 'the generally recognised principle of co-operators, that the societies shall divide the fund known as profit equitably between the capitalist, the worker and the purchaser', Mitchell replied that they did, but in a different way, through members' purchase of goods. 'And thus, if you get the combination of shoemaker, joiner, and every other artisan class combined in a common bond, everybody gets a share of his own and other persons' productions, because they strengthen the business by the trade which they give to it.'

Divisions of labour within the work place (and payment of wages) characteristic of large-scale industry were tolerated within the CWS system in ways which subsequent socialists have found scandalous. This has been one of the sources of the lingering bad odour associated with Mitchell's memory. Indeed, modern divisions of labour were championed within the CWS in ways which made men like Ben Jones close cousins of the Fabian collectivists who admired them so. There was an unsentimental determination not to be driven to the wall by private competitors through refusal to use the production methods characteristic of large-scale industry. Ben Jones was quite explicit about this in *Co-operative Production* (1894), as was Mitchell's successor at the Wholesale, Thomas Tweddell from Newcastle.

> The era in which it was possible for a few men to profitably engage in manufacturing operations is fast becoming traditional. In all the principal trades, and in many of the smaller ones, the drift is irresistible in the direction of concentration. For good or ill, we have entered an era of big capitals, operating through gigantic factories, these again equipped with perfect tools, manned by well-drilled armies of men, and forming part only of perfect and far-reaching organisations. If that has been the tendency in the past, it will more than ever be the tendency in the future, for Nature is democratic in her methods, and refuses to work cheaply for the few. Cooperators must learn from these facts that if they are to win permanent success in manufacturing industry, they will have to enlist the aid of large capital and the most perfect organisation. And these auxiliaries hitherto have ranged themselves rather on the side of powerful federations of consumers than on the side of the self-governing, profit-sharing workshop. Indeed that institution has seldom been able to command either the capital, the power of cohesion, the faculty of organisation, or one of the essentials of permanence or success, and to seek to supplant the modern capitalist by its means is, to my mind, like opposing a pop gun to the rifled ordnance of the Elswick works.[114]

Supplanting the modern capitalist, in these kinds of working-class accent, might well send a shiver down the spine of the most liberal-minded, middle-class co-operative patrons. *'The rifled ordnance of the Elswick works'* indeed! There was, of course, serious argument about co-operative production taking place at this time, to which I have already alluded. It was between the 'Christian Socialist' advocacy of self-governing workshops (with bonus-to-labour, profit sharing, etc.) and the CWS notion of *all* production being conducted in large-scale factories governed by the CWS General Committee, the CWS itself being owned and controlled as a federation of local Co-operative Societies. In the CWS system, the benefits of co-operation were to be realised by the worker-as-member (along with all other members), rather than by the worker-as-producer in his own, self-governed workshop. This was a serious debate, both sides of which are still relevant to anyone interested in the connections that complex co-operation in an era of large-scale industry will require. In this chapter, I want to insist on two things: first that the Mitchell/CWS – sometimes known as 'federalist' – approach was a serious argument, an ideal, even a theory. History has not, so far, allowed it to be. Secondly, I want to return to an earlier theme: that in Mitchell's day the conflict was a North–South one; more seriously, that it was a conflict between different class attitudes and allegiances.

Edward Owen Greening was a leader of the Southern, Christian Socialist, anti-CWS camp. In 1889 he gave a lecture on his version of 'Complete Co-operation'. At this time, Greening was pleased with himself and with his Labour Association's advocacy of 'the essential principle of co-partnership' against the CWS. He told how he was visiting Leicester some time after an infamous strike by CWS workers against their own Society. In 1887, 60 or 70 workers from the CWS shoe works had applied to the Labour Association for advice on starting a schismatic Society of their own. Greening and friends 'took the trouble' to procure the rules of Godin's 'Familistère' and to translate them into English, 'omitting those parts which an Englishman would not understand or appreciate'. The New Leicester Co-operative Boot Factory had done well, thought Greening, out-pacing the CWS works. This is how he told it:

> When I went into that workshop ... I saw the men at work, and I saw everywhere the evidence of the wonderful results of the reconciliation of capital and labour. For instance, there was one man stamping out those ornamental fringes they put round the top of ladies' boots, 'gimping', I think they call it, by swinging round an immense lever; and he was swinging it round at a tremendous rate. He never stopped all the time I was talking to him. I said, 'You are working very hard; don't you stop that all day?'. He said, 'No; in the Wholesale Society they have got a steam engine to do this work, and I have got to get as many dozen a day done by this machine as their steam engine turns out, so I can't stop till I've got my number.' You could see the reason for it. His heart was in his work.[115]

I cannot help imagining Thomas Tweddell or Mitchell asking where else this worker's heart might be in a couple of years' time, if the independent Society failed to install modern machinery. Nor would Mitchell have read Greening's boast about return on capital in the same light. Whereas the CWS was receiving 3 to 3.5 per cent interest on capital in their works, the new Leicester Factory was, apparently, paying 20 per cent on capital. 'So the capitalists don't suffer', said Greening in his lecture. But that was not what Mitchell and Tweddell meant by reconciliation of the interests of labour and capital.

Mitchell told the Royal Commission on Labour that 'we endeavour to conduct our productive establishments with the highest regard to efficiency of workmanship, combined with sufficient remuneration and comfort of the worker ... the best goods, made under the best conditions'. But I have not found him talking so hardheartedly as Thomas Tweddell or Ben Jones about the division of labour. A research project is needed on the conduct of the CWS Productive works in Mitchell's time and after it, starting with the biscuit factory at Crumpsall (1873-1986). I have been through the relevant CWS Minutes, and made a sad visit to Crumpsall in search of records during the summer before it closed. Details, I suspect, will have to come from local newspapers. It is perhaps interesting that, on his death, the Chartist, Secularist Thomas Hayes from Failsworth – appointed first Manager at Crumpsall in 1873 – was celebrated as that 'rare type of democrat who combined great activity for the co-operative movement with the daily practice of its central principle in his everyday life'. It may be indicative of a slightly softer attitude in Mitchell than in Tweddell that, on Hayes's death in 1912, it was alleged that Mitchell had said that he was appointed 'not because of his knowledge of the bakery business but because of his sincerity, industriousness and reliability'.[116] And there are signs in subsequent Productive Committee Minutes of conflicts at Crumpsall between the imperatives of productivity and softer, co-operative ways.[117]

There was trouble at the Leicester Shoe Works in 1886-87. This led to the fiercest period of dispute between the Christian Socialists and the Mitchell/CWS system. Employees at the CWS factory in Leicester had complained of low wages in letters to the *Co-operative News*. They also complained that work of an inferior type was being put out to Enderby, in a form of sub-contracting (sweating). Mitchell stuck to the constitutional forms of CWS government, demanding loyalty in a strike which was obviously embarrassing to one for whom (as later in the Soviet Union) strikes were seen as literally incredible. How can a worker strike against himself? He wanted 'authorised statements', not letters of complaint. He tried, too hard, to keep the strike out of Committee reports and, therefore, not discussed at Quarterly Meetings. He set up a sub-group of the CWS Committee to hear complaints. This was unacceptable to protagonists of the strikers such as Edward Owen Greening who wanted a committee of investigation independent of the CWS. Such independence, in anything, went against Mitchell's ideas. It would be to go outside the system. How was it possible to be independent of a body of which one was a member? Thus, while he welcomed trade unions, he refused to concede to workers on CWS ships the right to control recruitment of crews and disciplinary procedures. He wanted to pay Union rates. But he also wanted the CWS committee, as servants in a common bond, to control their own servants in the Productive Works without any loss of autonomy to a body outside the system, whether trade union or otherwise.[118]

Mitchell was angry when the clickers and riveters in Leicester declined to state their case to the CWS Committee: 'was that a respectful way in which to treat the Committee who were their masters having engaged them in the name of the delegates?'.[119] Acting in the name of the delegates obviously meant being entitled to ask for complete loyalty to the Committee, within a closed system (a community) of which all were – or at least could be – members. 'The Committee desired and endeavoured to treat all their servants with the greatest respect and consideration possible, but if the delegates came to the Quarterly Meetings and set the authority of the Committee on one side, then the Committee could have no control over their servants.' All within the CWS system were to be masters of each in order to be servants of all, servants of all in order to be masters of each. This could not be expressed in a system of workers' control.[120]

Unity and loyalty were paramount Mitchell values, stronger even than their subsequent expression among working-class people in twentieth-century Labour Party politics. Concentration of trade in a single channel was his dream:

> My desire is that the profits of all trade, all industry, all distribution, all commerce, all importation, all banking and money dealing, should fall back again into the hands of the whole people. If co-operators will manage their enterprises in such a way as to concentrate all their trade in one channel, I am certain that this can be accomplished.[121]

Anything less than this would be to 'squander' possibility. It was important that no money should leak from the system; 'all co-operative money would be gathered up to be used purely for co-operative purposes'. That was the point of the bank.[122] It was important too that there should be 'an absolute faithfulness' by Societies to their own productive works. This was a continuation of the old tactic of exclusive dealing.[123] Loyalty was demanded from Societies to the Wholesale and from members to Societies: it has lingered in Co-op advertisements ever since. Thomas Woolfenden clearly did not like it when he received a letter from the Committee of the Rochdale Equitable Pioneers Society on 16 April 1881 telling him that over the previous four quarters his purchases from the Society had been less than the minimum fixed in the Rules. His case, he was told, was an 'aggravated one' because he was a member of the Educational Committee and a CWS representative. He was asked for an explanation. On April

20th, he gave it.[124] 'From a variety of causes I have not done so much as usual but I need not enter into that here except to say that, if you kept a better butter, I should do more in that alone than would meet the requirements of the rule. Mrs. Woolfenden prefers the best Kiel Butter which we get at the bottom of the Walk which is better than yours at the same price. I could put up with yours, but she cannot.'

But Thomas Woolfenden had his pride. He was not going to grovel in order to keep his offices in the Society,

> which I have not sought and which I am ready to give up at any time the members may think fit: if this is not satisfactory and if you wish to take advantage of this my first breach of the rule, I do not grudge the pleasure. My only regret will be in parting company with an institution which with all its faults I regard as the most potent influence in raising the social condition of the class to which I belong, more particularly to its educational appliances.

For Mitchell, means were united with ends *through the movement,* with all its constitutional inventions and disciplines. If you did not take the movement seriously (despising the store) as a way of life rather than as an idea, and as a real-life association of large numbers of disagreeing, and sometimes disagreeable, working people, then you did not take Mitchell seriously. It was through active membership of a common movement, based upon thousands of horizontal links of federation, that the person, the member, was to achieve an equitable share of (dividend in, plus democratic control over) the rationalities of co-operative production, distribution, and exchange. As a servant, the member might have to obey, say, the Productive Committee of the CWS, but as fellow servants in a common system the members of such a Committee had a different call on the loyalty of the member than a private, capitalist, irresponsible, unelected tyrant. 'We are, of course, subject to strikes and trade disputes, but liability to these is reduced to a minimum because the Committee are at all times accessible to the work people in case they have any representations to make and to discuss matters with them', said Mitchell to the Royal Commission in 1892. It was through active membership of a movement that the producer and the consumer came face to face, as the same person. In a complex society, direct relations required complex forms: membership of one or another could not but be messy. It was held to be advisable that, while employees as Co-operators should control the Movement, they should not, as workers, control the works, or even (as employees) the shop. If they did, vested interests would grow up. To the extent that the works or the shop prospered, those exclusively controlling and profiting from them would become capitalists or 'gentlemen who would get rich out of co-operators and then we should have to begin the work of co-operation again'.[125] None of this is to suggest that because this was the vision, all of it would be delivered. Not being an island entire to itself, the CWS was vulnerable to all the deformations indicated in the laws of (bourgeois) sociology. 'We encourage all our work people [meaning, in this instance, workers in the productive works] to become members of the local stores', said Mitchell in 1892. But he did admit to the Royal Commission that, while there were some work people on the committees of individual productive works, and certainly some on the committees of retail Societies, there were no work people from any of the Productive works on the Committee of the CWS.

However imperfect the system of production in which, as Mitchell saw it, 'the Wholesale occupied the highest ground', it was a whole by which independent producer co-operatives, and even productive units attached to local Societies, could be judged as second-best parts. They needed replacing by CWS units which would feed directly into the single system. Size was put to him as a problem: the CWS was big. Mitchell was unafraid: they were not yet, he would point out, as big as Government itself, and Government seemed to manage.[126] Decisions which seemed pragmatic to his detractors involved him in what he saw as 'great constitutional principles'. When he wanted to refuse the entry of the Co-operative Sundries Manufacturing Society into the CWS in 1891, Neale taunted him, 'why be afraid of 2 or 3 pills?'[127] The CSMS wanted to manufacture, and to supply from other manufacturers, groceries, drugs, patent medicines, etc. Some of its 120 articles would be encroaching on existing CWS production. Allies and friends in business were involved, but Mitchell was adamant. He reached for John Bunyan to say that one small leak might sink a ship, one sin would keep a sinner out of heaven. They were in a 'representative institution'. This was utterly incompatible with the admission of any 'private interests'. 'If a person comes here in the capacity of a representative, and he is a private shareholder in some other society, then you have a private interest conflicting with a representative interest.' It was in these settings that he looked most pig-headed to people who disagreed with him.[128]

Within the single system, production was important to Mitchell, in a way which the familiar label 'consumers' co-operation' has served to conceal. He put it an unfamiliar way round: 'we are striving that this wealth which is made in distribution shall belong to those who produce'.[129] 'Co-operation was the one true redemption for the social evils of human life, because it declared that the profits made by every kind of industry belonged to the people who made them (Applause).'[130] He was stung into putting it together in a single speech when Thomas Hughes criticised the CWS in the inaugural address of the 1887 Congress.[131] Mitchell mounted a hugely ambitious defence of his system. He wanted the Wholesale to establish works in every town where they would pay. He wanted them to make everything that their members wore. He wanted co-operation to be 'permanently successful'. 'He advised cooperators never to be satisfied until they got control of the entire producing, banking, shipping and every other, interest in the country.' The whole was brought into play when seemingly trivial parts were being talked about. When considering the replacement of a tea merchant with whom they had been dealing for years, in 1878, a paper to the General Committee spoke of how 'we must climb to the climax of a perfect organisation'.[132] In his 1887 speech, Mitchell put it thus:

> To whom does profit and the increment of value belong? We hold that, as it was created by the industrious classes, it belonged to them. Profit was made by the consumption of the people, and the consumers ought to have the profit. *But what was the difference between the people* and *the industrious classes?* [my emphasis].

He advised co-operators not to be satisfied until they got control of the entire producing, banking, shipping, and every other interest in the country. If the circle could only be completed, forms would be found wherein there would be no difference between 'the people' and 'the industrious classes'. That was the gap that Mitchell was trying to close. Tom Mann: '[M]ay I put it this way, that your distributive co-operation is merely preliminary to productive co-operation?' Mitchell: 'That is so.' Tom Mann: 'Then productive co-operation is exactly what you are driving at?' Mitchell: 'Exactly.'[133]

'Ours is a complete system in itself bound together by a common bond for the best interests of mankind.'[134] Until completion, in what Percy Redfern called 'the final form of industry', internal class conflicts, or, as Mitchell called them, 'special interests', would have space to grow within the Movement, as they did outside. 'In co-operation there were no class interests.'[135]

This was the case against bonus-to-labour, profit sharing, and the like. Mitchell told the Royal Commission that they 'will only tend in the direction of creating a new order of capitalists'. Distributing profits among a select few would create a working-class aristocracy.[136] At a meeting at Congress in 1894, he argued with his opponents:

> Co-operation ought to be based on the principle of united interest with the societies, and not individuals. Some persons taught that the individual should be the basis ... It was not a sound principle to appropriate profit to specially selected persons, on the basis of class interests; such a plan was opposed to the genius of genuine co-operative thought and action which had characterised the Movement since its commencement.[137]

If profits derived from the work place, they would be sectional. The whole community, the entire body politic, should share in any surplus derived from production. It would be better for everyone to have a bit than for some, for instance those nearest to the flour mill or those who worked in it, to have a lot. To Mitchell, personal wealth was not particularly desirable anyway: he disliked it with an old-fashioned plebeian radical temper.[138] It was important for everyone to be comfortable. It was important, too, to have a system in place whose dynamic worked in the right direction, rather than one which might have temporary advantages (say for those living in Leeds, or on top of a coal mine, or for anyone who married the miller's daughter) but which would have to be revolutionised all over again once wealth had accumulated in a particular channel. Mitchell's project was to find the single (for him necessarily federal) form which was also the universal one. He was not to be satisfied with anything less.

There was much ceremony at the opening of the Wholesale Society's Flour Mill at Dunston-on-Tyne in April 1891: processions, meals, and music. As always, there were speeches. At the end of the day Mitchell got up to make a final, seemingly spontaneous speech, which attracted direct heckling by Edward Vansittart Neale. Mitchell was in an ebullient mood, deep into the romance of statistics. He calculated that the industries in federation with the Wholesale had, to that date, made a profit of £70,000, allowing for interest, depreciation, and losses. They employed about 2,000 workers in their productive works. 'Now he asked them whether it was more in the interests of working men that that £70,000 should be divided amongst 70,000 people rather than 2,000 people? (Mr. Neale: "No"). He said yes, and it was more in the interests of mankind (Cheers). They had made capitalists enough in the past. They wanted to make capitalists universal.' He then explained that in one of the CWS industries it took about £50 to employ a man, in another £87, another £114, another £372, and so on. In the Flour Mills, it would take nearly £1,500 of capital for every man that could be employed. In two corn mills where 200 workers were employed, last year they had made a profit of £40,000:

> He asked them would it be in accordance with common sense that 200 people should take £40,000? That was not co-operation. It was diametrically opposed to the spirit and genius of co-operation, that they should divide the profits of working men

amongst a few people. He thanked them very cordially, and he should not have made those remarks but for the feeling that they were bound to know both sides of the question, in order that they might understand what it meant.[139]

It is generally forgotten that the voices arguing for co-partnership during the late nineteenth and early twentieth centuries included arch enemies of the Co-operative Movement such as W. H. Lever, and that there were theoretical, principled, working-class voices arguing strongly against it.[140]

Politics, and associational practice

Mitchell's politics related to mainstream party politics, but were not primarily about them. He once suggested that the Conservatives had done as much for Co-operation as the Liberals. He ran for office as a Radical Liberal in local election campaigns in Rochdale in 1893 and 1894. This was at a time in the town when old-style Liberalism was being attacked by a growing Independent Labour presence, and when alliances between the ILP and Radicals were being promoted. On the Radical side, State Socialism was seen as an obstacle to alliance.[141] At his adoption meeting in 1893 Mitchell was recommended as an 'excellent representative of both labour and capital (Laughter and Applause)'. There were obvious advantages, seen as such by the local Liberal press, in running such a candidate at such a time. 'Mr. Mitchell is not exactly a wage earner just now ... but he is in the truest sense a man of the people.'[142] He was narrowly defeated by the Conservatives, and again in 1894, having stated 'what he most desired' as 'the working man exercising control over the forces of the nation'.[143] After the second defeat, the *Rochdale Observer* praised him thus: 'He is not a good electioneer. He offered his services to the ward, but that was all; he would not flatter his friends, he would not canvass the indifferent, he would not cajole the unwilling. This is admirable, but it is not electioneering.'[144]

Mitchell advocated Co-operative Parliamentary representation rather early, at the Congress of 1877. He returned to the theme at Lincoln in 1891. In part, he saw the Movement as an interest among other interests, needing seats near to the centre of power in order 'to influence the government of the day in favour of co-operative legislation.[145] But it was more than that, locally and nationally. It was about control: bringing co-operation into politics rather than politics into co-operation.[146] As with trading, Mitchell was not satisfied with half measures. When the Mayor of Lincoln came to open an exhibition of Co-operative products at the 1891 Congress, Mitchell presented him with the CWS *Annual*. He then took the opportunity to remind him that there were 6,000 members of Lincoln Cooperative Society. Ever ready with statistics, Mitchell said that they contributed £700 a year towards the Corporation. The Mayor was obviously embarrassed. He said he was impartial and would open exhibitions for private trades people, if asked. Mitchell finished his speech by declaring that 'Co-operators should strive to get the government of the towns they represented more under their own control'.[147]

The language of Mitchell's politics was in a plebeian radical tradition dating back to the early nineteenth century, and before. They were 'engaged in an enterprise which had a great future', he told a meeting at the Huddersfield Congress in May 1888, 'embodying government based on the universal voice of the people'. 'The people' was a favourite expression of his, and 'the people of England'. 'What we wanted was that capital and its profits should belong to the people, it was through co-operation that this would be accomplished, and when that day dawned it would be a bright and glorious one for the people of England (Applause).' They were to work for 'the time ... not far distant when the vast cooperative body would have some control over the social and political policy of the nation (Applause)'.[148] One of their entitlements to control was, he said in 1882, that 'they contributed largely to the taxes of the nation and as a body they had no voice in the expenditure of those taxes'.[149] His interest in the National Debt was also in this tradition, as was his concern that the people, not diplomatists, should make treaties. Now that 'the principle of reconcilement of interests' was in motion in their Movement, it 'would leave little work for armies and navies as it came to be applied in the future to the greatest of human affairs'.[150]

It was the details of associational form that mattered, and the relationship between detail and democratic principle. Preoccupation within the CWS with small sums of money, as a way of curbing the audacity of elected persons, has already been considered. In 1874 there was a debate within the Movement over the mode of appointing the Central Board of the Co-operative Union. Up until then, the Board had been elected by delegates at Congress, with each Society having equal representation. William Nuttall wanted to introduce a block vote scheme, whereby each Society would get an extra delegate for every 500 members. The terms upon which E. O. Greening opposed this innovation were interesting. He said that it would do away with 'parliamentary government' and introduce a foreign system, 'a kind of democratic ultra-despotism, voting by mandate'. Mitchell, however, backed the idea, which was not in the end carried. It was 'what the radicals of this country had fought for for the last century – namely equal electoral districts and power concentrated in localities'.[151]

Mitchell's ultimate vision was original, if not entirely thought out. This was teased out of him by Professor Marshall and Tom Mann in front of the Royal Commission on Labour. Space, he conceded (to Tom Mann) should be allowed for municipalities to do whatever it could be shown that they did best. Mitchell was not dogmatically against *any* State activity. He had, after all, been Secretary to the government-financed Science and Art Classes for many years in Rochdale. 'It would all depend on the circumstances of the case.' But he was concerned in ways which paralleled his doubts about independent producer co-ops. He was concerned about area, or location, and incipient, new inequalities. In October 1892, Tom Mann pressed him to support local State control where it could be effective as an agent of democratic control over production. Mitchell was wary:

> [I]f I understand your question aright, I should say no, because a corporation controls only a limited area, and a wider area would be contributed to the advantage of a limited area in the case you put. *Our principle is the widest area possible for the distribution of advantages* [my emphasis], and if the question were put to me on the basis of the corporations of the land where joining together for the combinations of their productions, it would be more in accordance with our line of action. But if one corporation is to engage in production, and receive within that corporation a special benefit to which it might be a hundred other corporations were to contribute to its advantage, I should not altogether adhere to that at once, whatever we might ultimately agree to.[152]

As far as most industry was concerned, all persons were to be Co-operators, affiliated through their local Societies to the aggregate Society, the CWS. Every person would have the power to vote for the Committee of the CWS. When he was asked by the Commissioners to generalise off the cuff, he proposed that in the co-operative society of the future it would be a matter of more or less direct election of a national, industrial, general committee of management. Marshall was sceptical: 'the result', he felt, 'would be simply a new form of management of certain industries by a Government for the people'.[153] He kept on suggesting that in Mitchell's scheme, citizens would have no more control over industry than they currently did over the national situation, which was less familiar to them than Quarterly Meetings in Manchester. At one moment there was an exchange with Gerald Balfour which provides us with a unique glimpse of the less-than-optimistic side of Mitchell. It is somehow reassuring to discover that such a side was there.

> *Balfour.* 'You contemplate the time when everybody in the country will be a member of your co-operative store?'
> *Mitchell.* 'I should like to do so, and I hope I may. I cannot say that my faith is over strong because of the selfishness of mankind, but I do contemplate that such a thing may be brought about by the universal distribution of knowledge of the highest kind.'[154]

The last phrase has an Owenite ring to it. But Mitchell pressed on with practicalities. He was not entirely clear about how direct or effective elections already were within the CWS. Much was left to the autonomy of Societies. But he implied that within his federation there would be, and was already, a greater degree of direct control than currently existed in the dominant arrangements of conventional politics:

> As it stands at present the constituencies elect Parliament, Parliament does not even elect the Government, except in one

way, by a sort of negative vote, but if the country were called upon directly to elect the Government – every post from the Prime Minister to the most humble positions then there would be a comparison to ourselves, if that was done.[155]

During one of his Rochdale campaigns in 1893, he had argued that 'all government should be conducted by elected executives, and, when elected, those executives should be favourable to the principles to which they gave adhesion when first they sought suffrage'.[156] At the Royal Commission he went rather deeper than his dinner:

> If the principle were carried out as I would have it carried out, every citizen would feel the influence of this great and powerful system, from the centre to the circumference, and they would feel that they were associated with something better than what is in existence today, and every citizen would be raised and would occupy a higher and nobler position.[157]

5. Towards a co-operative university

Co-operatives are voluntary organizations, open to all persons able to use their services and willing to accept responsibilities of membership ...

> *1st principle: voluntary and open membership, International Co-operative Alliance (ICA) Statement of Co-operative Identity 1995*

If manure be suffered to lie in idle heaps, it breeds stink and vermin. If properly diffused, it vivifies and fertilizes. The same is true of capital and knowledge. A monopoly of either breeds filth and abomination. A proper diffusion of them fills a country with joy and abundance.

> *Poor Man's Guardian, 3/15, 1 June 1834, p. 146*

Sooner or later this country must face a comprehensive form of education beyond school ... and make it available to all ...This will be achieved through a bloodier battle than that for the comprehensive reform of secondary education.

> *Eric Robinson, 'A Comprehensive Reform of Higher Education', in Higher Education Review, 3/3, Summer 1971, pp. 1927–2011*

Knowledge, states, and markets

There are many reasons for thinking that now is a good time to be considering – more than that, acting on – the idea of transforming higher education (HE) in the UK in a co-operative and mutual direction. In this chapter I will select just one reason and use it to identify some of the wider issues involved: it is that ideas and knowledge matter more and more in the world we live in, as do the forms of association through which they are produced and distributed. My approach to co-operation, which is committed as well as conceptual, is illustrated with historical and current instances, as well as from my own experience. Ideas and examples are clustered in five overlapping sections which are not linear or chronological.

In 1969, Boris Ford, professor of education at the University of Sussex, asked 'What is a university?'[1] He regretted that this is 'a topic which most of us who work in them seem content to avoid'. This is no longer so. 'The idea of a university' is in play as it has not been since John Henry Newman's work in 1854, or before him that of Wilhelm von Humboldt.[2] Deeply felt answers have been coming from academics with very different points of view.[3] In working through this issue from the point of view of co-operative and mutual enterprises (CMEs), we have much to learn about the intellectual as well as financial difficulties that any coherent, ethical *idea* of a university, with its own values and principles, continues to face in 'the West'.

A definition of co-operation relevant to HE is a good place to start. The *Statement of Co-operative Identity* (1995) by the International Co-operative Alliance contained one. When reading the whole *Statement* with a single university or a global HE network in mind, key concepts stand out: autonomy; voluntary and open membership; and member ownership and control. Co-operation is relevant to education because by its nature learning is a two-way, mutual activity. Knowledge is something that you can give to others without losing any of it yourself. 'All education which is worth the name involves the relationship of mutuality.'[4] A *de haut en bas* system, particularly in England, has always been marked by a fear from the top that too much 'Higher' for too many of the 'Lower' involves either a waste of money or a loss of position. As the Master of the Rolls asked during the legal battle preceding the 1902 Education Act, which abolished School Boards as rare examples of direct democracy in England and prevented them from controlling any Higher Grade work beyond elementary education: 'Why should I teach my ploughboy Greek?'[5]

I have spent much of my life in or near education, from joining a pre-school run by the Parents' National Education Union[6] in 1945, to retiring from Ruskin College Oxford as Principal in 1997. I taught at the University of Sussex from 1966 to 1989. Since 1997 I have worked in a variety of ways with the Co-operative College and with the Co-operative Heritage Trust. In each of these places the form as well as the content of learning has been a central concern.[7] In opportune conditions for CMEs, it may be time to follow Brecht's advice: 'nor should you let the Now blot out the Previously and Afterwards'.[8]

For most of my time there, Sussex represented an innovative and, in retrospect, a co-operative and mutual idea of how a new university should organise itself, and how that connects with what it teaches, learns, and writes about. Yet Asa Briggs's inspirational 'New Map of Learning' lasted no longer than 25 years. Ever since it was abandoned by a subsequent Vice-Chancellor, I have recognised that 1960s and 1970s enthusiasts like myself, assuming a 'secular trend towards increasing academic self-government',[9] neglected the internal work necessary to sustain a different model of the university, based on co-operative and mutual *membership*, in competitive, market-convergent times.

We tended to use our pre-1996 Research Assessment Exercise habitus,[10] defended as 'academic freedom', to work externally: in my case organising for community and labour history in associations like the Federation of Worker Writers and Community Publishers. We resisted Planned Programme Budgeting[11] but allowed management to marginalise the ideal of cross-grade, communitarian self-government. Our radicalism tended towards *alternative* rather than fully *oppositional* construction. Academics continue to disdain management as 'admin' and are wary of excessive 'teaching loads' in order to defend their 'own work'. It may be that intellectuals, like the professional and managerial class more generally, have little elective affinity with CMEs. Writers as they would like to be, non-scientific academics prefer on-the-page connections to on-the-ground constructions, and whole systems rather than knowable, slow-cooking Societies. But this may point us in a particular direction as far as transforming higher education is concerned.

These tensions are discernible historically. It would be worth considering how far 'adult education', treated as an isolated department rather than as the whole HE enterprise, unintentionally functioned to let a comprehensive, democratic transformation of HE off the hook between 1945 and c.1979.[12] It was a rare and famous strike in 1909 about the nature and direction of knowledge, led by staff, which lay at the heart of the history of Ruskin College.[13] And the idea of specifically workers' equivalents to universities shaped the pre-history of Ruskin as a College founded in 1899, as it did the Co-operative College in 1919.[14] Such notions floated in the

European air during the late nineteenth century. *Universités Populaires* had been encouraged by the followers of Emile Durkheim in France, and Marcel Mauss' work remains central to theorising mutuality.[15] The central intellectual problem for any co-operative university has to be knowledge itself, the power which flows from and into its dominant *divisions of labour* in the sense in which Durkheim used that term.[16]

In what ways are our times good as well as opportune? More and more, ideas are seen as material: the concepts of 'knowledge worker' and 'knowledge economy' have been current since the 1960s.[17] This hardly needs saying in universities nowadays. It has long been assumed in co-operatives: 'bread, knowledge and freedom', as William Lovett, the storekeeper of the First London Co-operative Trading Association, wrote in the title of his autobiography.[18] In this way, CMEs can be seen as movements for lifelong learning which offer models for brain-workers today.[19] The generation of new knowledge and consciousness through these co-operative forms is becoming essential to sustaining modern, 'economic' co-operatives *as* co-operatives. There is a sense in which large-scale co-operatives and mutuals, for instance in the financial sector during times of capitalist crisis, need to become learning organisations – specialist universities – in themselves. The alternative is to take the line of least resistance: the capitalist road. Member-consciousness is the (organic) capital of co-operatives and mutuals, a point well understood among successful networks of co-operatives and credit unions across the world where education was seen as co-terminous with co-operation.[20]

During the early twenty-first century, universities are commonly defended by their funders and managers in terms of bread rather than truth, generating useful knowledge for the UK's competitive position in a global race. They might equally be evaluated in terms of the originality, morality, or sustainability of the ideas that they produce, distribute, and exchange. Or in terms of the special relations between the private freedoms and public responsibilities which their charters and statutes, including their licence to confer degrees, are drawn up to incorporate – by no less an arm of the state than the Privy Council. How universities are governed matters. Put another way, it matters to what extent people in them dare to make states, but not quite as they choose, rather than submit to abstract notions of 'the state' and 'the market'. The fully 'public university' makes its own 'circumstances', its own markets and states of affairs, changing as well as understanding The Market and The State.

Complex relations between the public and the private to make things differently, and to make things happen, are the stuff of present-day co-operatives and mutuals. CMEs are full of externally derived market and state contradictions in and against which their members make spaces to produce, distribute, and exchange goods, social relations, and ideas. Such enterprises are economic, yes, but for what kind of economy? An economy of the common good? They are businesses, yes — no more heavily state-funded than, say, British Aerospace – but also voluntary and open associations of members. 'A co-operative', says the 1995 *Statement,* 'is an autonomous association of persons united voluntarily to meet their common economic, social, and cultural needs and aspirations through a jointly-owned and democratically-controlled enterprise'.

Co-operative characteristics: possibilities for universities?

As suggested at the start, autonomy, ownership, and control by members in 'voluntary and open membership' characterise co-operatives. How far can we re-think universities and HE systems along these lines?

Autonomy?
It matters whether we conceive of autonomy in terms of individual institutions or of federated activities across a wider system. Certainly, there is a long history of institutions striving for autonomy, whether that be in terms of civic status or, more recently, in status groups such as the Russell Group which promote league-table autonomy. Universities seek autonomy as fast as they reasonably can, whether from local authorities or from the Council for National Academic Awards, or from joint ownership by 'parent' universities. Reading, Exeter, and Southampton all gained their independence from University of London or Oxford examinations. Former components of the University of London regularly 'win' degree-awarding powers. More recently, Suffolk University Campus gained its 'freedom' from the academic, research, and financial underwriting that it had previously enjoyed from the Universities of Essex and East Anglia. Imagine a minimalist 'university', on a regional or even national scale, to which autonomous units could prepare and present candidates. Why go it alone rather than help to form an open, co-operative university network designed for learners and learning in our times? There is potential for students, teachers, managers, and support staff to *socialise* massive, open, online courses (Moocs), to prevent autonomy at a single institutional level working for competitive sameness rather than for co-operative difference. Imagine a university – 'universal' was a favourite Owenite word – as a complex local *and* global cluster of federally linked mutual societies of diverse sizes fit for their purpose and for meeting members' needs. Some might be as small as seminar rooms;

others as large as science parks and with no social or technical obstacles to communication between them or, for that matter, with anyone else who wishes to learn to follow the argument wherever it leads.

From the point of view of forming co-operatives with organic, meaningful memberships, Co-operative and Mutual Enterprises (CMEs) could provide universities with services (teaching, assessment, research, or any other type of supply) for purchasers across an open system, rather than within one closed institution. A North East Music Co-operative (NEMCO) was set up in Newcastle upon Tyne in 1995, offering music/instrumental tuition across the North East, providing a pioneer example from the school sector. Once there are enough such co-operatives (in language learning, world-market literacy, study skills, public history, memory work, life writing, gender studies, etc.) and once they have been shown to engage their members in mutually improving, productive ways, a co-operative and mutual higher education system would become visible.

Open?

Like autonomy, openness is a key co-operative value: 'open and voluntary'. Instead of the Open University (OU) competing as an autonomous establishment, *one* university among others, could there not be an open HE system for which the OU could still provide the matrix? The story of the *containment* of Harold Wilson's original thoughts about the University of the Air needs to be written. He imagined 'a new educational trust bringing together many institutions and organizations', rather than an independent and autonomous institution that granted its own degrees.[21] The taming by universities of Gordon Brown's University for Industry (UfI), among other examples, might reveal a similar story. It would be in the long-term interests of students and their National Union to organise 'anti-enclosure' research and development – action research perhaps[22] – not only on university governance but also on the 'ownership' of degrees and other post-compulsory qualifications. The vision would be to 'make universities irrevocably part of the knowledge commons'.[23]

Openness to – and then ownership by – everyone, 'the people', was part of the idea of a university long before the Open University opened in 1971. In 1900 the Social Democratic Federation (Shoreditch branch) used 'Oxford and Cambridge and other endowed seats of learning (as) the rightful inheritance of the people' as an argument against the foundation of Ruskin as a separate 'workers' college'.[24] Given the Oxford and Cambridge Acts of 1571 and 1877, they may have had 'civil or common law' on their side.[25]

The new universities of the 1960s were more open than their predecessors in the UK, at least in promoting new ideas, re-thinking internal organisation, and generating traffic between academics and outside interests; not least in the creation of centres, institutes, and 'units', on and off campus, for modern records, development studies, creative writing, science policy, and business studies. But that generation of 'old-new' universities were also set in quite traditional moulds, determined to win their spurs as 'proper universities', as was the OU.

Might it be possible to develop a vision of a regional and comprehensive post-compulsory education system in which all local citizen-beneficiaries had automatic membership rights, linked to mutually beneficial cultural institutions: libraries, theatres, galleries, and sports centres, with front-room learning centres on every estate or group of streets? No more competitive admissions processes on which individual universities spend so much spirit, sifting and grading. For that matter, a mutually constructed Open University Validation Service (OUVS) and a mutually owned assessment/ examination service working to agreed criteria might reduce the elaborate examination and grading processes on which individual universities spend up to a whole term from a student's point of view. Instead we could encourage openly available, voluntary membership in teaching and learning societies, federated into comprehensive, regional universities of teachers and learners, all able to research and write, learn and teach, within a nationally available credit system – a co-operative and mutual Council for National Academic Awards (the CNAA, 1965–1993).

Ruskin College illustrates the problems and possibilities well. In the early 1990s, the College, under pressure from the then new Further Education Funding Council (FEFC), replaced its two-year diplomas with one-year courses. In response, Ruskin sought open, external, transferable validation and accreditation through the Open University Validation Service, a successor body to the CNAA. The one-year Certificate of Higher Education (Cert HE) provided 120 credits out of the 360 needed to achieve a degree, to which was added, for some subjects, a second-year Dip HE programme, making 240 credits in all. Hence the College's interest in two-year foundation or associate degree programmes. Ruskin became one of OUVS's success stories. Its Advisory Board, on which I served, had some of the excitement, but with less of a single-institutional focus, that must have attached to the original Planning Committee for the OU, which began work in 1967. By 2013, it was possible to study for a full degree at Ruskin, funded from further and higher education sources, linked to different external networks and accreditation routes.

Ruskin was one beneficiary of a national credit framework. This developed from the 1980s, from a base in further education colleges such as Nelson and Colne College, and eventually became the Open College Network (OCN). It spread to polytechnics such as Preston Polytechnic, now UCLAN, reflecting Eric Robinson's vision for 'People's Universities'.[26] Robinson's 'integrated colleges scheme' would have allowed an individual student, indeed a whole class of students, to gain degrees or other qualifications without buying into the Oxford, Sussex, or any other exclusive 'brand'. Ruskin became a small part of that potentially co-operative and mutual system. The idea remains only half finished because it lacked political backing from any government, and because no university is bound to 'recognise' a student's credits. They are not legal tender, in the sense of being fully portable across a wider, open, university system.[27]

There were moments of hope, such as when Ruskin and the other Long Term Residential Colleges for Adult Education (LTRCs) were given their unique Adult Education Bursaries in 1975. Soon after that, there was also a chance for the University of Sussex to join with the College of Education across the road and with Brighton Polytechnic as it then was, to make moves towards regional, comprehensive arrangements for HE in Sussex. The University gave no sustained, collective thought to the matter. The result is two contiguous, autonomous universities: Brighton and Sussex – now with a joint Medical School (2002) as a symbol of the comprehensive co-operation that might have been. Regional arrangements in Sussex and elsewhere would also have made sense of LTRCs, region by region: flexible bursaries for late returners to learning, including homeless people, for whom residence and tutorial support is necessary and well suited.

Ownership?

Whereas members of CMEs do and must own the future of their ultimately 'private' enterprises, even at the risk of democratic decisions to de-mutualise them, there is no reason why the public assets that enable universities to function should be owned in the same way. They need to be held 'in trust' for their users and beneficiaries, in a range of publicly accountable forms such as those now being implemented within the Schools Co-operative Society. 'Ambiguity of ownership' has led to 'governance hazards' which 'include the appropriation of academic resources for managerial gain at the expense of social interests'.[28] Top managers love property-development schemes, whether in higher or further education, not always with manifest educational benefit.

The question then remains: should user-members, or a wider set of beneficiary-member/owners, be seen mainly as entire, self-governing institutions ('the university'), or could lessees also be smaller consortia of teachers, learners, researchers, writers, technicians, or craftspeople who 'unite voluntarily to meet their common economic, social and cultural needs and aspirations through a jointly-owned and democratically-controlled enterprise'? In 1962, in a book which grew from teaching a class for the Workers' Educational Association (WEA), Raymond Williams addressed the problem of ownership in relation to democratic control in the newspaper industry, another site of autonomous and powerful baronies in British culture. His approach could equally well apply to HE. In many cases it already does: public ownership (local, regional, national, community, or trust) of land and other large-scale assets, with users as long-term lessees. 'It is the duty of society to hold these means [of communication] in trust for the actual contributors, who for all practical purposes will control their use.'[29]

Members?

The *Statement of Co-operative Identity* mentions members and membership 17 times. Without members, co-operatives cease to be such. Hence the work led by Graham Melmoth, CEO at the Co-operative Group (previously Co-operative Wholesale Society) from 1996 to 2002, to make individual membership meaningful once again in consumer co-operative societies. Many of these were in danger of de-mutualising themselves owing to lack of member engagement. As President of the International Co-operative Alliance (ICA), Melmoth had started the process which resulted in the *Statement*. He then put it to work in educational programmes designed by the Co-operative College for employees and other members of Societies.

At this stage of the argument, to do equivalent – if more preliminary – work in HE is more a matter of asking questions than offering answers. Co-operative schools have multiplied rapidly, forming into clusters which have the potential to develop federated Co-operative Educational Trusts, member-governed partnerships or co-operative education authorities. As the network develops, there is increasing scope for trade in goods and services, curriculum development, and active democratic governance. But even in this dynamic movement it would be fair to say that schools, let alone universities, as full-blown, member-governed co-operatives, scarcely exist in the UK as yet. As was the case in full-blown co-operative banks, enabling legislation would be a necessary preliminary.

Which are the most promising units in higher education, below the level of the whole university or system within which member-ownership and member self-governance can grow? How best can we draw on surviving, if atrophied, governance models such as elected, sovereign Senates, in order to 'vest beneficial ownership and control in students and employees and help prevent excessive managerial predation'?[30] We must also recognise that students are not perpetual, and that faculty members are as footloose as footballers. This means that any stakeholder-governed model for HE would require staid, continuing membership by academic and support staff, local authorities, professional communities of interest (global as well as local), businesses, and voluntary associations.

A useable past?

As always in the UK, there is a useable past to draw on. Moving between universities and co-operatives, I offer four points from the past and present of each, all of them relating to membership and to *belonging* in the sense of feeling-part-of as well as owning.

First, old-old universities like Oxford still describe staff and students as members, perhaps more frequently and with more inherited meaning than new ones. 'The University' of Oxford is something of an abstraction: tourists continue to look for it in vain. The co-operative adult educator N. F. S. Grundtvig (1783-1872) and the co-operative labour historian G. D. H. Cole (1889-1959) each identified colleges at Oxford in the 1820s and the 1920s respectively, not the university, as proto-co-operatives, presenting their members to the University (the 'Group' in Co-operative terms), preparing them for examinations or for studying at other colleges.[31] Colleges continue to be self-governing, using the language of membership and association: fellowship, election, common room, congregation, wardenship, etc. Publications such as the *Oxford Magazine* continue to protest at every executive encroachment by vice-chancellors who want to act as chief executives. To their members, including the students whom the Colleges (not the University) admit, Colleges are more meaningful than any anciently chartered whole. Is such thinking always, and only, archaic? In a more modern register, the 2008–09 HE Funding Council and Lincoln University *Learning Landscapes* project was similarly concerned with the co-production and management of learning, defining students as well as staff as producers of their own 'arrangements' for learning at university, within carefully designed, disaggregated spaces, rather than as passive consumers of a whole-institutional offer.[32]

Secondly, to go back to the nineteenth century and the co-operative movement, mutual improvement societies were among the earliest, simplest, and smallest of CMEs. The sense of belonging and often informal membership that they generated was strong and remarkably productive of learning at every level.[33] These groups of ambitious adult learner-members combined eclectic high-level learning with basic literacy. In the digital age, their experience becomes relevant all over again. What would a hi-tech mutual improvement society look like?

It is tempting to get over-excited by the Age of Google, as if *any* technology could re-make social relations, or learning, on our behalf. *An avalanche is coming: HE and the revolution ahead.*[34] Connectivity matters, but how? Exactly the same debates about openness, and about the commercial pressure to enclose courses to generate revenue, are raging within the massive open-online-course movement itself: 'Will Moocs be the scourge or saviour of higher education?'[35] Discontinuous possibilities *are* opening up in this field, but on a relatively small scale – apart, that is, from the millions of individuals each at their interactive terminals. Gaia University is an example of a web-enabled, global federation of small groups of learners. Scaled-down, sustainable ways of life and courses on permaculture design are its reason for existence.[36] Similarly, the Khan Academy has been promoted as 'free world-class education for anyone, anywhere', potentially heralding the end of campus life.[37]

Thirdly, co-operators are well placed to insist, as does Gaia, on the primacy of social relations in learning, and as the OU did from its beginning, with its summer schools and tutorial support in a network of regional centres. The 'branch' of a consumer co-operative society in the north of England at any time during the late nineteenth century was the very model of a modern learning centre.[38] The Workers' Educational Accociation's tutorial-class system, invented by R. H. Tawney, Albert Mansbridge, and others, remains exemplary: its famous book-box system would nowadays have multiple platforms to add to the printed page. Joining a tutorial class then entailed becoming a member of a local branch, part of a wider district, both federated into a national association.[39]

Co-op UK's predecessor, the Co-op Union, had an elaborate Education Department which channelled co-operative societies' self-imposed education dividend through to the Co-operative College. From the mid-nineteenth to the mid-twentieth century an active member could participate in mutually accredited lifelong learning within the movement rather than the state system, moving from qualification to qualification.[40] During the 1990s, Unison offered multi-level learning to its members through Unison Open College, as well as the WEA, the OCN, Northern College, Ruskin College, and other member-sanctioned FE and HE partnerships. The OCN was, in effect, a co-operative mutual validation and accreditation network, owned and controlled by its members, its services provided from each to all, and all to each.

Fourthly, back to university. Campuses sometimes look coherent. But even in a now rare single-site university, they are peculiarly centrifugal, fissiparous places, full of cellular, individualistic energies, well-guarded 'academic tribes and territories'.⁴¹ Anyone who has worked on one knows that they are by nature more like covered markets or department stores, full of independent franchises, than airports or supermarkets, however much increasingly well-paid executives try to make them otherwise. The recent but rapidly growing literature on university management can be read as sometimes sensitive, sometimes crass attempts to corral the campus into a command organisation.⁴² The characteristic size of effective units in universities has been considered in a sensitive way.⁴³ But management difficulties and campus discontents perhaps indicate the potential benefits of co-operative and mutual enterprise in this setting. By nature CMEs grow federally, multiplying horizontal lines of belonging rather than vertical lines of command. I watched an early contribution to the 'science' being made at Sussex, shortly after management consultants (in this case McKinsey, who had never been asked by a university before) had been called in to recommend how to 'manage' a university.⁴⁴ This was at approximately the same time as the first-ever separate building for Management, 'Sussex House', was erected. And the Students' Union successfully called for action research towards real self-government at every 'level' of the university. This took the form of an elected Committee of Inquiry into the Organisation of the University of Sussex. Its Final Report is still worth reading by democrats.⁴⁵

Human agency and the idea of a university

At the same time (1970) that E. P. Thompson attacked what he called 'The Business University' at Warwick, he was leading an exceptionally productive, co-operative, and mutual Centre for Social History.⁴⁶ The collective memory fades quickly. Human agency – Thompson's main historical, moral, and political preoccupation – is critical to the field of co-operation and mutuality in a way that state policy is not. By this I mean people, would-be members and lifelong learners, taking action to build on residual and emergent ideas of higher education in and against dominant ideas, not necessarily on a large scale. At different times and places during my working life, academics have proceeded further towards 'the co-operative university', cell by cell, than would now be known about by most students or seen by policymakers as contributing to the UK's competitiveness: 'jobs and growth'.

In 1970s Brighton, mutualising developments in HE were actively under way. *The Idea of a New University: an Experiment in Sussex*[47] lived on until the early 1990s. Asa Briggs's 'new map of learning' was expressed through self-governing schools of study which replaced departments and fostered conscious, critical mutuality within and between disciplines. While students' programmes belonged to schools, faculty members could teach across them, rather than being clustered by specialism. Disciplines or 'subject groups' worked with clipped wings. The bias was towards studying problems and testing professionalisms against possible futures. School-based or critical 'contextual' courses accompanied every 'major' course. There was an arts-science programme in which every student had to participate. Academic and intellectual divisions of labour were studied as social problems rather than promoted as career opportunities. It is not surprising that research on the social history of co-operation thrived in such a setting and, in response to student demands, new courses evolved through dialogue.[48] The sociology of knowledge – those organisational forms through which knowledge is altered, produced, distributed, and exchanged, along with the disciplinary and departmental boundaries – is inseparable from its content. This is what 'knowledge is power' means: different knowledges from and for different arrangements of our powers of production, distribution, education, and government.[49]

There is still space for the co-operative idea. Such has been the restlessness in education policy in England and Wales during the last one hundred years that it would be odd indeed if 'the Co-op' was to remain invisible among other entrepreneurs in this field. These have included the militantly anti-state University of Buckingham or the short-lived, anti-populist notion of a University of Bloomsbury, which was to rely on top-of-the-market fees.[50] Many companies, from Lloyds Bank to McDonald's, have created their own less-than-universal universities. While at Ruskin College, I served on the Board of the Heart of England Training and Enterprise Council (HOETEC) with John Neil, founder of Unipart and its University. 'The U' stood for just-in-time knowledge, designed for a New Business Agenda (NBA). It had the chutzpah to challenge, in Oxford, the notion of 'warehousing knowledge'. This was seen as wasteful, like stockpiling automobile spare parts. In comparable ways, it would not be odd for large-scale consumer co-operative societies in the UK to work with the Co-operative College to form a co-operative education branch of their businesses alongside their farms, pharmacies, funerals, food, travel, and legal services – and for that branch of Societies' work to achieve a higher return on capital employed than groceries. That could be one setting for a co-operative university: not itself a co-operative, but with member ownership and governance achieved through a wider co-operative society or group.

Towards the co-operative university?

So far as I know, there are not many current examples of 'the co-operative university' in full working order. This is why ancient, faith-based examples of co-operation and mutuality in higher learning may still be useful reference points. It is also why down-to-earth work on 'co-operatives, mutuals and the idea of membership' and on 'organisation for member-controlled enterprises' needs to be better known in the academy.[51] The question for today may not be how to articulate the idea of an entire university and begin to draw up constitutions, but how best to learn from the fate of anticipatory cells, including inevitable defeats, to inform future possibilities. Alongside the *universal* in 'university', the proud word 'college', or even 'school', as in schools of study, exam schools, and so on, may turn out to be important, as may the co-operative word 'Society' – much used by students to organise their own interests.

In 1989 I was appointed to the post of Principal of Ruskin College by a twenty-strong interview committee composed of member-governors. This followed an open meeting of all staff, who had listened to and questioned all short-listed candidates, ranking them for the committee. Is this how vice-chancellors are appointed? The appointment of chief and other executives is an issue which has recently been identified as a 'morally lazy' aspect of university governance.[52] Ruskin's governing members' constituent organisations were entitled to seats on the Council according to the number of scholarships and bursaries they offered to members of their own organisations, whom they had approved to study at the College. They also commissioned and supported research and development from the College's expert units: the Trade Union Research Unit (TURU) and the Trade Union International Research and Education Group (TUIREG). Ruskin's member organisations included trade unions, the Co-operative Union, the International Co-operative Alliance, and the Working Men's Club and Institute Union – an organisation with an honourable, if exclusively male, educational history including the CIU 'Club Diploma'. In this way, the College worked with *its* members to develop courses, conferences, and research opportunities for *their* members. The Co-op College still does. As happens when forms of funding change, in co-operatives as well as in educational institutions, some ideas survived and others were defeated when, as a condition of continued state funding after the Further and Higher Education Act of 1992, the College was told to transfer sovereignty from its Council to a smaller Executive. Should we have done so?

Between 2001 and 2007, with the active help of their local co-operative society, the University of Lincoln Students' Union worked as a co-operative society. In 2007, the change from a CME into a charitable company limited by guarantee was caused by changing student cohorts, by the cost of insurance and other costs of not conforming to more recognised models, but above all by legislative changes stipulating what student unions were and were not allowed to do. 'The State' is no more innocent than 'The Market'. Historically, for many years the Chief Registrar of Friendly Societies fought to prevent co-operative societies allocating funds for their own, educational purposes.

Examples of campus co-operatives are legion and need to be assembled. Case studies of their success as businesses, but also of their containment as cherished but no more than niche institutions, need to be collected. As often happens within regional ecologies, in Lincoln in 2010 another anticipatory cell formed: a remarkable teaching and learning co-operative named 'The Social Science Centre'. This will be well able to speak for itself, offering *'free,* co-operative higher education', 'organised on the basis of democratic, non-hierarchical principles, with all members having equal involvement in the life and work of SSC'.[53] The Centre's name may be seen as a direct heir of the Owenite understanding – indeed invention

– of *social science* as critique of the anti-social or *dismal science* of competitive political economy.

Mondragón in Spain is probably the most integrated contemporary reference point for activists as well as intellectuals in this field. Jointly owned by its academic and administrative staff, the University was founded from a group of co-operatives dating back to a technical school in 1947. It now has 9,000 students. To become fully fledged members, staff have to work in the University for at least two years and then pay Euros 12,000 to buy into the university's capital. This can be withdrawn on retirement. There is a governing General Assembly, a thirty-strong representative body, made up of equal numbers of staff, students, and interested outside parties. The Assembly even has the power to sack members of the senior administrative team.[54] Income differentials within the university are kept within 3 to 1, an interesting contrast to developments at the apex of British universities.[55]

The idea of a university and the idea of what constitutes a co-operative and mutual society or CME are both in play as they have not been before in my lifetime.[56] Running through both are conflicts and struggles central to the rest of the culture.[57] How should production of a central social good be organised or, to put it in the active mood, how should we producers and consumers – social stakeholders every one of us – arrange our own powers?

Acknowledgements

Invaluable help in researching and completing this chapter has been given by Ursula Howard, Tom Woodin, Mervyn Wilson, and, most recently, Dan Cook of the University of Bristol Graduate School of Education, who did a fine consultancy project for the Co-operative College on *Realising a Co-operative University*. In just the same way that comparative courses in Labour Movements, Aristocracies and Elites, Armies and Politics, and other 'General Subjects' in History were offered as part of the History degree at Sussex, a course on Co-operation, Mutuality, and Higher Education in the UK and internationally is now urgently needed at HE levels of teaching and learning.

6. Co-operation, mutuality, and the democratic deficit – or re-membering democracy

> Democracy is the logical differentia or the major feature which distinguishes Co-operation as a system of economic organisation ... it is hardly possible to conceive of Co-operative societies existing or working under any other than a democratic system of government.
>
> W. P. Watkins, *Co-operative Principles Today and Tomorrow* (Manchester: Holyoake Books, Co-operative Union Ltd, 1986), p. 54.

Does the project of co-operative and mutual enterprise offer new kinds of social relations which may be uniquely important for democracy? Would it be overstating the case to reverse W. P. Watkins' sentence, four decades after he wrote it, and to say that it is hardly possible to conceive of democratic societies existing or working in the modern world without Co-operative Societies?[1] 'In the modern world' is not a phrase that appears in Watkins' text. Such has been the speed of globalisation during the past forty years that the words 'modern' and 'world' carry ever-increasing weight.

This chapter, rooted in British experience, takes as its subjects the limitations of 'democracy' when symbiotic with modernisation and globalisation, and the importance of Co-operative and Mutual Enterprises (CMEs) as membership organisations well adapted for dealing with those limitations. At the end of the eighteenth century, John Wesley, Methodism's prophet, said that *the world is my parish.* Early in the twenty-first century, it is increasingly the case that, carefully explored, any parish in the world — including the UK — has something to say about the globe itself.

A distinction between project and practice runs through my argument. 'Practice' refers to existing 'goings on', for example, in democracies or in CMEs.[2] Project' refers to possibilities immanent in 'democracy', 'co-operation', and 'mutuality'. While it is important to make this distinction analytically, in real time practice and project, project and practice, are interwoven. Their weave is the stuff of history. This chapter argues that the project of democracy is valuable; that democratic practices in democracies have been diluted; and that the project is worth recalling with some urgency. The pressure to forget 'classical' democracy increases *pari passu.*

Projects such as democracy, co-operation, and mutuality are valuable in their own right, not regardless of practice but because practice, when dilute, needs to draw on project as concentrate. Co-operative and Mutual Enterprises when less than fully co-operative and mutual need to draw on co-operation and mutuality — hence the importance in recent Co-operative history of the *Co-operative Statement of Identity and Principles as approved at the International Co-operative Alliance (ICA) Congress, Manchester, September 1995.* If all CMEs had been perfect embodiments of Co-operative Values and Principles by the mid-1990s, what need would there have been to restate values and principles? What need for the Co-operative College UK to devise international learning programmes based on the project that the 'Co-operative Statement' summarised? It is not my purpose to claim more for the practice of CMEs than is accurate. They have been subject to the same pressures as democracies. Rather, I want to evaluate the project of co-operation and mutuality at a time when it can be said with some plausibility by global democrats that 'democracy will always be something of a mess'.[3] In the modern world, as it has taken shape since Watkins was writing towards the end of his long life as a prophet and practitioner of Co-operation,[4] a 'democratic deficit' has become widely acknowledged, recently with some alarm.[5] A worrisome number of people no longer seem to feel that their democracies belong to them as fully responsible citizens, or that they are members of, or belong to, their democracies sufficiently to vote, let alone to participate in other ways. This chapter focuses on how understanding CMEs and the project of co-operation and mutuality can offer ways in which more people can become more complete citizens by means of identifying with or participating in the project. The argument is divided into four sections:

1. The project of modern democracy, as distinct from other forms of democracy.
2. The project of co-operative and mutual enterprise.
3. Trends in modern democracies which are worrying from a democratic point of view: the dismemberment of democracy.
4. The re-membering of democracy: the contribution of CMEs.

1. Modern democracy, as distinct from other forms of democracy

This section separates the dominant form in which 'democracy' is projected today (the phrase used most commonly is 'representative democracy', but this tells only part of the story) from other forms of residual or emergent democracy.[6] These other forms are marginalised as either 'earlier' or 'primitive' forms.[7] At other times, they are put on a 'classical' pedestal.[8] Or they are patronised as 'participatory' or 'direct' democracy. But, in modern times, they are still available as practice, sometimes latent, sometimes manifest, but sufficiently present — not least in the form of CMEs — to offer a critical handle on the increasingly dominant modern forms of democracy. It is at least plausible to suggest that they may have something democratic to offer to modern 'representative' democracies.

If a working definition of democracy is rule by the people (the *demos* in Greek, as opposed to rule by the theos, the aristos, the plutos, the oligos, etc.), it is a more ample project than modern democracy, as the latter came to be defended in and exported from 'the West' (and 'globally') during the second half of the twentieth century. There is of course no fixed definition of the word.[9] Democracy is a 'keyword' in the sense that Raymond Williams used the term. That is to say, it is a word through which social struggles, rather than semantic squabbles, take place. In Williams' sense, democracy is as 'key' as any word in the contemporary vocabulary: 'No questions are more difficult than those of democracy.'[10] Deep Western assumptions lie buried under it.[11] Twentieth-century politicians fell over each other to own it. The 'people' were told that they already owned it, even in situations where this was clearly not the case, as in the People's Democracies of Eastern Europe from the 1950s to the 1980s. Self-government by all human beings working in association with one another is not the same thing as a single-party State ruled by an appointed élite. Nor is it the same thing as representation by representatives free to decide what they choose, even if those representatives have been elected.

To list twelve of its characteristics, modern democracy as project can be described in the following terms.

LIST A

- *'Representative' in character*

  The adjective 'representative' is ubiquitous in modern democracies in order to distinguish them from more radical forms of democracy. The insistence on this usage of the term is associated with Edmund Burke, whose aim it was to distance democracy from its French Revolutionary versions. His trenchant views about representatives' freedom from constituents' opinions and from local 'purposes and prejudices', and about Parliament not being 'a *congress* [his emphasis] of ambassadors from different and hostile interests', remain profoundly influential in the West, particularly in the USA and UK. Behind such continuing anxiety to make democracy safe for 'general reason' (Burke) — and safe from the radicalism of Rousseau and Paine — lie the history and sociology of 'representation' as a complex and significant keyword in its own right.[12]

- *Based upon a 'separation of powers'*

  The insistence on a separation or division of labour in modern Western democracy includes its legislative, executive, and judicial powers. Separations between these powers provide a touchstone as significant as the Burkean idea of representation. They extend into other divisions of labour: for instance, between business and politics, industrial relations and politics, private life and public life. These divisions are:

- based upon a concept of liberty predominantly seen as

freedom from outside interference, the State commonly being seen as antithetical to, or as a subtraction from, the individual;[13]

- 'cameral', which means centred on chambers, houses (of Parliament, etc.), senates, and other permanent institutions that acquire a quasi-sacred aura. The institutions of this form of democracy are characteristically built to look old, in Gothic and Classical styles. The institutions multiply precedents and invent traditions. In Britain the late nineteenth century was a fertile period for 'the invention of tradition' in order to vaccinate against the sacred aura of Parliamentary and other institutions being dissipated by the extension of the franchise to working people.[14]

Modern democracy as project is also:
- 'General' – by which is meant generalised to everyone by means of 'occasions'; the general occasions of modern democracy being known in Britain as general elections.
- Mediated by political parties. Party organisations compete for votes in professional, mechanised, business-like ways. In the UK, party 'machines' and their caucuses have been known as such and identified as businesses ('manufacturing opinion') since the early 1870s. Modern Western representative democracy has come to be associated with, or even defined in terms of, parties.[15] It is important to remember that for much of the early history of modern democracy in its 'liberal' form, 'classical' democrats like John Stuart Mill profoundly distrusted parties. There is an extensive, democratic, liberal, classical but anti-party literature.[16] The classic analysis of the 'iron law' of oligarchy as illustrated by parties *qua* organisations was provided by Roberto Michels in *Political Parties* (1913).

Modern democracy is also:
- Generative of a separate sphere of activity known as 'politics' (which also becomes a separate social scientific discipline) and of people known as 'politicians'. The phrase 'the political class' has recently come into use.[17] In modern democracies, it is regarded as important to keep the 'political' separate from the 'social', as well as from the 'economic'. 'Social' democrats had to reinvent the connection during the late nineteenth and twentieth centuries. The ultimate draining of meaning from the word 'social' happened, perhaps, when it began to overlap with the word 'private', as in usages among the political class such as 'I like to keep my social life private'.[18] In modern 'social science', the economic, the political, and the social acquire their own separate academic disciplines or departments, known as economics, political science, and sociology. In Owenite social science, the intention had been to bring them together. This residual tradition was continued by John Ruskin, J. A. Hobson, C. Wright Mills, and many others. In modern capitalism — and integral to its definition as capitalism — a relatively autonomous 'economic' demesne was carved out. The empirical separation of that demesne over time and by capitalists (a new word of the 1850s) had growing implications for politics, for social science, and for democracy. These implications were, incidentally at this point, the problem that Co-operators addressed.

Modern democracy as project is also:
- Reliant upon experts, professionals, and managers who have multiplied and theorised a special place for themselves as a professional, managerial class (or PMC) since the third quarter of the nineteenth century.[19]

- Individual, celebrating and conscripting individuals' private secret choices and identities on paper, in booths, by post, electronically, and by means of lists of registered voters and numbered citizens. As well as celebration of individual choice, modern democracy relies upon the conscription of individuals by means of identification (cards), state-istics (census), numbering (tax numbers), naming (second names), and conscription to the military. Compulsory voting is discussed favourably in modern democratic discourse. In one or two modern democracies, this conscription of the citizen has been done. Taxation to fund political parties is also debated.

Finally, modern democracy as project is:
- Consumer-oriented, with citizens exercising individual 'choice' between parties, with parties, between government departments seen as providers of policies, with citizens as their purchasers.
- Focused on nation-states in such a way that national adjectives can be used to describe it: for example, British, German, American democracy.
- A finished fact or structure that is either there or not there. When it is there, it becomes a priority to protect it by means of 'security' and 'defence'. When it is not there, modern democrats think that it can be exported wholesale and as imperium to other countries, or to their own 'first nations', regardless of those nations' cultures and inherited forms of popular participation and control.

Democracy is increasingly framed (projected) in the above terms, but democracy need not be like this. It is only necessary to scratch the surface of the pre-'modern' history, the non-'Western' geography, and the class sociology of democracy to recall that, in the case of each of the twelve characteristics listed above, democracy can be different. Re-membering the history, geography, and sociology of democracy is necessary because one particular form of democracy (labelled 'modern' here) has become increasingly powerful since the end of the Cold War. It now overlays 'democracy' as a more general category so overwhelmingly that democracy of any kind other than its modern variant can become invisible or, when it is seen, is often regarded as subversive of democracy itself as understood in 'the modern or civilised world'.

Taking each characteristic in the first list in turn, democracy can be any or all of the following:

LIST B[20]
- Delegatory in character, emphasising the directness of accountability, or mandate, that exists between representatives, or delegates, and electors. Rights of recall may be built into the relationship between delegates — even MPs — and electors. Some decisions may be delegated away from representatives, or made the subject of referenda that flow from citizen initiatives. In the history of the Labour Party in Britain there have been high-pitched struggles about who has the right to take what decisions within the Party and between the Party and other decision-making forums.[21]

Democracy can also be:
- Based upon a fusion rather than a division of labour between 'powers'; with the most democratic individual and collective 'arrangements' between citizens being seen as those through which humans — all humans — conceive (legislate), do (execute), and adjudicate (judge) together, in association, and for themselves.

For democratic purposes, it may also be seen as important to integrate arrangements for self-defence with other powers, or arrangements for self-government, rather than professionalising such arrangements. This was one of the components of democracy in early 'soviets' and one of the sources of resistance to 'standing' armies. It remains one of the sources of the citizen's 'right to bear arms' in those democracies where this is defended. However, it is important not to romanticise these fusions or integrations of powers. As they work out in practice, they may result in confusion or worse. Unalienated justice and self-defence are often antipathetic to the modern sensibility.[22]

Democracy can also be:
- Based upon concepts of liberty that rely on presences rather than absences: freedom *to* rather than freedom *from*. These 'positive' concepts of liberty may be based upon rights, or they may be based upon practices (or even 'virtues' or the responsibilities of self-government).[23]

Positive concepts of liberty see freedom (liberty, independence, etc.) as a status or state of affairs that needs to be publicly arranged for people (as in rights conferred by laws and legislation and therefore by states), or by people for themselves (as in self-government, which also results in states of various kinds). In this discourse, plurals are important, hence individuals and states. 'The State' in the singular and as an abstraction was born twinned with 'the individual'. So far from preceding 'the State' and being diminished by it, individuals may be seen historically as dependent for their individuality on 'an art of social *organisation* [my emphasis] satisfying and reconciling certain vital human needs which are different'.[24] Such an art of organisation or association may be seen as cultural activity that is as complex and as available for critique and creativity as any other art form.[25]

Democracy can also be:
- Reliant on specific 'congresses' (to use Burke's unfavoured word, much favoured by working-class associations), 'conventions', 'assemblies', 'meetings', 'societies', 'associations', and 'parliaments'. Parliaments need not be singular, 'standing', or permanent, any more than armies or building societies. Informal or spontaneous assemblies, demonstrations, and so on may also be part of democratic communication. Such 'politics out of doors', as Gladstone called it, is seen as a 'right' in modern democracy but, as such, it can be withdrawn in emergency and made illegitimate when seen as direct action ('politics direct').

Democracy can also be:
- General by means of everyday, rather than occasional, decision-making devices. These devices may include general councils, general committees, general assemblies, general meetings, general petitions, general conventions, referenda, plebiscites, polls, ballots, juries, forums, and commissions, as well as general elections. Elections may be multiple and specific as well as monopolistic and singular. Sovereignty may be dispersed or shared rather than enclosed; although sharing (mutualising?) sovereignty presents difficulties akin to those of doing the same with 'ownership'.
- Suspicious of 'parties', particularly in their modern 'machine' top–down forms. Parties have been seen, by liberal democrats and others, as clogging rather than enabling democratic communication (see List A).

- Resistant to a separate sphere of professional activity for politics and politicians. Adequately democratic individual and associational forms have been judged (certainly within CMEs) as those through which the political, the economic, and the social are put together or associated rather than divided.
- Suspicious of experts, professional, and managers, at least in their role as a *nouvelle couche sociale* (the PMC). The PMC grew discontinuously during the twentieth century as one of that century's major features. Professionals and managers and theorists working from their perspectives became highly influential in terms of modern democratic theory and practice. Their theorists affected CMEs and the wider Labour Movement, in particular via Sydney and Beatrice Webb.
- Public or social, rather than private or individual, celebrating people's choices as exercised with other people, face to face, rather than as anonymous absentees or by appointed proxies.
- Producer- or production-oriented, with citizens defined as people who make decisions together in association with consumers (who are in fact themselves in another role). Policies may be seen as choices made and agreed among 'us', rather than products developed by experts and sold to us by 'them'.

Participation is one word for this active process of making, but it is a weak, vague term in modern democracy, capable of meaning very little joint activity.[26] The fact that the term 'participatory democracy' can be used at all in modern democracy suggests that its opposite (non-participatory democracy) is seen as falling meaningfully within the category 'democracy'.[27] The *demos* can be said to rule without participating. Similarly, 'popular' democracy is used to distinguish it from some other kind of (unpopular?) people's rule.[28] Another word overused in modern democracy is 'partnership'. 'Ownership' better describes co- or mutual decision making. How can people own decisions and the means of producing them? This is a question asked of modern democracy by democrats who do not like finding themselves on the wrong end of decisions.

Democracy can also be:
- Federal, or trans- or supra-national, with 'states', 'republics', and even 'nations' being seen as capable of quasi-autonomy within a wider democracy or democratic 'union'.
- An unfinished process that — even when founded in historic, sacred declarations (of independence, etc.), bills (of rights, etc.), constitutions, revolutions, and settlements — remains patient of reinvention or transformation. Democratic history and structures may be seen as having not yet completed their development. Still less may dominant forms of modern democracy be seen, particularly in the United States — *pace* Francis Fukayama and The End of History — as the terminus of history itself.

The differing characteristics of democracies in Lists A and B have been theorised in an extensive literature.[29] The history of conflicts and struggles concerning different kinds of democracy in different social formations has been written, albeit in more detail for some places and periods than for others. List B has been kept alive or re-membered by social movements and, more recently, by 'networks'.[30] To anticipate, the Labour Movement, which includes the Co-operative

Movement as one of its 'wings', has been a fecund source of social inventions, many of which have built upon List B in order to contest the limitations of List A.³¹

During the Cold War, from the late 1940s to the late 1970s, limiting democracy to its modern forms in List A was considered to be important for democracy's defence and security, particularly in the United States. Over-participation might, it was feared, overheat democracy, leading to deformations such as Communism or Fascism. The phrase 'lowering of expectations' was much used to describe the task of political leaders. 'Apathy' was an index of satisfaction. Too little of it would be dangerous.³² 'Freedom' for citizens was redefined as licence not to be citizens, to go to work (for wages), to consume leisure time and leisure goods (for prices), and to let govermnents get on with what they do best.

During this period, the extent to which modern democracy had become democracy's specifically capitalist or 'free market' form ('Western' and 'global') became apparent.³³ This makes modern democracy's active occlusion of other modes of political or democratic production intelligible. J. A. Schumpeter's *Capitalism, Socialism and Democracy* (1942) provided explicit theorisation of modern democracy as competition between élites for power to produce policies for 'the masses'. The means of production of policy were to be political parties organised much like rival chains of supermarkets. 'Classical' theory was made to seem dated, dystopic, and dangerous.

However, the dangers of a growing democratic 'deficit' — identified as such during the 1980s — to the survival of modern democracy, perhaps to the survival of modern capitalism itself, became widely acknowledged during the 1980s and 1990s in place of Cold War emphases on the dangers of a democratic 'surplus'. Democratic audits produced disturbing results. Too much apathy, too little participation, too few resources for a journey of hope,[34] too little membership and belonging — or a surplus of membership and belonging of some kinds rather than other kinds — were seen as dangerous by the beginning of the twenty-first century, even by holders of political power in modern democracies who owed their position to it.

2. The project of co-operative and mutual enterprise

This section identifies the project of co-operative and mutual enterprise mainly in terms of 'belonging' and membership. The distinction is maintained between project and realised achievement, or between the reach of co-operation and mutuality and the grasp of CMEs. Members and membership are at the heart of the project.

2.1. CMEs have members

Without membership, co-operatives and mutuals cease to be such, and fall outside the category Co-operative and Mutual Enterprise. People belong to CMEs, and CMEs belong to them, otherwise the acronym is meaningless. Membership and therefore, in some sense, belonging, is the defining feature of the project of co-operative and mutual enterprise.[35] The question is: in what sense? The answer can be broken down into separate elements.

2.2. Making membership meaningful

The ambitious project of co-operative and mutual enterprise is to make membership meaningful, bringing with it the reality as well as a sense of belonging.[36] Real belonging is related to 'owning' in its management-speak sense, as well as in its material sense. The project of making membership meaningful in a material sense is more difficult in some contexts and at some times. That we are 'members one of another' (to quote St Paul) is easier to observe as a fact about the human species, *qua* species, than it is to live out at any general or universal level of inclusivity. Sometimes Co-operators get disheartened. But the difficulties inhere in and describe the context as much as they describe the limitations of members who try to make their belonging fully material. Defeat, when it occurs, is not all Co-operators' fault and is not the same as failure. To anticipate a later argument, rneaningfully democratic membership, belonging, and the inventive practice of association that goes with them are what is most important about CMEs for democracy. They are where modern democracy is most in deficit. (There is another sense in which membership, of deformed kinds, is where modern democracy is most in surplus. The deformation refers to varieties of 'total', 'fundamental' membership and belonging that are less than (or anti-) democratic.[37] This will be developed in Section 3.)

2.3. Members and their needs

The project is to satisfy members' needs by producing, distributing, and exchanging goods and services. 'In a broad sense a ... co-operative society exists every time that a number of persons feeling the same need join together collectively to satisfy it better than they could do by individual means.'[38] 'Through co-operation, people express mutual needs that translate into common goals.'[39] For the most part, these needs have been articulated by CMEs in terms of the sustenance and sustainability of the species, rather than in individual and psychological terms. The needs met have been for food, shelter, sociability, insurance against rainy days, and learning. 'Need' is a more characteristic preoccupation of CMEs than 'demand'. Meeting needs is more characteristic of their project than gratifying desire. This accounts for some of the problems that the Co-op *qua* business encountered in the context of the history of retailing, and capitalism more generally, from the early twentieth century onwards. Unlimited desire became capitalism's stock-in-trade. It also accounts for the opportunities open to Co-operatives and other CMEs in the early twenty-first century, at a time when ethics, responsibility, and sustainability have made a comeback.

2.4. Associating needs

In a CME, members unite voluntarily to 'meet their common economic, social and cultural needs and aspirations'.[40] This phrase draws together, or associates, economic, social, and cultural needs. This is the project of co-operative and mutual enterprise. The word 'cultural' in the Definition of a Co-operative in the 1995 *Statement of Identity* serves a similar purpose. 'Cultural' is a word that integrates elements in a 'whole way of life'.[41] The phrase in the 1995 Statement also specifies the needs as 'common' or, to use a phrase for common ownership, 'held in common'. It makes clear the comprehensive and integrative ambition that has always informed the project of membership and belonging in the Co-operative Movement: to become members one of another, each for all and all for each, across a wide range of species-sustaining needs.

2.5. Members' voluntas, or will

The word 'voluntary' is fundamental to the project of co-operative and mutual enterprise. Members are not compelled but choose to belong to 'an autonomous association of persons united voluntarily'. Full co-operation between human beings, as in CMEs, 'can only result from the engagement of their will'.[42] Co-operation and mutuality between human beings in CMEs is more than 'natural' — and, therefore, able to be relegated to an earlier 'state of nature'. It is more than compulsory and, in that sense, involuntary. The project of co-operative and mutual enterprise involves choice, a decision to consciously socialise a society (or, in psychoanalytic terms, a personality) rather than — as must inevitably also happen at an unconscious level — to be socialised by it. Members are projected as potential subjects, rather than as the objects that many of them (us) have had to become at work, in the home, and in the marketplace.

2.6. 'A hinge upon which history turns'

Appropriate associational forms have to be brought into being by members before such voluntary belonging is open to large numbers of ordinary people or, aspirationally, to everyone. To bring them into being in early CMEs was the innovative project of working people in Britain at the turn of the eighteenth and nineteenth centuries. When becoming a full member of a secular association that aims to change the world is open to large numbers of people hitherto not seen as active makers of their own futures, and when membership is projected as a future possibility for every human being, the project becomes, in E. P. Thompson's phrase, 'one of the hinges upon which history turns'.[43] Associations that offer opportunities for 'members unlimited' may be seen as decisive interventions and major social inventions towards the universalisation of democracy as self-government.[44]

2.7. Transformation via the 'ordinary'

The alchemical dream was to find a way of turning base metals into gold. This dream occupied human imagination and proto-scientific practice for many centuries. The co-operative and mutual vision is to make associations that turn ordinary ways of meeting basic human needs, together and today, into a transformed tomorrow (the gold known among Co-operators as 'the Co-operative Commonwealth'). The project of co-operative and mutual enterprise is to make the vision visible in part before it can be seen as a whole, to realise the future in the present, the result in the process, the end in the means, the ideal in the material, desire in necessity, what will be then in what is now.

Members in a consumer co-operative and in other CMEs such as the Workers' Educational Association (WEA) or a Friendly Society may purchase their membership, expressed as shareholding, bit by bit by buying daily necessities in a branch store, or by paying for a class whose topic has been chosen by the learners, or by saving in good times. But democratic membership entitlements are available instantly. 'If we could but see a day of it', wrote William Morris on page one of *News from Nowhere*, 'not a dream but a vision'. This is what CMEs provided, to end the permanent state of probation within which so many radical and religious reformers have lived.

2.8. Members as owners

By definition, in a CME the members own the enterprise. Co-operative and Mutual Enterprises are 'jointly owned enterprises'. On the face of it, this is an innocent fact. CMEs belong to their members, and members belong to CMEs. Nothing in the modern world seems simpler, more to be desired, and more central to that world than ownership. But the seemingly simple fact of ownership among and between members of CMEs, amid a wide range of historically changing meanings of ownership, discloses a project that is by no means simple. 'Private' ownership, for instance in land, and commodification of most things by the opening of the twenty-first century (leisure, sport, politics, desire, etc.) was not established without centuries of struggle. The project of co-operation and mutuality asks a central question: can such meanings be generalised and thereby transformed, in the sense of becoming open to general choice, general election, by the many, not the few? Can universal inclusivity be achieved ('jointly') with and among all people, rather than without and at the expense of some people? Is 'deliberate liberalism' (G. J. Holyoake) achievable without the characteristic twentieth-century slide into State socialism, national socialism, soviet communism, and so on? Can the 'private' become the 'general' (common, social, public, etc.) by means of transforming the most central capitalist fact of all, namely *ownership*?

These key questions about ownership are at the centre of the project of co-operative and mutual enterprise. They are still open questions. They have also been at the centre of the history of ownership itself. The questions themselves (let alone the answers) become difficult to grasp in modern capitalism, because the project of co-operative and mutual enterprise is pre-capitalist and in that sense residual. It is also post-capitalist and in that sense emergent. It comes before and after the 'private' and the 'public' in the dominant modern meanings of those keywords. The project inherits and works with pre-capitalist ideas of 'moral economy'. It invents and works with post-capitalist ideas of 'social economy'. No wonder it has problems in the age of 'political economy'!

Is the project of 'mutuality' (or a state of mutual ownership or socialised ownership) the same as private ownership? Public ownership? Common ownership? Co-ownership? The answer is 'Yes, but ...'.

Is the project the same as individual ownership? Collective ownership? State ownership? National ownership? No, but ... . Edgar Parnell's 1999 classic, *Reinventing Co-operation*, insisted that Co-operatives are 'private' and have nothing to do with 'collectives'. Yes, but ... the book is well subtitled *The Challenge of the Twenty-First Century.*

Does the project represent forms of social relations that are very old and at the same time very new? Yes, but those social relations will take some research and development. Co-operative and mutual enterprise cannot 'fit in' without changing either capitalism or the project of co-operation and mutuality. This is an awkward situation to be in. Abstracting ownership as 'public', 'national', and 'State' is easy. It was done during the twentieth century by capitalists as well as by social democrats and communists. Mutualising ownership is more ambitious. Hands have to be visible, with fingers interlocked – as in old Friendly Society symbols. Active socialisation is achieved through construction and struggle, here and now, not by sleight of hand, as in Adam Smith's 'hidden hand'.

2.9. Members as governors of democratic organisations controlled by their members[45]

Edgar Parnell defined co-operatives as 'enterprises *run by* [my emphasis] their members, providing services to their members, for the benefit of their members'.[46] The project of co-operative and mutual enterprise is for CMEs to be governed by their members, in a manner most simply described as democratic. Each CME should be a democracy, which then 'works together (with other CMEs) through local, regional, national and international structures' to establish, in the words of the sixth Principle (1995), 'co-operation among co-operatives'.

This is achieved by means of rules, agreed in Rule Books, whose amendment requires due and democratic process. The rules vary across time and between CMEs. The age, scale, and scope of each enterprise make an inevitable difference, alongside freely chosen variation. In some CMEs, at some periods of their development, democratic governance is active, initiatory, and 'from below'. At other times, governance is reactive, with members approving or vetoing executive decisions taken 'from above'. Divisions of labour and specialisations elaborate over time. Elaboration is an opportunity for democratic Societies (as it is for modern society itself) to grow large and complex. For the project of co-operative and mutual enterprise, however, such divisions also represent a problem. Indeed, the project is partly about that problem. How can divisions of labour not be competitive divisions between humans, as in class divisions, and become co-operative divisions of work? Examples of divisions and specialisations include those between General Meetings (or Councils) of members and Committees of Management; or those between Committees of Management, Boards of Directors, and Members; or those between all of these and Executives; or those between Executives and General Managers and (Company) Secretaries. The Executive may in effect be the Chief Executive Officer (from the early 1960s onwards) or Executive/ Leadership Teams (from the early 1990s onwards). In early, small, or specialist co-operatives, for example housing co-operatives, it is hard to prise all or any of these functions apart from the membership.[47]

From the point of view of control by members, these tensions are related to and made more complex by contradictions between 'the centre' and 'branches', or localities. Federal forms are characteristic of the ways in which the project of co-operative and mutual enterprise seeks forms within which such contradictions can be realised, or find room to move. These are not easy to invent, or to operate when found. In the mid-nineteenth century in the UK, working-class associations with 'branches' were not within the law. Friendly Societies had struggles to find legal, let alone viable, forms of local plus national association. Democracy itself, as it develops, struggles with the same contradictions, seeking to discover spaces within which contradictions can be realised rather than collapsed.

2.10. Equity between members

Members in a CME may purchase their shareholding bit by bit, for example by buying goods in a branch store of a consumer Co-operative Society and leaving their dividends on deposit. They must subscribe a minimum in order to be members, even if their share is not fully paid up. They may not, in most instances, subscribe more than a prescribed maximum. By subscribing the minimum, they become full members — as full as those who subscribe more or have subscribed for longer. In that sense, members are equal.

'Equitable' is in the title of many co-operatives, building societies, clubs, and friendly societies. The human nexus is considered to need conscious protection against the cash nexus in organisations that work in a capitalist context and that deal with millions of people and millions of pounds: hence the entitlement to step-by-step, collective and individual growth, or collective self-help and, hence, the perceived inequitability — for the project of co-operative and mutual enterprise — of 'profit' rather than 'trading surplus'. Profit is seen as having been extracted from, rather than generated with, someone or something. This goes back to the labour theory of value and the Owenite neo-Ricardians. The socialisation of profit is achieved by CMEs, not by returning it to an abstract 'community' (as in a 'Bencom') but to material members who can then decide what happens to it.

The idea of Equity and its practical realisation were clearly of great importance to these pioneers. The meaning that they attached to the term is not the jurist's, who has to rectify divergences of law from natural justice; nor yet the businessman's, who is concerned with the rights of shareholders to the profits of joint-stock companies; but rather that distributive aspect of justice, briefly discussed by Aristotle in Book V of the *Nicomachean Ethics*, which is involved in the exchange of the products of one man's labour against those of another.[48]

Later comers into the Society join under the same conditions and enjoy the same rights as the first member; they even pay the same sum as share subscription. How very different is the position in ordinary joint-stock companies, where anyone wishing to become a shareholder must buy a share, i.e. get one transferred to him or her by an old shareholder, and if the company is in a flourishing condition he or she will have to pay a much higher price than the original subscriber paid, perhaps ten times as much! This is because in ordinary joint-stock companies the number of shares is limited, whereas in co-operative societies the number is unlimited, and the share register is always open.[49]

2.11. Mutuality

Once again, *co-operation* and *mutuality* define the project: co-operatives and mutuals refer to the practice. But a further refinement might be to see *mutuality* as the project of *co-operation*.

There are differences within the category 'CME' between (on the one hand) co-operatives and (on the other) mutuals in which mutuality is 100 per cent achieved. While membership is essential to co-operatives, its meanings may differ from those in fully mutual enterprises, i.e. in enterprises that trade exclusively with and for their members. In 100 per cent mutual enterprises, members alone receive the surplus, as well as owning and governing the mutual in a circle within which there is — in principle — no 'structural differentiation' between users, beneficiaries, employees, and members. The same can be, but is not necessarily, true of co-operatives. For instance, some housing co-operatives, credit unions, and producer or 'worker' co-operatives are fully mutual. Historically, some retail Co-operative Societies had the word 'mutual' in their names. Some retail Societies in Europe trade exclusively with their own members.

Within the category 'co-operative', and certainly within the history of large-scale CMEs, there have been, in practice, many varieties of membership and belonging. Some members have confined their participation to the economic sphere, some to the political sphere, and some to the social. But the project of co-operation and of mutuality has been to bring these together, or to mutually relate them one to the other in a culture or state of mutuality.

All mutuals are co-operative: some co-operatives are mutual. The degree to which co-operatives (and mutuals) attain mutuality provides a performance indicator by which the extent to which their project is realised may be measured. If the meanings of membership in mutuals may be clarified by how they differ from (some) co-operatives, the meanings of membership in CMEs may be further clarified by how they differ from the meanings of membership in other forms of 'not for profit' and 'for profit' enterprises or associations that have 'members', and by how they differ from the meanings of membership in still other forms of 'membership organisations' or associations.[50]

3. The dismemberment of democracy: trends in the practice of modern democracy that are worrying from a democratic point of view

Many millions of members have belonged, and continue to belong, to CMEs. Their membership is and was the quintessence of co-operative and mutual enterprise. 'In a co-operative members are much more than customers, as important as these may be to any business, they are the owners of the co-operative, and the very reason why the co-operative exists.' These millions of members — 'probably at least half the world's population is in some way involved in or affected by some form of co-operative economic activity'[51] — remain the owners, the beneficiaries, and — at least in project — the democratic governors and controllers of their CMEs. Their project grows in importance given the context that will be described in this section.

In the two preceding sections the focus has been on projects — of modern democracy and of co-operation and mutuality respectively. In this section and Section 4, the focus is on practices, first in modern democracies and then in CMEs. But in history's 'heat and thundering noise', as E. P. Thompson put it, no such analytic distinctions can prevail for long.

There are trends in modern democracy that are sufficiently worrying from a democratic point of view to suggest the need for remedies. To the extent that rule by the people, or self-government by all human beings working in association with one another, remains the goal of democracy, modern democrats have problems. The absence of 'belonging' provides one yardstick by which to identify these problems. 'Dismemberment' is one way of summarising the worrying trends in modern democracies. The term is used here because it links with the project (Section 2) and practices (Section 4), sometimes residual, sometimes emergent, that inform CMEs.[52] Membership, belonging, and the re-membering of democracy via CMEs are the themes of Section 4.

Eight trends stand out. These trends are related to each other, sometimes in contradictory ways. For example, the absence of belonging in modern democracies, in some forms, relates to its presence in other, deformed, types of belonging.

3.1. A democratic deficit

It became widely acknowledged during the late twentieth century that democracy was in deficit. Democrats expressed this in the economic language of 'deficit', which had been uncovered by a democratic 'audit'. Historians, philosophers, and cultural critics writing in Britain during the second half of the twentieth century traced the origins of the deficit further back than the 'modern' period, to the 1650s and before. They identified 'long revolutions' responding to deep caesuras in the democratic project, or paths that constitutional theory and practice (in the British case) failed to take following the Civil War.

These critics (who for the most part ignored co-operation and mutuality) identified a dilution of the theory of representation; a departure from classical or republican democracy (Quentin Skinner's 'neo-Roman' concept of liberty) and a declension from inclusive ideas of liberty, independence, freedom, and self-government. They saw these dilutions and departures — the strongest word for them used by thinkers such as William Cobbett and Thomas Paine in the nineteenth century was 'corruptions' of democracy — as inherent in utilitarian liberalism from the late eighteenth century onwards. The 'social' was drained from democracy. Liberalism became less liberal, conceptually and practically, until 'liberalisation' could refer to taking 'controls' away from processes that were seen as exclusively economic. This was, in part, because of nineteenth-century liberalism's growing connections, including those of the Liberal Party, with new interests who could adopt it as *their* ideology, namely the new manufacturing class of the industrial revolution, scientific naturalists like T. H. Huxley and Herbert Spencer, and later the new professional and managerial class of the 'nineteenth-century revolution in government'. Their tendency was to enclose democracy, excluding those who did not already possess property in households, lands, intelligence, or expertise.

By the final quarter of the twentieth century, tight private forms and loose public forms of belonging were not producing the participatory, democratically active citizenry that liberal democrats such as John Stuart Mill had proposed. Mill also saw the Co-operative Movement as the 'futurity' of the fully liberal democratic project, once that project was extended by working people. Mill, a classical liberal democrat, thought that producer co-operatives would achieve the goal of 'uniting the greatest individual liberty of action with the common ownership of the raw material of the globe, and an equal participation of all in the benefit of combined labour'.[53]

By the end of the century, masses of people in modern capitalisms participated as 'members' in many kinds of tight, private units of association, and in some kinds of loose public ones, including their nation-states. But participation in democratic activity as citizens was not a dominant component of their portfolios of active 'belonging'. Membership often meant no more than the paying of a subscription or the closing of a facility to non-members. Sub-cultures became more adhesive than common cultures, families more binding than cities, sects more meaningful than churches. The phrase 'liberal democracy' lost more and more of its roots in 'classical' liberalism. People — 'the masses' — were no longer even expected to aspire to be more than individual consumers, rather than associated producers of their own futures. Perhaps the majority of humans had always been this way. But the classical liberal democratic project, before contracting into List A (section 1 above), had been designed to address this fact, mainly by means of open-ended, liberal education with 'the sky as the limit'.

Twentieth-century social democrats took part in this lowering of expectations in the name of a fast-expanding State. Increasingly, the State paid their wages. A division between those who took decisions and managed their execution (representatives and executives) and 'most people', who lived with (consumed) the results, began to be seen as a permanent, desirable, natural division of labour. It was as if modern democracy had become the best that democrats could hope for. Political parties became less and less like federations of semi-autonomous, proudly independent artisan workshops (branches, constituency associations), and more and more like centralised machines for policy production and distribution. Citizens became de-skilled consumers buying or rejecting 'policies' at general elections. Modernised political parties encouraged this. Apathy became a widespread phenomenon.[54] Low turnouts, not just for elections, became normal. Leisure and entertainment technologies and domestic comforts encouraged them. The technologies were used more powerfully for leisure and entertainment in their 'mass' forms than for any other, entirely possible, purposes — including the strengthening of democracy. Technology was developed in demotic but not in democratic ways. Even where the outward forms of democracy were present, the practice of democracy — as active belonging to and membership of 'society' and of Societies/Unions (etc.) — became more limited. During the economic 'golden years' of the 1950s, 1960s, and early 1970s, as argued above, non-participation was welcomed as an index of consumer/voter satisfaction But from the second half of the 1970s, gathering pace during the late 1990s, non-participation became so pronounced as to be seen as threatening, even to already elected holders of political power.

3.2. Non-voting, non-voters

In many modern democracies there is a trend away from voting in general elections or their nearest equivalents (for instance, presidential elections), the centre-pieces of representative democracy. The UK provides a convenient example in which, as powers were moved to the centre, local elections suffered in an even more pronounced way than general elections.[55] Representative democracy has increasingly become 'single occasion' politics: the occasion of voting for a representative, a Party, or a 'Leader' provides its democratic content. Accountability rests more and more upon these intermittent, single occasions. Between the occasions, MPs dislike it if they are thought to be 'delegates'. Governments increasingly manipulate legislatures, Prime Ministers' Cabinets, Party Leaders' Parties, Parties' Constituency Associations, and so on down the line.[56]

If citizens do not vote on the general occasions into which their democratic input has been concentrated, where does democratic legitimacy come from? In what sense can people be said to belong to, or be in active membership of, 'their' society? Citizens who are supposed to 'own' or to feel that they belong to their society and it to them were not behaving as if they felt that they or it did. And citizens do not for the most part belong to political parties. Students of 'social capital' suggest that they (we) do not belong to many other socially ambitious, or even privately sociable, associations either.[57]

3.3. Other kinds of 'single' growth

In this changing ecology, other kinds of 'singular' politics grew during the last quarter of the twentieth century. These were less comfortable for representatives than the single-occasion routines of representative democracy. Instead of concentrating, would-be political impulses dispersed along disassociated, dismembered lines. These included:

- 'single issue' politics, by means of which participants pursued a single objective, sometimes altruistic and sometimes not (for example, stop-the-war, or not-in-my-back-yard campaigns) regardless of their effect upon the whole gamut of future-oriented issues;
- 'single social group' politics, by means of which participants pushed the interests of one group (for example, road users), regardless of their effects upon the whole gamut of overlapping and/or conflicting groups (for example, children);
- 'single identity' politics, by means of which participants expressed the meanings of an identity (for example, sexual orientation) or a 'sub-culture' (for example, musical taste), regardless of their effects upon the whole gamut of identities within as well as beyond the sexual or sub-cultural group concerned;
- 'single leader' politics, by means of which participants promote the role of a single figure, often attached to an '-ism' and a group of '-ites' (for example, Thatcher-ism, Blair-ites), regardless of their effects upon the whole gamut of constitutional forms (cabinet, parliament, local authorities, parties, etc.);[58]
- 'single organisation' anti-politics, by means of which participants built a single organisation based upon a uniform, 'fundamental' set of beliefs or ideology (for example, a religion or a religious denomination or sect) which purported to be totally sufficient for its members' meanings and human purposes (for example, their salvation), regardless of the effects upon the whole gamut of civil, voluntary, or public organisations.

3.4. 'Westernising' democracy

There has been a global trend towards the establishment of representative democracies in a growing number of nation-states.[59] However, representative democracy in the world context of the late twentieth century tended to freeze 'democracy' into a single set of practices, institutions, nations, into a single point of the compass: 'the West'. This was because modern democracy was extended across the world after the collapse of the Soviet Union. In this context, there were no challenging alternatives.[60] That is to say, no alternatives that at least offered hope for a different, fuller kind of democracy or popular self-government. People's Democracies, Unions of Socialist Republics, Soviets, and Communisms were *not* democratic in practice, nowhere near. Nevertheless, many anti-democratic regimes grabbed the title of 'Democracy' or 'Democratic' during the third quarter of the twentieth century. Often they were the carriers of the hopes of many people, parties, and social movements who thought that they could, should, and would become democratic in a fuller, more inclusive sense than modern democracy. In a world in which such alternatives failed or were defeated, and in a world of a single super-power — with a military capacity greater than the 27 next-most powerful countries combined[61] — defining its own, modern, Western democracy as 'the end of history', actually existing, democratic institutions, states, or nations came to be seen as all that is, or could ever be, democratic. Dystopia replaced utopia: commonwealths became a thing of the past. 'History', in Fukuyama's sense, had ended: 'There is no alternative.'

3.5. Global Public Limited Companies (PLCs)

As a counter-trend to this extension of formal, representative democracy in the world, there was another global trend that affected all nation-states, including the United Kingdom, during the same period. This trend was for capitalist companies, public and private, to grow beyond nation-states in size and in power.[62] Globalisation, world free trade, and the market state became familiar labels for this trend towards the end of the twentieth century.[63] It meant that an increasing proportion of public decisions that had been accessible, in principle, to political, representative, democratic decision making — even if its occasions were limited — were now made in private. Unelected, commercial, supra-national settings such as PLC board rooms predominated, with economics winning out over politics. Free markets began to narrow the effective remit of free elections. Within PLCs, power shifted from owners to executives. An 'ownership vacuum' was identified in PLCs, whose shareholders and Boards behaved less and less like governing members.[64]

The World Trade Organization's General Agreement on Tariffs and Trade (GATT) Agreement on Services heralded quasi-statutory limitations on the proportion of national provision of social and other services that nation-states could ring-fence for public provision. Private, international competition was to be introduced into national health services, education systems, welfare services, utilities, transport, and communications, as if these were economic industries like any other. Such industries were to be removed from political (hence representative democratic) control. Globalisation and privatisation went hand in hand, taking more and more decisions into settings where they could be controlled democratically, if at all, only in less and less direct ways. At the same time, 'world' organisations themselves were at best notionally democratic.

During the final quarter of the twentieth century, the effects of such a trend were magnified by unprecedented economic growth and technical change, particularly in Information and Communications Technology. This was not accompanied by parallel growth in world political, democratic institutions. Supra- or inter-state organisations with direct citizen access remained comparatively weak.[65] The writ of market forces and free-market competition and choice was thus extended as never before. At its most extreme, it appeared as though politics itself, or even 'society' and the 'social', could be put out to global, competitive tender along with other 'utilities'.

3.6. Regulation

There was a continuing counter-tendency during the last quarter of the twentieth century in the UK, as elsewhere, for states at the national level to regulate the private (companies, families, etc.), the associational, the voluntary, the co-operative, and the mutual. As the term 'nationalisation' receded, so the term 'regulation' and the profession of 'regulator' emerged. Regulators were mostly appointed by governments, seldom elected, although the phrase 'self-regulation' was preferred by powerful sectors. States also got to regulate at the international level — for instance, in the European Union (EU) — and at a global level — for instance, in the World Trade Organization (WTO) and the World Bank. This tendency could be interpreted as a counter-tendency to the hegemony of the global PLC, although its effect was to encourage the largest of these to grow larger. Regulation, even of the most benign kind — for instance, regulation of hours of work or 'standards' — tends to favour enterprises that are large enough to afford compliance.

But the trend towards regulation was also an alternative to strategies based upon ownership. Ownership, it was argued, did not matter any more. Control could be achieved without it — an extraordinary change in the capitalist conversation. Private versus public debates were said to be old hat. Enthusiasts for 'social enterprise' also argued this, against co-operative and mutual ownership, in the 'new political' settings of the late 1990s and early 2000s. 'Social democrats' had done the same from the 1890s to the 1950s, from Eduard Bernstein in pre-1914 Germany to Anthony Crosland in post-1945 Britain. Contrary to former impulses (and constitutional commitments) to public, national, and State ownership, and *pace* those still committed to co-operation and mutuality, regulation and regulators could do the job. Proxy or surrogate owners acted for real ones, like proxy voters in a PLC. Representatives in a PLC setting need no longer be elected.

Increased regulation in a free-market era should not be surprising. The effective freedom of dynamic markets as Adam Smith described them is rooted in legal incorporation and legal contract, in public regulation and public infrastructure. Markets and states are never mutually exclusive. Markets also make rules. States also make commercial transactions. In all but the most anomalous periods of history, it is wiser to ask 'what kind of market?' and 'what kind of State?', rather than to search for one or the other. The market and the State exist as exclusive alternatives only to ideologists, from Right and Left. To anticipate Section 4 below, CMEs work to rearrange both. If CMEs fail or are defeated, or if it begins to look as if co-operation and mutuality might succeed, CMEs tend to be annexed by either the market or the State. They effectively disappear as CMEs. Their project becomes hidden, even from themselves. They either go so public as to move into the State apparatus, or they go so private as to become domestic or informal.

A propensity to regulate, license, limit (liability, for example), tax, subsidise (training and education, for instance), and establish minima (such as health and safety regulations) was expressed in legislation. 'Incorporation' was one instrument. By means of incorporation, an organisation or body of persons (for example a municipality, a college, a company, or a CME) becomes a legal or corporate 'individual' separable from the individuals belonging to it as members. Alienation of responsibility becomes possible. This is incompatible with an unincorporated, face-to-face, fully voluntary or mutual association.

As the scale and scope of transactions and interactions multiplied in the modern period, corporations grew and multiplied, making such alienation an ever-larger presence in society. 'Society' itself became corporate. This was a central concern of the founding fathers of classical social theory: Marx, Weber, and Durkheim.[66] Enterprises and associations that were adapted for the modern landscape, and which had been selected within its ecology (or, in cultural terms, its morphology), grew large in scale and in scope, as did incorporated CMEs. It remained possible to be unincorporated. But the penalty for remaining fully private (unregulated, unincorporated) – a *gemeinschaft* of members, all of whom belonged heart and soul – was to become marginal in scale and in scope.

There were benefits of compliance, as there were costs; the same applied to non-compliance. The ecology within which the 'voluntary' operated altered, as did the 'associational', the co-operative, and the mutual. This meant that voluntary organisations had difficult choices to make. These choices can be mapped historically. How 'voluntary' could voluntary organisations afford to be, and how much real ownership could their members have if the organisations wished to do more than operate in the interstices of dominant 'public' and dominant 'private' forms? How could the ambition behind

'Voluntary Action: a Method of Social Advance' (Beveridge) be re-membered when organisations — voluntary and other — were subject to such dismembering tendencies?

The social relations that were increasingly regulated, often in spite of calls for de-regulation, included the following:

- *Financial liability:* who was responsible, liable, or able to benefit, and by how much, among members, employees, and others in different organisations (among them, CMEs) and in particular organisational contingencies?
- *Professional competence:* who was an 'approved person', fit and proper to take part in the governance and management of different organisations (among them, CMEs), and with what qualifications or training?
- *The division of labour between organisations:* which organisations (among, for example, different kinds of CME registered as Industrial and Provident Societies) were licensed to do or were legally prevented from doing what things?
- *Competition:* what could certain organisations do (among them CMEs and, in this case, Trade Unions) or, more pertinently, not do, if they were to avoid acting illegally with particular reference to the restraint of trade? How freely could they compete with dominant forms of enterprise and association? Could all associations behave like any associations, or was the playing field not so level?

Regulation appears to be an obvious social good: protecting choice, protecting competition, empowering consumers, incorporating organisations (including CMEs) in order to enable them to grow. But, by its very nature, regulation always creates problems for losers, as well as opportunities for winners. It is never neutral. To anticipate Section 4 below: from the point of view of CMEs, the question is: who or what was being protected? Members? Competitors? Regulation was inevitably experienced in contradictory ways. It was used internally by one kind of CME against another, and within single types of CME, such as Co-operatives. It was used by one CME against another, for example, by Co-operative Societies that gained from there being no legal basis for trading areas versus smaller Societies that suffered. Administrative and legal regulations were experienced as burdensome or protective, depending on the position and power of the observer, and depending on the size of the organisation/corporation.

3.7. Selection, artificial not natural

In this, as in all ecologies, there was a tendency for some kinds of association to flourish and others to falter or to fail. Competitive business models flourished, growing larger in scale and in scope. Increase in scale carried with it its own liability, for instance, to R. Michels' 'iron law of oligarchy', and its own liability to divisions of labour between officials and rank and file, or between cadres of semi-professional activists and ordinary members. Models that were instrumental to the individual's needs and identities flourished. These needs could be internalised and redefined as not being a member of or belonging to anything except my own 'subjectivity': 'me, me, me'. Specialist organisations that were differentiated structurally and performed only one function flourished: for example, banking, making home loans, or insuring against sickness. Singularity did well (see above), for example, in organisations campaigning only on a single issue, such as pressure groups. Some kinds of tight, exclusive models of association also flourished. In the absence of general belonging, humans seek specificity. It is as if humans take their 'surplus consciousness'[67] — that is to say, their (our) consciousness which is not deployable within the dominant, modern forms of society — elsewhere. We thereby dismember or deform the 'public' and reinforce or re-form the 'private'. Deficits accumulating among one set of associational forms accumulate as surpluses among another set.

There is an ecology of 'belonging' and of 'membership' in the modern world that has ugly and dangerous elements — deformations — within it. Belonging remains an evident human desire, even a demand. It is currently expressed within modern societies in at least four forms, each of which may be read as de-formations from a fully, or generally, democratic point of view. Each of these four forms co-exists with a widely acknowledged 'democratic deficit'. In this context, this means first a deficit, among the array of all existing organisations, of organisations that are formally democratic; and second, a deficit among formal democratic organisations or organisations in which a large number of people/members practise democratic participation.

These are the four forms of 'belonging':

- Familial, or domestic belonging, known as belonging to 'the family'.
- 'Sub-cultural', denigrated as 'tribal' belonging, including hyper-active membership within 'cultures of exclusion', including drug cultures.
- Millennial, or sectarian, belonging, known as membership of faith-based communities. These are very tightly, even totally, participatory, with membership occluding everything else in members' lives. Fundamentalism is too narrow a term for such forms of total belonging against society, not to society.

- Ethnic, or 'national', belonging, where membership of the 'nation' — in this particular sense of nation — inheres not in people who live in a place but in people of one ethnicity and/or of one belief. Such people may belong to each other so closely that they indulge in a 'cleansing' of other groups or people — seen as The Other — especially those, on the face of it, that are near to them.

To anticipate Section 4 once again, the importance of these forms in this context is that all of them may be strongly contrasted with CMEs.

3.8. Inequality

There was a tendency for inequalities to grow. This was one of the most striking features of late-twentieth-century global history, as well as of life in late-twentieth-century Britain. Statistical evidence is not difficult to find.[68] The social relations that resulted are more difficult to analyse. Inevitably, they are relations of domination and subordination, of power and relative powerlessness. 'Capacity building' and 'empowerment' became issues for power-holders in modern democracies as inequalities grew. The included became apprehensive about the excluded. How would the excluded behave if they had no capacity other than their humanity, and no power other than their power to associate with each other, in a context where people who had capacity and power enjoyed it on a hitherto unimaginable scale? What 'terror' might be unleashed, needing 'counter-terror' or global war to contain it? How could capacity and power be multiplied in ways that were sustainable, inclusive, bit-by-bit but also universal, and democratic? Could it be done by means of mutual forms?

4. The re-membering of democracy: the contribution of CMEs

Sections 1 and 3 established that a re-membering of democracy may be necessary from a democratic point of view. Whether the offer of Co-operative and Mutual Enterprises can be well enough articulated, or prove sufficient to address modern democracy's deficit, can become evident only in practice. This section suggests ways in which CMEs have a unique offer to make to democracy, empirically as well as essentially, in practice as well as in project. However, no project is rendered worthless because it fails to achieve full realisation at any single point in its history: the worth of all projects derives from the goals that they set, by which their own performance in practice may be criticised. Are the goals worth pursuing? In this instance, are the goals democratic? And are they democratic in the specific ways that modern democracy needs if it is to reduce its deficit?

That CMEs themselves require democracy may be taken as axiomatic by this stage. Democracy is an unfinished process for them, as it is for democracies. CMEs, too, are subject to the trends outlined above in Section 3. CMEs are surrounded by systematic, contextual pressures that work against co-operation and mutuality. Pressures on CMEs include those of incorporation, specialisation, and capitalisation, each of which constrains the mutualisation of membership. CMEs can resist these pressures, but they cannot avoid them.[69] In the UK, during recent times, they may even be bought and sold, or 'privatised' like any other commodity.

Against such a background, the eight problem headings of Section 3 will be used in order to clarify the opportunities that are the subject of this section. The items in List B in Section 1 will also be amplified for the ways in which items on that list may be 're-membered'. As a reminder, these were the headings in Section 3:

1. Democratic deficit
2. Non-voting, non-voters
3. Other kinds of singular growth
4. Westernising democracy
5. Global PLCs
6. Regulation
7. Selection
8. Inequality

Under each of these, a research and development programme is called for from the point of view of the actual and potential contributions of CMEs. Initial pointers will have to stand in for such a programme here, as signs to be entered on the map of 21st-century Co-operative Studies.

4.1. Democratic deficit

CMEs' unique opportunity to contribute to addressing the democratic deficit is *to address the problem in 'useable' ways and at salient, accessible points, in time and place.*

Time: now is clearly an appropriate time to address this problem. The concept and practice of 'now' has already been explored as the focus of the unique offer made by CMEs as forms of association that do not postpone the realisation of democracy until some future date 'when the economy is right', 'after the election', 'after the revolution', or 'when we are in power'. They practise it now.[70]

The advantage of CMEs for 'subordinate' people is that they constitute un-alienated, do-it-yourself democracy. They do not assume that democracy and citizenship are something else, going on somewhere else at some other time (for example, election time).

From a research point of view, the right time to focus on is the historical period during which the democratic deficit took root: the two hundred years between c. 1650 and c. 1850. This was the period during which liberty (freedom, independence) came to be defined in negative, *freedom from,* terms and in terms of (State-derived) 'rights', rather than as self-government. This was also the time when voluntary association and civil society took root in the UK, of which 'membership unlimited' in CMEs, as mutually owned, private and public, self-governing associations of 'ordinary people' became a prominent part. Historical research is urgently needed to make the connections here and to draw out the potential offer of co-operation and mutuality with particular reference to 'ownership' and 'sovereignty'.

The opportunity for CMEs is to examine their own roots in this 'early modern' to 'pre-industrial' period. Such history is part of their social capital, useable for the purposes of growing a wider, fuller democracy than modern forms of democracy have turned out to be. 'We must accept the importance of history while at the same time refusing to allow it to become a prison warder preventing an escape to a better future.'[71] Liberty, freedom, and independence for the many rather than for the few require inter- or mutual dependence. CMEs came into being as associations through which working people could access the classical democratic idea at its strongest, holding it to its *inclusive* promises in a world of mass, large-scale, capitalist industrialisation.

Place: the most appropriate place at which to address the democratic deficit in modern times is the point of consumption. This is where the promise of modern democracy is strongest and most modern, but also where it most fails to deliver anything other than the most attenuated, thinnest, most 'market-oriented' forms of democracy. The point of consumption, after all, is where consumers are made, and where consumption happens. The image of people as 'consumers' is a dominant one in modern democracies. It is a more limiting image than earlier images, such as user or customer.[72]

The point of consumption is also where some of the strongest and most successful CMEs have come through in the consumer, retail, or distributive trades. They have unlimited promise for humans as more than consumers. This is notably the case in the UK in 'the Co-op' and in the former CWS, now the Co-operative Group CWS Ltd. If a 'consumer democracy' can ever be built, CMEs are best placed to do so. The opportunity is to reassemble citizens and citizenship (choice) around the proudest points of modern democracy (the place of choice), but in associated rather than individualist ways, inflecting the image (and the facts) of consumption towards richer words like custom, customer, use, need, fairness, responsibility, and union, between consumption and production, consumers and producers. 'For a CWS that is the people in its unity with their well-being, all the future waits.' 'Since and before 1863, leaders in CWS history have stood for reorganising trade, for equalising the world's advantages, and for extending the division of surpluses to an unlimited and equal membership.'[73]

The CWS saw itself as a consumer democracy not because it saw democracy as limited to consumption, but because in a society where democracy was being limited in that way, societies (Co-operative Societies) of consumers could add democratic value in the economic setting from which democracy had been most obviously subtracted. In practice, of course, the Society was never an entirely functional consumer democracy. Some of its managers behaved like many other managers, preferring to be left alone to manage. And some members had external, political fish to fry. From the mid-1980s onwards, however, the CWS began to address these internal dysfunctions. It began to see itself not only as part of the problems of the wider democratic polity in the UK and the world — reflecting wider democratic decay and the atrophy of liberal ideals — but also as a potential contributor to their re-memberment. 'New political' outsiders also began to see the CWS and its successor, the Co-operative Group, as part of the solution, as part of a revived interest in co-operatives and mutuals as democratic forms from the late 1990s onwards.[74]

4.2. Non-voting, and non-voters

CMEs' contribution to addressing this problem is *to reconnect voting with real returns for the voter*. This is done in CMEs in two ways.

First, CMEs restore directness to the links between representatives and represented. They always work best when these are fully material, rather than abstract. Working people's movements and associations have always been inventive as regards procedures for selection, mandating, delegation, and report-back. The Burkean idea of the freedom of representatives to do as they like between elections has always been a problem for CMEs and similar associations. Leaving it to others, whether those others are professional representatives or professional managers or party machines run by political professionals, has always been seen as a problem rather than a rational, modern opportunity within CMEs.[75]

Second, CMEs can, in principle, reconnect the economic, the social, and the political. The Society or association within which the voter exercises his or her vote is owned by the members. It delivers on all three of those fronts in ways that may be decided or interrogated by members at half-yearly intervals. These intervals were originally quarterly, but never annual, still less quinquennial. The 'Dividend' is directly accessible and open to allocation by members to the community as well as to themselves. It is individual and economic, but also social. 'The important point is that democracy requires wide ranging commitment and participants need to know that they are indeed efficacious — their participation brings results.'[76] Voter turn-out in CMEs, particularly in large retail Co-operative Societies and in Building Societies, was poor and became increasingly so during the third quarter of the twentieth century. In co-operative societies in the UK, membership itself also declined step by step with the abolition or dilution of the Dividend from the 1960s onwards.

4.3. Other kinds of singular growth

CMEs' contribution to addressing this problem — or the unique opportunity that co-operation and mutuality have in this problem area — is *to put things together that are becoming increasingly singular, or separate, in the culture of modern democracy.* The opportunity is for a democratic politics that is more than single-occasion, single-issue, single-social-group, single-leader, single-identity, or single-organisation politics, as described in Section 3.3. The unique offer of a CME such as the CWS in the late-twentieth-century ecology — given the facts set out in Sections 1 and 2 — was that the CWS constituted a large-scale organisation relevant to meeting such an opportunity. Its scale and complexity matched the scale and complexity of society itself, thus making its practice oppositional, whether members and managers wanted it to be or not, rather than safely alternative.

Membership in CMEs, at best, constitutes democratic practice that is more than occasional, cross-issue, cross-group, cross-identity single leaders. It is also, at best, federalist in its organisational and ideological approach (i.e., exemplifying Co-operative Principle no. 6: Co-operation among Co-operatives). In Co-operative Societies, large and small, and in a slow, incremental process of renewal from the mid-1980s onwards, there have been accessible opportunities to build democratic practice bit by bit. At best these opportunities have constituted more than the single-occasion routines of representative democracy.

4.4. Westernising democracy

CMEs' contribution to addressing this problem is *to offer democracies that are unlimited by geographical place as well as by historical period*. The democracy of CMEs is not closed or limited to institutionalised political representation and its intermittent occasions. Co-operative and mutual democracy may be forbidden by a regime, but it is not limited to a single type of regime. It may be constructed bit by bit, away from 'the centre' in and against any regime that allows it space. It is also 'prefigurative', in the sense that feminists used the term during the 1970s. It is not Western in the sense that it is finished, needing only defence or security in order to perpetuate its quasi-sacred institutions. It is a dynamic, open, voluntary, human possibility that requires creative, collaborative, continuous, bit-by-bit development and social construction *sans frontières*. 'Democracy is process, and is not simply present or absent. It is always in flux and has ebbs and flows.'[77] The alternative, sometimes seen as 'the enemy within' in modern democracies when they are threatened, is the idea of social movement (the co-operative movement as part of the labour, working-class, or originally the *social*, movement). While such movements exist as clusters of would-be democratic, associationist forms, no closure or 'end' or final institutionalisation of modern democracy can be achieved. While movements (now commonly seen as networks) exist, it is more difficult to put History in a sealed vault and forget it.

4.5. Global PLCs

CMEs' contribution to addressing this problem — or the unique opportunity that co-operation and mutuality have in this problem area — is *to make connections available in a landscape in which divisions are increasingly apparent and in which inherited connections (such as nation-states other than the largest) are increasingly fragile.*

Interest in 'civil society' increased from the late 1980s onwards as the volatility and the fragility of nation-states became more apparent. Global Civil Society Organisations (CSOs) joined CMEs in the late 1990s as available connectors in a landscape in which divisions were increasing. This interest increased with the break-up of the Soviet empire. 'Global civil society' was seen as a source for 'global governance'.

Unless links could be forged between popular agency and global structure, democracy could not possibly develop in dynamic ways. Similarly, places, or accessible locations, needed connecting if self-government was ever to be realised in a world order whose centres of power seemed not only centralised but also remote. If self-government was to be realised as more than an individual ideal, exclusive and individualist forms needed openings into inclusive, interdependent associations. Associational forms that citizens could join were needed, through which market and State, production and government, abstract society and actual Societies could be connected. Associational forms with the capacity to build the 'social' — and hence 'society' — into an entity strong enough to include the 'economic' and the 'political' globally as well as locally were not common, hence the late-twentieth-century salience of the CWS, of CMEs, and of CSOs. Only through such agencies could 'the future', which Percy Redfern had seen as 'waiting' in 1938, be kept from waiting for ever.

4.6. Regulation

CMEs' contribution to addressing the problem of regulation is *to be among the winners so that the problems of democracy become the problems of co-operative and mutual enterprise*. As we have seen, regulation is not going to go away in a market state, still less in a State market, and it favours, or selects, some forms rather than others. There is no reason why CMEs should not grow large in this setting. History shows that there is every reason why they should – and did. CMEs became successful, large-scale, and broad in scope, and they offered rational solutions to the problem of meeting basic human needs.

A 'co-operative and mutual advantage' thus became apparent in significant areas of enterprise. So much so that 'business co-operation' developed among entrepreneurs and enterprises that had no affiliation to values and principles beyond those of business success in modern capitalisms.[78] Some Co-operators proposed that Co-operatives should be regulated under Companies Acts (with appropriate adjustments) rather than, as had happened in Britain since the early nineteenth century, under Friendly Society and then Industrial and Provident Society legislation. 'Social enterprise' also became mainstream in Britain during the late 1990s, with enterprises claiming 'social-ness' by pointing to their intentions, or to what they did with their profits, or to their values loosely defined, rather than to mutuality or to specifically co-operative values and principles (including, of course, mutual ownership and democratic control by members). During this period 'social enterprise' was welcomed in the 'new politics' rather more than CMEs and became a term more used than 'the social economy'.

The opportunity in this setting is for the problems of size and success that visit all enterprises in modern capitalisms to become the problems of large-scale CMEs, and thus the available solutions to those problems embedded in the project of co-operative and mutual enterprise. The problems have been rehearsed in this chapter. They are those of the economic winning out over the social; professional competence in tension with democratic control; the division of labour between organisations; competition; finding successful federal structures; accessibility versus central direction; and rational direction versus autonomy. The opportunity is for those problems to be solved — or space found for contradictions to be realised — within member-owned enterprises in the fullest sense of ownership.

4.7. Selection

CMEs' contribution to addressing the problem of 'artificial selection' is *to grow as a strong presence in an ecology within which thick deformations (or a surplus) of membership and belonging co-exist with, or flourish because of, the thinness of modern democracy — its deficit.* An ecology in which the forms outlined in sub-section 3.7 flourish is one in which CMEs are also able to flourish, but without taking on all the same characteristics. It is an ecology that cries out for co-operation and mutuality.

The contrasts should by now be obvious. The privacy, lack of civility, lack of interest in (and sometimes explicit hostility to) participatory democracy at a federal, general level (as opposed to within their own forms) of families, tribes, sects, special-interest groups, and 'nations' is a striking characteristic.

Families, tribes, sects, and 'nations' are not about co-operation and mutuality, even between themselves and cognate forms, let alone between themselves and (to them) dissonant forms. Their energy comes from working against allies — the closer, the more opposition — rather than from working with them in order to constitute a wider society.

Their identity comes from having few or no allies. Their membership, their forms of belonging, are shut, not open; compulsive and compulsory, not voluntary. Tightness and exclusivity characterise them. 'Mutuality' within may be strong, but mutuality between, especially where difference rather than homogeneity is in play, is weak. In Robert Putnam's terminology in *Bowling Alone* (2000) and in the explosion of literature on 'social capital' that followed, such forms of social capital *bond,* but they do not *bridge.*

As meaningful co-operative membership became an explicit, deliberate, and self-conscious project during the second half of the 1990s among powerful consumer Co-operatives, it became more overtly available as a corrective to both the deficit and the surplus described in this chapter. 'Privatisation' of mutuals from the 1980s onwards had helped. It made for greater self-consciousness and pride among CMEs, particularly when the CWS publicly fought off predators. Certainly from 1997 onwards, the CWS at the leadership level, together with Co-operative Societies in membership of the CWS such as Lincoln and Oxford, Swindon, and Gloucester, and an alliance between the Building Societies Association (BSA), the Association of Friendly Societies (AFS), and the United Kingdom Co-operative Council (UKCC), all contributed to a renewed recognition of 'mutuality' and CMEs as a common resource that was available for wider, deeper, democratic development.

4.8. Inequality
CMEs' contribution to addressing this problem is *to act as organisations with a built-in tendency to diminish inequalities, or to brush against their grain rather than to reproduce them.* It is at this point that the 'origins of modern social theory' (Giddens) in the 'classical' sociological tradition of Marx, Weber, and

Durkheim need to be revisited, first for what they have to say about co-operation and mutuality, and second for what they do not have to say, but point towards, in relation to CMEs.[79]

The problem and the opportunity for co-operators and mutualists interested in the value of CMEs in the wide world, rather than as marginal alternatives to dominant forms, can be well illustrated by going through the index in scores of books where there should and might be references to 'Co-operatives' and/or 'Mutuals', only to find that they are few and far between. There are many resources for a journey of hope in the classics of social thought. Examples include Marx on 'the associated mode of production'; Weber on the early modern, deeply mutual, 'sectarian' forms of association that have an affinity for world-changing activity among their members; and Durkheim on forms such as producers' guilds that provide possible vehicles for 'organic solidarity' even when the terrain is steeply sloped against their users. Even when dominant interests, fortified by economic 'laws', are stacked against co-operation and mutuality, and especially because at-a-stroke change was shown during the twentieth century seldom to work in the interests of those on whose behalf it was made, it may be possible to prefigure and then to generalise democracy as self-government by means of CMEs. The project and the practice are worth further action research.

7. Theorising co-operative studies: obstacles and opportunities for twenty-first century co-operative and mutual enterprises

This chapter outlines some problems and opportunities faced by the Co-operative Movement as it moves into the wide-open, theoretical and practical spaces of a twenty-first century would-be 'social' world. As Co-operative Studies gain in confidence, seven preliminary questions are identified:

1) Are the questions of who does Co-operative Studies, and for whom, more fundamental in this field of study than in others?
2) Is practice integral to any theory that informs Co-operative Studies?
3) Do Co-operative and Mutual Enterprises (CMEs) embody a set of practices that constitute a theory of the transition to a post-capitalist society?
4) Can co-operatives be seen as a species within a genus of associational forms for which the acronym 'CME' is appropriate?
5) Does the degree to which CMEs attain 'mutuality' provide a performance indicator for their project?

6) Are the central issues raised in the writings of the founders of 'modern social theory' implicit in the practice of CMEs but less explicit, so far, in their theory — for example, Marx on class, Weber on active associational forms, and Durkheim on organic solidarity?

7) When we are thinking towards a discipline called Co-operative Studies, are we also thinking about issues which have moved to the centre of 'natural' history, or Darwinian Studies?

In the UK, where this chapter comes from, large-scale CMEs acted defensively and were treated as archaic in the wider field of 'business' from the late 1950s until the mid-1990s. The 1995 International Co-operative Alliance (ICA) Statement of Identity, Values, and Principles was a sign of a sea-change. The chapter uses mainly British/European and mainly labour-movement-based Co-operative experience to provoke more confident thinking among CMEs in a more positive context.

Introduction

The tap root of this chapter is local ('localist'?): in Oxfordshire, England, where I live. Many of its references come from my training as a British historian. All my life I have tended to follow Sven Lindqvist's injunction to community activists and historians during the 1970s, to 'Dig Where You Stand!'. So do many Co-operators. This may be because Co-operative and Mutual Enterprises (CMEs) are associations of people, unlike capitalist enterprises which, because they are associations of capital, tend to be restless and rootless, displaced and displacing.[1]

In view of the chapter's Eurocentricity and its base in British labour-movement-based co-operatives, it was as well that my thoughts were tested at the international conference on 'Mapping Co-operative Studies in the New Millennium', held at the British Columbia Institute for Co-operative Studies in May 2003. Thanks to Ian MacPherson, a spoken version of what follows served as the keynote address for that conference. During the following four days, delegates from many places in the world told me — from their own perspectives — how my ideas could be extended or reconsidered. With such help, I produced this written text, retaining my ambitious title. The conference was opened by a First Nation Canadian who welcomed us on to his people's historic land. By the end of the conference, I recognised that, while the European sociologists upon whom I draw remain important for the future of co-operation and mutuality, so too are the non-European cultural/intellectual traditions and the agrarian, women's, and other co-operative and mutual movements about which I say very little.

The title is ambitious, but 'theorising' in this context means something quite modest. My aim is to be suggestive rather than definitive. Only in the final two sections of the chapter, on social science and on natural science, will I explore theories at any length. Co-operative Studies in the twenty-first century need to be confident rather than diffident when exploring ideas. This is perhaps the largest contextual change in the situation of Co-operative Studies in the twenty-first century. From the mid-1990s onwards there was a sea change in the situation of the Co-operative Movement, symbolised by the International Co-operative Alliance's approval of a new 'Co-operative Statement of Identity and Principles' at the ICA Congress in Manchester in 1995. Before then, although a large-scale, world-wide business, the consumer Co-operative Movement had occupied a somewhat defensive position, in the UK and elsewhere, ever since the mid-1950s. The ambition of figures like J. T. W. Mitchell has had to be rescued from the condescension of posterity, even within his own movement. Some CMEs made major breakthroughs between the 1950s and the 1990s. Credit Unions in Ireland and the Mondragon complex in Spain are two of the most well-known examples.[2] But when the consumer movement showed signs of believing in 'the co-operative difference' during the mid-1990s, and when it began to relate to other sectors in co-operative as well as in business-like ways, the whole context for co-operative and mutual study, as well as for co-operative and mutual practice, began to improve. In Britain, the Co-operative College's return to Manchester signalled a new lease of life. My intention here is to think aloud about Co-operative Studies in the new context, in such a way as to make CMEs more available for critical, creative thought in general, but particularly among Co-operators.[3]

Co-operative Studies and the 'Social'

This emphasis — particularly among Co-operators — is important. It points to theory as well as to practice. 'Who?' and 'for whom?' are radical questions to ask about any intellectual undertaking. For Co-operative Studies, they are defining questions.

In Co-operative Studies who does the thinking and how they (we) do it matters more than it does, for example, in astronomy. The move from 'they' to 'we', from the third person to the first, is also significant, although it is an awkward one to make in an academic text. Academic convention is to avoid the first person, particularly the first-person singular. One way of stating the objective of Co-operative Studies is: to make the first-person plural — 'we' — a fully meaningful subject, so that 'we the peoples' can be said materially and without rhetoric.[4] In other words, to make 'us' (we all) an inclusive, active, fully realised, voluntary, and open presence in the world, as our own subjects rather than as other people's objects, as 'men and women of Co-operative quality'. In the confident words of the Communist Manifesto of 1847-8, 'we shall have an association in which the free development of each is the condition for the free development of all'.[5] I use 'we' throughout this text whenever the present tense is also used. As W. H. Auden wrote in his United Nations Hymn, 'Till what it could be / At last it is'.

This is a tall order. The answer to the question 'who?' sought in Co-operative Studies is: we all, everyone, all for each, and each for all. The answer to the question 'how?' sought in Co-operative Studies is: together, in open and voluntary association, mutually and co-operatively. These cannot be simple matters to follow through, intellectually or practically. To arrive at such answers will be to brush against the grain of individualist, competitive capitalism. But it is important to insist that, in the case of Co-operative Studies, the first-person plural represents theoretical commitment rather than rhetorical decoration. This need not be the case in other fields of study, for example Cultural Studies. The theory is difficult and not yet fully articulated, nor is the practice.[6] When we are thinking towards a discipline of Co-operative Studies adequate for our times, we are thinking about a set of practices which need to be researched and developed together, co-operatively not individually. Given the surrounding educational and academic culture, at least where I come from, and given how that culture distributes rewards for research and development (careers, assessment, grants, etc.), competitive individualism is easier.

Knowledge for Co-operative Studies necessarily includes the sociology of knowledge, or social science. It is no accident that 'social science' was a term invented not in the academy but by early-nineteenth-century Owenite Co-operators. They coined the term as a critique of the 'dismal science' of competitive political economy. Working-class advocates of social science in Britain, associating in what became the Co-operative Movement, saw political economy and its manufacturers as anti-social.[7] They wished to replace anti-social, competitive science and practice, then known as political economy, methodologically and substantively. Co-operative and mutual knowledge — or 'associative intelligence', as early Co-operators called it — had, as its vocation, the making of a 'science' which could be owned as 'ours'.[8]

Sociality — or, a key word in Co-operative Studies, 'association' — remains the aim and object of Co-operative Studies in a way that need not be true, for instance, of business studies or management studies. Co-operative and mutual knowledge comes from and returns to what became known during the nineteenth century as the social movement, or *le mouvement sociale*.[9] The 'movement' was fundamental to it. Such a movement is being referred to again during the early years of the twenty-first century, in a global context.[10] Co-operative and mutual knowledge was also a constituent of what became known during the nineteenth and twentieth centuries as the social economy, or *l'économie sociale*.

The theory of a set of practices whose theory is that they are practices not a theory

When we are thinking towards a discipline called Co-operative Studies, we are thinking about a set of co-operative and mutual practices whose theory is that they are practices not theory. This is not a puzzling paradox: it points directly to the substance (what) of Co-operative Studies, as well as to the sociology (who) and the methodology (how).

Practice matters to (or is material to) Co-operative Studies. Practice had to matter for most of the people who constituted the Co-operative Movement during its earliest days. To them, 'position' meant something involuntary and on the ground. It referred to their position in the labour market, in or out of a work place. It referred to their 'position in society'. Position was not something in the head and freely chosen, as it is for people who are paid to have a position or to take a view, as in 'my position on value is …'. Co-operators' position is that we tend not to be dominant in capitalisms. This is because of forces as yet beyond our control. At worst the position of Co-operators has been 'residual' in capitalism, at best 'emergent'.[11] But we also tend not to dominate because of our beliefs, our values, and principles. Co-operators cannot be 'in power' in the conventional sense of that phrase. We cannot constitute a regime. If we were to arrive at a position to be in power, we would transform power by sharing it. Power would not remain the same thing. Sovereignty is altered if it is shared. So is ownership. They are reconstituted as transformed sets of social relations. Because Co-operators have tended to be labour, or working people — with their labour as their capital, socialised as 'social capital' by their Societies — they have tended to be sub-ordinate rather than super-ordinate people. This is what Co-operators struggle to change by means of CMEs, while also struggling to move on to equitable terrain, without the subs and the supers, the 'high', 'low' antinomy which disfigures the present landscape.

The labour theory of value among early co-operative economists in Europe was significant not because it was a theory of value, correct or incorrect, but because it was a labour theory of value. It began from a position: that of humans without a great deal to lose, but with the human capacity to produce things and to generate value by means of labour power. Labour can be associated in the passive sense and as an object, or labour can associate itself in the active sense and as a subject. This can happen in a variety of ways, some of them more 'social' than others. The labour theory of value attempted to change the relations, perceived as anti-social, through which things were predominantly being produced in competitive society. 'Capitalism' was named as such several decades later, some time after the vocabulary of socialism.[12] Early co-operative economists such as William Thompson (1785-1833) considered that competitive relations involved the extraction of value from labour and its appropriation by capital, rather than its equitable and mutual sharing. Their goal was the socialisation of 'trading surplus' by means of associations of people exercising the associative intelligence of their members.

This explains why theoreticians and politicians detached from the Movement are problematic for Co-operators; they are not 'organic' to it.[13] Similarly, policy can be a problem for CMEs, as well as offering opportunities. Readers of Shakespeare's history plays will recall 'policy' as the word that describes what kings and courtiers sought to stay in power. Shakespeare almost always used the word pejoratively, as a critique of contemporary politics.[14] Since then, the word has tended to refer to things done to or sold to one set of persons (usually ordinary people) by another set of persons (usually professionals and managers). Policy remains predominantly a 'from above' word, rather than a word which has any affinity with co-operation or mutuality. We now inhabit a political world in which policies from above — including 'social policy' and 'social enterprise policy' — are rampant. They come from Departments of State as well as from academic departments, and from local government as well as from supra-national institutions. They are not necessarily helpful for CMEs. It is not always clear whether it is advantageous to the co-operative and mutual project to be included within a particular policy framework. Inclusion can have penalties for co-operation and mutuality if it is made to 'fit' dominant State or academic categories. Policy makers in the UK have difficulty fitting CMEs even into the category of social enterprise, let alone not-for-profit enterprises.[15] Co-operative Studies is thus probably not best seen as a branch of either Policy Studies or of Political Studies even if, in modern universities, students of Co-operative Studies are in no position to be fastidious about their location. They are often subsumed into 'business studies', 'management studies', or 'social policy': seldom itemised on their own.

Time has also been important to Co-operators, alongside position or place. If the place for CMEs has had to be, to quote the poet William Carlos Williams, 'the true core of the universal', so has 'now': here and now. Co-operators' construction of power has had to be such that power can be produced and shared among them — 'arranging the powers' in the words of the Rochdale Pioneers[16] — with whoever is in power. 'Then' has to be built out of Now if ever it is to be built by, rather than for, Co-operators, or if ever 'we' are to come into existence for ourselves. Similarly, the future has to be built in the present; the ideal has to be carried in the material, the idea in the practice. Otherwise 'then' will always remain as someone else's future: dismembered and incorporate. If tomorrow is to be ours, owned and managed by us, it has to be built from today, here and now, rather than by them, over there, and then.

The contrast is with regimes and 'rulers' who, like many such in the past, have tried to escape time by guaranteeing their succession — promoting their sovereignty for all time — establishing their proprietorship 'time out of mind'. The contrast is also with politicians who, like many such in the present, 'take' or 'capture' power and turn it into an expensive and exclusive commodity by means of elections and other party practices whose costs rise until they are out of ordinary people's reach. Co-operators have to arrange powers, to make them, learn about them, and exercise them, every day and where we stand.

The Co-operative Movement's alchemy is to have invented forms of association through which daily necessity (here and now) for food, shelter, insurance, learning, sociability, and recreation can be turned by everybody into desirable ways to live (there and then). Co-operative Societies are prefigurations of society: the limbs of a different body politic. The universal human need for food, shelter, insurance, and so on is the bare metal that Co-operators and Mutualists intend to turn into gold by means of extraordinary social inventions: Co-operative and Mutual Enterprises. The ordinariness of this intention is important. The tools being used are everyday tools, rather than time-lords' magic wands.

There is a profound sense for Co-operators that what we want is already there/here. Such thinking, of course, extends beyond CMEs. In English terms, it was well expressed by William Blake. It goes back to John Milton and, more widely and deeply, to a Judaeo-Christian antinomian inheritance. CMEs are 'available forms', to use a term developed by Raymond Williams, when theorising Cultural Studies.[17]

To realise what John Stuart Mill described as our 'futurity' would be a deep and epoch-making change. It is out of reach, in one sense. But it would also be quite ordinary and, in another sense, it is therefore to hand: 'That awareness of light, of song, of human liberty, which are there close enough to grasp, yet seemingly always just out of reach in the harsh close-up world of deprivation and struggle'. The fit is never perfect: 'Some of us are cursed with the urge to be making assertions that are either too big or too deep to fit into the box of current relations.'[18] Philip Pullman's best-selling trilogy *His Dark Materials* draws on Blake and Milton, among others. One way of reading the trilogy is as a study of mutuality. On the final page of *The Amber Spyglass*, Lyra talks with her daemon about the difference between the republic of heaven and the kingdom: 'The kingdom is over, all finished ... where we are is always the most important place.'[19] That is what Co-operators discovered, by necessity. For Co-operators, the other must be ourselves, whereas in other forms of enterprise — politics and religion — there can be, and frequently is, displacement on to an alienated other, at worst The Other.[20]

The first objective of the Rochdale Pioneers was 'to establish a store for the sale of provisions ...'. Their fifth objective was 'to *arrange the powers* [my emphasis] of production, distribution, education and government'. This was what 'this Society shall proceed' to do, with the qualification 'as soon as is practicable'.[21] A modern activist in the Co-operative Group (CWS) Limited remembers a co-operative central store in Liverpool during his childhood. It was decorated with inscribed tiles on which 'Boot Repairs' was given the same prominence as 'Liberty' and 'Equality'.[22] For Charles Gide:

> ... co-operation keeps its striking characteristic of being at the same time highly idealistic and very practical. It is at once Martha and Mary, Don Quixote and Sancho. It follows the blue bird, but instead of seeking it in the Fortunate Islands, shuts it up in a shop. It sets before itself the reformation of the world; it begins by sweeping the pavement before its own door.[23]

A theory of the transition

The transition to socialism, sometimes abbreviated as 'the transition', and the transition from feudalism to capitalism, sometimes abbreviated by historians as 'the transition problem', were central scholarly concerns — and not only for socialists — for many decades. They became less so at the end of the 1980s, following the collapse of the Soviet Union and its empire.

When we are thinking towards a discipline called 'Co-operative Studies', we are thinking about a set of practices which constitute a theory of the transition to a post-capitalist society. The theory has always been largely unacknowledged as such by socialist scholars. It also remains largely untheorised among CMEs. One of the preoccupations of Co-operative Studies in the twenty-first century will be to sustain any idea of transition in modern times and then to determine how to turn our own ideas into more than assumptions, thus making them available for research and development.

From the early 1990s onwards, 'the transition' to a future other than capitalism became unfashionable to think about. Socialisms seemed to have terminated. In the United States, 'the end of history', or 'endism', meant that there were to be no further this-worldly transitions. History had terminated in 'the market' or Western democracy. Any new moral world other than the new economy, or globalisation, tended to become a matter for religious eschatology, rather than for day-to-day construction.

Nevertheless, a distinctive theory of transition remains visible within, and integral to, the practice of CMEs. The theory focuses on the here and the now and is part of the alchemy already noted. As such, it is a critique of hitherto dominant socialist ideas. Hence the explicit critique of 'socialist ideology' among advocates of 'the new mutualism'. Associationism of a co-operative kind is one among a range of opposed socialisms.[24]

For Co-operators and Mutualists, there is no fracture between means and ends — results and processes — of the kind which has kept so many socialists incapable of acting in the present because they are over-mortgaged to the future. Mass labour movements were too often frozen in permanent contradiction between what their members actually did from day to day, what their leaders 'demanded' that other people or the State should do, and what they said that they believed in.[25] Co-operators are critical of political parties in nation states and of states of mind in which postponement is accepted as inevitable by professionals and managers who have interests vested in such postponement. In these situations, it will be all right, the professionals say, but after something else has happened: after the next election; after the revolution; after 'the bottom line' has been corrected so that 'overheads' can be 'carried'; after 'the base' has reached a condition from which the new 'superstructure' will immaculately follow; after 'growth' reaches a level at which 'redistribution' becomes manageable; or after economic 'means of production' have been developed so that social 'relations of production' can be considered.

For Co-operators, it is not 'after' or 'when' anything. It is *now* that we begin to 'arrange the powers'. The distribution of corn, flour, and bread, or how phone calls are paid for, become part of such arrangements. 'Arranging' is a different sort of verb from 'nationalising' or 'seizing' or 'demanding'. We do it for ourselves rather than demanding that 'progress' or 'history' do it for us. 'The transition' is a matter of constructing what 1970s feminists called 'prefigurative forms'. These are associational forms which anticipate, in present Societies (CMEs), what future 'society' can be.

CMEs, Co-operatives, and/or Mutual Enterprises

When we are thinking towards a discipline called Co-operative Studies, we are thinking about a cluster of associational forms larger, in the UK, than The Co-op and larger, anywhere, than Co-operatives. The Co-op was the first integrated retail and manufacturing chain in the UK. As a powerful social and business invention in its own right, and one made by working people, it became such a powerful presence in the culture that it tended to eclipse Co-operatives in general, let alone Mutuals in general. These had already been eclipsed by giant 'Orders' of Friendly Societies, another extraordinary social invention made by working people.

The associational forms within the potential remit of Co-operative Studies include Friendly Societies. But they also include Building Societies, Educational Associations, Club and Institute Union clubs, Credit Unions, and, in some of their aspects, Trade Unions. This cluster of forms has a common history in the UK, the land of the first industrial revolution. It commenced, legally, with Societies registered as Friendly Societies during the 1790s. The Rochdale Pioneers (pioneer Co-operators) and the Tolpuddle Martyrs (pioneer trade unionists) were registered, or sought registration, as Friendly Societies. Most Working Men's Clubs — the whole cluster was overwhelmingly male in its leadership and membership — also registered as Friendly Societies, which they were allowed to do until the 1990s. The Friendly Society rather than the Co-operative Society is, in many ways, the archetype or *ur* form of CME, at least in the UK. As such it remains greatly under-researched.

This cluster of associational forms may be seen as a genus of which each kind of Society may be seen as a species. To continue the biological analogy, there are then varieties within the species, and creative hybridisation between them. In different national cultures or ecologies, classifications are different. This can make international comparisons in Co-operative Studies difficult. Even though the species have grown further apart, partly as a result of incorporation or State action, there are still acknowledgements of the genus, sometimes from surprising individuals within various species. In Britain, the President of the Club and Institute Union still speaks at the Union's Annual Congress of Clubs as democratic mutuals, firmly within the CME cluster. Trade Unions were theorised by Demos, a think tank, during the late 1990s as 'employee mutuals'. Friendly Societies and Credit Unions in Britain drew closer together when incorporation became less restrictive towards the close of the twentieth century. From about 1997 onwards in Britain, there were interesting signs of species wanting to grow together again. Joint meetings were held between the trade associations of Co-operatives, Friendly Societies, and Building Societies. The 'family' metaphor began to be used, first within The Co-op, then between consumer Co-operatives and other varieties of Co-operative, and then between Co-operatives and Mutuals. Gender equality and ethnic diversity also began to be recognised as high priorities among CMEs, which had not been good at supporting or promoting either.

There are three reasons for thinking that 'CMEs' as a label for the cluster will add value. The first is to assist the process of coming together, or mutualisation, between Co-operatives and Mutuals. Without a distinct but inclusive flag of our own, we tend to get internally divided. Specialist incorporation of sub-species of CMEs has served to reinforce division; so have professional and managerial self-interest, as individual Societies grew larger and larger.[26] Structural differentiation has been as evident in the history of co-operation as it has in the history of competition.[27] This should be the subject of a research programme in Co-operative Studies. Labels for varieties within the co-operative species proliferate: housing co-operatives, finance co-operatives, care co-operatives, producer co-operatives, agricultural co-operatives, business co-operatives, consumer co-operatives, and so on. The split between producer and consumer and between worker and retail co-operatives in the UK became antagonistic, roughly between the 1880s and the 1980s. Neither camp theorised co-operation sufficiently, in general. Both camps failed to recognise each other as having even a particular theory of co-operation. A key element in a general theory would have been mutuality (Co-operative *and Mutual* Enterprises), and this concept was under-employed (in the UK) during those one hundred years. An encouraging sign of the times during the first years of the twenty-first century was that 'mutuality' came back into the culture, from outside the Movement as much as from within. Politicians and policy makers in Britain began to fall over themselves to approve of it.

The second reason for thinking that 'CMEs' as a label for the cluster may add value is opportunistic. When Co-operative Futures, a Co-operative Research and Development agency growing from a retail Society in England, published 'Mutuality: Owning the Solution' in 2000 as a report on a year's work by what is now the Midcounties Co-operative, the aim was to enter a national conversation on the ecology of enterprise in the UK. SMEs (Small or Medium-sized Enterprises) had been loud voices in this conversation during the 1980s and 1990s. Government policy, training initiatives, and enterprise strategy in general had focused on SMEs. The acronym became familiar. The objective was for CMEs to enter the same discourse.

From the late 1990s onwards, this began to happen, but under a variety of names. The International Labour Organization (ILO) and the European Union (EU) included Co-operatives in their plans and protocols. The World Social Forum and Global Justice Movement included Co-operatives and Mutuals in their drive towards Fair and Ethical Trade. The Report of the Co-operative Commission in the UK used the term CMEs, while asking questions of The Co-op in its drive to become more co-operative and more mutual.[28] There were government reports from, for example, the Cabinet Office and the Department of Trade and Industry in the UK which acknowledged the place of CMEs even when they used a variety of terms such as Not for Profit Organisations and Social Enterprises.[29]

The third reason for thinking that a clear label for the cluster, from the co-operative and mutual side, would add value is that modern policy makers need a handle. The CME label serves as a corrective for another one which became as widely used as 'SME' under New Labour in the UK: 'Social Enterprise'. CME stiffens 'Social Enterprise', which otherwise has a tendency to include all enterprises that simply say that they are social rather than anti-social. Without a clear subset of Co-operative and Mutual Enterprises, 'Social Enterprise' suggests that intention is all, and that ownership, membership, and governance are immaterial in the modern world. While CMEs can pick up wind by sailing with Social Enterprises and with new vessels such as Global Civil Society Organisations (GCSOs), and with older ships such as Voluntary Organisations, it can be risky. The risks are diminished to the extent that recognition is achieved for CMEs and for Co-operative Studies as the focus of a distinct cluster of associational forms.

Mutuality as project

Co-operative Studies focus on project as well as practice. The project may be described with abstract nouns: co-operation and mutuality. The practice, by contrast, is described with concrete nouns: co-operatives and mutuals.

'Mutuality' is a word which has a beauty of its own, but it has not been a 'keyword' in English, in the sense that Raymond Williams defined keywords. Keywords, in this sense, are words such as 'class' and 'culture', through which struggles between antagonistic clusters of social potential have been articulated.[30] 'Mutuality' has been less of a keyword in English than *mutualité* was in nineteenth-century France.[31]

The beauty of mutuality is apparent when it is used, for example, to identify the nature of lifelong learning as a distinctively mutual good. Mutuality draws attention to goods with a built-in resistance to commodification. For example, 'Knowledge is something that you can give to others without losing any of it yourself'. Moreover, 'by its very nature learning is a … mutual activity …. We generally learn from and with others. I cannot buy learning, I can only buy assistance to learn … [it] is an activity which in many cases can only benefit an individual if it also benefits someone else.'[32]

But, however attractive it may be, mutuality remains elusive. There is no legal definition in British law of 'mutual', any more than there is of 'privacy'. It has recently been suggested that mutuality may be 'a good term because it has not been used much since the nineteenth century'. For this reason we can 'stop thinking of mutuality in all or nothing terms', and liberate it to draw attention to an unfinished project, rather than to a realised achievement.[33] Mutuality may prove useful as a description of the project of co-operation, unrealised until 'the circle is complete' between members within Co-operatives and Mutuals and between all Co-operatives and Mutuals.

While all Mutuals are co-operative, not all Co-operatives are mutual. The degree to which Co-operatives or Mutuals attain mutuality provides a performance indicator by which the extent to which their project is realised may be measured. 'Mutuality' would be one envelope for all Key Social Performance Indicators (KSPIs) for Co-operatives.[34] There may be practical reasons why few CMEs are fully mutual at any one time. But their distance from mutuality represents a problem for Co-operative Studies to address, rather than an opportunity to be celebrated, as it might be in Business Studies. Demutualisation happens within a CME some time before its members agree to sell out. In Business Studies, CMEs may be seen as 'a curious form of organization that seems to be a quaintly out-dated form that, it is assumed, cannot possibly compete with the ubiquitous, and triumphant, joint stock company'. In Co-operative Studies,

> a lot of work remains to be done to specify the type of organization that can be efficient and effective on the one hand, and ethically responsible and trustworthy on the other ... Existing mutuals are only a rough guide to this ... and a poor guide to what a truly stakeholder-controlled organization would look like. They have a long way to go to restore the sense of involvement that mutuals used to provide when they were small and based in real geographical communities. What we need are some bold experiments in mutuality that are completely new.[35]

While membership is essential to Co-operatives, its meanings may differ from those in 100 per cent mutual enterprises – that is, enterprises which trade exclusively with and for their members. In these mutual enterprises, members alone receive the surplus, as well as owning and governing the mutual, in a circle within which there is – in principle – no structural differentiation between users, beneficiaries, employees, and members. The same can be true of co-operatives. But it is not necessarily so. For example, some housing co-operatives, credit unions, and producer/ 'worker' co-operatives are fully mutual. Historically, some retail Co-operative Societies in Britain had the word 'mutual' in their names. Geographically, some retail Societies in Europe trade exclusively with their members.

Typologies of all enterprises and associations that have 'members' will be helpful for Co-operative Studies in the same way that typologies of sectarian, denominational, and church forms of organisation were helpful for Religious Studies. If the meanings of membership in Mutuals may be clarified by how they differ from some Co-operatives, the meanings of membership in CMEs (as a cluster of associational forms) may be further clarified by how they differ from those in other forms of 'not for profit' enterprise, and by how they differ from Private or Public Limited Companies (PLCs) and variants of the PLC form.

In the history of large-scale CMEs, there have been many varieties of membership and belonging. Some members have confined their participation to the economic sphere, some to the political sphere, and some to the social. But the project of co-operation and of mutuality has been to bring these together, or to relate them one to the other mutually. The project may be described as mutualising different types of belonging. When we are thinking towards a discipline called Co-operative Studies adequate for our times, we are thinking about a set of projects and practices that have been actively and unhelpfully divided from each other by forces external to CMEs. These 'modernising' forces produced separate meanings for the economic, the social, and the political that we have to employ as Co-operators working in the 'real' world. But we do not have to 'act out' those meanings, as if they are all that reality is. Thinking through what 'mutuality', 'membership', and 'belonging' mean when stretched to their fullest extent will help.

This is necessarily difficult, because it involves 'brushing against the grain', as Walter Benjamin called it, of systems — market capitalisms and State socialisms — in which types of belonging are systematically held apart. The difficulty may inhere in the concept of mutuality itself at a time when both modern capitalism and the modern State are so mature. This is the challenge of the concept of mutuality in Co-operative Studies. There is necessary awkwardness and a sense that Co-operatives and Mutuals do not fit. This derives from the fact that when we are thinking towards a discipline called Co-operative Studies, we are working with inherited, pre-capitalist, and, in that sense, residual categories, as well as with projected, post-capitalist, and in that sense emergent, categories. For example, CMEs cannot fit into dominant usages of the 'private' or the 'public'. Co-operation and mutuality preceded both and will succeed both. CMEs cannot fit into dominant categories of ownership, such as common ownership, national ownership, State ownership, private ownership, public ownership, individual ownership, and collective ownership. These categories have become so dominant that they hide other meanings or practices that none the less are still alive.

From the margins to 'Modern Social Theory'[36]

Such is the centrality of Co-operative Studies to an authentically 'social' science that it would not have been surprising if the papers for the conference 'Mapping Co-operative Studies' had been about aspects of society and social theory implicit, rather than explicit, within Co-operative and Mutual Enterprises. The question 'What are CMEs about, other than themselves?' has many answers. All of them release CMEs into mainstream Social Studies, rather than confining them to Co-operative Studies, if seen as tributary.

The answers cannot be followed through here in the way that they will be in a full programme of twenty-first century Co-operative Studies. Among the wider themes which the study of CMEs raises are these: the deconstruction of 'ownership', 'membership', and 'governance'; the deconstruction of the 'public' and the 'private';[37] democracy, management, and the division of labour in large-scale organisations; federal organisation; and complex co-operation with a small 'c', as contrasted with 'simple co-operation'.[38] Embracing all these themes, CMEs are about the possibility of extending to everyone in modern complex societies the central promises of liberalism, as opposed to allowing those promises to turn sour, enclosed by an élite.

Moving from a cosy, internal, 'alternative' stance on such issues to an engaged, outward-looking stance can be uncomfortable. Being engaged, or 'oppositional' in this sense means working in the wide open spaces of social knowledge. During the last decade of the twentieth century, CMEs, at the same time as they became known as such, moved out of a corner where they had rested for decades — in the UK since the 1970s — into the mainstream. 'Mainstreaming' became a phrase employed by modern Co-operators.[39]

From the outside looking in, it remains true that the indexes of social scientific and historical books and periodicals in which generic issues concerning co-operation and mutuality are central often omit an entry for either Co-operatives or Mutuals. This could be an interesting starting point for a research project in Co-operative Studies. From the inside looking out, however, neglect among CMEs of the central issues in social science and in social history that their practice raises became less common during the 1990s. This could also provide the basis for a research project. Between the late 1970s and the mid-1990s, it was unusual for social scientists, historians, or policy experts in Britain to focus on Co-operatives or Mutuals, except as dysfunctional antiques. At the end of the twentieth and the beginning of the twenty-first century there was a renewal of positive engagement from both sides.

Anthony Giddens's *Capitalism and Modern Social Theory: An Analysis of the Writings of Marx, Weber and Durkheim* quickly became a classic, achieving 24 reprints and selling 100,000 copies between 1971 and 2001. By the close of the 1990s, Giddens was also known as the leading thinker behind 'third way' politics across the developed world. A third way between market and State, private and public, individual and communal, and rights and responsibilities became attractive. CMEs had travelled this way for many years, starting out before the first and second ways had been set. Perhaps for this reason, 'new political' advocates of the third way from the late 1990s onwards, including Giddens, neglected their pioneer role. CMEs had been mixing market and State, private and public, individual and communal, and rights and responsibilities for two hundred years before 2000. This was part of what their early missionaries meant by their 'New View of Society' and 'New Moral World'.

Implicit in the practice of CMEs, but less explicit in their theory, were some of the central issues raised in the writings of Marx, Weber, and Durkheim. One way of helping students of Co-operative Studies to move confidently in from the margins will be to select issues from each of these classic founders of modern social theory and to put them on the emerging map of Co-operative Studies. Three questions to put will be: Are these issues still interesting and important from the point of view of the future of co-operation and mutuality? Is Co-operative Studies a good way of 'seeing' these issues? And, putting it the other way, are these issues a good way into Co-operative Studies?

Such questions cannot be answered adequately here. One issue central to each of these thinkers will, however, be selected as an example and entered on the map of Co-operative Studies. This is designed to encourage further work.[40] Further work will, of course, move beyond these early classics into twentieth-century functionalism, modern critical theory, post-modernism, and — perhaps above all — into the anthropology of non-Western societies.

Marx and class

For Karl Marx *class* was a central issue. He used the concept in ways that differed from the ways in which it had been used previously and from the ways in which it was to be used subsequently.

Marx used 'class' to refer to a set of oppositional possibilities that were carried by a group of people united by the fact that they were materially able to carry forward that set of possibilities. People who formed a class were in an economic (and social) position *vis à vis* production to construct new social (and economic) relations. Classes were not always conscious of themselves as such. They did not always act as such. Another class generally stood in their way. Classes existed in a full sense, for Marx, only in relation to other classes.[41] The 'possibilities' of which classes become the historical bearers are oppositional in the sense that they are in conflict with those carried by another class. Occasionally conflict turns into struggle.

The middle class, or bourgeoisie, was the most factual example of a class that Marx had to hand, although a working class was forming fast in England, where Marx did a great deal of his work. In the case of the working class or proletariat, it was not only that the jury was out during his lifetime: it has not yet returned to court with a final verdict. In modern, national economies, 'the working class' as 'proletariat' is no longer an obvious presence. Globally, is there an emergent, would-be social formation which has the objective capacity — no matter whether such capacity is realised or not — to 'sweep away the old conditions of production' and to construct 'an association in which the free development of each is the condition for the free development of all'? The trial continues. Fresh evidence is forthcoming every day from times and places of which Marx could know nothing.

What has this got to do with Mapping Co-operative Studies? CMEs provide an excellent testing ground for 'class'. They can be examined through its prism and, vice versa, the concept of 'class' can be examined through the practice and the project of CMEs.

From the early days in the history of the formation of the 'middle class', with their economic and political project, namely large-scale competitive capitalism, thousands of working people proposed another way of doing things. They sometimes saw themselves, and were more often seen by the middle class, as the working class or 'classes'. They proposed to make economic and political relations more social. They lived through the shift from moral economy to political economy and offered a sequel: social economy. They brought into being a cluster of associational forms, epitomised by CMEs, and they formed a social movement. The movement was social but — in so far as it was epitomised by CMEs — it was also economic. Such duality was its major characteristic.[42] Can such a double optic ever come into clear focus?

To try this out, CMEs used materials that were to hand *now,* within newly forming industrial capitalism, rather than waiting for *then*. This was noted above. CMEs acted against, but were also deeply within, the competitive system, scattering their seeds within many of the same freshly ploughed furrows. Anything new which is to amount to more than a dream can never be conceived immaculately. A new and different 'mode of production' (Marx's 'associated mode') was offered, capable of forming a new view of society and an actual new society. In some respects the new society was also to be old, carrying the markings of an inherited 'moral economy'.[43]

Was this to turn out to be possible? Marx watched early developments keenly, at first through the eyes of Engels, who was living in Manchester during the 1840s, the 'shock city' of the age, and the region for co-operation.[44] His subsequent work was always informed by the history and theory of its possibility. Neglected sections of *Capital*, Volume 3, deal with the possibility of the 'associated mode of production' succeeding capitalism. Throughout his work there are favourable references to co-operation as project and as practice, alongside political attacks on thinkers such as Lassalle and Proudhon.[45]

What happened between the mid-nineteenth and early twenty-first centuries? What will happen by the 2040s, when our children and their children produce the world cities of their age? Can *class* as concept help our understanding of what has already happened from the point of view of CMEs? Can it assist our continuing intent, as Co-operators, to change the world? Were CMEs epitomes of class formation? Can CMEs enlarge an understanding of class as concept and as practice? For Co-operative Studies the only certainty is that the case is not closed. The questions remain open and voluntary, in the sense of open to our mostly pessimistic intellects, and open to our mostly optimistic wills as Co-operators.

Weber and associational form

For Max Weber, the *Protestant Ethic* as it related to the *Spirit of Capitalism* was a central issue. It provided the title of his best-known book.[46] Associational forms which were characteristic of Protestantism — namely independent, autonomous, self-governing churches or sects — preoccupied him as one among many 'religious rejections of the world and their directions'.[47]

Weber's life work was to investigate how and why modernity broke through where and when it did. The spirit and organisation of capitalism, he thought, was fundamental to the modern world, and fundamental to capitalism were 'rationality' and 'bureaucracy'. He was interested in the historical sociology of why people obey or give power to other people, and how one phase of the history and sociology of those reasons gives way to another. Why people co-operate, in that limited sense, or act in deliberate accord with other people, is another way of expressing his main problematic. Protestant associational forms, which had parallels in other world religions, played a critical part in the generation and diffusion of modernity.

There were times and places, Weber thought, when people followed the practice of other people, or groups of people, as authorities, because they always had done so (traditional society). There were other times and other places when people followed leaders because of their personal qualities (charisma). To cut a long story short, the modern world took shape in parts of Western Europe and America, in the 'early modern' period. In real time, the patterns of traditional, charismatic, and rational authority overlapped, but it was important for Weber to distinguish analytically between them in order to map their history and geography.

The modern world became one in which people gave authority to other people because of the calculability of the regulatory systems (bureaucratic rationality) embodied in the emerging organisational or associational forms of that world. Rational calculation of the relations between means and ends could increasingly be made in modern societies. This, for Weber, defined rational, bureaucratic, capitalist society. If a person did a, b, or c in a political, legal, or religious setting – for example vote, go to trial, or join a church – x, y or z result could rationally be expected to follow: for example, an election result, due process, or salvation. The Calvinists' psychological situation was complicated. They knew their ultimate destiny was pre-ordained, but also that it was unknowable. So they 'acted out' as rationally as they could, urgently looking for signs of salvation. This resulted in dynamic, ordered, worldly work, mutually supported by fellow members of Protestant sects and churches.

The world in which more and more humans lived was thus transformed between c.1600 and c.1800. We have lived with the results ever since. Weber, like Marx and Durkheim, was more struck than we tend to be today by the oddity of the modern world. For them, that emergent world could not be explicable simply in terms of human individuals or God's or History's purpose. It was, above all else, historical and therefore patient of change. 'Whereas utilitarian philosophy places man outside of history, seeking to interpret human social action in terms of a-temporal concepts of utility and the pursuit of self-interest', these thinkers were social and historical.[48] An historical 'confrontation' was taking place before their very eyes 'between the dissolving "traditional" society and the emergent "modern" type'.[49] Explaining the discontinuities through which the modern world was still coming into being, and being accepted by people, needed, they argued, explanation. This was their vocation. It enabled some limited projection of future possibilities.

Could the modern world be made better, by its own lights? That is to say, could the possibilities which the modern world had disclosed for the first time in human history be realised? Could a succeeding class (the working class) universalise and thereby transform the promise of the middle class (see Marx above)? Or would barbarism succeed? Could a whole society of 'organic solidarity' for all (see Durkheim below) be realised following the disclosure of its possibility (Durkheim's definition of the transition to modernity)? If so, existing, unequal aggregations of power would turn into a fully realised, individuated, but also socialised community. Or would egoism, insatiable demand, and *anomie* on the one hand, or mechanical, purely economic socialism on the other hand, succeed? In Weber's case, would bureaucratic rationality and capitalist organisation develop in such a way as to trap humanity in an 'iron cage', or could such a trap be sprung by similar types of associational forms which had enabled modernity to break through in the first place?[50]

Among the associational forms which contributed to the breakthrough in early modern Europe, religious organisations were, for Weber, pre-eminent, hence *The Protestant Ethic and the Spirit of Capitalism*. This text may be seen as the deposition for the analytical, comparative, and historical trial which Weber conducted throughout his work.

In summary, Weber's findings with respect to associational forms were the following: that associational forms of all kinds are powerful agencies of creativity and social change; that sects and sect-like religious organisations are extraordinary associational forms; that they are capable of generating and sustaining unusual quantities of shared, dynamic, world-transforming behaviour among their members; that they deal with the theodicy problem, or people's consciousness of the unequal distribution of life chances; that they are also capable of generating less active religious rejections of the world, resulting in complete withdrawal; that the directions which their members take depend on many variables in cultures and societies (ancient Judaism, China, India, Europe, and America), including the power or lack of power of officials, priests, and other professional and managerial classes inside and outside religious organisations; that it was in early modern Protestant Europe, and then in America, that an 'ethic' was shared among members of Protestant churches which enabled Calvinistic theologies to precipitate this-worldly, world-changing capitalistic behaviour; that embryos of such a (Protestant) ethic and such a (capitalist) spirit had existed in other cultures, including Catholic cultures, and in other epochs of human history; but that it was the particular 'elective affinity' — established by Weber in his best-known book (borrowing the concept from Goethe) — that diffused modern capitalist behavioural patterns until they became the norms of the modern world.

What has this got to do with Mapping Co-operative Studies?
CMEs provide a possible testing ground for the idea that particular species of associational forms provide a key variable in generating and sustaining epochal change. Could CMEs be the basis for another 'revolution of the saints', or will fundamentalisms succeed first, with their ambition to freeze time? Ideal-type mutuals have much in common with sect-like forms, as direct, face-to-face, membership organisations whose members own and govern their associations, elect officials, and actively problematise divisions of labour inside their Societies and in society, rather than passively reproducing them. As CMEs grow larger and more complex, their patterns of development may be compared with those of sects which often turn into large-scale, complex denominations and

churches.⁵¹ CMEs might usefully be examined through this prism, and the prism might usefully be examined through the practice and project of CMEs. CMEs represent a cluster of associational forms, forming a social movement. Could there be an elective affinity between CMEs and a whole 'new view of society', as different from competitive capitalism as capitalism was from its predecessors? Early Co-operators thought so. Could forces and relations analogous to those that led to 'the rise of capitalism' produce that system's successor, as R. H. Tawney hoped? The questions remain exciting enough to put. For Co-operative Studies the only certainty, again, is that the case is not closed. History has not ended. The questions remain open and voluntary in the sense of open to our intellects and open to our wills, as Co-operators.

Durkheim from mechanical to organic solidarity
For Emile Durkheim, *organic solidarity* was 'the essential basis of the modern social order'.⁵² But how does it develop? How can individuals develop in humanly differentiated ways at the same time that society develops as a coherent (solid) whole? *Individualisation* plus *socialisation* was Durkheim's answer. Are there variants of individualism which are capable of growing in the arms of variants of socialism, and vice-versa? 'The key to Durkheim's whole life's work is to be found in his attempt to resolve the *apparent* [my emphasis] paradox that the liberty of the individual is only achieved through his dependence on society.'⁵³

This problematic may explain why Durkheim had such resonance in the 'new politics' of the late 1990s and early 2000s, particularly through Giddens's reading of his work. The late 1990s was a period when politics was about individual plus community, market plus State, rather than one or the other. The new politics shared with Durkheim an attempt to find a way between old polarities. That 'the collective interest is only a form of personal interest', or that 'altruism is merely a concealed egoism', became inadequate alternatives to policy makers, as they did to social thinkers (and to evolutionary biologists: see below).[54]

Durkheim had a sense as powerful as that of Marx that he was living in transitional times. In Durkheim's case, the journey was between traditional and modern society. Traditional societies were characterised by *mechanical* solidarity, modern societies by *organic* solidarity. This was not a *fait accompli*. The potential of organic solidarity had been disclosed in modern history. But its full realisation remained as an objective for Durkheim, as against other possibilities, and as against obstacles which stood in its way. 'It is fundamentally important to recognize ... that organic solidarity, at the present juncture, is emergent rather than fully actualized.'[55] Among the obstacles to its fuller emergence, he thought, was inequality. Durkheim thought that the legislative abolition of inherited wealth would help. But civil society had a role to play, as influential as that of the State. In modern society 'our ideal is *constantly* [my emphasis] to introduce greater equality in our social relations, in order to ensure the free unfolding of the socially useful forces'. Durkheim was particularly interested in guilds, or associations by trade and profession. (Such constancy, towards greater equality of social relations, is, of course, the agenda of CMEs.) In any event, equality — or the equal chance for all individuals to become such, rather than to remain where social accident had put them — was best achieved not by revolution, but by continuous association.

So what is organic solidarity? And what could its actualisation have to do with Co-operative Studies? Organic solidarity describes the 'ties of co-operation between individuals or groups of individuals' in a single economic system in which communities have become interdependent rather than isolated. The functioning of such a system (society or organism) depends upon what students of CMEs call 'mutuality', but which Giddens, expounding Durkheim, calls 'the reciprocal relationships which the various specialized organs of the body have with each other'. These relationships multiply as modern society develops, in what can be seen as an objective growth in co-operation and mutuality waiting to become subjective by means of CMEs.

Such relationships are not spontaneous, or not entirely so. They are humanly chosen, and in that sense open and voluntary. The Durkheimian project is to make them more so. As the modern replaces the traditional, and the organic the mechanical, 'the state is for individuals no longer like an external power that imparts a wholly mechanical impetus to them'.[56] But the relationships which characterise organic solidarity also amount to more than the sum of individual choices. They are social. They are obligations as well as choices, socially determined as well as the consequence of individual determination.

The 'social' takes on a life of its own in appearance and in reality. This becomes the subject matter of sociology. More or less conscious, more or less socialised relationships are produced by means of human association in active interplay with the state. Associations, including the State, also take on a life of their own. They appear inaccessible to rational choice and self-conscious determination. In traditional societies they actually are inaccessible – hence traditional religion, which projects human agency on to external divinities or gods outside the machine. Individuated humans living in modern organically solid societies, who have internalised their own divinity, will no longer need to project beyond society. Their 'religion' will be in society and, ultimately, in their selves.[57]

External forces need bringing back to their human homes. This will result in society becoming conscious of itself, or socialised in human, individuals' consciousness. It is a task which requires not only a transformed society in general but the agency of human associations or Societies. Conditions for such associational solidarity may be favourable or unfavourable at different times and in different places. Social development, with sociology as its map-maker, will allow humans to 'become rationally aware of the principles which govern the social world', hence the possibility of modern democracy.[58]

Durkheim was particularly interested in the role of *occupational associations* or guilds in France.[59] Channels of communication needed to be cut between the various component parts of modern society. Individual freedoms depended on agencies in civil society which could counterbalance the state. Durkheim was also interested in regulation. This was one of the functions of the state. In Durkheim's view, however, regulation was of two kinds: economic and moral. It is the moral which is of particular interest to CMEs. Durkheim agreed with the socialists of his day that economic co-ordination of market functions was necessary to avoid disconnection between production and consumption and other forms of crisis endemic in modern economies. While the division of labour was incompletely developed, and while individuals had not found productive work that matched their capacities, there would be friction. These would be within the workplace, between capital and labour. They would also be between producers and consumers. Again, this is of particular interest to CMEs, whose agenda is to connect producers and consumers.

Durkheim did not think that economic regulation by the State would be sufficient: hence his critique of socialism in its dominant economic and statist forms. Dominant forms of socialism were, he thought, too one-sidedly mechanical. Moral regulation was crucial. In the era of organic solidarity, this could no longer be left to the 'elementary forms of the religious life' and to a collectivised conscience. Concrete forms of the moral ideal needed to be developed through which systemic frictions would recede: 'A morality of co-operation was developing'.[60] In modern society its forms were different from those in traditional society, less collective but more deliberately social. For instance, the repressive law of traditional society had given way to restitutive law.

Students of Co-operative Studies could pursue the idea that there is an element of mutuality within the entire history of modern law, just as there is in the emergence of contracts, insurance, and other modern practices. If 'mutuality' were to stand in for a host of other words more often used in these settings, such as reciprocity, trust, or restitution, it would have the result that co-operation and mutuality, and their articulation in CMEs, could be repositioned in the history of ideas as forward looking. CMEs are too easily represented, by activists as much as by academics, as backward-looking traditional forms. Some of their adherents are deeply conservative. In Ferdinand Tonnies' terminology, co-operation and mutuality tend to get buried with *Gemeinschaft*, rather than being seen as integral to the further development of *Gesellschaft*. 'Early' societies have a great deal to teach modern Co-operators, particularly about how to practise democracy, but co-operation and mutuality need not be seen as archaic.

The *division of labour* — or who did what, and what people felt about it — was very different in traditional society from what it became in modern society. This was a major preoccupation of Durkheim. The differences between traditional and modern divisions of labour get to the heart of those between mechanical and organic solidarity. The division of labour is also at the heart of what concerns CMEs. Our problematic in advocating Co-operation is, as John Ruskin put it, to transform the division of labour from division between humans, which it is in competitive society, into the division of work among humans, which it becomes in co-operative society.[61]

In traditional society, solidarity was 'mechanical', in the sense that there was no choice about it. Individuals conformed or they were repressed. They were not expressed, as individuals. In traditional society, the ideal 'was to create or maintain as intense a shared life as possible, in which the individual was absorbed' — in other words, *Gemeinschaft* co-operation.[62] Moral consensus, or a *conscience collective* (*commune*), subsumed individual consciousness, which was simply a microcosm of the collective. There was only restricted opportunity for individual members of society to develop specific and particular personality characteristics, occupations that matched their natural capacities, or beliefs which articulated their needs as 'one-off' people.[63] 'Labour is divided spontaneously only if society is constituted in such a way that social inequalities exactly express natural inequalities.'[64] Spontaneity, in this sense, takes a great deal of organising. CMEs are well adapted for such a task, not all at once, but 'constantly'.

This is a tall order, radical at any time. It is impossible when the division of labour is rudimentary, as in traditional societies when it is less specialised. Each local group in traditional society — family or clan — was a functionally equivalent and independent productive unit. There was no interdependence across a single, social, national, or global economic system. In such a situation, conflict between groups over scarce resources was more likely than intensive or extensive co-operation. Co-operation can only multiply and extend as the mutual dependence between more and more individuals extends, or as the actual connections between more and more individuals become more extensive as well as more intensive. The organic metaphor is important here. In a modern society or complex organism, the removal of one organ will affect a large whole. In a simpler setting, the whole that is affected will include a very much smaller number of individuals. In traditional society, one family or clan, and most individuals, can substitute themselves for one another without much widespread, dysfunctional effect.

If organic solidarity is a long revolution rather than a finished fact for Durkheim, what prevents it or stands in its way? What can be done, here and now, to remove obstacles? And what are the connections here with an emerging map of Co-operative Studies? Three further connections may be suggested.

First, CMEs are unusual membership organisations. They encourage belonging in more than superficial ways. In CMEs, belonging is based on ownership or possession — antidotes to alienation. Belonging in CMEs is based on material attachment plus (learned and taught) psychological or spiritual attachment — antidotes to Durkheimian *anomie*. This sense of belonging is a conscious value in CMEs, to be deliberately cultivated rather than passed on as tradition. Shared knowledge of how the whole works is to be achieved by means of knowledge about how its separate parts function, federated as they are in a Movement. Complete rather than partial (political) citizenship is the result.

Second, contrary to conventional wisdom about the 'voluntary' and the 'civil' in capitalist societies — and even more contrary to the conventional wisdom concerning ownership — the people to whom early CMEs belonged, in very large numbers, were working people rather than middle-class people.⁶⁵ CMEs brought into being a working-class 'public' and the public spaces (buildings, etc.) that went with it. They achieved this almost at the same time as, and as a challenge to, the dominant definitions of the 'public' and 'public places' that middle-class modernisers were bringing into being during the late eighteenth and early nineteenth centuries.⁶⁶

The challenge of CMEs lies precisely in the fact that they picked up tools predominantly being used to construct large-scale, complex, industrial capitalism and used them to create a more inclusive, more solid set of Societies (or 'Co-operative Commonwealth') just as large and complex. The tools used by CMEs were modern, but they also came from an older, pre-political, or 'moral', economy. It goes without saying that the project remains uncompleted. Whether it can be completed is an open question. It was aligned with Marx and Weber, as well as with Durkheim, in the specific sense that existing movements and tendencies were being employed by CMEs rather than millennial, revolutionary fantasies.

This explains why CMEs have never had an easy ride, and why enabling legislation concerning them (in the UK, Industrial and Provident Society Acts) is always, at the same time, disabling. CMEs work at one and the same time as part of the modernising, productive forces of society, and as agencies for transforming those forces. 'In every society there are collective currents of change. Modifications of belief and attitude, which take place at the level of infrastructure: in the "lower layers" of society.' A society can be called 'democratic', according to Durkheim's usage, to the degree to which a reciprocal relation is established between these 'unconsciously evolved movements and the more articulate and deliberate activities of the state'.⁶⁷

Third, CMEs represent actually existing, not utopian (or 'communist' in Durkheim's use of that term), 'concrete forms of moral ideal'. If society is, as Durkheim thought, 'a unity which displays characteristics that cannot be reduced to those of its component individuals', and if 'this unity is primarily moral', CMEs may be seen as being formed from — and may act as carriers of — moral ideals which have evolved with the development of society. When consensual values are no longer expressed in terms of traditional religious symbolism, they get projected on to bloated states and their leaders. Such values need more accessible matrices to enable a *conscience collective*. The task is to regulate rather than to prevent modern divisions of labour, articulating demand with need rather than with egotistic individualism.[68] The inheritance of family wealth, for Durkheim, represented a survival into the modern age of traditional forms of collective property. Property needs to be articulated in individual but also in social terms. CMEs represent forms of shareholding as membership, rather than as transferable commodities.

Do CMEs offer a way in which modern societies can move through the traditional, the mechanical, and the collective, in Durkheim's meanings of those terms? Seen the other way, would the 'traditional', the 'mechanical', and the 'collective', as sociological terms, be well tested in the context of Co-operative Studies? Do CMEs offer ways to remove the obstacles that accumulate within modern societies: 'third ways' not solely dependent on the market or the state? Inequalities of wealth, power, and status congeal in modern societies in ways conceived as class-related (Marx), organisational (Weber), and mechanical (Durkheim). Are CMEs well adapted for addressing these inequalities, here and now?

Even though CMEs are largely unconsidered as such in Durkheim's work and in that of Giddens (they are largely absent from the indexes of their books), do they address both Durkheim's and Giddens's problematics? The questions are important enough to be posed. For Co-operative Studies the only certainty, once again, is that the case is not closed. History has not ended. The questions remain open and voluntary in the sense of open to our intellects and open to our wills as Co-operators.

To the centre of 'natural' history, or evolutionary studies

When we are thinking towards a discipline called Co-operative Studies, we are thinking about issues which have moved to the centre of natural history. Darwinian studies — earth science as well as evolutionary biology — became a popular field during the last quarter of the twentieth century. Major theorists and practitioners wrote for general readers, as Darwin and T. H. Huxley had done.[69] In doing so, they raised issues that have implications for society as well as for science. These resonated with issues raised not only in social theory such as Durkheim's, but also in the project and the practice of CMEs. This made it easier for Co-operators to make connections between how change takes place at the most minute and the most general levels. One contributor to 'the new mutualism' suggested that humans have been 'hard-wired' for co-operation, in the genetic make-up which is the result of their deep historical past.[70]

It also made it possible for people outside CMEs, business people as well as social scientists, to make connections between their own work and co-operation and mutuality. It made cross-referencing easier between the maps of social studies and of biological and geological studies. Natural scientists and social scientists were thinking about comparable general models of change such as Niles Eldredge and Stephen Jay

Gould's 1977 'punctuated equilibria' model. This suggests that while stasis is normal, and a lively rather than an inert achievement among living beings, it is punctuated by episodes of discontinuity which are sometimes catastrophic. During these periods, whole environments, entire ecologies, are transformed. Impermanence has an effect on the moral and political imagination, as well as on scientific accounts of how things happened.[71]

'How history happens', for Co-operative historians living in the same intellectual culture as scientists, could now include universes as well as locales, 'kingdoms' far removed from the animal kingdom, unimaginable levels of deep time as well as modern times, and unimaginable quantities of tiny units: for example, bacteria. As social science criss-crossed evolutionary science, *how different things had been* fuelled thinking about *how different they would be.* Then, contingency challenged inevitability. How different things might have been fed into how different they could be: the precise shapes of the future depending on collective, associated activity, on who and what got together, where and when. The debates that took place within radical social history during the 1970s began to take place within Darwinian studies instead. Debates between schools of historians, concerning structure versus agency in human affairs, and between determination as the setting of limits to how people make their own history and determination as one-way causation between base and superstructure, began to take place between evolutionary biologists.[72] This shift of terrain from social history to evolutionary history meant, perhaps surprisingly, that more rather than fewer openings were made in the direction of Co-operative Studies. Co-operation and mutuality in 'nature', supposedly red in tooth and claw, began to be discussed once again, to stimulate their discussion in society, and in 'culture' (a term used in both fields of study).

It is of some historical interest that Co-operators have always reinforced their social commitment by reference to natural science and to long periods of time. 'Jubilee Histories' of local Co-operative Societies in Britain that were published from the late nineteenth century onwards were often set in surprisingly wide stretches of nature and deep stretches of time, as were the opening addresses of Co-operative (and Trade Union) Congresses. They appealed to Co-operators' imaginations as well as to facts.[73] Owenites thought of new worlds even while they turned a single estate into a community. One estate belonging to a maverick landlord prefigured millennial change everywhere: New Harmony. Early Co-operators thought in universals. They thought of the human family as one: the 'Universal Family of All Peoples and All Nations'. They also thought in details concerning how ventilation was best achieved, how work was best supervised and paid for, and what educational systems best engaged humans to learn.[74]

Nineteenth-century Co-operators were equally interested in scientific and social findings. Working-class thinkers had not yet been schooled by twentieth-century professionals into separating the two.[75] Evolution, a word that Charles Darwin did not coin, was important to Co-operators because it seemed to promise progress from 'lower' to 'higher' forms, including forms of association: if evolution could be discovered to take place through co-operation or mutual aid rather than by means of competition, so much the better. This was reinforced by two important scientific experts: Alfred Russel Wallace and Peter Kropotkin. Wallace, who accidentally forced Darwin to rush the publication of *On the Origin of the Species* (1859) by almost pipping him to the post on natural selection, had strong radical connections to Owenite socialism. Prince Kropotkin was an anarchist living in exile in Brighton who wished to reconstruct the Russian state even more thoroughly than the early Bolsheviks. His *Mutual Aid: A Factor of Evolution* (1902) was both influential and widely circulated. Interestingly, *Mutual Aid* was employed by Matt Ridley, not a socialist, as the prologue to his *The Origins of Virtue* (1996). Ridley is a zoologist and economist, and a social interpreter of scientific and mathematical thinking.[76]

In *The Origins of Virtue,* Ridley uses game theory to show that co-operation works better than other strategies to maximise humans' advantage: 'The more we co-operate, within strategies of reciprocal altruism that punish selfishness and suckers, the more society prospers.' David Rogers, a scientist as well as a Co-operator, built on Ridley in his pamphlet *New Mutualism: The Third Estate:*

> [Ridley] explains that the most effective game theory strategy to be devised is one called "Firm but fair," a programme written by Marcus Frean of Cambridge University. "Firm but fair" co-operates with co-operators, is forgiving by returning to co-operation after defection by an opponent (rather than indulging in repeated recrimination), destroys free riders (the hedonists who look only to their own self-interest at the expense of others), and punishes suckers who do not retaliate when a defection from co-operation occurs. Given that human relationships mostly involve frequent and repeated interaction, co-operative strategies lead to the greatest benefits for *all* [my emphasis] ... The more we co-operate, within strategies of reciprocal altruism that punish selfishness and suckers, the more society prospers. We are also very good at spotting potential co-operators and potential hedonists through communication with others. This is our genetic heritage, underpinned by our strong emotions that tend to lead us to co-operate and go to the aid of others even when

the reward is not immediate, or where there may be a real risk to us. For Ridley, emotion encourages altruism and underpins it. Just as the computers evolved games that "understand" the benefits of co-operation so too did the human species through its evolution.[77]

Our history, including very deep stretches of time, is thus released into our consciousness as capital, working for sociality rather than for mutual destruction.

During the second half of the nineteenth century and much of the twentieth century, Darwin's work in *The Origin* was appropriated as a resource for theories of competition and individualism. It was explicitly used to oppose co-operation and collectivity. Competition as fact and as metaphor ran deep in Darwin's own thought and language.[78] Malthus's unsentimental model of population struggle to the death in situations of finite resource helped Darwin to arrive at the idea of natural selection in the first place. But Darwin cannot be held responsible for the ways in which individualist, competitive capitalism subsequently fed from his work after the 1850s. The cruel *laissez-faire* excesses of socio-biology and the cruel interfering excesses of eugenics were not Darwin's. 'Nature red in tooth and claw' and 'the survival of the fittest' were not his phrases. The selfish human individual of utilitarian political economy — still less the gene which Darwin did not know about — was not for him a model for all biological individuals.

During the final quarter of the twentieth century, co-operation, mutuality, and their relatives using other names such as 'trust' began to come back into Darwinian studies. Altruism (sometimes selfish), symbiosis, mutual dependence, and integration came through where emphasis had previously been on disintegration into the smallest possible atomistic and independent units. As in Durkheim's critique of utilitarian individualism, notions that 'the collective interest is *only* [my emphasis] a form of personal interest' and that 'altruism is *merely* [my emphasis] a concealed egoism' began to give way to subtler interplays with less insistence on either/or and more allowance for not only/but also. From the social scientific side, hybridisations such as 'co-opetition' were made to match the fact that issues close to the project and the practice of CMEs began to surface again in the life sciences. Other new words will be coined by natural scientists as much as by social scientists, on a rapidly forming 'island of meaning' called 'trust'. 'Selfish means doing things for me; altruistic means doing things for you; groupish means doing things for us.'[79]

Gaia theory provides one example of the late-twentieth-century scientific imagination extending towards mutuality. Gaia is 'the hypothesis, the model, in which the earth's living matter, air, oceans and land surface form a complex system which can be seen as a single organism and which has the capacity to keep our planet a fit place for life'.[80] This theory, with its sense of wholeness, mutual interdependence, and co-responsibility across a planetary 'community' of related phenomena, stimulated Brett Fairbairn, a leading specialist in the history of Co-operation, to reinterpret one of the largest movements in Co-operative History, the late-nineteenth- and early-twentieth-century German Co-operative Movement.[81]

James Lovelock, who conceived Gaia theory and then developed it with microbiologist Lynn Margulis, works with a holistic, ecological systems perspective. The planet is seen as a 'total ... being'. 'Living creatures acting together in evolved patterns of co-operation respond to changes and regulate the planetary environment in ways that ensure their own collective survival.' Social movements such as the Co-operative Movement may then be 'read' in analogous ways. Brett Fairbairn 'implies that just as Gaia is a response to a competitive-individualist bias among evolutionary scientists, a systems perspective could correct for a competitive-individualist bias among historians'.[82]

Tempting as it is, 'science' with all its modern prestige should not be summoned to prove anything in co-operative studies or any other social or cultural studies. To avoid easy transfer from one field to another, however, is not to inhibit putting different discourses on the same map of human knowledge to their mutual advantage. Conclusions in different fields are arrived at within the same changing cultures.

8. Towards co-operative politics: using early to generate late socialism

This chapter uses the distinction between politics and anti-politics deployed by Gregory Claeys in *Citizens and Saints* (1989) to define what pre-1850 Owenites and Co-operators meant by 'socialism'. Building on their anti-politics, or 'associationism', the chapter identifies an inheritance of specifically co-operative politics which may be useable by co-operators in our time. 'Early' socialists (a better label for Owenites and Co-operators than 'utopian') started from the 'economic' world of thought and action; showed the determination and capacity to *produce* society rather than be determined by it; were committed to education, but in a sense of the word long buried by schools and colleges; and refused to separate moral reformation from social reform in ways not unrelated to many modern 'extremists'. If we are to develop an adequate 'late' (too late?) socialism, by means of modern co-operative and mutual enterprise, it may be worth revisiting Owenism with the help of historians like Claeys who work within the Cambridge school of intellectual history rather than the Communist school of labour history.

A large literature about 'socialist politics' has grown up around the assumption that nothing very worthwhile or historically meaningful was written on the subject before Marx and Engels began their own explorations.[1]

Introduction

It was as part of the story of co-operation and mutuality during the early nineteenth century that the word *socialism* came into English in 1827.[2] For the next twenty years in Britain, the word indicated one of many strands of Owenite belief and practice and/or co-operation among working people. Socialism during the early nineteenth century had a very distinctive meaning, much of which had been lost by the early twenty-first century. Retrieval might be to the advantage of modern co-operators, remembering that the antagonist of socialism for early co-operators was *individualism*.[3] In our times too, individualism is a more widely acknowledged enemy than capitalism.[4] Individuals, with what we would call our own individuality, were not a problem for Owenites: indeed, the early socialist project was to give back to each and every individual (a word which originally meant 'undividable from') the full range of human capacities which systematic, individual*ist* competition was taking from them.[5] It may be important to remember that, while there were *capitalists* around during the first half of the nineteenth century – not enough of them, in fact, for co-operative socialists, who wanted to turn every labourer into a capitalist – *capitalism* was not labelled as such until the 1850s.

This chapter will search for early nineteenth-century material for reviving a specifically *co-operative* politics – a co-operative socialism – which could still come into its own, proud of differing in critical ways from other kinds of politics and other socialisms. These other kinds of politics – all erstwhile rivals of co-operative politics on the Left – include, in rough chronological order: revolutionary; social democratic; labour; pressure-group and single-interest politics. It is from all of these that effective, new/old co-operative politics needs to be distinguished. If we could use *early socialism* to identify the unique offer which could again be made by *co-operative* politics, it might help towards making a socialist politics adequate for our times. Nothing is more urgent. Names may not matter. Jean Dubuffet's insight about art may also be true about socialism: 'it loves to be incognito. Its best moments are when it forgets what it is called.'[6]

To anticipate: co-operative politics would prefigure what its advocates want, rather than demanding it from others; its advocates would make things in associations rather than policies in Parties; they would be posited in particular kinds of membership/belonging, and they would be powerfully post-capitalist because of being rooted in pre-capitalism.[7] To modern Politicians, including Labour Party people, distinctively co-operative politics/co-operative socialism would probably be dismissed as un- or anti-politics. Such a caricature needs to be resisted as much by co-operators as by historians of co-operation. It is the fully political outlook which lay behind co-operators' critique of 'capital-P' Politics that we need to retrieve, for the sake of accurate history as well as good, future-bearing politics. Our times, after all, are as crisis-ridden as Owenites and early co-operators felt theirs to be, and our Politicians are as partial as theirs.

A tribute

Thanks to the work of Gregory Claeys, to whom this essay is something of a tribute, we can now appreciate Owenite practices and ideas *politically* in a less condescending way than used to be common on the Left. The fact that Claeys worked within the Cambridge school of intellectual history, rather than the Communist and post-Communist school of Labour history, makes it easier to work politically *with* Owen and the Owenites instead of *after* them. We can recover their meanings, using them to challenge our own, rather than allowing them to be overlaid by those of their would-be mature successors.

Claeys is conceptually as well as empirically alert. He uncovers a large-scale, innovative, working-class, non-violent, transformational and 'moral' socialism which is richer than that which post-1848 'revolutionary' socialists liked to relegate as 'reformist'. The revolutionary/reformist fault-line which ran across the Left from the mid-nineteenth century onwards was always shallower than it seemed. The test of fully politicised class consciousness does not have to be revolutions of the 1789 or 1917 types or, in the UK, electoral victories for Labour such as those of 1945 or 1997. Instead, 'mature' class consciousness, born of conflict as well as struggle, can eventuate in continuous associations or societies – 'unions' of many kinds, including co-operatives and mutuals – of which William Lovett's autobiography is such a singular record.[8] Power may have to be dispersed by means of active co-operation and mutuality a long time before it can be 'won' or 'seized' with any degree of positive or permanent effect for working people. Being 'in' or 'out of' power is not the same as altering the nature of power with any degree of advantage for the majority.

In *Citizens and Saints* Claeys also argues against the well-known Labour History antonym 'utopian/scientific'. He prefers 'early' socialism to 'utopian', at a time when an adequate 'late' socialism is urgently needed. It may already be too late to avoid anything other than a period of barbarism later in the twenty-first century. My contention, however, is that something like the self-sustainability of early socialism might contribute towards preventing this. The modern politics of sustainability, for example, beginning with Transition

Town Totnes in October 2005 and now spread to more than one hundred localities, is, without knowing it, quite close in a number of respects to early socialism in Britain.[9]

Claeys organises his work around an analytical distinction between 'citizens' and 'saints': roughly speaking, between politics and anti-politics, allowing for tectonic shifts in the meaning of politics. This distinction, which it may be helpful to draw out into contrasting ideal-types, is so productive that it could enable him and others to move through the *narrative* of socialism in Britain from 1827 to the present day, in the thorough way that Sidney and Beatrice Webb moved through the narrative of trade unionism towards their *History of Trade Unionism* (1894).[10] The Webbs were then able to publish their analytical masterpiece, *Industrial Democracy* (1897).[11] These two books 'still stand as the greatest achievements in the fields of study they inaugurated'.[12] When his narrative is done (it is already much more than a narrative), I have great but unfairly projected expectations of a 'Socialist Democracy' book from Claeys, building on the work of Cambridge-school intellectual historians of democracy and political theory such as John Dunn.[13] This could be as useful as *Industrial Democracy*, playing with the categories 'political' and 'anti-political' as the Webbs played with the categories 'primitive' and 'expert'. After all, Claeys continues to publish on an almost Webbian scale.[14]

Association, politics, and anti-politics

Working mostly with *Citizens and Saints*, I will characterise 'early' or 'associationist' socialism in Britain in my own terms, using Claeys' work to develop my own on 'the three socialisms'.[15] His research extends what I continue to call *associationism*, helping to differentiate it from the other two socialisms that I proposed: *statism* and *collectivism*. Statism equates a magnified central or local State with socialism. Collectivism, as developed particularly by the Webbs (once more with individualism as its antagonist) celebrates the rise of the professional and managerial class *as* socialism. It favours states and other 'collectives' run by experts which bear no necessary resemblance to co-operatives or to mutuals. I still want to stimulate interest among historians and co-operators who retain hopes of a distinctive co-operative politics, and who still want to work as socialists, with or without the name, in the twenty-first century.

My argument is that co-operative politics, if they are to be adequate for modern times, which are surely as epochal as Owen's, will be associational in type. They will need to challenge ordinary Politics, even Labour Politics, more than the Co-operative Party and Co-operative Politicians currently dare to do. And they will have many characteristics to carry forward from Owenite/early socialist models in the UK and the USA.[16] Above all else they will be rooted in their own activities in their own associations: Societies, co-operative and mutual enterprises, rather than projected on to Parties, Politicians, Policies, and the practices which now confidently define what it is to be Political. As the Emperor Trajan feared in his correspondence with Pliny, who had dared to recommend citizens' fire-brigades to him, and as the rulers of modern China also recognise, it is *association* itself, regardless of ideology, that threatens to replace statism as much as it challenges collectivism.[17]

Ideal-type politics

It may be helpful to get categories clear first. Politics as ideal-type may be said to sit at one end of a spectrum on which, at the other, sit 'anti-politics'. In modern times Politics in this sense has become a 'vocation' for what has recently become known as 'the political class'. As such, Politics becomes specialised and professional and, since the second half of the nineteenth century, generally the perquisite of Party 'machines'. 'Modern Politics' describes a specific body of thought and activity clearly separable from 'economics', 'industrial relations', 'voluntary work', 'religion', and so on, all of which grew into their distinct, modern forms as part of the same, industrial-revolution division of labour, or – to use a term from functionalist sociology – 'structural differentiation'. The history is fascinating, important, and relatively recent. Nineteenth-century liberals were often highly suspicious of Party Politics, from a democratic point of view. Since then, the 'political game' has become so much a part of the everyday furniture of our times – limiting the idea of 'democracy' itself – that further definitions need not detain us.[18] 'Politics' is well described as what 'don't knows' have in mind when they close the door on a pollster or a canvasser with a 'not today thank you, we're not political here'. Ideal-type politics are also well captured by what Political people and Parties are accused of doing in 'non-political' settings, namely 'playing politics'. Boundaries have become so well established that when socialists of any kind challenge them, they are greeted either with incomprehension or with accusations of authoritarianism.[19] John Dunn has suggested that socialism is particularly hard to assimilate because it is such a uniquely political philosophy that boundaries get blurred. Politicians panic: if everything is politics, where is Politics? When Politics in ideal-typical form enters Co-operative Societies, particularly as Party Politics, it has been recognised as a cuckoo in the nest. The 'No Politics, No Religion' rule in co-operative societies was devised, however, not against Government or God as such, and not against individual, strongly based beliefs and affiliations beyond co-operatives. It was devised to counter the cacophony which breaks out when individualist, unfit-for-purpose Politics is imported into multi-part choirs of association, or disturbs – a cherished early socialist word – harmony.

Anti-politics as ideal-type

At the opposite end of the spectrum sits ideal-type anti-politics. Less easy to identify in its pure form than ideal-type politics, it rejects anything which calls itself, or which may usefully be called, 'politics'. For whatever reason, extreme anti-politics prefers to exist alone or in a group, without intended political effect or participation: on top of a pillar in the desert, in a withdrawn church or sect ... or in any posture which casts out the things that are Caesar's. The salvation which anti-politics intends, if any, is moral, whether in this world or the next. Today, adversaries of anti-politics sometimes picture them in hiding, in a cave on the borders of one country or another, perhaps setting out towards 'Western democracy' with a bomb on their back. 'Refuseniks' was an older way of talking about them from a Total-Political, statist point of view. Anti-politics is often moralised into 'apathy', a term much favoured by Political folk who forget that 'anti-politics is as much a theory of politics as any other'.[20] Claeys' use of 'saints' as his label for the anti-politics end of the spectrum, to contrast with 'citizens' at the other end, is apt. The roots of anti-politics run deep into religion, although religious soil has, of course, also nourished deeply political plants. In the Judaeo-Christian tradition, it is the things of God that are commonly contrasted with those of Caesar. Christ's avowal that 'my kingdom is not of this world' was theorised for Catholic Christians in deep and lasting ways by St Augustine during the late fourth century, working in North Africa:

> Let us pine for the City where we are citizens ... By pining we are already there ... I sing of somewhere else, not of here ... The citizens of Babylon hear the sound of the flesh, the Founder of Jerusalem hears the tune of our hearts.[21]

Many modern Muslims might agree, sometimes with devastating personal and political consequences. Otherworldliness may also be found, more surprisingly perhaps, in the history of socialism, with socialist organisations sometimes playing a similar role to 'the church' of St Paul or St Augustine: waiting for something to happen, of which they cannot be the main agents.[22] A contemporary explanation 'for why the Socialists did not take part officially in the 1837 elections was that "their kingdom is emphatically not of this world"'.[23] One of Robert Owen's many impulses was to transcend politics entirely, although, in spite of the words that Owenites used, one must always be careful not to remove *this* world and the *social* from their ideas of 'salvation' and 'redemption'.

Real-world politics and anti-politics in early socialism
Politics
To move from categories into real time: if there was some almost ideal-type politics in the actual history of Owenism and early socialism, it was usually not at the extreme, Machiavellian, end of the spectrum. And it had generally had more to do with Robert Owen himself than with Owenite socialism among his followers. Owen liked to appeal directly to heads of state whenever he could, inviting them to use Political Power to achieve his ends, at a stroke. He was more impatient for all-at-once change than co-operators later learned to be. This was a source of his disdain for daily working-class practice, as though ordinary people were not capable of changing the

world in ordinary ways, like arranging their own powers differently – or keeping shop. Like many later socialists, Owen was unwilling to accept world-change in the quotidian forms in which co-operators produced, distributed, and exchanged it – and certainly not if High Politics could deliver a New World, for everyone, for all time and all at once.

It was, however, a creative, eclectic, un-functionalist, un-Western Marxist view of the State – as separable from society, rather than 'governing' society – which encouraged Owen to try to use the State from the top down rather than feel shaped by it. This impulse was part of a widespread disconnect between State and society after 1750.[24] To attempt to arrange things with and through State servants was on a continuum, for Owen, with 'arrangements' to be made with and by other people in other ways. While railing against 'politics', he often insisted that 'the real science of government is to form arrangements to produce the greatest amount of improvement in the state, and to secure the highest degree of happiness for the whole population'.[25]

In the end it was only after 'repeated failures (that) Owen finally became convinced that *only* the state could commence the new moral world'.[26] But 'commence' is significant. Once land had been publicly acquired, the producers and exchangers of change would be working people husbanding that land with spades, building communities, in and through technically inventive forms of associated production. Owen stood for election to Parliament many times. But, like J. S. Mill in 1865, this was more for the sake of argument or Public Address than to join any Political cadre.

Anti-politics
More pervasive than ideal-type politics, there was also some *almost* ideal-type anti-politics in the real world of Owenism/

early socialism. 'Owen's wish to *transcend* politics was central to his life's work.'[27] The *trade* unionists who came together in extraordinary numbers in the Grand National Consolidated Trade Union (GNCTU) shared his aspirations. They were proud that 'politics, that care-worm of the heart, never yet lurked in our lodges'. Political language insinuated 'politics into a system which ought to be strictly social'. The re-placement of political power was assumed in the pivotal letters on 'Associated Labour' by 'Senex' in the *Pioneer* in the Spring of 1834, but that was not where the *action* lay for James Morrison or J. E. Smith, the joint authors of these letters which, surely, found an echo in the passages in *Capital* Volume 3 which deal with the 'associated mode of production'.[28] Morrison was committed to the organisation of independent production by labour and for labour, but 'labour' inflected thus:

> we have determined that REFORM shall commence from within. *We govern within ourselves* [my emphasis] and conceive it to be a duty to acquaint ourselves with the principles of government, consisting of good internal regulations. We feel that to regulate trade, or the several branches of labour by which we live, will most speedily regulate government.[29]

Debates on the meaning of democracy between O'Brien, the GNCTU, and Owen himself remain a vital resource for thinking about and developing the politics of anti-politics today.[30]

Owen's opinion that the Charter would merely 'make all petty politicians' was widely repeated among his followers. One such preferred 'universal suffering and animal parliaments' to universal suffrage and annual parliaments.[31] Owen could be devastatingly impolitic in the organisations that he touched, including the first series of Co-operative Congresses from 1829 to 1832, the GNCTU from 1833 to 1834, and the community at Queenwood (Harmony Hall) in Hampshire in 1839. E. P. Thompson judged that he 'simply had a vacant place in his mind where most men have political responses'.[32] He had a tendency to confuse what he wanted to happen outside himself with the power of his own, almighty reasons. He and some of his followers *did* believe in quasi-miraculous, supra-Political change at some moments in the movement's history. During such times, they believed in change innocent of ends pursued by rationally chosen means. There were to be millennial happenings, arising from an outlook called 'pre-political' by E. J. Hobsbawm.[33] Exemplary words or deeds were seen as capable of contagious effect, such as the simple act of founding New Harmony in the USA in 1825 or laying the foundation stone for Queenwood in 1839. The latter was inscribed 'YM 1', or Year of the Millennium One. Political follow-through was thought to be unnecessary. David Green, for example, a leading figure in the Leeds Redemption Society, was always hostile to the insinuation of political views into the socialist movement.[34] He said that he

> always felt it a very difficult and delicate task to mix up politics with communism ... Communism is of no party; it knows of no politics. The miserable distinctions of Whig, Tory, or Radical, belong to the old world. They could not exist in a new social state ... I esteem politics as but a meretricious ornament to communism. The Redemption Society cannot recognise any faction in the political world, and more especially as it includes amongst its members men of all grades and politics. To introduce politics, would be to introduce another element of discord.[35]

Political growth points in anti-politics

For such as Green, 'faction' and 'party' could not be redemptive, any more than 'competition' could. They would reproduce an old, anti-social state of affairs. 'Communism knows of no politics.' If we listen more closely, however, we can detect the presence of politics in associations such as the Leeds Redemption Society even if, as St Augustine might have said, not yet. It was from anti-politics like theirs that socialism as an 'available form' for everyone could grow. '*At the present stage of progress,*' Green wrote, 'there is not any *necessary* connection between politics and association.' 'Labour' had to 'prove itself *by practical illustrations over and over again* [my emphasis] that it is organisable'. 'When association has demonstrated itself to such an extent as to have become an important element of society, government must take cognisance of it. But that is the task of the future age.'

Government would, as it were, have to move over, displaced by associated self-organisation or self-government. Green's *was* a political strategy, but not the same strategy as demanding universal suffrage and annual parliaments. To stay with this single example among many, his strategy was to prove, practically and continuously, that labour is (we are) organisable in its (our) own interests, and thereby to make the connection between politics and labour's (our) chosen associational forms *necessary* – thereby altering the very nature of politics.

By subscribing to 'union', 'community', 'association', a whole politics – a *society* worthy of the name – could be produced, distributed, and exchanged. This society would be very different from what representative democracy later became. Many associationists thought, and continue to think, that such a society is best attainable by withdrawing demand for (as in

William Morris's 'policy of abstention'[36]) a rapidly emerging supply of representative or parliamentary democracy. It is surely revealing how parliamentarians in Britain continue to defend parliament and parliamentary sovereignty with more passion than they address popular democracy. It is as though they are either unaware or afraid of the difference between the two. Whether or not they have been 'enfranchised', ordinary people have often demonstrated a preference for building – often with enormous artistry and depth of culture – 'giant theatres of associated life' or 'parliaments of labour' which arrange their own powers for themselves.[37] The political class, Left and Right, then dubs these associations un- or anti-political, or they legislate to ensure that they stay in their silos. Hence the long stream of Acts of Parliament which tell co-operative and mutual enterprises of all kinds – credit unions, clubs, trade unions, friendly societies, building societies – what they can and cannot do. Sociologists try to see such enterprises 'functionally', with subordinate roles within a 'system' which, in fact, it is their project to replace. Industrial and Provident Society legislation needs to be seen at one and the same time as enabling and licensing, liberating and controlling.

> Early socialist political thought has remained unexplored often because it has been dismissed as 'unpolitical'. But this, precisely, is part of its significance for the history of socialism.[38]

It is from conjunctions between anti-politics and politics, achieved in actually existing associational forms and large-scale social movements, that we may be able to describe historically, and develop politically, a useful line of theory and practice in the UK and elsewhere. This has its roots in early socialism and self-conscious 'moral economy' which lived on in extraordinary associations such as the Co-operative Wholesale Society and the Royal Arsenal Co-operative Society and survives, somewhat buried, in ordinary, 'un-political' Co-operative and Mutual Enterprises today. Such enterprises saw themselves as constituting the change that they were working for: 'Be the change', as Mahatma Gandhi put it later. This useable inheritance is still available to us now, to fill the craters left by the failure – sometimes the defeat (which is not the same thing) – of later socialisms.

It was in the middle parts of the spectrum where politics and anti-politics met that the substance, as opposed to the ideal types, of Left politics between c. 1800 and c. 1850 lay. Claeys invents the category 'social radicalism' for this conjunction. He deploys its details in highly original ways in the central chapter of *Citizens and Saints*.[39] Owenites repositioned radicalism with 'newly-created "social" ideals', seeking 'to join political means to social ends as well as to link the moral and economic analysis of socialism to republicanism'.[40]

Claeys sees social radicalism as a separable body of ideas, but then also as a 'component' in the mix of many individual and organisational outlooks. He blends taxonomy with history, to their mutual benefit. There were, of course, differences between many creative social radicals about *timing* – as to whether political reform preceded or followed economic activity on its way to making *society* social. There were also differences concerning *community* – as to whether it was the precondition or the result of society: whether Socie*ties*, communities, co-operatives, and unions brought full sociality into being or depended upon it. But in most cases what *we* are constructing *now* came before what *they* – what we now call 'the political class' – must be asked to do *then*.

Government meant what *we* can do among ourselves, co-operatively and mutually, as much as it means what *they* –

the government – must be asked to do. Co-operatives and mutuals were more than campaigns.

Owen's insistence upon the futility of parliamentary reform was repudiated by many of his working-class followers by the late 1820s. A select group of these attempted *in a successive number of organisations* [my emphasis] to unite radical objectives [many of them Political] with an Owenite programme of co-operation and community-building.[41]

These organisations included the British Association for the Promotion of Co-operative Knowledge (1829–1834), the National Union of the Working Classes (1831–1834), and the Grand National Consolidated Trades Union (1834). My point of difference with Claeys is that whereas he sees most shades of social radicalism as remarkable but over and done with soon after the 1850s, I see them – with the help of Peter Gurney's work, among others – as potential contributions to that 'great arch' of socialism's cultural revolution which was still being constructed throughout the nineteenth and twentieth centuries and which awaits completion.[42]

The flavour of the anti-politics of the GNCTU has already been conveyed. Un-parliamentary it was. But un-political? Just how un- or anti-political was, for example, the 1834 House of Trades scheme, taken by James Morrison and Elisha Smith directly from Owen's plan for a national extension of the GNCTU? In late 1833, Owen proposed the democratisation of production, folding 'politics' into 'economics' in ways which have been attempted several times and in several places in the world since the 1830s. Owen proposed that Union branches

> would form themselves into two lines of parochial, country and provincial lodges; the first consisting of parochial lodges of

builders, shoemakers, tailors etc. etc., respectively appointing a delegate [NB: delegates not representatives] to represent them in the provincial lodge (of which there will be four). The second line of lodges will consist of the united trades formed into provincial, county and parochial lodges, as with those of the respective trades, whose business it will be to superintend the interests of the various workmen in their respective communities ... The superintendents, *who will supply the place of masters* [my emphasis], will be men elected for their skill and integrity.[43]

An earlier historian of the GNCTU, W. H. Oliver, thought that, among trade unionists, a 'plan for universal co-operative production' was being put forward from which new democratic arrangements 'inevitably' arise.[44] Claeys attributes more of the positive, democratic thinking which informed these arrangements to Robert Owen's fertile brain than to any inevitability. *Citizens and Saints* rescues Owen as a creative contributor to democratic thought, just as *Machinery, Money and the Millennium from Moral Economy to Socialism* rescues many early-nineteenth-century Ricardian and socialist thinkers as creative contributors to 'new economic' thought. There were trade unionists who proposed that Chartist demands like annual parliaments, universal suffrage, and no property qualifications could grow direct from the associational life of the GNCTU, rather than be demanded from and 'granted' by Parliament. Democracy was to be constructed rather than demanded, produced rather than given. Such activists argued against Bronterre O'Brien's political emphasis, as they saw it.

> Even if Owen never explicitly said that the union was to replace parliament, his position was nonetheless much closer to this (considering that he regarded the organisation of production

as the chief task of government, next to education), and much more egalitarian than historians have hitherto indicated.[45]

Starting from what we would call 'the economy', John Gray (1799-1883), John Francis Bray (1809-1897), and William Thompson (1775-1833) have been rescued in Claeys' *Machinery, Money and the Millennium* and in *Citizens and Saints*. They have been retrieved not as precursors but as practitioner-theorists of new-old, co-operative relations of production which anticipated and sought to bring together what we now call 'economics' and 'politics'. As such, they were *social* scientists contesting what they identified as a less than fully social or positively anti-social science.

Associational forms were being brought into being which could create as well as propose; exchange[46] as well as produce; and deal in a sense of futurity for working people as well as in products necessary for sustaining life. Such associations were the means of production and means of belonging, as well as forms of inclusive ownership for members and associates. These inclusive forms of ownership and belonging differed in detailed ways from emergent, exclusive, public and private forms of ownership and *not* belonging. Consciously invented means of belonging define 'religion', as Emile Durkheim (1858-1917) proposed, with his roots in French, Saint-Simonian associationism. So it is not surprising that 'religious' constructions were not uncommon in early socialism and that they survived into the subsequent history of the co-operative movement. Radicals altered their positions over time, including on the sociality, or mix of politics and economics, that they favoured in one set of circumstances rather than another.[47] This makes them more than frozen precursors unable to melt into Marxism or Social Democracy. John Gray may 'merit recognition as the originator of the idea of the modern planned economy'.[48] But his early, under-consumptionist work was all about productive, creative, universal *labour*. Labour theories of value majored in *labour* in day-to-day practice as well as in *value* in eternal theory.

> ALL would be productive members of society; excepting only the persons *absolutely required* in unproductive occupations ... Immoral professions, or those derived from the immoral effects of the present system, would be superseded and would in turn release more productive labour.

The end of wasteful competition would mean that

> *Everything that deserves the name of wealth shall instantly be accessible to all:* for then we should have as much wealth as we have the POWER OF CREATING![49]

Bray's capital letters and italics are not just quaint, any more than the long titles chosen by Owenites for their associations, or the long title-page of William Lovett's autobiography. They indicate the pitch, tenses, and tone that they preferred. George Mudie, editor of the *Economist,* was a critic of Owen's labour exchanges of 1832 and of the French producer workshops of 1848 in ways which anticipate 'revolutionary socialist' dismissals of early socialism ever since. In his *A Solution of the Portentous Enigma of Modern Civilization* addressed to Louis Bonaparte in 1849, Mudie regretted

> a direct tendency to create the Organised Labourers into competitors and rivals of the present Productive Capitalists now sustaining and carrying on all the business operations of society.

How often from the mid-nineteenth century onwards did co-operators have to listen to this criticism from socialists! This was why co-operators, for the most part, preferred not to call themselves socialists from that time onwards:

> productive associations of labour must necessarily prove abortive, in consequence of all the determined opposition and hostility which (they) could not fail to encounter from all the powerful parties who would be deeply and indeed vitally interested in defeating (them).

So, likely defeat the first time round was turned into 'necessary' failure and for all time. Nevertheless, Mudie shared with Bray and with the socialism of his time an activist, 'physical' conception of what 'productive classes' could do if only adequate arrangements of production were made with them and by them. He went into some detail about what these arrangements should be, to

> enable the most suitable place in the Organisation to be found for every one, and every one in the Organisation to find his most suitable place.

He proposed a kind of internal market for labour, avoiding direct competition with capital: 'the market for all the productions, or the demand for them (would be) found in satisfying the wants, the duties, and the obligations of the Organised Labourers themselves'. This was a market which could 'never fail', and the supply of which could not 'injuriously affect any portion of the national interests'.

Co-operation, in other words, could only begin with co-operators, not with the whole society as competitors.[50] This was a perspective that many Co-operators adopted as the Co-operative Wholesale Society grew during the second half of the nineteenth century into one of the largest businesses in the world.[51]

Some characteristics of early socialism

Allowing for overlap, the anti-political politics of early socialism had four characteristics which are still relevant. First, they started from the 'economic' world of thought and action, that is from what 'civil society' originally meant to the political economists. Secondly, they showed the determination and capacity to *produce* society, rather than to be determined by it. Their project was to meet fundamental human needs in Societies, preventing society from becoming a Thing and thereby reducing Itself, in Margaret Thatcher's way, to 'individuals and families'. Thirdly, they were committed to education, but in a sense of the word long buried by schools and colleges.[52] Finally, early socialists shared a refusal to separate moral reformation from social reform in ways which were not unrelated to many modern 'extremists'.

A basis in the material or 'economic' world of thought and action
Early socialism rejected what would later become the a-social, a-political isolation of economics. This was made possible by the willingness of Owen and his contemporaries to enter the world of competitive political economy in sufficient intellectual depth and with sufficient brio to counter it with co-operative, 'social' knowledge or *science*. Early socialist thinkers and their associations set out from the material rather than from the ideal. They began – just as they wished to end – with making, producing, distributing, exchanging: in other words, with activities which would now be known as necessary and basic. They understood government

and education as being on a continuum with production, distribution, and exchange, and thus equally available for *making* by means of 'associated labour'. Hence the Pioneers' commitment to 'arranging the powers of production, distribution, education and government'. Each of these four activities was later undertaken mainly by professionals, experts, and managers rather than by members and associates of co-operatives, having been conceptualised as abstract nouns. For early socialists, producing, distributing, etc. were active verbs taking the first person plural as subject: *we all ... will produce, arrange the powers of ...* because they are powers which everyone has. Early socialists dealt in human powers more than in State-derived rights.[53]

It was from such an accessible, material base that early socialists debated with radicals and republicans who saw contemporary problems and solutions in terms of good governance and civic virtue, and with Chartists who saw the franchise and fair elections as the main priorities.[54] In practice many radicals wanted to exercise more than the public virtues for which they stood, and many Chartists wanted more than the political democracy for which *they* stood. But the radical and Chartist bias towards politics helped to define a language and structure of primarily *political* inclusion for the many who, willingly contained within such a language, quickly became 'the masses'. Against this bias, early socialists believed that politics should properly be about economic matters, as practised by labour.[55]

Making society by means of Societies

Early socialism was rooted, of course, in associations. The most characteristic of these have kept their shape until now, as productive *Societies* which are member-owned, member-governed, and, in project at least, member-controlled. The active impulse towards member ownership/member control is demonstrated by the fact that the Owenite associational forms which were *not* member-owned or member-controlled (including Owen himself!) generated intense internal struggles 'from below', precisely about member ownership and member governance, indeed about democracy itself.[56] Debates between Owen and Owenites were an essential part of the history, which is also our resource. Examples include local Branches, Communities, Halls of Science, Unions (Grand National Consolidated and otherwise), and early Co-operative Congresses, all of which were full of debate and pressure, sometimes successful, sometimes not, towards belonging and control by a would-be active membership.

Early socialist associations produced, distributed, and exchanged material goods. They also created social relations in opposition to the anti-social ones by which they were always surrounded and sometimes infected. Conceptual divisions of labour like those between 'politics' and 'economics' were one thing. But there were also practical divisions of labour, like those between producers and consumers, or managers and members, or shopping and learning, which also needed to be put together on a daily basis. The associations that resulted differed from the organisational forms which now get corralled into a 'sector': as 'voluntary organisations', 'social enterprises', and charities. With or without the label 'socialist', and often taking a co-operative and/or mutual form, early socialist associations grew in and against other Owenite initiatives. They were proudly working-class, self-generated, actively independent, 'from below' associations, often taking off against the wind of Owen's impatient waywardness.

Such associations became increasingly difficult to define in terms other than their own. Competitors still try to make them fit into categories to which they do not belong. They do not fit easily into dominant 'business', 'voluntary', or 'political' categories; although they are businesses, they are voluntary, and they are political. Members have sometimes been tempted to let them collapse into dominant versions of these categories, mainly through inactivity. Antagonists have often tried to encourage them to do so, mainly through regulation. It is noteworthy that co-operatives and mutuals as independent, mostly working-class associations have lasted longer than most other categories of enterprise or association coming through to us now from the early nineteenth century. They have survived as Societies and 'Unions' of many kinds: co-operative, friendly, building, credit, trades, club-and-institute. and so on. During the early nineteenth century, such Societies and Unions constituted <u>the</u> *social movement* or, in France, *le mouvement sociale*. The social movement preceded *the labour movement* to which it became politically subordinate during the late nineteenth century as one of that movement's three 'wings' and known as the 'consumer' wing. The other wings were the 'citizen' wing led by the Labour Party and the 'producer' wing led by *Trades* Unions, with the former increasingly in command.[57]

Member-owned, member-governed Societies saw themselves as entities capable of re-forming a complete, new/old *social* order, using the word 'social' in a stronger sense than is common today. Industrial and Provident Societies saw themselves as making a *new moral world*. They became known as 'I and Ps' for regulatory purposes, to distinguish them from capitalist Companies. They were oppositional in stance and hegemonic in ambition, rather than safely alternative or subordinate. While voluntary as a matter of principle, they were not 'voluntary organisations' in today's sense of *not*-business, *not*-State organisations: in other words, they were not confined within what has recently become known, against earlier usages of the term, as 'civil society'. As their enemies acknowledged, they constituted 'a State within the State'. Rather than licensing them to function, democracy would flow from their functioning. William Hawkes Smith's confidence went as far as to say that

> in truth, provided personal freedom be permitted in a country, it matters but little to the success of the co-operative scheme, what particular forms and institutions prevail. A community of mutual interests, be the Government what it might, must be, within itself, essentially and practically a democracy.[58]

The intention was not to leave 'business' and 'the State' in place, with a sprinkling of the 'social' added to each of them, as in 'social enterprises' or 'social democracy'. The project was, literally, trans*form*ational, constituting *different* forms of enterprise, as different forms of democracy.[59]

Education
Owenism was full of the language of *circumstances*. As notorious as Thatcher's nostrum on 'society' was Owen's proposition that 'the character of man is formed for and not by him'. It is less well known that Owen and his followers majored, quite specifically, in the *education* of circumstances, and that this is how they used the word *education*. The education of circumstance was what the construction of 'society' meant, first by means of communities, later by means of co-operative and mutual Societies. This is what member-owned, member-governed Societies were *for:* multi-dimensional, interactive, mutual education. This is what socialists were supposed to *do:* discover and practise the politics of detail, so that members, loosening their competitive, individualised, and collectivised ('working *class*') chains, could *become* their

own circumstances, thereby leading each other out (*e-ducere* in Latin). We will 'surround ourselves with circumstances', 'circumstances that will make (us) intelligent, rational and happy'.[60]

> The knowledge he ['man'] has acquired – that he is under the control of circumstances – forms itself a new circumstance, which will give him the power to control a large range of circumstances relative to himself.[61]

It was the task of communities and of co-operatives to educate their members enough in the social science of co-operation to create their own, new circumstances. Socialism was social experimentation, social discovery, social *movement*. Education would 'end the unconscious determination of character by circumstances'.[62] 'Society shall be *taught* to govern circumstances.'[63] Familial achievement, political reform, and even economic justice were not enough. As Owen's future partner in New Harmony said when he first met him at New Lanark, only an education which could 'drown the self in an Ocean of Sociability' would be sufficient to create the moral environment of the new world.[64]

This was why education was at the heart of the early socialist project, and with far fewer sorting and grading connotations than it has today. This may be the most useful of all Owenite meanings for us to listen to now.[65] Owen and his followers bled *education* into *government*. Education pointed to our understanding of the natural and social worlds and human nature and nurture in them, rather than any sequence of qualifications. It developed what G. J. Holyoake called our 'associative intelligence'. *Social science* was the main Owenite term for these understandings. Such science was to replace government as hitherto practised.

The Owenites were the first to popularise the notion of 'social science' in Britain, and clearly intended the concept to replace the older sciences of government as well as the practice of 'politics' generally.[66]

Government was identified not with Politics as in Godwinian anarchism, but with *society* and thus with the task of education. Through education, society could be constructed not only as current limitation but also as future possibility. Early socialists were never afraid to contest dominant meanings and philosophies, whole ways of seeing and living in the world which they rejected. No one could afford for anyone to be deprived of the best available moral and social knowledge. If education was unequal, divisions of labour which were less than fully human would develop. This is what human membership, one of another, meant. It was best expressed in bridging bodies like deliberate communities and open and voluntary co-operatives, rather than in bonding organisations like families and nations. Hence 'the educational principle of government'. In the end 'the world will be governed by education alone'. Although his behaviour in the old immoral world could be autocratic, Owen saw this as only temporarily necessary. Equality had to be established before everyone could participate. This required education. Transitional forms of government, even if unequal to the point of autocracy, could provide improved education, or what we might call consciousness raising, towards a time when more adequate 'society' could educate – transform – 'government' altogether. Without mutuality, taught and learned in Halls of Science, 'society' would be unknowable except as circumstance: it would have been abstracted, alienated from associated human 'arrangement'. In a word, it would have been de-mutualised.

Social reform included moral reformation

So the re-formation of society was what early socialist politics consisted of: new and different forms of association, federally linked in order to replace familial and national boundaries. Government in these settings included self-government, including the moral regulation produced by 'public opinion'. This was most effectively formed in communities of a certain size.[67] There were appropriate functions for individuals to perform at different stages of their lives. Age was a better way to move into and out of eligibility for formal, governmental functions than competitive bidding for power between parties, factions, and interests.[68] The latter could only reproduce individualism.

Owen was unafraid to challenge *family* and *nation* as the fixed points that they later became in socialist discourse. It was for the same reason that Owenites were also suspicious of *class* when deployed by their antagonists. Any focus for membership and belonging which subtracted from humanity itself, serving as an inhibition on universal community rather than one component of it, was to be transcended. The early socialist challenge to lesser nuclei was moral as well as scientific, behavioural as well as conceptual. 'Family', as in the universal family of all human beings, was important to Owen. But not the small or nuclear family. This was the site of the competitive selfishness that was cause and effect of the crisis of the times.

> Every family made a little exclusive world seeking its own advantage ... With these persons it is *my* house, *my* wife ... *my* children .... Children are taught to consider their own individual family their own world. We all know that when a family party converse together, they speak freely upon subjects which as soon as a stranger accidentally enters amongst them

he never hears ... But by a community education, you may all acquire the same general and particular ideas and feelings: consequently, into whatever circle you enter, you would still be in your family circle, and would converse with each other as freely as with a husband, wife or child.[69]

Early socialists were unafraid to raise the moral and intellectual cost of entry to the movement by making these moral as well as intellectual challenges to capitalists and to their *dismal science* of competitive political economy. 'The social mode of improvement', as it was described in 1856, demanded the education and moral improvement of all those who were to assist in the building of the new society, and thus the renewed pursuit of public virtue, and of 'the knowledge of right and wrong, of true and false modes of action, and the culture of good habits'. The work of Claeys and J. F. C. Harrison has shown how Owen was committed to a higher moral purpose than inherited partisanship, and how he wanted to refashion ideas of public, national, and international interest in order to ensure peace, justice, and well-being for everyone. Such a project survives, of course. Indeed, it is being revived in the third decade of the twenty-first century, but at some distance from socialism and from co-operative politics. Moral language tends to be deployed now as culture-war rhetoric by statists and fundamentalist marketeers seeking to rally voters to their side rather than to the side of their opponents, or else it is seen by voters and non-voters as a private, individual, or familial alternative to political activity. It is deployed every day away from 'the' State, rather than towards a different kind of state. For early socialists it was intrinsic to a carefully considered anti-politics from which a new politics could grow.[70]

Notes and References

Notes to Chapter 1

1. The phrases are those of E. R. T. Morse, a Reading co-operator, in *Reading Co-operative Record*, 17 February 1904, and Thomas Rigby, a Bury co-operator, in *The Origin and History of Co-operation in Bury, 1855–1905* (Bury, 1905).
2. The phrases are from W. H. Brown, *The Co-operative Manager* (Manchester: National Co-operative Managers' Association, 1937), p. 15, and *Co-operative News*, 25 April 1891, on the opening of CWS Flour Mills, Dunston-on-Tyne.
3. *The Co-operator*, March 1863, Address to Co-operators from Rochdale Pioneers, accompanying a set of model rules that they issued following the passing of the Industrial and Provident Societies Act of 1862.
4. The cancer image is in W. T. Carter, *Co-operation a Remedy*, a pamphlet (Manchester: Co-operative Union, 1885).
5. T. W. Mercer, *The Co-operative Movement in Politics*, a pamphlet (Manchester: Co-operative Union, 1921).
6. Catherine Webb (ed.), *Industrial Co-operation: The Story of a Peaceful Revolution*, 1st edn (Manchester: Co-operative Union, 1904); 8th edn, 1919, p. 2.
7. From an article in the CWS *Annual* for 1902. In this article even the word 'sold', as in buying and selling, is put into inverted commas as being not quite appropriate for co-operative exchanges. The whole movement at this time was a living critique of the commodity form itself.
8. G. J. Holyoake, *Self-help by the People: The History of the Rochdale Pioneers,*

10th edn, revised and enlarged (London, Swan Sonnenschein, 1907), p. 12.
9. The 'close community' phrase is from the article cited in n. 7 above.
10. At the Congress of 1874, see *Co-operative News,* 25 April 1874, p. 230. I owe this reference to Peter Gurney.
11. From a speech made in Reading in 1898 by the Honorary Secretary of the Southern Section of the Co-operative Union, Adam Deans.
12. See Holyoake, op. cit., p. 73.
13. Rigby, cited in note 1 above, p. vi.
14. 'The Labour Movement must work to show that the alternative society does exist and can be achieved without national catastrophe which itself could lead to the triumph of a system which is the very opposite of democratic socialism. ... There will never be a "convenient" time to alter the structure of existing society.' Royal Arsenal Co-operative Society, *The Role and Problems of the Co-operative Movement in the 1980's,* a pamphlet, May 1977.
15. Senex, in *The Pioneer,* 22 March 1834, Letter II, 'To the productive classes'.
16. D. C. Jones, 'The Economics of British Producer Co-operation', unpublished PhD thesis, Cornell University, 1974.
17. Percy Redfern, *The New History of the C.W.S.* (London, J. M. Dent and Manchester, CWS, 1938), p. 55; 'the whole community' is my emphasis.
18. Thomas Rigby, *The Origin and History of Co-operation in Bury, 1855–1905* (Bury, 1905).op. cit., pp. 7 and vi.
19. For Mitchell, see Chapter 4 in this volume.
20. Samuel Smiles, *Character* (London: John Murray, 1871).
21. Webb, op. cit, p. 122.
22. M. Fothergill Robinson, *The Spirit of Association* (London: John Murray, 1913), p. 350.
23. Raymond Williams, *Marxism and Literature* (Oxford: Oxford University Press, 1977).
24. CWS, *Annual,* 1886, p. 115.
25. For which see K. Marx, *Capital,* vol. 3 (Harmondsworth: Penguin

Books, 1981), pp. 571-2, and my two contributions to Tom Bottomore ed., *A Dictionary of Marxist Thought* (Oxford: Blackwell, pb edition, 1985) on 'Co-operative Association', pp. 95-6 and 'Working-Class Movements', pp. 528-531).

Notes to Chapter 2

1. As Natalie Davis put it in an important theoretical Introduction to her *Society and Culture in Early Modern France* (London: Duckworth, 1975), pp. xvi-xvii: 'It (research) was also a matter of recognizing that forms of associational life and collective behaviour are cultural artefacts, not just items in the history of the Reformation or of political centralization. A journeyman's initiation rite, a village festive organization, an informal gathering of women for a lying-in or of men and women for storytelling, or a street disturbance could be "read" as fruitfully as a diary, a political tract, a sermon, or a body of laws.'
2. Against 'the selfish misconception that induces you (the bourgeoisie) to transform into eternal laws of nature and of reason the social forms springing from your present mode of production and form of property — historical relations that rise and disappear in the progress of production — this misconception you share with every ruling class that has preceded you'. Karl Marx and Frederick Engels, *Manifesto of the Communist Party* (1848), in Karl Marx, *The Revolutions of 1848: Political Writings, Vol. 1*, ed. David Fernbach (Harmondsworth: Penguin, 1973), p. 83.
3. 'Let us uproot this habit of thinking of individuals according to certain artificial so-called "classes". Nothing is more unjust and nothing could be more dangerous.' Lord Leverhulme (W. H. Lever), *The Six Hour Day and Other Industrial Questions* (London: G. Allen & Unwin 1918), p. 294.
4. Asa Briggs, 'Middle-Class Consciousness in British Politics 1780-1846', *Past & Present* 9 (1956), pp. 65-74.
5. Such as the atomised, mechanised world of E. M. Forster's frightening

story 'The Machine Stops' (1909), or the better-known, drugged world of Aldous Huxley's *Brave New World* (1932).

6. The quotations in this paragraph are all from Karl Marx, *Capital: a Critique of Political Economy*, vol. I, Ch. 15, section 9, 'The Health and Education Clauses of the Factory Acts' (1867; Harmondsworth: Penguin, 1976), pp. 610–35.

7. J. M. Baernreither, *English Associations of Working Men* (London: Swan Sonnenschein, 1889), p. 11.

8. Philip Corrigan derived from Marx (but I cannot find it in Marx's work) the helpful sequence from moral > political> social economy in his fecund 'State Formation and Moral Regulation in Nineteenth-Century Britain: Sociological Investigations' (PhD thesis, University of Durham, 1977). This thesis is still abundantly worth reading.

9. See, for example, the excellent article by Gareth Stedman Jones, 'Engels and the Genesis of Marxism', in *New Left Review* 106 (Nov.–Dec. 1977), particularly pp. 85 and 102–3. 'Theoretical ability, even when possessed in as exceptional a degree as in Marx, is a necessary but not sufficient condition of a theoretical revolution, especially in the social domain. For such revolutions to occur, disturbing phenomena are also necessary, which not only point to the inadequacy of the existing theoretical problematic, but are suggestive of the raw components of a new theoretical structure. It was Engels in his writings of 1844 and 1845 who provided these decisive new components.' The importance of Engels' contribution derived less from his moments of theoretical originality than from his ability to transmit elements of thinking and practice developed within the working-class movement itself in a form in which it could become an intrinsic part of the architecture of the new theory. 'It was the process itself rather than the intervention of the philosopher which had awakened workers to a consciousness of the class position, and which he hoped would lead to the emergence of a "proletarian socialism".'

10. Karl Marx, 'Letter to the Labour Parliament' (1854), in *Surveys from Exile: Political Writings, Vol. 2*, ed. David Fernbach (Harmondsworth:

Penguin, 1973), p. 278. See also the section in Karl Marx, *Grundrisse* (1858), ed. M. Nicolaus (Harmondsworth: Penguin, 1973), pp. 704–706, on the 'contradiction between the foundation of bourgeois production ... and its development'. These pages consider 'to what degree the powers of social production have been produced, not only in the form of knowledge, but also as immediate organs of social practice, of the real life process'. 'Forces of production and social relations – two different sides of the development of the social individual – appear to capital [and to many modern Marxists – S. Y.] as mere means, and are merely means for it to produce on its limited foundation. In fact, however, they are the material conditions to blow this foundation sky-high.' I was led to these pages by Philip Corrigan and Derek Sayer, 'Class Struggle, Moral Relations and Political Economy', *Radical Philosophy* 12 (1975), p. 18.

11. Marx, *Capital* vol. I, p. 171.
12. Marx, *Grundrisse*, p. 107.
13. Marx, 'Letter to the Labour Parliament'. For the honourable history of such forms, see T. M. Parssinen, 'Association, Convention and Anti-Parliament in British Radical Politics, 1771–1848', in *English Historical Review* 88 (July 1973), pp. 504–33; and for O'Connor's defence of one of them (the 1839 Chartist Convention) see *Northern Star* 22 June 1839, p. 8: 'To the existence of that Convention, you are to attribute the difference between our present revolution and any revolution which has hitherto taken place among nations. (Cheers). Look to the several French revolutions. They failed of producing the promised result because men attacked abuses, and fought for a shadow, without being prepared with a substitute. (Cheers). Your case is now different for, upon an emergency, you have a Parliament which would act, and one whose orders you would obey or to appoint *instanter* another, whose orders you could more cheerfully obey. (Loud cheers). Herein then lies all the difference: you cannot move without the consent of all. You cannot move partially, because you are one link in the great chain. (Cheers). There is an end to sectional agitation; you are each

answerable to the other for the manner in which you shall handle this cause. (Cheers).' Quoted in J. A. Epstein, *The Lion of Freedom: Feargus O'Connor and the Chartist Movement, 1832–1842* (London: Croom Helm, 1982), p. 139.

14. Royden Harrison, 'The British Labour Movement and the International in 1864', *Socialist Register* 1 (1964), pp. 293–308.
15. Marx, 'Inaugural Address to the International Working Men's Association' (1864), in *The First International and After: Political Writings, Vol. 3*, ed. David Fernbach (Harmondsworth: Penguin, 1974), pp. 79–80.
16. So that the third of the Provisional Rules of the International, drafted by Marx, read: 'That the economical emancipation of the working-classes is therefore the great end to which every political movement ought to be subordinate as a means.'
17. Marx, 'Inaugural Address', p. 80; Marx, *Capital*, vol. I, p. 413, n. 58.
18. Marx, 'Inaugural Address', p. 79.
19. Marx, *Capital*, vol. I, pp. 412–13 and following.
20. See Marx, 'The Association for Administrative Reform (People's Charter)' (1855) for a comparison of the implications of universal suffrage in Britain and in France, made necessary because 'the continentals are prone to under-rate the importance and meaning of the English *Charter*'. Marx's point underlines that of Feargus O'Connor in note 13 above. Whereas in France, owing to historical development and social structure, suffrage reform was a mere political question, in Britain it had become a social one: since 1842 'there has no longer been any doubt as to the meaning of universal suffrage. Nor as to its name. It is the *Charter* of the classes of the people and implies the assumption of political power as a means of meeting their social requirements. That is why universal suffrage, a watchword of universal fraternisation in the France of 1848, is taken as a war slogan in England. There the immediate content of the revolution is universal suffrage, here the immediate content of universal suffrage is the revolution.' In Karl Marx and Frederick Engels, *Articles on Britain* (Moscow: Progress

Publishers, 1975), pp. 235, 236.
21. Frederick Engels, 'The Abdication of the Bourgeoisie' (1889), in Marx and Engels, *Articles on Britain*, pp. 395–400.
22. 'Educated' in the sense of what Marx calls Hegel's 'very heretical views on the division of labour'. In his *Philosophy of Right* he says: 'By educated men we may *prima facie* understand those who ... can do what others do' (Marx, *Capital*, vol. I, p. 485 n. 51). As large-scale industry develops, the proportion of such people, for capital (but potentially also for labour), presumably increases greatly.
23. 'The mind which believes only in its own magic strength will disappear. For the revolutionary struggle is not fought between capitalism and mind. It is fought between capitalism and the proletariat.' Walter Benjamin, *Understanding Brecht* (London: New Left Books, 1973), p. 103.
24. Karl Marx and Frederick Engels, 'Circular Letter to Bebel, Liebknecht, Bracke, *et al*.' (1879), in Marx, *First International and After*, pp. 374–75.
25. Marx, 'The Eighteenth Brumaire of Louis Bonaparte' (1852), in *Surveys from Exile*, pp. 146–7.
26. Marx, *Grundrisse*, p. 278.
27. Philip Corrigan's clarity in 'State Formation and Moral Regulation', p. 378, helps here: 'Just as Marx was able to refer to a "political economy of Labour" which was different from that of Capital, so we can point to different moral relations. The dominant moral order works — i.e. is in being — because it is based upon a material order (that is a world) *held one way up* by historically specific relations of production and State apparatuses formed for their maintenance. In experiencing that moral order, the working classes also experience the power and force which holds the world one way up. *Their experience of the State is therefore quite analytically separable from their role performance which sustains that order without internalizing it* [my emphasis, S. Y.]. For this reason apart from the tensions and structural crises of the world-wide mode of capitalist production — the State apparatuses of modern Britain are constantly engaged (flexibly and subtly) in reproducing and enforcing a moral

order. These investigations have shown how that order was both a selection from available alternatives (moral economy, social economy) and acted to suppress or marginalize other images of social life.'

28. Two essays in E. J. Hobsbawm's *Revolutionaries* (London: Weidenfeld and Nicolson, 1973) pose this question of interpreting the second half of the nineteenth century in Britain very sharply: 'Lenin and the "Aristocracy of Labour"', pp. 121–29; and particularly 'Karl Marx and the British Labour Movement', pp. 95–108. In the latter, Hobsbawm suggests a revolutionary (Chartist etc.) phase for British labour, followed by the 'phase of modest reformism which succeeded it in the 1850s, 1860s and 1870s during which it became clear (to Marx-Engels) that they could no longer expect very much from the British labour movement'. Hobsbawm can see that 'looking at the mid-Victorian decade with the wisdom of hindsight, we can observe that the retreat concealed elements of a new advance', but for him that advance consisted of anticipation of the continuous *organisation* of the socialist/trade union revival of the 1880s onwards, as opposed to the earlier 'succession of waves of militancy'. Hobsbawm's judgement of the second phase is clear, and it can stand as representative of a whole school of labour history – not just Marxist – and not yet spent: 'It (the British labour movement) still led the world in a special form of organization, namely trade unionism and probably also in the narrower form of class consciousness which simply consists in recognizing the working class as a separate class, whose members have different (but not necessarily opposed) interests to other classes. However, it had abandoned the effort and perhaps even the hope of overthrowing capitalism, and accepted not only the existence of this system, seeking merely to improve the condition of its members within it, but also, and increasingly, it accepted with certain specific exceptions – the bourgeois-liberal theories about how much improvement could be achieved. It was no longer revolutionary, and socialism virtually disappeared from it.' Marx, he argues, 'recognized the adaptation of the labour movement to the bourgeois system; but he regarded

it as a historical phase, and indeed, as we know, it was a temporary phase. A socialist labour movement in Britain had disappeared; but it was to reappear.' It is towards qualifying and enriching such partly true judgments that the second half of my chapter here is directed. Hobsbawm goes on to argue that this reformist phase for British labour, while increasingly disappointing for Marx-Engels, did not lead Marx into Fabianism/revisionism: 'They may have led him to become pessimistic about the short-term prospects of the working class movement in western Europe, especially after 1871. But *they neither led him to abandon the belief that the emancipation of the human race was possible nor that it would be based on the movement of the proletariat* [my italics]. He was and continued to be a revolutionary socialist.' The question that now needs posing is this: if the italicised sentence above constitutes qualification for being revolutionary, do not many 'reformist' working people, co-operators and others, during this second phase, also qualify, along with Marx?

29. Asa Briggs, *Mass Entertainment: the Origins of a Modern Industry* (Adelaide: Griffin Press, 1960).

30. J. T. W. Mitchell (1828–95) is the subject of Chapter 4 below. He was 'the most remarkable personality that the British Co-operative Movement has thrown up' (according to Beatrice Webb, *My Apprenticeship* (Harmondsworth: Pelican, 1938), p. 406 n. 1). Bastard son of a beer-house and lodgings keeper, he worked as a piecer in a cotton-mill from the age of 10, remained in the textile industry until he was 45, then worked for the Co-op movement. He was re-elected chairman of the Co-operative Wholesale Society from 1874 to 1895, quarter by quarter. 'Throughout these twenty-one years of complete absorption in building up the most varied if not the largest business enterprise in the world at that time, Mitchell lived on the minute fees, never exceeding £150 a year, that this vast enterprise then allowed its Chairman, in a small lodging at Rochdale, his total estate on death amounting to the magnificent sum of £350 17s 8d.' See also Percy Redfern, *John T. W. Mitchell, Pioneer of Consumers Co-operation* (Manchester: Co-operative

Union, 1923); and Joyce M. Bellamy and John Saville (eds), *Dictionary of Labour Biography,* vol. 1 (London: Macmillan, 1972), pp. 241-42.

31. I have not followed recent work on Friendly Societies, relying on the pioneer work of P. H. J. H. Gosden, *The Friendly Societies in England 1815-1875* (Manchester: Manchester University Press, 1961), and *Self-Help: Voluntary Associations in Nineteenth-Century Britain* (London: Batsford, 1973); see also Barry Supple, 'Legislation and Virtue: An Essay on Working Class Self-Help and the State in the Early Nineteenth Century', in Neil McKendrick (ed.), *Historical Perspectives: Studies in English Thought and Society in Honour of J. H. Plumb* (London: Europa, 1974), pp. 211-54, and Geoffrey Crossick, *An Artisan Elite in Victorian Society, Kentish London 1840-1880* (London: Croom Helm, 1978), ch. 9, pp. 174-198.

32. For concern, as late as 1928, about changes in the format of Congresses of the TUC such as introducing the rostrum instead of speaking from the floor, see Walter Citrine, *Men and Work: an Autobiography* (London: Hutchinson, 1964), pp. 248-49. For a typically 'smart', modern dismissive, cynical tone about Congresses, see Peter Jenkins, 'Annual Ritual of Democracy', *Guardian,* 5 Sept. 1967.

33. For tensions within the Reading Co-op, for example between the editor of the *Reading Co-operative Record* (Esrom) and the Trade sub-Committee, over the ideological/political education of the adverts in the *Record,* see Stephen Yeo, *Religion and Voluntary Organizations in Crisis* (London: Croom Helm, 1976), pp. 283-9.

34. See E. J. Cleary, *The Building Society Movement* (London: Elek, 1965), particularly Ch. 6, 'Starr-Bowkett Buildings Societies', pp. 101-115.

35. Hilary Wainwright, 'The Labour Party's Monopoly of Working-Class Representation: its Conditions and its Limits', paper presented to the 1977 Conference of Socialist Economists.

36. This situation and the specific choices faced and made by associations of many kinds in a single town (Reading) – religious, leisure, welfare, educational and political – between 1890 and 1914 are a major theme of my *Religion and Voluntary Organizations in Crisis.*

37. Faced by deficit in 1911, the Reading WEA appealed to branches in other towns to raise a 1d. tax on members to save 'the pioneer branch': they were unusually self-conscious about vice-presidential domination and its subordinating tendencies. Gradually, however, they lost autonomy: see Yeo, *Religion and Voluntary Organizations in Crisis*, pp. 235–241. For the Statist background to the WEA becoming a Responsible Body in 1924 (as opposed to the WEA reasons), see Raymond Challinor, *The Origins of British Bolshevism* (London: Croom Helm, 1977), p. 261.
38. Rich material for making up one's mind on these questions is in Geoffrey Crossick's 'Social Structure and Working-Class Behaviour' (D Phil thesis, Univ. of London, 1976); and his *An Artisan Elite*. He produces fascinating evidence, such as that 12 per cent of Royal Arsenal Cooperative Society members were unskilled or semi-skilled in the period 1872–80, and that 'It was a central tenet of friendly society exclusiveness that this independence and this capacity for self-government must theoretically be attainable by all' (*An Artisan Elite* p. 196); and that 'It is clear from both the national and the local evidence that the elitist position of the aristocracy of labour rested upon earnings differentials and relative job security' ('Social Structure and Working-Class Behaviour', p. 182). But, with a lot of careful argument and qualification, he would probably disagree with my sentences here.
39. Yeo, *Religion and Voluntary Organizations in Crisis*, p. 286, and Board of Trade Labour Department, *Report of Workmen's Co-operative Societies in the UK*, Cd. 698 (1901), pp. xviii–xix, for examples of Co-operators discussing the problem of moving beyond their better-paid base.
40. The analogy is with manufacture and machine production or large-scale industry in Marx, *Capital*, vol. I, p. 504: 'Manufacture produced the machinery with which large-scale industry abolished the handicraft and manufacturing systems in the spheres of production that it first seized hold of. The system of machine production therefore grew spontaneously on a material basis which was inadequate to it. When the system had attained a certain degree of development, it

had to overthrow this ready-made foundation, which had meanwhile undergone further development in its old form, and create for itself a new basis appropriate to its own mode of production.' See also Antonio Gramsci's view that what makes intellectuals/philosophy 'organic', what makes ideas into material forces, and what unites theory and practice are adequate-for-labour parties or movements or, in the language of my chapter here, associational forms. Parties or 'the party' are/will be more or less adequate-for-labour forms of 'political', and other, production. *Selections from the Prison Notebooks,* ed. Quintin Hoare and Geoffrey Nowell Smith (1934; London: Lawrence and Wishart, 1971), pp. 330–31 and elsewhere.

41. Just as it is 'quite possible that socialism will remain a sect till the very eve of the last stroke that completes the Revolution, after which it will melt into the new society', William Morris, *Commonweal,* 3 July 1886. I owe this reference to Ian Bullock.

42. See Bentley Gilbert, 'The British National Insurance Act of 1911 and the Commercial Insurance Lobby', *Journal of British Studies* 4 (1965), pp. 127–48; W. J. Braithwaite, *Lloyd George's Ambulance Wagon: being the Memoirs of William J. Braithwaite, 1911–1912* (London: Methuen, 1957); and Chapter 3 which follows.

43. B. T. Hall, *Our Fifty Years: the Story of the Working Men's Club & Institute Union* (London: CIU, 1912), Ch. XI.

44. John Saville, 'Trade Unions and Free Labour: the Background to the Taff Vale Decision', in Asa Briggs and John Saville (eds), *Essays in Labour History* (London: Macmillan, 1960), pp. 317–50.

45. Barry Supple, 'Legislation and Virtue', p. 227.

46. M. Carr-Saunders et al., *Consumers' Co-operation in Great Britain: an Examination of the British Co-operative Movement* (London: George Allen & Unwin, 1938), p. 469.

47. Corrigan, 'State Formation and Moral Regulation', cited above.

48. For which see Paddy Maguire, 'Co-operation and Crisis: Government, Co-operation and Politics, 1917–22' and Neil Killingback, 'Limits to Mutuality: Economic and Political Attacks on Co-operation during

the 1920s and 1930s' in Stephen Yeo ed., *New Views of Co-operation* (London: Routledge, 1988), pp. 187-206 and 207-228.

49. See Karl Liebknecht's reaction to 'politics as the art of the possible'. 'The extreme limit of the possible can only be attained by grasping for the impossible. The realized possibility is the resultant of the impossibilities which have been striven for. Willing what is objectively impossible does not, therefore, signify senseless fantasy-spinning and self-delusion, but practical politics in the deepest sense. To demonstrate the impossibility of realizing a political goal is not to show its senselessness. All it shows, at most, is the critic's lack of insight into society's laws of motion, particularly the laws that govern the formation of the social will. What is the true and strongest policy? It is the art of the impossible.' Quoted in Rudolph Bahro, 'The Alternative in Eastern Europe', *New Left Review* 106 (Nov.-Dec. 1977), p. 31.

50. I will tell this tale in an essay to be called 'Class Struggle and Associational Form'.

51. 'Socialism does not claim to speak the truths of an abstract society: it portrays the relational understanding of social formations from a particular, materialist and thoroughly experiential basis. The material base of socialism is simultaneously its moral base: how direct producers are, and the thousands of struggles involved in understanding what it is to be a direct producer under the dictatorship of the bourgeoisie' (Philip Corrigan and Derek Sayer, 'Class Struggle, Moral Relations and Political Economy', in *Radical Philosophy* 12 (1975), pp. 21-22. Or, for an older, late-Owenite view by R. J. Derfel: 'Instead of wasting time, energy and money on palliatives, which under existing conditions will be palliatives to some only, whilst they are bound to be aggravations to others – all reformers, and especially all socialists, ought to unite their efforts to establish the new society side by side with present institutions, so that the superiority of the new may show the inferiority of the old, and that will be the best way to get rid of it. ... The new society must be established ... by its evident superiority over the old. I can see no way to replace individualism and competition, except by

showing in actual everyday life, the great superiority of organized co-operation in labour for the common good, and a community of interest in the results.' R. J. Derfel, *An Unauthorized Programme* (Manchester, 1895).

52. Stephen Yeo, 'Some Problems in Realizing a General Working-Class Strategy in Twentieth-Century Britain', a paper presented to the British Sociological Association annual conference, 1977. The distinction between 'abolition' of contradictions and finding forms 'within which they have room to move' is based on Marx, *Capital*, vol. I, p. 198. 'We saw in a former chapter that the exchange of commodities implies contradictory and mutually exclusive conditions. The further development of the commodity does not abolish these contradictions, but rather provides the form within which they have room to move. This is, in general, the way in which real contradictions are resolved. For instance, it is a contradiction to depict one body as constantly falling towards another and at the same time constantly flying from it. The ellipse is a form of motion within which this contradiction is both realized and resolved.'

Notes to Chapter 3

1. W. J. Braithwaite, *Lloyd George's Ambulance Wagon: being the Memoirs of William J. Braithwaite, 1911–1912* (London: Methuen, 1957), p. 116.
2. B. Kirkman Gray, *Philanthropy and the State, or Social Politics*, ed. Eleanor Kirkman Gray and B. L. Hutchinson (London: P. S. King, 1908), *passim*.
3. A. V. Dicey, 'The Balance of Classes', in *Essays on Reform* (London: Macmillan, 1867), pp. 67–84.
4. E. P. Hennock, 'Social Security: a System Emerges', *New Society* 7 March 1968.
5. Karl de Schweinitz, *England's Road to Social Security* (Philadelphia: University of Pennsylvania Press, 1947).
6. Barry Supple, 'Legislation and Virtue: An Essay on Working Class

Self-Help and the State in the Early Nineteenth Century' in Neil McKendrick (ed.), *Historical Perspectives: Studies in English Thought and Society in Honour of J. H. Plumb* (London: Europa, 1974), pp. 211–54.

7. P. H. J. H. Gosden, *The Friendly Societies in England 1815–1875* (Manchester: Manchester University Press, 1961), and *Self-Help: Voluntary Associations in Nineteenth-Century Britain* (London: Batsford, 1973).

8. Philip Corrigan, 'State Formation and Moral Regulation in Nineteenth-Century Britain: Sociological Investigations' (PhD thesis, University of Durham, 1977), 333–4.

9. Quoted in J. H. Treble, 'The Attitude of the Friendly Societies Towards the Movement in Great Britain for State Pensions, 1878–1908', *International Review of Social History* 15 (1970), p. 274.

10. Quoted in Joseph Chamberlain, 'Old-age Pensions and Friendly Societies ', *National Review* 24 (1895), pp. 592–615.

11. Or the end of the 1950s, by which time 'the welfare state' was congealing as fact and phrase.

12. In R. M. Titmuss, *Problems of Social Policy* (London: HMSO, 1950).

13. Like that of Karl de Schweinitz, cited in note 5 above.

14. W. H. Beveridge, *Voluntary Action: a Report on Methods of Social Advance* (Allen & Unwin, 1948), pp. 320, 324.

15. Stephen Reynolds, and Bob and Tom Woolley, *Seems So! A Working-class View of Politics* (London: Macmillan, 1911), p. xv.

16. See note 21 below. Celebratory china pieces, plates, tiles, egg cups, etc. were much used before and during the 1914–18 war, perhaps particularly in association with Lloyd George?

17. *Tit-Bits*, 23 May 1911.

18. Sir Henry Bunbury, 'Introduction', in Braithwaite, *Lloyd George's Ambulance Wagon*, p. 18.

19. Reynolds and Woolley, *Seems So!*, p. xxv.

20. For W. H. Beveridge in his famous report, *Social Insurance and Allied Services* (London: HMSO Cmd. 6404, 1942), 'the term "social insurance" implies both that it is compulsory and that men stand together with

their fellows' (para. 26).
21. Bentley Gilbert, 'The British National Insurance Act of 1911 and the Commercial Insurance Lobby', *Journal of British Studies* 4 (1965), pp. 127–48.
22. *Clarion*, 14 July 1911.
23. Gilbert, 'British National Insurance Act', p. 143.
24. *Labour Leader*, 10 September 1898 through to 15 April 1899.
25. Gilbert, 'British National Insurance Act', pp. 128, 148.
26. Sidney Webb and Beatrice Webb, *The Prevention of Destitution* (London: Longmans, 1911), pp. 169–70.
27. Beatrice Webb, *Our Partnership* (London: Longmans, 1948), pp. 468, 430, 473–4.
28. Braithwaite, *Lloyd George's Ambulance Wagon*, p. 47.
29. Lucy Masterman, *C. F. G. Masterman: a Biography* (London: Nicholson and Watson, 1939), p. 342.
30. E. P. Hennock, 'Social Security: a System Emerges', *New Society* 11 (7 March 1968), p. 337.
31. R. W. Harris, *National Health Insurance in Great Britain 1911–46* (London: Allen & Unwin, 1946), p. 17.
32. Gilbert, 'British National Insurance Act', p. 147.
33. Masterman, *C. F. G. Masterman*, p. 223.
34. *Clarion*, 28 July 1911.
35. Ernest Gowers, *Plain Words: a Guide to the Use of English* (London: HMSO, 1948), pp. 12–13; Masterman, *C. F. G. Masterman*, p. 385.
36. A. V. Dicey, 'Introduction to the Second Edition', *Lectures on the Relation between Law and Public Opinion in England during the Nineteenth Century* (2nd edn., London: Macmillan, 1914), p. xl.
37. Dicey, 'Introduction', p. lxxvi.
38. Braithwaite, *Lloyd George's Ambulance Wagon,* p. 266 (Bath: Cedric Chivers, 1970 edition) p. 266.
39. F. H. Keeling], *Keeling Letters and Recollections,* ed. by E. T[ownshend] (London: G. Allen & Unwin, 1918).
40. *Keeling Letters,* pp. 71 (1910), 59 (1910), 42 (1908).

41. *Keeling Letters,* pp. 59–60.
42. Kirkman Gray, *Philanthropy and the State* is a wonderfully honest register of the times.
43. *Keeling Letters,* p. 126 (1912).
44. *Keeling Letters,* p. 138 (1912).
45. *Keeling Letters,* p. 46 (1909).
46. *Keeling Letters,* p. 152.
47. Braithwaite, *Lloyd George's Ambulance Wagon,* pp. 217–18.
48. Braithwaite's diary, in *Lloyd George's Ambulance Wagon,* pp. 180–81.
49. David Englander (ed.), *The Diary of Fred Knee* (Manchester: Society for the Study of Labour History, 1977).
50. *Justice,* 1 July 1911.
51. *Justice,* 21 October 1911.
52. Braithwaite, *Lloyd George's Ambulance Wagon,* p. 188.
53. Braithwaite, *Lloyd George's Ambulance Wagon,* pp. 196, 206; *Justice,* 21 October 1911.
54. Beatrice Webb, *My Apprenticeship* (London: Longmans, 1926), pp. 124–5 (diary entry 12 January 1884).
55. Dicey, 'Introduction', pp. xc–xci.
56. Sidney Webb, 'The Reform of the Poor Law', *Contemporary Review* 58 (1890), p. 104.
57. L. T. Hobhouse, *Liberalism* (London: Oxford University Press, 1911), p. 128.
58. R. J. Holton, *British Syndicalism 1900–14: Myths and Realities* (London: Pluto Press, 1976).
59. *Clarion,* 16 June 1911; 23 July 1911.
60. John Berger, *A Fortunate Man: the Story of a Country Doctor* (London: Allen Lane, 1967), p. 99. See also my 'On the Uses of "Apathy"' in *Archives Européennes de Sociologie* (vol. XV, 1974, no. 2) pp. 279–311).
61. Reynolds and Woolley, *Seems So!,* p. 67.
62. Reynolds and Woolley, *Seems So!,* p. xxv.
63. Reynolds and Woolley, *Seems So!,* p. xii.
64. Reynolds and Woolley, *Seems So!,* p. xix.

65. Reynolds and Woolley, *Seems So!*, p. xxv.
66. Reynolds and Woolley, *Seems So!*, p. xii.
67. Reynolds and Woolley, *Seems So!*, pp. 112–13, 278.

Notes to Chapter 4

1. 'By one who knew him', *Co-operative News,* 23 March 1895, p. 297.
2. For an earlier attempt to get at 'the place of the Cooperative Wholesale Society in the proletarian forces of the world' via consideration of J. T. W. Mitchell, see James Haslam, 'Pioneers and Leaders', *The Wheatsheaf,* May 1923, p. 76.
3. For conveniently presented data on the size and growth of the CWS, see Percy Redfern, *The New History of the CWS* (London, J. M. Dent, 1938), 'Statistical Supplement', pp. 531–547.
4. The nearest I have come to Mitchell and Socialism named as such by him is in a personal copy of the *Handbook* of the Edinburgh Co-operative Congress, 1888, which has a rare example of Mitchell's handwriting in it. The *Handbook* was in the possession of the Library and Information Unit of the CWS in Manchester, from whom I had much help in writing this chapter before all the material in the possession of the CWS (later the Co-operative Group) was transferred and catalogued into the National Co-operative Archive in Holyoake House, Manchester, cared for by the Co-operative College Library team, from whom I have always had expert and generous help. Referring to a sermon that he had heard on Sunday 13 May 1883, Mitchell noted down the texts, and then 'the socialistic experiment of Jerusalem may have been a failure. But it ought not to discourage us in doing what we can to bring about some plan of [illegible word] among men. Not only must we bear our own burdens but also each other's burdens.' Haslam ('Pioneers and Leaders') wrote that Mitchell 'gave indication of being an evolutionary socialist who might have written some such volume as *Merrie England* if he had had Blatchford's great literary skill'. At

Mitchell's funeral, his pastor at Milton Congregational Chapel, the Revd. J. Hirst Hollowell, called the Co-operative Movement 'the most successful of all embodiments of the Socialistic spirit' (*Rochdale Observer*, 23 March 1895). The CWS *Annual*, 'put out by the Committee each year', expressed its project thus in 1886: 'In the present Annual it is our main purpose to explain the growth of thought in connection with human progress, the ideas of the philosophers and the struggles of the workers. We make no pretense to state the minute particulars of all forms of socialistic thought ... Our aim more specially is to place in the hands of the reading portion of our working population a sketch that will enable them to apprehend a subject which has perhaps a stronger claim than any other on the serious attention of all classes of our population.'

For the labile 'Left' language in and around Mitchell and the CWS, see Mitchell's extraordinary performance in 1890 in front of the *Royal Commission of Labour* described below (and referenced in note 109). The language included 'federal production', 'rather on the lines of a commune', a 'complete system'. And for John Watts on 'communism', see note 6 below.

5. See an address to the Bolton Co-operative Society at the opening of their Reading and Conversation Rooms in 1877, quoted in F. W. Peaples, *History of the Great and Little Bolton Co-operative Society Ltd: showing 50 years' progress, 1859–1909* (Manchester, 1909), pp. 103–4.

6. The quotes by Mitchell on Owen are from Mitchell's testimony to the Royal Commission on Labour on 25 October 1893, for which see 'Evidence before R. C. on Labour', PP 1893–4 XXXIX pt. 1 [C. 7063-i], pp. 15–47, Questions 1–405'; and from Mitchell's speech as President of the Co-op Congress of 1892, as reported in *Co-operative News*, 11 June 1892, p. 609. The 1892 Congress speech contained an historical account of co-operation in Britain back to 1792, going on through the first Congresses of 1831–35 of which Mitchell knew the details. At the 1869 Congress, the first of the new series, Owenites such as Henry Travis and William Pare harked back to the 1830s. Mitchell, delegate

from Rochdale, related to them thus: 'he did not see any insuperable difficulty in the way of realising the better state of co-operative life which had been foreshadowed, provided we began low enough and proceeded by natural growth', quoted in Arnold Bonner, *British Co-operation: the History, Principles and Organisation of the British Co-operative Movement* (revised edn., Manchester: Co-operative Union, 1970), p. 80. That Mitchell's doubts about Owen were well founded perhaps needs no arguing nowadays, but for their justification see Owen's reaction to finding six or seven Co-operative Societies trading in different parts of Carlisle in 1836: 'to my surprise, I found there 6 or 7 co-operative societies ... doing well, as they think – that is, making some profit by joint stock trading. It is, however, high time to put an end to the notion very prevalent in the public mind that this is the social system which we contemplate or that will form any part of the arrangement in the New Moral World', quoted in W. Henry Brown, *A Century of London Co-operation* (London: The Education Committee of the London Co-operative Society, 1928), p. 19. In 1884 Mitchell showed his friend William Maxwell the actual plan of Owen's proposed 1822 industrial village/colony which was to have been sited near Liverpool. Maxwell later wrote to W. Henry Brown, telling him that this plan made a deep impression on him, as he was 'at that time considering a scheme I intended to carry out in the Scottish CWS which, two years afterwards, took form at Shieldhall'; see W. Henry Brown, *A Century of Liverpool Co-operation* (Liverpool: Liverpool Co-operative Society, 1930), pp. 32, 37. One of the lines of descent for Mitchell's Owenism, in the sense that I am proposing it here, was through Dr John Watts (1818–1887), the slightly paralysed (and therefore unfit for manual work) son of a Coventry ribbon weaver who became an Owenite missionary. Watts spoke at the first of the new series of Congresses which Mitchell attended in 1869. He was also a speaker at the National Association for the Promotion of Social Science on Co-operation; see *Transactions ... 1860* (London: John W. Parker, Son and Bourne, 1861), pp. 873–4. He wrote a major series of articles to open the *Co-operative*

News in 1871 in which he put forward much of what Mitchell later (already?) represented, and in which he theorised Co-operation as a transition to Communism. For Watts' influence, see Percy Redfern, *John T. W. Mitchell, Pioneer of Consumers Co-operation* (Manchester: Co-operative Union, 1923). Watts and Mitchell were still seeing each other in the 1880s; see CWS General Committee, Minutes 8 Feb. 1884, p. 581. Watts intervened at the 1873 Congress on behalf of CWS production against people like Ludlow. A good social / intellectual biography of Watts is needed as much as one of Holyoake.

7. *Co-operative News*, 20 Oct. 1894, p. 1168.
8. Haslam, 'Pioneers and Leaders', p. 76; *Co-operative Congress Report 1894*, p. 138. All references to Co-operative Congress Annual Reports in this chapter can be enjoyably traced in a series of magnificently printed, annual volumes in the National Co-operative Archive in Holyoake House Manchester. Just to pick one up is essential, to feel its weight, all 650 pages of it; the pride of the Co-operative Union and its membership in the means and relations of production of member-led democracy; the verbatim reports of every speech; the photos of the different towns (each year a new one) in which Congress was held; the open, explicit, 'accountable' financial data; the taste of what a working-class civil society (overwhelmingly male at the governance level) could and did look like. Each year the full Congress Report was published at and by Manchester: Co-operative Union Limited, Holyoake House, Hanover Street.
9. R., 'Candid Friendship', *The Wheatsheaf*, Feb. 1922, p. 20, a piece on Beatrice Webb, referred to how 'J. T. W. Mitchell, whom she still regards as a genius, became her friend'. When Mitchell turned down the prestigious invitation to become a Director of the Manchester Ship Canal in 1895, the *Co-operative News*, 16 Mar. 1895, p. 277, used the decision to point up the difference between Mitchell's *exclusive* devotion to public causes and the tendency among younger men to ask 'whether this great slow-moving machine of democracy is worth making sacrifices for'. The *News* saw this as a major problem of the

times. For this incident see also CWS General Committee Minutes, 1 March 1895 – 21 June 1895. Beatrice Webb, *My Apprenticeship* (London: Longmans, Green, 1926), p. 360 n. 1.

10. *Co-operative News*, 11 Dec. 1880, pp. 308–12.
11. *Rochdale Observer*, 3 Apr. 1895.
12. William Maxwell, 'The Late John Thomas Whitehead Mitchell', in *The Co-operative Wholesale Societies Limited England and Scotland ANNUAL for 1896* (Manchester: The CWS Limited, 1 Balloon Street and the Scottish CWS Limited, Morrison Street, Glasgow) pp. 392–414 [henceforth cited as Maxwell, 'Memoir'], at p. 397: this memoir is the most personal piece of writing we have about Mitchell. Maxwell was Mitchell's equivalent within the Scottish CWS, had obviously been inside Mitchell's home, went with him to the USA in 1884, and wrote as if he had spoken quite intimately with Mitchell. In the Edinburgh Congress Handbook referred to above, Mitchell recorded his purchase that day of work by Crabbe, Burns, and Shakespeare. He would quote from Bunyan, see *Co-operative News*, 21 Mar. 1891, pp. 268–72. My observations on the Co-operative Congress Reports in n. 8 above apply, even more so, to these magnificent CWS Annuals.
13. Funeral and Memorial Services for Mr. J. T. W. Mitchell, Milton Chapel March 20th and 31st 1895, *Addresses by Rev. J. Hirst Hollowell* (Rochdale, 1895), in Rochdale local history collection; *Rochdale Observer*, 23 March 1895; *Co-operative News*, 23 March 1895.
14. *Co-operative News*, 27 Mar. 1895, p. 297, an appreciation 'By one who knew him'.
15. Maxwell, 'Memoir', see n. 12 above. They had met in temperance, political, and Co-op work in Rochdale. The friendship grew closer when Howard's wife and Mitchell's mother died in the same year, 1855. They lived together for a while. Howard remarried, and then in 1861 moved to Liverpool to a new job. Until the end of his life, Mitchell kept a room in John Street, Rochdale for Howard to visit, better furnished than his own.
16. The story of this relationship comes from Maxwell, 'Memoir', pp. 401–

2; and from Redfern, *John T. W. Mitchell*, p. 32.
17. *Rochdale Observer*, 23 Mar. 1895.
18. Maxwell, 'Memoir', p. 400.
19. *Rochdale Observer*, 20 Mar. 1895.
20. Webb, *My Apprenticeship*, p. 359 n. 1.
21. *Handbook of Co-operative Congress* (Rochdale: 1892), p. 154. I am unsure whether delegates had a printed Handbook each year at every Congress.
22. Prospero, *Mitchell the Leader*, The People's Papers no. 4 (Manchester: Co-operative Wholesale Society, 1928), p. 6.
23. Maxwell, 'Memoir', p. 394; *Rochdale Observer*, 20 Mar. 1895.
24. Maxwell, 'Memoir', p. 395.
25. Redfern, *John T. W. Mitchell*, p. 49. At the time of his Presidency of the Rochdale Congress in 1892, the piece on him in the *Rochdale Observer* saw the L and PYS liquidatorship as 'the only flaw in the ointment of Mr. Mitchell's relations with the Pioneers, and when he can give them a good report, as all hope he soon may, they will be perfectly satisfied with him'; 4 June 1892.
26. The convention was set by Sidney Pollard, 'Nineteenth-century Co-operation: from Community Building to Shopkeeping', in Asa Briggs and John Saville (eds), *Essays in Labour History* (London, Macmillan, 1960), pp. 74–112; but then see Philip N. Backstrom, *Christian Socialism and Co-operation in Victorian England: Edward Vansittart Neale and the Cooperative Movement* (London, Croom Helm, 1974).
27. CWS General Committee Minutes, 22 March 1895 and other entries.
28. T. W. Mercer, *Towards the Co-operative Commonwealth* (Manchester: Co-operative Press, 1936), p. 93: 'if ever a man incarnated the spirit of an institution, John Mitchell did'.
29. *Co-operative News*, 30 Apr. 1892: 'Now for the first day's President we are to have Mr. Mitchell the "spouse" of the Wholesale, and was there ever a more loving husband or a father that ever looked after his progeny better?', quoted in H. B. Wilkinson, *Old Hanging Ditch: its Trades, its Traders and its Renaissance* (London and Manchester: Sherratt

& Hughes, 1910), p. 228; see also Maxwell, 'Memoir': 'someone has said that the Wholesale Society was his spouse and their members his family'; see also *Co-operative News*, 23 March 1895: 'Friendships he has sacrificed, rather than sacrifice, in his estimation, the Wholesale and its interests. He cared for it – for he was a father in this respect at least just as the parent cares for his child.'

30. *Funeral and Memorial Services for Mr. J. T. W. Mitchell* (1895), see note 13 above.
31. See my *Victorian Agitator, George Jacob Holyoake: Co-operation as 'This New Order of Life'*, Volume 1 of the series *A Useable Past* of which the present book is Volume 3. Holyoake theorised association more deliberately than anyone else near to Mitchell; see Peter Gurney, 'George Jacob Holyoake: Socialism, Association and Co-operation in Nineteenth-Century England', in Stephen Yeo (ed.), *New Views of Co-operation* (London: Routledge, 1988), pp. 52–72 and Peter Gurney, *Co-operative Culture and the Politics of Consumption in England, 1870–1930* (Manchester University Press, 1996) ch. 5. In his *Organisation: Not of Arms but of Ideas* (London: J. Watson, 1853), p. 13, Holyoake also used the marriage metaphor, but not in a reductive way: 'Let him who takes an associate, at the same time understand that he takes a master. It is equally true of marriage, of friendship, as of confederation. Companionship implies the intention of mutual service, service includes mutual submission ... Organisation is a vow; it involves a plan of life.'
32. CWS General Committee Minutes, 2 May 1884 onwards.
33. I am taking some of my information here from a hostile source, Wilkinson, *Old Hanging Ditch* (London and Manchester, 1910) a copy of which was lent to me by the late Roy Garrett of the Cooperative Union, of which he was the expert and co-operative Librarian for many years.
34. General Committee Minutes, 23 May 1884, p. 206.
35. 'By one who knew him', *Co-operative News*, 23 Mar. 1895.
36. *Co-operative News*, 13 Sept. 1879, p. 596.

37. For the Leman Street story, see *Co-operative News*, 13 Sept. 1879, pp. 595–7; for the Pitman incident, see *Co-operative News*, 12 Mar. 1881, pp. 161–6.
38. *Co-operative News*, 14 June 1884, pp. 553–4.
39. General Committee Minutes, 20 Dec. 1884.
40. General Committee Minutes, 29 Dec. 1884.
41. For attendance at General and sub-Committee meetings: 7/6d. per meeting and 3/9d. extra if a second meeting was attended on the same day. Conferences: 5/-, and for overnight stay an extra 7/-. It was also resolved 'that the Chairman be not paid but honorary'. In future, quarterly balance sheets issued by the Society, amounts received by each Director for railway fares, and other expenses were to be inserted.
42. *Co-operative News*, 11 June 1892.
43. The same 1892 Presidential speech, but I have taken this extract from Wilkinson, *Old Hanging Ditch*, p. 231.
44. *Co-operative News*, 13 Dec. 1879, p. 805.
45. For Crabtree, see Joyce M. Bellamy and John Saville (eds), *Dictionary of Labour Biography, vol. 1* (London: Macmillan, 1972), pp. 88–9.
46. *Co-operative News*, 10 Sept. 1881, pp. 601–5.
47. *Ibid.*, p. 614.
48. See a speech in Dundee on 17 Sept. 1881, in *Co-operative News*, 1 Oct. 1881, p. 659.
49. The piece was called 'Caesarism and Federation', and is quoted at length in Backstrom, *Christian Socialism and Co-operation*, p. 113.
50. *Co-operative News*, 9 Sept. 1882, p. 616. The issues were substantial. They included a CWS grant to the Amalgamated Society of Railway Servants, see *Co-operative News*, 9 Sept. 1882, p. 606; and Mitchell's views on the CWS Committee's powers over employees, concerning a strike at the Heckmondwike Shoe Works.
51. *Rochdale Observer*, 27 Mar. 1895, p. 2.
52. Mitchell later spoke from this experience on a number of occasions. At the Quarterly Meeting of the CWS Newcastle Branch (*Co-operative News*, 8 Sept. 1883) he used the L and YPS story to emphasise his case

that Co-operative production could only be successful if the Societies were loyal and bought the goods. In other words, selling outside the Movement was, in this case and for Mitchell, necessary not desirable. At the Lincoln Congress he said: 'he was a firm believer in Co-operative production in which the Wholesale occupied the highest ground. As the liquidator of a productive society, he knew the difficulty of disposing of goods.'

53. Maxwell, 'Memoir', p. 405.
54. *Co-operative News*, 9 June 1883, pp. 511–19.
55. *Co-operative News*, 8 Mar. 1884, pp. 187–191.
56. *Co-operative News*, 8 Sept. 1883, pp. 795–7, 802–3.
57. Backstrom, *Christian Socialism and Co-operation*, p. 213.
58. *Co-operative News*, 23 Mar. 1895, p. 297.
59. Benjamin Jones, *Co-operative Production* (Oxford: Clarendon Press, 1894), p. 111, quoting from a Report of the Society for Promoting Working Men's Association.
60. *Transactions of the National Association for the Promotion of Social Science: Norwich Meeting, 1873* (London: Longman, Green, & Co., 1874), p. 516.
61. Co-operative Congress, Oxford, 1882, p. 3.
62. Throughout most of Mitchell's life, Congress tended to be under the aegis of the Christian Socialists, and the *Co-operative News* more susceptible to the CWS position. But each is an invaluable source for the other position.
63. Backstrom, *Christian Socialism and Co-operation*, p. 211.
64. Beatrice Webb, *My Apprenticeship* (London, Longmans, 1926), pp. 359–61 (diary entry for 28 March 1889).
65. Webb, *My Apprenticeship*, p. 368 (diary entry for June 1889).
66. In *The Economist* in 1821, Philadelphus, a middle-class Owenite, defended the practices of the Co-operative and Economical Society of London against 'men (who) ... have already endeavoured to ridicule our idea of mending the world by such carnal means as beef and pudding'. 'We shall see', he added. He was attacking reformers who saw the answer as Political – in this instance, suffrage reform – together

with those who advocated at-a-stroke revolution, concentrating on men's hearts and minds rather than on material, associational forms. Against such views Philadelphus set permanent association, through which the common people could 'unite heart and hand for the acquisition of those things, the value of which is palpable to the senses, namely the good things of this life'. As he saw it, no authority had the right to prevent the common people associating in this way, and furthermore 'it is entirely within their power'. It was an available form. In a debate between a Pemberton Co-operator (William Carson) and John Doherty in July 1830, Doherty had a go at Co-operative trading: 'when he heard men talk about getting profit from every mouthful they eat, he confessed his opinion was somewhat changed. According to this doctrine, all they had to do was to sit down and eat all before them in order to become completely happy (laughter). The more they eat the richer they would become.' For Philadelphus's views, see *The Economist*, 27 Oct. 1821; for his identity, see Gregory Claeys, *Bulletin of the Society for the Study of Labour History* no. 43 (autumn 1981), p. 14. For the Carson–Doherty debate, see Robin Thornes, 'The Early Development of the Co-operative Movement in W. Yorkshire, 1827–1863' (D.Phil. thesis, University of Sussex, 1984).

67. *Co-operative News*, 27 Apr. 1878, p. 264; 4 May 1878, p. 281.
68. A tribute from an artist – Miss Nora Batson – who had been commissioned to do a portrait of Mitchell for the CWS: see *Co-operative News*, 23 Mar. 1895, p. 296.
69. Maxwell, 'Memoir'.
70. Hirst Hollowell in his funeral address, quoted above.
71. His friend Abraham Howard, quoted by Hirst Hollowell, and in the Maxwell 'Memoir', p. 413.
72. A piece written by William Robertson, a reporter on the *Rochdale Observer* for the *Handbook for Co-operative Congress, Rochdale 1892*.
73. Halstead was later secretary to the Co-operative Productive Federation. His reminiscences are in *The Cooperative Official*, vol. III, no. 31 (Oct. 1922), p. 179.

74. Cutting from the *Daily Chronicle*, in a press cuttings volume in the Manchester Central Reference Library, Manchester Newspaper Cuttings, 1889–1896, vol. 3, F.942, 7889.M119, p. 127. For another eye witness at a Quarterly, see the London Correspondent of the *Bradford Observer* at the Feb. 14th 1891 meeting, quoted in *Co-operative News*, 28 March 1891, p. 305; and see also *Rochdale Observer*, 20 March 1895.
75. Maxwell, 'Memoir', p. 407.
76. Mr. Shillito, Vice-Chairman of the CWS, in his graveside address at Mitchell's funeral.
77. Robert Holt, President of the Rochdale Equitable Pioneers, in the *Rochdale Observer*, 3 April 1895, at the first meeting of the REP following Mitchell's death.
78. Haslam, 'Pioneers and Leaders'.
79. For this terminology, see Stephen Yeo, 'Three Socialisms: Statism, Collectivism, Associationism', in William Outhwaite and Mike Mulkay (eds), *Social Theory and Social Criticism: Essays for Tom Bottomore* (Oxford: Basil Blackwell, 1987), pp. 83–113; 'Notes on Three Socialisms, mainly in late nineteenth and early twentieth century Britain', in Carl Levy (ed.), *Socialism and the Intelligentsia* (London, Routledge, 1987), pp. 219–70; and 'Socialism, the State and Some Oppositional Englishness', in Robert Colls and Phillip Dodd (eds.), *The Idea of Englishness: Politics and Culture, 1880–1920* (London, Croom Helm, 1986), pp. 308–69.
80. Sidney and Beatrice continued to study Co-operation throughout their lives, in separate treatments of the Movement in Britain as well as in their works on *Industrial Democracy, A Socialist Constitution, Soviet Communism*, etc. Derek C. Jones has focused on their analysis of producer co-operation in a critical way in 'The Economics of British Producer Co-operatives' (D.Phil. thesis, University of Cornell, 1974), pp. 3–48, 57–9, 74, 277–9, 292, 342–5; see also his 'British Economic Thought on Association of Labourers 1848–1974', in *Annals of Public and Co-operative Economy* 47. I (1976), 5–36 and 'British Producer Co-operatives and the Views of the Webbs on Participation and Ability to Survive', in *Public and Co-operative Economy* 46.1 (1975), 23–44.

81. *My Apprenticeship*, Chap. VII, section on 'The Co-operative Movement'. This section needs reading in its entirety for the beautifully expressed ambivalence of Beatrice, as well as for her novelist's eye trained on well-known figures in and around the Co-op Movement during the late 1880s and early 1890s.
82. Quoted in 'Notes on *The Co-operator*', in T. W. Mercer, *Cooperation's Prophet: The Life and Letters of Dr. William King of Brighton, with a reprint of The Co-operator, 1828–1830* (Manchester, Co-operative Union, 1947), p. 183.
83. *Co-operative News*, 23 May 1891, p. 495.
84. *Co-operative News*, 20 Oct. 1894, p. 1168.
85. Redfern, *John T. W. Mitchell*, p. 43.
86. James Haslam, *Accrington and Church Industrial Co-operative Society Limited: History of Fifty Years' Progress, 1860–1910* (Manchester: Co-operative Newspaper Society, 1910), pp. 61–3, also reported in *Co-operative News*, 14 Nov. 1874.
87. *Royal Commission on Labour*, p. 33, Q. 153.
88. *Co-operative Congress, Newcastle 1880, Report.* A meeting at Gateshead Town Hall, 17 May 1880.
89. Speech at Conference of Co-operators in the Northern Section of the Central Board, in the Mechanics Institute, Chester-le-Street, in *Co-operative News*, 3 Aug. 1878, pp. 500–03.
90. *Handbook for the Co-op Congress in Rochdale, 1892*, p. 154.
91. REPS General Committee, Minutes, 5 Jan. 1857.
92. I am taking this from Prospero, *Mitchell the Leader*, p. 7; there is also a sympathetic account of the controversy about what was then called 'bounty to labour' in Benjamin Jones, *Co-operative Production*, pp. 260–65.
93. The controversy broke through into G. J. Holyoake's paper *The Counsellor* in 1861. This was the paper which lasted for a brief time, between the demise of *The Reasoner* and the start of *The Secular World*. It is on open shelves in the basement of the Bishopsgate Institute Library, now a major repository for Co-op material. *The Counsellor* asked

William Cooper, financial clerk of the REPS, to do a survey among religious denominations in Rochdale on the bonus-to-labour question. The results were reported in Sept. 1861, p. 7. *The Counsellor* stirred it up by advising Co-operators to keep away from the Hard Shells, as the Independents, they said, were called in Lancashire, and the Gutta Perchaists, as the Wesleyans were known, 'until the principle of the participation of profits is established'. Abraham Howard, President of the REPS, then had to rebuke Cooper for being party to bringing religious differences into Cooperation, Nov. 1861, p. 18. In the REPS Minute Book, the moving letter of rebuke by Howard is written out in full. It is one of those bits of handwriting which has the power to take one right back into the moment where it came from. I was led into this controversy by the *Dictionary of Labour Biography, vol. 1* entry on William Cooper, 1822–1868.

94. *Rochdale Observer*, 4 June 1892.
95. *Co-operative News*, 20 Oct. 1894, p. 1168. 'That we do not allow any of our rooms at Leicester Shoe Works for the use of dancing as requested by the employees of the works', was a resolution recorded in the CWS General Committee Minutes, 5 Dec. 1884, p. 13. But I do not know enough of the background to be able to read this properly.
96. It was at the opening of the Flour Mills at Dunston. *Co-operative News*, 25 Apr. 1891, p. 390: 'They said that they had gone on their own footing for many years past, and that they intended to remain "a peculiar people, zealous of good works" (Loud cheers).'
97. Opening an exhibition at Tynemouth, see *Co-operative News*, 20 Aug. 1892, p. 920.
98. There was a nice example of this when a deputation of the Labour Association came to Manchester in 1885 to press 'true co-operative principles' on the CWS; see *Co-operative News*, 10 Oct. 1885, p. 935. Mitchell's smile on this occasion, if I am not mistaken, had an edge to it. He listened to the arguments of Neale, Greening and co., said that they might differ over methods but not goals, offered to print what they had said, and finally said that they in the CWS were glad to have

had that interview 'because they had been able to gather the views and sentiments of those with whom they did not come into frequent contact'. See also Mitchell's tribute to Edward Vansittart Neale at the Dewsbury Congress of 1888, in *Co-operative News*, 26 May 1888, p. 492, a year in which Neale was President of Congress. At a time when dispute between the two sides was at its height, Mitchell said: 'They might have differences of opinion as to means to an end, but he trusted their end was the same. (Hear hear). They might travel on different roads, but he trusted that when these roads were gone over they might accomplish the work they desired, and that work was that the industrious class of this and every other country should at last find that what is called profit and increment of value shall find their way into the pockets of the industrious classes. (Hear hear and Applause) That was what their friend Mr. Neale had worked for, and he trusted that what Mr. Neale desired might be accomplished, though they might not always walk on the same road.' Ben Jones made eclecticism into a class principle in an interesting way which contrasts strongly with the opponents of the CWS among the Christian Socialists – of whom, incidentally, Neale was the most open to the different-routes-but-same-destination view put by Mitchell above. Mitchell was also capable of being harshly exclusive.

99. Samuel Smiles, *Self-Help: with Illustrations of Conduct and Perseverance*, with a centenary introduction by Asa Briggs (1859; London: John Murray, 1958), p. 284.
100. A phrase of the Rochdale Pioneers of 1844, in a statement of their 'objects and plans'.
101. General Booth, *In Darkest England and the Way Out* (London: Salvation Army, 1890), p. 142. In the Appendix, pp. xxiii–iv, of this book (which was ghosted by W. T. Stead) there was an account of 'The Co-operative Experiment at Ralahine'.
102. Booth, *In Darkest England*, p. 230. Many thanks to Peter Gurney for this reference on management. I was led back to *In Darkest England* by it, to find the E. T. Craig lineage.

103. *Co-operative News*, 25 Apr. 1891, p. 389.
104. Listed in Redfern, *John T. W. Mitchell*, pp. 69–70.
105. In a volume of newspaper cuttings, 1888–96, in Manchester Central Reference Library, vol. 3, F942, 7889, M.119, p. 127.
106. *Co-operative Congress, Glasgow 1876, Report*, p. 5.
107. Redfern, *John T. W. Mitchell*, p. 35.
108. *Rochdale Observer*, 4 June 1892.
109. *Royal Commission on Labour*, p. 22, Q. 43.
110. *Co-operative Congress, Carlisle, 1887, Report* p. 7.
111. *Co-operative Congress, Bristol 1893, Report* p. 132.
112. *Co-operative News*, 7 Apr. 1877, p. 16.
113. *Co-operative Congress, Huddersfield 1888, Report* p. 10. For this notion of a common bond used in a moving argument against religious and political differences within Co-operation, see Rochdale EPS General Committee Minutes for Quarterly Meeting on 6 Jan 1862, letter by Abraham Howard rebuking William Cooper and others over *The Counsellor* row: 'the present Co-operative Movement does not intend to meddle with the various religious or political differences which now exist in society but by a common bond namely that of self-interest to join together the means, the energies and talents of all for the common benefit of each'.
114. Thos. Tweddell, 'Two reasons why Co-operation succeeds', *The Wheatsheaf* vol. II no. 8 (Feb. 1898), p. 114.
115. 'Complete Co-operation', pp. 186–202 of *Co-operative Life* (London: Co-operative Union, 1889), a reprint of a series of lectures given in the Working Men's College, London. The anecdote is on p. 192.
116. *Co-operative News*, 16 Mar. 1912, p. 327.
117. CWS, Productive Committee Minutes, 14 March 1895. A new-broom manager at Crumpsall was trying to deal with more lax methods which seemed to be associated with Hayes. Two visitors from the Productive Committee had gone to Crumpsall to sort out some aggravation. 'Messrs. Hayes and Procter in the first place stated that Mr. Marshall did not understand co-operative ways, by which they

appeared to mean that co-operative employees should have a certain amount of laxity allowed them, such as coming a few minutes later in the morning etc., to what they would have in working for a private firm.' Marshall was concerned to increase productivity and cut down on overtime. He said that in the handmade-biscuit department, 'with half the hands he could turn out the same amount of work'. On March 21st Hayes and Marshall had to attend the PC. A reconciliation was attempted; 'it was understood that Mr. Hayes and Mr. Marshall would consult together and that Mr. Hayes would carry out any suggestions which were made of a practicable character and which would be an improvement'.

118. See *Co-operative News*, 14 Sept. 1889, pp. 982–991.
119. *Co-operative News*, 12 Mar. 1887, p. 246.
120. I have taken the story of this strike from the *Co-operative News* and the CWS General Committee Minutes. It can be followed in more detail in Jones, *Co-operative Production*, and in Backstrom, *Christian Socialism*. It would be worth researching in more detail as part of wider work on CWS production, perhaps starting with all the labour disputes referred to in Jones.
121. Percy Redfern, 'The Mitchell Centenary and its Significance', *The People's Year Book* (Manchester: CWS, 1929), pp. 15–16.
122. *Co-operative News*, 23 Oct. 1880, p. 697.
123. *Co-operative News*, 8 Mar. 1884, p. 79.
124. The entire correspondence was copied in long hand into the REPS General Committee Minute Books, see Committee Meeting, 21st April 1881, in a way which, as with the Abraham Howard letter in *The Counsellor* case above, gives one a real feeling of direct contact with the people involved.
125. *Co-operative Congress, Lincoln 1891, Report*, p. 104
126. *Co-operative News*, 3 Aug. 1878, pp. 500–03, speech at a Conference of Co-operators in the Northern Section of the Central Board.
127. *Co-operative News*, 21 Mar. 1891, pp. 268–272.
128. See, for instance, his opposition to the CWS giving a donation to the

National Co-operative Festival in 1893, on the grounds that this was an event promoted by the Agricultural and Horticultural Association and a few private individuals, not authorised by the Movement (*Co-operative News*, 17 June 1893, Quarterly Meeting, pp. 646-652); and for his opposition to production by large retail societies more or less in opposition to the general federation, see Redfern, *John T. W. Mitchell*, pp. 52 ff. The unsorted Greening papers in the Co-operative Union Library would be valuable sources for these episodes.

129. *Royal Commission on Labour*, p. 32, Q. 150. Years later, in his *Mitchell the Leader*, 'Prospero' commented, 'the new idea of abolishing profit and all special interests in profit, by using the CWS as the means of the whole body of consumers producing for themselves, was not grasped'. Similarly, Percy Redfern wrote in 1928 that 'if the consumers' theory is not felt to be radical and challenging, it is simply because so few of us have yet taken it seriously, and so fail to see where it is pointing' ('John T. W. Mitchell, A Centenary Appreciation', in *The Cooperative Review*, II (1928), pp. 176-180).

130. *Co-operative News*, 13 Sept. 1884, p. 834.

131. *Co-operative Congress, Carlisle, 1887, Report*, p. 7.

132. CWS General Committee Minutes, volume covering 29 June 1878-4 Sept. 1880.

133. *Royal Commission on Labour*, p. 45, Qs. 372-3.

134. *Royal Commission on Labour*, p. 40, Q. 293.

135. *Co-operative News*, 13 Sept. 1884, p. 832. Mitchell was launching a lifeboat at Tynemouth, called 'Co-operator, 1'.

136. *Co-operative News*, 13 June 1891, pp. 609-10; and *Co-operative News*, 19 May 1894, p. 530: 'He did not want a section of co-operators to be elevated at the expense of the rest, that would be creating a privileged and wealthy aristocratic class. Profits should go to the entire body politic.'

137. The 1894 speech was at a meeting at Congress (see *Co-operative Congress, 1894, Report*, p. 138) celebrating the Jubilee of 1844. I owe this reference to Gill Scott.

138. See his speech at the 10th Quarterly Conference of Midland Co-operative Societies in Leicester, in *Co-operative News*, 16 Jan. 1875, pp. 29–30.
139. *Co-operative News*, 25 Apr. 1891.
140. In 1912 Lever was to print an address on co-partnership which he had delivered to none other than E. G. Greening's Agricultural and Horticultural Association. Not surprisingly, his tone was not unlike that of General Booth, quoted above. The Scottish Co-operative Movement, where it was a live issue during the 1890s and early 1900s, is the best place to pick up the working-class and socialist case against co-partnership. See *The Scottish Co-operator:* 19 Aug. 1904, p. 772; 4 Nov. 1904, p. 1245; 18 Nov. 1904, p. 1093; 25 Nov. 1904, p. 1116; 16 Dec. 1904, p. 1192; 6 Jan. 1905, p. 20. 'Is it not possible that he (the anti-bonusite) may be pervaded by something nobler than greed?', asked one correspondent, who expounded a long case against 'making a favoured class inside the Co-operative Movement'. 'Is it not possible that he may be pervaded by the spirit of principle?' (*Scottish Co-operator*, 19 Aug. 1904, p. 772). In April 1905 'Democritus' wrote out the case against in a very trenchant letter: see *Scottish Co-operator*, 28 Apr. 1905, pp. 407–8.
141. See a long letter by Charles Oakeby in the *Rochdale Observer*, 21 Oct. 1893, p. 4.
142. *Rochdale Observer*, 4 Nov. 1893, p. 4.
143. *Rochdale Observer*, 24 Oct. 1894.
144. *Rochdale Observer*, 3 Nov. 1894, p. 4. For an attack on private shopkeepers by Mitchell during this second campaign, see *Rochdale Times*, 1 Nov. 1894.
145. 'They not only wanted leasehold enfranchisement, they wanted power to compel landlords to let land for co-operative purposes', *Co-operative Congress, Lincoln 1891, Report* p. 2.
146. A formulation by William Maxwell, at the Congress of 1897; see Sydney Elliott, *Sir William Maxwell: A Pioneer of National and International Co-operation* (Manchester, Cooperative Union, 1923).

147. *Co-operative Congress, Lincoln 1891, Report* p. 3.
148. Public meeting at the Cooperative Congress in Plymouth, 1886, in *Co-operative News*, 19 June 1886, p. 581.
149. *Co-operative News*, 13 Apr. 1882, pp. 204-5, speech at the coming-of-age celebrations of the Huddersfield Industrial Co-operative Society.
150. *Co-operative News*, 27 Sept. 1884, p. 857, and p. 860. For Mitchell's internationalism, see *Co-operative Congress, Newcastle-on -Tyne 1880, Report* p. 42 and a speech of welcome to French Co-operators at the *Co-operative Congress, Oldham 1885* and a speech at the opening of the London CWS building, Leman Street, in *Co-operative News*, 12 Nov. 1887, pp. 1138-9. Co-op Congress proceedings have generally been more international in flavour than those of the TUC.
151. *Co-operative Congress, Halifax 1874, Report*, pp. 21-2.
152. *Royal Commission on Labour*, p. 46, Q. 392.
153. *Royal Commission on Labour*, p. 40, Q. 287.
154. *Royal Commission on Labour*, p. 41, Q. 299.
155. *Royal Commission on Labour*, p. 40, Q. 289.
156. *Rochdale Observer*, 4 Nov. 1893, p. 6.
157. *Royal Commission on Labour*, p. 40, Q. 288.

Notes to Chapter 5

1. Boris Ford, 'What is a University?', *New Statesman*, 24 Oct. 1969.
2. I drafted this chapter in 2015 when the idea of a university was in more creative play, as opposed to the economics and government spending on an entire system of Higher Education. So my references here need more updating than I am able to give them: Robert Anderson, *British Universities Past and Present* (London: Hambledon Continuum, 2006); Alasdair MacIntyre, *God, Philosophy, Universities: A Selective History of the Catholic Philosophical Tradition* (Lanham, MD: Rowman & Littlefield, 2009); Michael Shattock, *Making Policy in British Higher Education 1945–2011* (Maidenhead: McGraw-Hill /Open University

Press, 2012); Harriet Swain, 'The free-wheeling universities' (in cafés, trailers, libraries, etc.), *The Guardian, Education,* 29 Jan. 2013.

3. Ronald Barnett, *The Idea of Higher Education* (Buckingham: The Society for Research into Higher Education and Open University Press, 1990); Peter Scott, 'The idea of the university in the 21st century: a British perspective', *British Journal of Educational Studies* 41.1 (1993), pp. 4–25; Michael Bailey and Des Freedman (eds), *The Assault on Universities: A Manifesto for Resistance* (London: Pluto, 2011); Stefan Collini, *What Are Universities For?* (London: Penguin, 2012); John Holmwood, *A Manifesto for the Public University* (London: Bloomsbury, 2011).

4. E. P. Thompson, 'Education and experience' (1968), republished in E. P. Thompson, *The Romantics: England in a Revolutionary Age* (Woodbridge: Merlin Press, 1997), p. 4.

5. Eric Eaglesham, *From School Board to Local Authority* (London: Routledge and Kegan Paul, 1956).

6. Essex Cholmondley, *The Story of Charlotte Mason, 1842–1923* (London: Dent, 1960).

7. Stephen Yeo, 'Social movements and political action: a preliminary view of a student initiated course', *Universities Quarterly* 24.4 (1970), pp. 402–422, and in Open University School and Society Course Team, *School and Society: a Sociological Reader* (London: Routledge and Kegan Paul, 1971); Stephen Yeo, 'A college for labour: towards an academic programme for Ruskin 1990–94', typescript, in Ruskin College Library (1990); Stephen Yeo, *Organic Learning: Mutual Enterprise and the Learning and Skills Agenda* (Leicester: NIACE, 2000).

8. John Willett and Ralph Manheim, *Bertolt Brecht, Poems 1913–1956* (London: Eyre Methuen, 1976), p. 307.

9. Graeme C. Moodie and Rowland Eustace, *Power and Authority in British Universities* (London: Allen and Unwin, 1974), p. 58.

10. Lisa Lucas, *The Research Game in Academic Life* (Maidenhead: Society for Research into Higher Education and Open University Press, 2006).

11. *Final Report of the Committee of Inquiry into the Organisation of the University of Sussex (1973)* (The University of Sussex, May 1973), pp.

27–38. I served on this Committee.
12. Lawrence Goldman, *Dons and Workers: Oxford and Adult Education since 1850* (Oxford: Clarendon Press, 1995); Richard Taylor and Tom Steele, *British Labour and Higher Education, 1945–2000: Ideologies, Policies and Practice* (London: Continuum, 2011).
13. C. Waugh, *'Plebs', the lost legacy of independent working-class education* (www.upstream.coop; post16educator.org.uk, 2009, accessed 11 June 2013); Jonathan Ree, *Proletarian Philosophers: Problems in Socialist Culture in Britain 1900–1940* (Oxford: Oxford University Press 1984); Harold Pollins, *The History of Ruskin College* (Oxford: Ruskin College, 1984).
14. J. A. Dale and L. T. Dodd, 'Ruskin Hall, Oxford', *Saint George: The Journal of the Ruskin Society of Birmingham*, 2/6 (1899), pp. 94–105; F. Merry, 'How to start a branch Ruskin Hall', *Young Oxford, a Monthly Magazine Devoted to the Ruskin Hall Movement*, 1.2 (1899), pp. 9–10.
15. Lucien Mercier, *Les Universités Populaires, 1899–1914: Education Populaire et Movement Ouvrier au Début du Siècle* (Paris: éditions ouvrières, 1986); Marcel Mauss, *The Gift: Forms and Functions of Exchange in Archaic Societies* (London: Routledge, 1922).
16. Emile Durkheim, *The Division of Labour in Society* (1893; New York: Free Press, 1997 edit. trans. W. D. Hall).
17. Peter F. Drucker, *The Landmarks of Tomorrow* (New York: Harper and Brothers, 1959).
18. William Lovett, *Life and Struggles of William Lovett in his Pursuit of Bread, Knowledge and Freedom with Some Short Accounts of the Different Associations he Belonged to and of the Opinions he Entertained* (1876; London: G. Bell and Sons, 1920).
19. Marzia Maccaferri, '"A co-operative of intellectuals": the Encounter between Co-Operative Values and Urban Planning. An Italian Case Study', in Anthony Webster et al. (eds), *The Hidden Alternative: Co-operative Values, Past, Present and Future* (Manchester: Manchester University Press, 2011), pp. 251–65.
20. J. M. Arizmendiarrieta, *La empresa para el hombre* (Bilbao: Alkar, 1984),

cited and translated in Claudia Sanchez Bajo and Bruno Roelants, *Capital and the Debt Trap: Learning from Cooperatives in the Global Crisis* (Basingstoke: Palgrave Macmillan, 2011); A. T. Culloty, *Nora Herlihy: Irish Credit Union Pioneer* (Dublin: Irish League of Credit Unions, 1990); Claudia Sanchez Bajo and Bruno Roelants, 'The Desjardins Cooperative Group: a financial movement for Quebec's development' and 'Ceralep Societé Nouvelle, France: David and Goliath in the global economy', in their *Capital and the Debt Trap*, pp. 152-75, 136-51.

21. Open University, 'The History of The OU', www.open.ac.uk/about/main/the-ou (2014; accessed 10 Jan. 2014).
22. Morten Levin and Davydd Greenwood, 'Pragmatic action research and the struggle to transform universities into learning communities', in Peter Reason and Hilary Bradbury, (eds), *Handbook of Action Research: Participative Inquiry and Practice* (London: Sage Publications, 2001), pp. 103-13.
23. Rebecca Boden, Penelope Ciancanelli, and Susan Wright, 'Trust universities? Governance for post-capitalist futures', *Journal of Co-operative Studies* 45.2 (2012), pp. 16-24.
24. Ree, *Proletarian Philosophers*, p. 191.
25. Dennis J. Farrington and David Palfreyman, *The Law of Higher Education* (new edn., Oxford: Oxford University Press, 2012), pp. 13-14.
26. Eric E. Robinson, *The New Polytechnics: the People's Universities* (Harmondsworth: Penguin, 1968); Robin Pedley, *Towards the Comprehensive University* (London: Macmillan, 1977).
27. Stephen Yeo, 'The pre-history and theory of credit', *Journal of Access and Credit Studies,* 1.1 (1998), pp. 53-69.
28. Boden et al., 'Trust universities?'.
29. Raymond Williams, *Communications* (Harmondsworth: Penguin, 1962), p. 122.
30. Boden et al., 'Trust universities?'.
31. A. M. Allchin, *N. F. S. Grundtvig: an Introduction to his Life & Work* (2nd edn., Aarhus: Aarhus University Press, 2015); A. W. Wright, *G. D. H. Cole and Socialist Democracy* (Oxford: Oxford University Press, 1979).

32. M. Neary et al., 'Final Report', learninglandscapes.lincoln.ac.uk (2009; accessed 14 May 2012); M. Neary and G. Saunders, 'Learning Landscapes and Leadership in Higher Education: the struggle for the idea of the university', Working Paper for the Centre for Educational Research and Development (Lincoln: University of Lincoln, 2010).

33. Lovett, *Life and Struggles of William Lovett*, pp. 35-6; J. F. C. Harrison, *Learning and Living 1790-1960: a Study in the History of the English Adult Education Movement* (London: Routledge and Kegan Paul, 1961); Jonathan Rose, *The Intellectual Life of the British Working Classes* (New Haven, CT: Yale University Press, 2002), pp. 58-91; Joint Committee, *Oxford and Working Class Education* (Oxford: Clarendon Press, 2008); Albert Mansbridge, *University Tutorial Classes* (London: Longmans, 1914).

34. Michael Barber, Katelyn Donnelly, and Saad Rizvi, *An Avalanche is Coming: Higher Education and the Revolution Ahead* (London: IPPR, 2013), available at https://www.ippr.org/publications/an-avalanche-is-coming-higher-education-and-the-revolution-ahead (accessed 28 March 2019); Robin Murray, *Co-operation in the Age of Google*, available www.uk.coop/ageofgoogle (2019; accessed 10 Jan. 2010).

35. 'Will Moocs be the scourge or saviour of higher education?' and 'Contact time a matter of degree', *The Guardian*, letters and emails 13 May, 16 May 2013.

36. Gaia University, www.gaiauniversity.org (2013).

37. Carole Cadwalladr, 'Goodbye to all this ... Is this the end of campus life?', *The New Review, The Observer*, 11 Nov. 2012, pp. 8-11; Khan Academy, www. khanacademy.org (2013; accessed 20 Jan. 2013).

38. Stephen Yeo, *Co-operative and Mutual Enterprises in Britain: Ideas from a Useable Past for a Modern Future* (London: LSE Centre for Civil Society, Report no. 4, 2002).

39. Mansbridge, *University Tutorial Classes*.

40. H. J. Twigg, *An Outline History of Co-operative Education* (Manchester: Co-operative Union, 1924); Linda McCullough Thew, *The Pit Village and the Store: Portrait of a Mining Past* (London: Pluto Press, 1985); John

Attfield, *With Light of Knowledge: One Hundred Years of Education in the Royal Arsenal Cooperative Society, 1877–1977* (London: Journeyman, 1981).

41. Tony Becher and Paul R. Trowler, *Academic Tribes and Territories: Intellectual Enquiry and the Culture of Disciplines* (2nd edn, Buckingham: The Society for Research into Higher Education and Open University Press, 2001).

42. Burton R. Clark, *Creating Entrepreneurial Universities: Organizational Pathways of Transformation* (London: IAU Press Pergamon/Elsevier, 1998); Rosemary Deem, Sam Hillyard, and Mike Reed, *Knowledge, Higher Education and the New Managerialism: The Changing Management of UK Universities* (Oxford: Oxford University Press, 2007); Michael Shattock, *Managing Successful Universities* (2nd edn, Maidenhead: Open University Press, 2010).

43. Gary Hamel, *The Future of Management* (Boston, MA: Harvard Business School Press, 2007).

44. John Fielden and G. Lockwood, *Planning and Management in Universities* (London: Chatto and Windus for Sussex University Press, 1973).

45. *Final Report ... Sussex* (1973).

46. E. P. Thompson, *Warwick University Ltd* (Harmondsworth: Penguin, 1971).

47. Asa Briggs, 'Drawing a new map of learning', in David Daiches (ed.), *The Idea of a New University: an Experiment in Sussex* (London: Andre Deutsch, 1964), pp. 60–80.

48. Yeo, 'Social movements and political action'.

49. Walter Benjamin, 'Eduard Fuchs, Collector and Historian', in Walter Benjamin, *One-Way Street* (London: New Left Books, 1979), pp. 349–86.

50. Clark, *Creating Entrepreneurial Universities*.

51. Johnston Birchall, *People-Centred Businesses: Co-operatives, Mutuals and the Idea of Membership* (Basingstoke: Palgrave Macmillan, 2011); Johnston Birchall and Richard Simmons, 'Member Participation in Mutuals: a Theoretical Model', in Johnston Birchall (ed.), *The New Mutualism in Public Policy* (London: Routledge, 2001), pp. 202–25; Edgar Parnell,

Co-operation, the Beautiful Idea: including a change agenda for co-operatives and mutuals (Oxford: Plunkett, Foundation, 2011); International Joint Project on Co-operative Democracy, *Making Membership Meaningful: Participatory Democracy in Co-operatives* (Saskatchewan: University of Saskatchewan, Centre for the Study of Co-operatives, 1995).

52. Melanie Newman, 'Use of headhunters to fill top jobs is "morally lazy"', *Times Higher Education,* 19 June 2008, http://www.timeshighereducation.co.uk/news/use-of-headhunters-to-fill-top-jobs-is-morally-lazy/402440.article (accessed 12 September 2012).

53. I learned about this remarkable initiative through personal contacts with Mike Neary and Joss Winn at Lincoln University and then by participating in a network of educational co-operatives built up over many years by Cilla Ross and the Co-operative College in Holyoake House, Manchester. In 2012 the College commissioned a thorough report, completed by Dan Cook as *Realising the Co-operative University: a consultancy report for The Co-operative College,* to explore the practical barriers to and enablers of a Co-operative University. A number of conferences were held, with up to 90 delegates from universities and from active co-operative and mutual initiatives working within and beyond university structures. The National Co-operative Archive and the lively documentation and records of the remarkable work towards a federated co-operative university, done while Cilla Ross was Principal of the College, are available in Holyoake House. Several doctorates await interested students of an initiative whose time will come. Start with Tom Woodin and Linda Shaw eds., *Learning for a Co-operative World: Education, social change and the Co-operative College* (London: UCL Institute of Education Press, 2019); Anca Volnea, 'Building a Co-operative University and gaining degree awarding powers' in *Co-op News,* April 2019, pp. 38–9; Tom Woodin ed. *Co-operation, Learning and Co-operative Values: Contemporary issues in education* (London: Routledge, 2015) pp. 144–146, in which I also list a fuller Bibliography for this chapter.

54. D. Matthews, 'Inside a co-operative university (Mondragón)',

Times Higher Education 2013, http://www.timeshighereducation. co.uk/features/inside-a-cooperative-university/ 2006776.fullarticle (accessed 29 September 2013); F. Molina and J. K. Walton, 'An alternative co-operative tradition: the Basque co-operatives of Mondragón', in Webster et al., *The Hidden Alternative*, pp. 226–250.
55. Boden et al., 'Trust universities?'.
56. Co-operative Free University, 2013.
57. Barber et al., *An Avalanche is Coming*; Penny Ciancelli, '(Re)producing universities: knowledge dissemination, market power and the global knowledge commons', in Debbie Epstein et al. (eds.), *World Yearbook of Education 2008. Geographies of Knowledge, Geometries of Power: Framing the Future of Higher Education* (New York: Routledge, 2007), pp. 67–84; Holmwood, *Manifesto for the Public University*.

Notes to Chapter 6

1. This chapter was conceived in order to clarify wider issues in the history of the CWS and the Co-operative Group which arose while I was working on J. T. W. Mitchell. The nearest I got to publishing on these issues was an eighty-page booklet for the Co-operative Congress of 2002: Stephen Yeo, *A chapter in the making of a Successful Co-operative Business: the Co-operative Wholesale Society 1973–2001* (Failsworth, Manchester in association with The Co-operative Group, 2002). My purpose was to establish a setting within which membership and belonging in the CWS could be understood and regarded as of social and political interest outside the CWS. This accounts for references to the CWS, particularly in Section 4 of this chapter. For a full business history of the CWS as it became the Co-operative Group, see John F. Wilson, Anthony Webster, Rachel Vorberg-Rugh, *Building Co-operation: A Business History of The Co-operative Group, 1863–2013* (Oxford: Oxford University Press, 2013).
2. For 'actually existing' as a concept, see Rudolf Bahro, *The Alternative*

in *Eastern Europe* (London: New Left Books, 1978), first published as *Die Alternative: zur Kritik des real existierenden Sozialismus* (Europaische Verlagsanstalt, 1977).
3. George Monbiot, *The Age of Consent* (London: Flamingo, 2003), p. 115.
4. W. P. Watkins served as Director of the International Co-operative Alliance (ICA) 1951–63 and as rapporteur of the ICA Commission on Co-operative Principles in 1965–6. Before that, he was a tutor at the Co-operative College UK 1920–29, before joining the staff of the ICA. He was one of the most prolific and thoughtful twentieth-century writers on Co-operation, including a time on the staff of *Reynolds News,* the Co-operative Sunday newspaper. From 1946 to 1950 he was Adviser on Co-operation to the West German Government, responsible for the rehabilitation of the movement in that country.
5. The alarm is widespread. A vivid articulation of alarm in Britain, and of co-operation and mutuality as a response from outside CMEs and from a highly placed politician, is David Blunkett's *Politics and Progress: Renewing Democracy and Civil Society* (London: Demos/Politicos, 2001). A Labour Party National Policy Forum Consultation Document on 'Democracy, Citizenship and Political Engagement', issued in 2001 following two massive electoral victories, was full of urgent alarm.
6. See Raymond Williams, *Marxism and Literature* (Oxford: Oxford University Press, 1977), pp. 121–8, for dominant, emergent, and residual.
7. The *locus classicus* for 'primitive' democracy as 'early' working-class practice and as highly participatory/direct/mutual is in S. and B. Webb, *Industrial Democracy* (London: Longmans, 1897).
8. The *locus classicus* here is J. A. Schumpeter, *Capitalism, Socialism and Democracy* (London: Allen and Unwin, 1943), particularly Part IV, chap. 21, 'The classical doctrine of democracy'. 'Liberal democracy' has sometimes stood in for 'classical', but on other occasions has been used from the Left to disparage 'bourgeois' democracy. For the complexities of 'liberal' democracy, see E. F. Biagini, 'Liberalism and Direct Democracy: John Stuart Mill and the Model of Ancient Athens',

in E. F. Biagini (ed.), *Citizenship and Community: Liberals, Radicals and Collective Identities in the British Isles, 1865–1931* (Cambridge: Cambridge University Press, 1996), pp. 21–44.
9. The *Concise Oxford Dictionary*, 5th ed. (Oxford: Oxford University Press, 1964) simply has 'state practising government by the people, direct or representative'.
10. Raymond Williams, *Keywords: A Vocabulary of Culture and Society*, rev. ed. (Fontana: London, 1983), p. 15, defines keywords as words the problems of whose meanings are 'inextricably bound up with the problems (they are) used to discuss'. 'Democracy' has the longest entry in the vocabulary, alongside the four other major keywords that informed Williams' entire *oeuvre:* 'industry', 'art', 'class', and 'culture'.
11. I became more aware of these following conversations at the BCICS Conference on 'Mapping Co-operative Studies in the New Millennium' at the University of Victoria in 2003, when talking with University of Saskatchewan delegates interested in First Nation links with modern Co-operatives.
12. Anthony Arblaster, *Democracy*, 2nd ed. (Buckingham: Open University Press, 1994). See pp. 79–86 for a brief introduction to a subject that has been best investigated by Quentin Skinner. His Ford Lectures in British History at the University of Oxford (2003) were on 'Freedom, Representation and Revolution, 1603–1641'. See also his *Visions of Politics*, 3 vols. (Cambridge: Cambridge University Press, 2002) and *Liberty before Liberalism* (Cambridge: Cambridge University Press, 1998). See also H. F. Pitkin, *The Concept of Representation* (Berkeley and Los Angeles: University of California Press, 1972).
13. This 'concept of liberty' became attached to Isaiah Berlin's iconic inaugural lecture in Oxford, *Two Concepts of Liberty* (Oxford: Clarendon Press, 1958). It reaches back to the Renaissance and to classical times; see also Quentin Skinner above.
14. E. Hobsbawm and T. O. Ranger (eds), *The Invention of Tradition* (Cambridge: Cambridge University Press, 1983).
15. Schumpeter's *Capitalism, Socialism and Democracy* accepts parties

as integral to the organisation of democracy as competition for government between elites; see 'Another Theory of Democracy', chap. 22, pp. 269–283.

16. Logie Barrow and Ian Bullock's *Democratic Ideas and the British Labour Movement* (Cambridge: Cambridge University Press, 1996) describes late-nineteenth- and early-twentieth-century debates within the British labour movement over the details of democratic form, including party organisation. Ian Bullock has published extensively on this theme since 1996. CMEs were integral to these debates within the labour movement. See also Lewis Minkin, *The Labour Party Conference* (London: Macmillan, 1980) and *The Contentious Alliance: Trade Unions and the Labour Party* (Edinburgh: Edinburgh University Press, 1991); and Paul Hirst, *Associative Democracy* (Cambridge: Polity, 1993, pp. 204–5) for a useful review of 'critiques of representative democracy that do not simply reject it'. See also M. Ostrogorski, *Democracy and the Organization of Political Parties* (London and New York: Macmillan, 1902) for a good example of the persistence of 'classical' models of democracy that are critical of Party forms, as were Liberals like John Stuart Mill and Socialists such as the members of the Social Democratic Federation (SDF) in Britain, in what was to become the 'Leninist' critique of liberal ('bourgeois') democracy. Henry Tam, a former policy head of civic renewal in the pre-1908 Labour Government, has published four committed and practical books since then, explaining the risks to democracy and how 'democracies' can be revitalised. Since I published 'A New Life: The Religion of Socialism in Britain 1883–1896' in *History Workshop: a journal of socialist historians* (Issue 4, Autumn 1977) pp. 5–56 and republished it for *A Useable Past* (Vol. 2) in 2018, I have not kept up with the excellent work by Mark Bevir, Jacqueline Turner, Anna Vaninskaya, and Thomas Linehan, critiquing and amplifying its themes.

17. David Marquand, *The Unprincipled Society* (London: Cape, 1988); Colin Crouch and David Marquand (eds), *Reinventing Collective Action: From the Global to the Local* (Oxford: Blackwell, 1995).

18. Harold J. Laski, *Democracy in Crisis* (London: Allen and Unwin, 1933), p. 64, refers to 'the restriction of the term "society" to the little group of leisured people who could make themselves notorious in the news by the conspicuous waste in expenditure of which they were capable by reason of their wealth'. John Bossy, 'Some Elementary Forms of Durkheim', *Past & Present* 95 (May 1982), pp. 2–18, is a more sustained analysis of the dilution/abstraction of 'society' (and of 'religion') in modern discourse.

19. For the Professional and Managerial Class (PMC), democracy, and socialism, see Stephen Yeo, 'Notes on Three Socialisms – Collectivism, Statism and Associationism – Mainly in Late-Nineteenth- and Early-Twentieth-Century Britain', in Carl Levy (ed.), *Socialism and the Intelligentsia, 1880–1914* (London: Routledge, 1987), pp. 219–270; and 'Three Socialisms: Statism, Collectivism, Associationism', in William Outhwaite and Michael Mulkay (eds), *Social Criticism and Social Theory: Essays for Tom Bottomore* (Oxford: Basil Blackwell, 1987), pp. 83–113, republished in *A Useable Past* Vol. 2.

20. To anticipate a later argument, readers familiar with the project of cooperation and mutuality and with the practice of CMEs will recognise connections between each of them and all the items in List B.

21. For representation, delegation, direction, and the role of experts in democracy, see S. and B. Webb, *Industrial Democracy* (London: Longmans, 1897).

22. See E. P. Thompson's reflections on 'The Rule of Law' at the end of *Whigs and Hunters: The Origin of the Block Act* (1975; Harmondsworth: Penguin, 1977), Pt 3, chap. 10, pp. 258–269.

23. Rights were the basis of the second of Berlin's 'Two Concepts …' and referred back to John Locke. Self-government is the basis for Quentin Skinner's 'third concept of liberty'. He has worked on this since 1981, establishing it historically and contextually, naming it 'republican' or 'neo-Roman' and distinguishing it from Berlin's first two concepts. The 'third concept' needs relating closely to the pre-history of CMEs. David Wootton, 'The Hard Look Back', *Times Literary Supplement* (14

March 2003), pp. 8–10, provides a useful overview of the 1,000-plus pages of Skinner's *Visions of Politics*.

24. W. P. Watkins, *Co-operative Principles Today and Tomorrow* (Manchester: Holyoake Books, Co-operative Union Ltd, 1986), p. 12.

25. Raymond Williams, *Culture and Society, 1780–1950* (1958; Harmondsworth: Penguin, 1961), pp. 285–324, makes this argument powerfully in a 'Conclusion' that is in a different, more political register than the rest of the book.

26. See Sherry R. Arnstein's 'ladder of citizen participation' in 'Participation and Planning', *The Journal of the American Planning Association* 35.4 (1969), pp. 216–224.

27. Carole Pateman, *Participation and Democratic Theory* (Cambridge: Cambridge University Press, 1970); David Held, *Models of Democracy* (Cambridge: Polity, 1987); David Beetham, *The Democratic Audit of the United Kingdom* (London: Charter 88 Trust, 1993). Beetham itemises some key principles and indices of democracy, thus showing the range of possible variation.

28. Hilary Wainwright, *Reclaim the State: Experiments in Popular Democracy* (London: Verso, 2003).

29. The works by Arblaster, Pateman, and Hirst cited above contain preliminary guides to an immense literature.

30. Among the many networks in this field are the 'new politics network' at www new-politics.net. This merged with Charter 88 in 2007, and the new politics weblink no longer functions. On 'partnerships', see Institute for Public Policy Research (IPPR), *Building Better Partnerships: the final report of the Commission on Public Private Partnerships* (London: IPPR, 2001), pp. 262–274, for a list of useful references.

31. Sidney and Beatrice Webb's work remains the richest sources for working-class democratic creativity at its apogee, even as they distanced themselves from it in the interests of what they saw as appropriate for an age of scientific and administrative expertise. The best modern guide to their work in this field is Royden J. Harrison, *The Life and Times of Sidney and Beatrice Webb: 1858–1905, the Formative Years*

(Basingstoke: Macmillan, 2000).

32. References to many sources for this paragraph may be found in Stephen Yeo, 'On the Uses of "Apathy"', *European Journal of Sociology* 15 (1974), pp. 279-311.

33. Eric Hobsbawm, *Age of Extremes: The Short Twentieth Century, 1914–1991* (London: Michael Joseph, 1994) and *The New Century* (London: Abacus, 1999), together with an extended review of Hobsbawm's work by Perry Anderson, 'The Age of EJH', *London Review of Books*, 3 and 17 Oct. 2002, provide one way into this complex question. The *New Century* is an extended analytical and thematic coda to the *Age of Extremes* with important material on democracy.

34. 'Resources for a journey of hope' is the title of the final chapter of Raymond Williams, *Towards 2000* (London: Chatto and Windus, 1983), pp. 241-269. In the same book, see also 'Democracy Old and New', pp. 102-127.

35. The word 'members' appears at least once in each of the seven Co-operative Principles in the 1995 Statement on Identity. According to Ron Roffey, *The Co-operative Way: The Origins and Progress of the Royal Arsenal and South Suburban Co-operative Societies* (South East Region, CWS, 1999), p. 109: 'Members are, in relation to the outside world, the Society'.

36. The International Joint Project on Co-operative Democracy, *Making Membership Meaningful: Participatory Democracy in Co-operatives* (Saskatchewan, Centre for the Study of Co-operatives, 1995).

37. Nicholas Deakin (ed.), *Membership and Mutuality: Proceedings of a Seminar Series Organised at the LSE Centre for Civil Society* (London: LSE Centre for Civil Society, Report Series, Report no. 3, 2002), pp. 17-20; Stephen Yeo, *Co-operative and Mutual Enterprises in Britain* (London: LSE Centre for Civil Society, Report Series, Report no. 4, 2002), pp. 32-5.

38. Charles Gide, *Consumers' Co-operative Societies* (Manchester: Co-operative Union Ltd., 1921), p. 2.

39. Johnston Birchall and Richard Simmons, 'Member Participation in

Mutuals: A Theoretical Model', in Johnston Birchall (ed.), *The New Mutualism in Public Policy* (London: Routledge, 2001), pp. 202-225; Richard Simmons and Johnston Birchall, 'What Motivates Co-op Members to Participate?' -- research carried out by Stirling University as part of a project entitled 'Creating and Supporting Stakeholder Members in Social Enterprises', draft report, June 2003, available from the Co-operative College UK.

40. Part of the Definition of Co-operatives in the 'Co-operative Statement of Identity and Principles as approved at the ICA Congress, Manchester, Sept. 1995'.
41. Williams, *Culture and Society 1780-1950*, cited above; see also his *Culture* (London: Fontana, 1981).
42. Watkins, *Co-operative Principles*, p. 4. Watkins having directed the ICA during times of conflict between compulsory and voluntary, 'Eastern' and 'Western' ideas of Co-operation, his book is particularly strong on voluntary commitment.
43. E. P. Thompson, *The Making of the English Working Class* (London: Gollancz, 1963), p. 24.
44. For 'social inventions as capital for CMEs to draw upon', see Yeo, *Co-operative and Mutual Enterprises in Britain*, pp. 38-45.
45. The second of the Co-operative Principles set out in the 1995 Statement.
46. Edgar Parnell, *Reinventing Co-operation: The Challenge of the 21st Century* (Oxford: Plunkett Foundation, 1999), p. 51.
47. For co-operation and the division of labour, see John Ruskin, *The Political Economy of Art* (London: Smith, Elder, and Co., 1857); Gide, *Consumers' Co-operative Societies*, pp. 5-7, 193-5, 237.
48. Watkins, *Co-operative Principles*, pp. 73-92, chapter 5 on 'Equity'. This remains one of the most thoughtful books on CMEs ever written.
49. Gide, *Consumers' Co-operative Societies*, pp. 75-6: 'Co-operative societies are like miniature republics, and one of their first principles is the equality of members.'
50. In 'not for profit' and 'for profit' enterprises that have members -- for example, companies limited by guarantee and companies limited by

shares – members have prescribed roles, unlike those in mutuals. One way of describing PLCs is as associations of capital, in contrast with CMEs, which are associations of people. See Gide, *Consumers' Co-operative Societies*, p. 79.

51. Parnell, *Reinventing Co-operation*, p. 7.
52. Summary terms such as possessive individualism, anomie, apathy, mechanical solidarity, alienation, commodification, privatisation, consumerism, and loss of social capital are more familiar in academic and policy-making circles than 'dismemberment'.
53. J. S. Mill, *Autobiography*, in vol. 1 of J. S. Mill, *The Collected Works*, ed. John M. Robson (Toronto: University of Toronto Press, London: Routledge and Kegan Paul, 1963-9); see also the posthumously published *Chapters on Socialism*, in *Collected Works*, vol. V.
54. Yeo, 'On the Uses of "Apathy"'.
55. Turnout in the 2001 General Election in Britain was 59 per cent, the lowest in any general election since 1918. For global references and material, see Richard Swift, *The No-Nonsense Guide to Democracy* (Oxford: New Internationalist Publications, 2002).
56. There was a failure from the Left of adequate critique and discourses for change, with democracy too often dismissed as only 'bourgeois', and 'centralism' too often embraced as 'democratic'. Co-operation and Mutuality as project and CMEs as practice were seldom seen, from the Left, as resources in this context, even by *social* democrats.
57. R. D. Putnam, *Making Democracy Work: Civic Traditions in Modern Italy* (Princeton, NJ: Princeton University Press, 1993) and *Bowling Alone: The Collapse and Revival of American Community* (New York: Simon and Schuster, 2000) have inspired widespread work on 'social capital', which is one conceptual framework within which to research and develop CMEs.
58. A former Deputy Leader of the British Labour Party wrote in 2003: 'the victory of personality over policy is almost complete. We are fast moving into a situation in which the party – as a democratic Institution – no longer exists. ...The cliché is "presidential". The

reality is the development of parties whose role is limited to choosing the candidate they think most likely to win. It is democracy that is at stake.' For more, see Roy Hattersley, 'Blair's a Winner as Labour Loses', *The Observer*, 23 March 2003.

59. 'According to Freedom House (headquarters Washington DC) the number of "liberal democracies" on the planet increased from 22 in 1950 to 44 in 1972; but between 1973 and 2000 it leaped to 85. In 2002 there were 119 "electoral democracies": a more elastic category.' For more, see Perry Anderson, *London Review of Books*, 17 Oct. 2002. See also 'Capitalism and Democracy', a survey in the 160th anniversary issue of *The Economist*, June 28–July 4 2003. One of the unintended (?) consequences of the end of World War II and then of the Cold War may come to be seen as the dilution of 'democracy'.

60. For a pre-1989, sophisticated expression of an alternative, see Rudolf Bahro, *The Alternative in Eastern Europe* (London: New Left Books, 1978), to which Raymond Williams' *Towards 2000* was, in part, a response from 'the West'.

61. *The Guardian*, 12 May 2003.

62. For figures, see *New Internationalist* (July 2001); P. Drucker, 'The Global Economy and the Nation State', *Foreign Affairs* (Sept–Oct. 1997), pp. 159–71); George Monbiot, *Captive State* (London: Pan Macmillan, 2001).

63. Wayne Ellwood, *The Non-Nonsense Guide to Globalization* (Oxford: New Internationalist Publications, 2001); Naomi Klein, *No Logo: No Space, No Choice, No Jobs* (London: Flamingo, 2000).

64. Robert Monks and Allen Sykes, *Capitalism Without Owners Will Fail* (London and New York: Centre for the Study of Financial Innovation, 2002).

65. Monbiot, *The Age of Consent* provides details on world organisations, governance, democracy, and access.

66. Anthony Giddens, *Capitalism and Modern Social Theory* (Cambridge: Cambridge University Press, 1971).

67. A concept developed by Rudolf Bahro in *The Alternative*.

68. Bob Sutcliffe, *100 Ways of Seeing an Unequal World* (London and New

York: Zed Books, 2001), provides graphic as well as statistical evidence for patterns of global inequality; David Ransom, *The No-Nonsense Guide to Fair Trade* (Oxford, New Internationalist Publications, 2001).

69. Incorporation, specialisation, and capitalisation provide examples of these pressures. If the essence of CMEs can be captured with the word 'mutuality', their presence, in all contexts that are not mutual (for example, in modern democracies), is inevitably surrounded by pressures towards loss of mutuality. These pressures are built into organisational success, if success is defined in terms of growth in scale and in scope. Size can become an independent variable, increasing the pressures to which CMEs are subject. CMEs can, of course, resist, in the name of co-operation and mutuality, but only by continual reinvention of themselves as the context changes. The effect of incorporation, specialisation, and capitalisation on CMEs constitutes their history, always requiring re-presentation as times change.

70. See Yeo, 'Theorizing Co-operative Studies: Obstacles and Opportunities for Twenty-First-Century Co-operative and Mutual Enterprises': Chapter 7 in this volume.

71. Parnell, *Reinventing Co-operation*, p. 11.

72. Raymond Williams, *The Long Revolution* (London: Chatto and Windus, 1961), pp. 296–8, has a sharp analysis of the image of the person as 'consumer'. See also David Marquand, *The Unprincipled Society* (London: Cape, 1988), pp. 29–30; and Nick Cohen, 'Buy Us — We're Labour', *The Observer*, 27 April 2003, which comments on Catherine Needham's *Citizen-consumers* (London: Catalyst, 2003).

73. Percy Redfern, *The New History of the CWS* (London: J. M. Dent, 1938), pp. 521–4.

74. Most obviously in *The Report of the Co-operative Commission: The Co-operative Advantage* (2001).

75. Capitalists wanting to take over the CWS in the late 1990s wished that members' representatives in members' meetings had been free to act less like delegates than they were. They saw Members Meetings — indeed 'procedure' as a whole — as distinctly awkward obstacles,

preventing a take-over that would have been easier in a PLC.

76. The International Joint Project on Co-operative Democracy, *Making Membership Meaningful: Participatory Democracy in Co-operatives*, p. 309. In Chapter 7, 'Theory', this study lists six areas where cultivation can occur. This list is important because it is rooted in actuality and in a literature review of key references, listed in p. 314 n. 11.
77. The International Joint Project on Co-operative Democracy, 1995.
78. Parnell, *Reinventing Co-operation,* is particularly strong on 'business co-operation' as a specific form of Co-operative, and on agriculture, where the form has been particularly strong.
79. This is dealt with in my 'Theorizing Co-operative Studies: Obstacles and Opportunities for Twenty-First-Century Co-operative and Mutual Enterprises' (Chapter 7 in this volume).

Notes to Chapter 7

1. A phrase of Charles Gide in *Consumers' Co-operative Societies* (1921), translated from the French by the staff of the Co-operative Reference Library Dublin (Manchester: Co-operative Union Ltd, 1921), p. 79; also used by Edgar Parnell in *Reinventing Co-operation: The Challenge of the 21st Century* (Long Hanborough: Plunkett Foundation, 1999). For the restlessness and rootlessness of capital, see Marshall Berman's reading of Marx in *All That is Solid Melts into Air: The Experience of Modernity* (London: Verso, 1983).
2. For an accessible modern account crossing all continents and all sectors, and with a useful bibliography (pp. 237–246), see Johnston Birchall, *The International Co-operative Movement* (Manchester and New York: Manchester University Press, 1997). Dynamic co-operation outside 'the Co-operative Movement', particularly from the 1970s onwards, also has to be brought into the picture, viz. 'community action', 'community politics', cultural, historical, ethnic, wholefood, and environmental collectives, etc. It was only towards the end of the

1990s in Britain that relations between these initiatives and 'the Co-op' began to be mutually reinforcing, largely through the work of the United Kingdom Co-operative Council (UKCC).

3. CMEs, as they were called in the Oxfordshire Mutuality Task Force Report, 'Mutuality: Owning the Solution' (Oxford: Co-operative Futures, 2000).

4. George Monbiot, *The Age of Consent: A Manifesto for a New World Order* (London: Flamingo, 2003), p. 67.

5. 'Men and women of Co-operative quality' is a phrase used in R. L. Marshall, *Co-operative Education: A Handbook of Practical Guidance for Co-operative Educationalists* (Manchester: Co-operative Union Education Department, n.d.). 'We shall have ...' concludes section 2 of the Manifesto of the Communist Party, written by Karl Marx and Friedrich Engels in 1847–8.

6. In Stephen Yeo, 'Whose Story? An Argument from within Current Historical Practice in Britain', in *Journal of Contemporary History* 21 (1986), pp. 295–320, and 'Difference, Autobiography and History', in *Literature and History* 14.1 (Spring 1988), pp. 37–47, I attempted to raise some of the issues from the point of view of social history.

7. Eileen Yeo, *The Contest for Social Science: Relations and Representations of Gender and Class* (London: Rivers Oram, 1995).

8. Ian MacPherson, 'Encouraging Associative Intelligence: Co-operatives, Shared Learning and Responsible Citizenship', in *Co-operative Learning and Responsible Citizenship in the 21st Century*, Co-operative College Papers, new series, no. 1 (Manchester: Co-operative College, 2003), pp. 11–19; P. J. Gurney, 'George Jacob Holyoake: Socialism, Association and Co-operation in Nineteenth-Century England', in S. Yeo (ed.), *New Views of Co-operation* (London: Routledge, 1988); Peter Gurney, *Co-operative Culture and the Politics of Consumption in England* (Manchester: Manchester University Press, 1996), pp. 29–37.

9. A defining work in the history of 'le mouvement sociale' (which remains the title of the French 'Labour History' journal) and from which Marx learned while he was in Paris, Lorenz von Stein, *Le Mouvement Sociale*

en France (1842) was translated as *The Social Movement in France* (New Jersey: Bedminster Press, 1964).

10. For the history of the terminology of 'the movement' in its 'anti-globalisation' setting, see Monbiot, *The Age of Consent*, p. 2.

11. For 'dominant', 'emergent', and 'residual' as useful terms in cultural studies and social history, see Raymond Williams, *Marxism and Literature* (Oxford: Oxford University Press, 1977), pp. 121–127.

12. For 'capitalism' (etc.), see J. Dubois, *Le Vocabulaire politique et social en France de 1869 à 1872* (Paris: 1963) cited in E. J. Hobsbawm, *The Age of Capital 1848–1875* (London: Sphere, 1977), p. 13: '*capitalism* hardly occurs before 1849 or comes into wider currency before the 1860s'. For the socialist vocabulary, see A. E. Bestor, 'The Evolution of the Socialist Vocabulary', *Journal of the History of Ideas* 9.3 (1948), pp. 259–302; and for entries on 'socialist' and related terms, see Raymond Williams, *Keywords: A Vocabulary of Culture and Society* (London: Flamingo, 1983).

13. In the sense of 'organic' used throughout the work of Emile Durkheim ('organic' as opposed to 'mechanical' solidarity) and Antonio Gramsci ('organic intellectuals').

14. See Sonnet 124 and the note to it in W. Shakespeare, *The Sonnets*, ed. G. Blakemore Evans (Cambridge: Cambridge University Press, 1996), p. 238.

15. *Private Action, Public Benefit: A Review of Charities and the Wider Not-for-profit Sector* (London: Cabinet Office, Strategy Unit, Sept. 2002), pp. 14–15: 'overview of the sector' with a diagram. There was some question whether a key Department of Trade and Industry (DTI) paper on social enterprise in the same year would include CMEs at all, which in the end it did, following pressure from Co-ops UK. See *Social Enterprise: A Strategy for Success* (London: DTI, July 2002).

16. 'Arranging the powers of production, distribution, education and government' were among the original Objectives of the Rochdale Pioneers in the 1840s and 1850s.

17. Raymond Williams, *Culture* (London: Fontana, 1981), pp. 148–180, 'Forms', and pp. 206–233, 'Organization'. Williams's work on culture,

class, and their formations will be essential for future work on CMEs as distinct cultural forms: it is a waste to see such work in cultural studies as only, or mainly, useful to literary studies and art. For working people in particular, as Williams also points out, organisation/association *is* culture.

18. Raymond Williams, *The Welsh Industrial Novel* (Cardiff: Cardiff University Press, 1978), pp. 18–19. The double quote is from a novel by Gwyn Thomas, *All Things Betray Thee* (1949).
19. Philip Pullman, *The Amber Spyglass* (London: Scholastic, 2000), p. 548.
20. 'Humankind must at last grow up. We must recognize that the Other is ourselves' were the concluding sentences of E. P. Thompson, 'Beyond the Cold War', in E. P. Thompson, *Zero Option* (London: Merlin Press, 1982), p. 188.
21. G. J. Holyoake. *Self-Help by the People: The History of the Rochdale Pioneers*, editions in 1857, 1878, 1893 (Sonnenschein, London) and 1907 (New York). This is the first and a still invaluable source, particularly for the Pioneers' ambition and culture. See also Stephen Yeo, 'A celebration of the modern personality of "Co-op. Original": Revisiting the Pioneers with the help of G. J. Holyoake, their first historian', in *Co-operative College Papers*, new series, no. 5 (Manchester: Co-operative College, 2005).
22. I owe this memory to an interview with Ian Pyper.
23. Gide, *Consumers' Co-operative Societies*, p. 10.
24. Stephen Yeo, 'Notes on Three Socialisms – Collectivism, Statism, and Associationism – Mainly in Late Nineteenth- and Early-Twentieth-Century Britain', in Carl Levy (ed.), *Socialism and the Intelligentsia 1880–1914* (London: Routledge, 1987), pp. 219–270; 'Three Socialisms: Statism, Collectivism, Associationism', in William Outhwaite and Michael Mulkay (eds), *Social Criticism and Social Theory: Essays for Tom Bottomore* (Oxford: Basil Blackwell, 1987), pp. 83–113.
25. Peter Nettl, 'The German Social Democratic Party 1890–1914 as a Political Model', *Past and Present* 30 (1965), pp. 65–95; Carl E. Schorske, *German Social Democracy 1905–17: The Development of the Great Schism*

(Cambridge, Mass.: Harvard University Press, 1963).
26. Parnell, *Reinventing Co-operation*, p. 5.
27. Neil Smelser, *Social Change in the Industrial Revolution: An Application of Theory to the British Cotton Industry* (London: Routledge, 1959), employs this Talcott Parsonian 'functionalist' concept.
28. *Report of the Co-operative Commission: the Co-operative Advantage*, 2001.
29. See the Reports cited in n. 15 above, together with *The Role of the Voluntary and Community Sectors in Service Delivery: A Cross-cutting Review* (London: H.M. Treasury, Sept. 2002).
30. Williams, *Keywords*, p. 15.
31. Related terms such as 'l'économie sociale' and 'le mouvement sociale' also retained harder movement-connected meanings in French for longer than their equivalents did in English.
32. For Mick Fletcher's work in this context, quoted from an unpublished paper, see Stephen Yeo, *Organic Learning: Mutual Enterprise and the Learning and Skills Agenda* (Leicester: National Institute for Adult and Continuing Education, 2000).
33. Johnston Birchall, 'Conclusion: The Future of Mutuality', in Johnston Birchall (ed.), *The New Mutualism in Public Policy* (London: Routledge, 2001), pp. 243–249.
34. Key Economic Performance Indicators (KEPIs) were one of the most interesting outcomes of the Co-operative Commission. The Co-operative Union, which became Co-operatives UK, developed them during 2001 for use and comparison among member Societies. Key Co-operative and Social Performance Indicators were prepared in draft form for the Co-operative Congress in Manchester in May 2003 by the National Centre for Business and Sustainability, working for Co-operatives UK.
35. Birchall, 'Conclusion', p. 243.
36. I take 'Modern Social Theory' from Anthony Giddens, *Capitalism and Modern Social Theory: An Analysis of the Writings of Marx, Durkheim and Max Weber* (Cambridge: Cambridge University Press, 1971).
37. 'To deconstruct does not mean to destroy, but to show that terms which

seem to be opposites (say, "man" or "woman") violently suppress the ways in which they are secretly in collusion': Terry Eagleton, 'Jacques Derrida', *New Statesman*, 14 July 2003, p. 31.

38. 'Simple co-operation' is used here in the technical sense of an early, 'primitive' 'stage' of development in which divisions of labour have not been elaborated in the same ways that they later became.

39. I first heard it used in the meetings of the Oxfordshire Mutuality Task Force, by Peter Couchman, then the Membership and Corporate Affairs Manager of the Oxfordshire, Swindon, and Gloucester Co-operative Society.

40. I should absolve Giddens here. What follows in the text is *my* take on the thought of Marx and Weber, and not that of Giddens. In the case of Durkheim, in whose work I have done less primary reading, what follows is rooted in Giddens' exceptionally lucid and original 'Durkheim's Writings in Sociology and Social Philosophy', which serves as the introduction to *Emile Durkheim: Selected Writings*, ed. A. Giddens (Cambridge: Cambridge University Press, 1972), pp. 1–50. On Durkheim, I have also learned much from Philip Corrigan, including his *The Great Arch: English State Formation as Cultural Revolution* (Oxford: Blackwell, 1985). See also the work of Philip Abrams.

41. E. P. Thompson, *The Making of the English Working Class* (London: Gollancz, 1963), Preface.

42. See also Thompson, 'Eighteenth-century English Society: Class Struggle without Class?', in *Social History* 3.2 (May 1978), pp. 133–165. Brett Fairbairn, 'History from the Ecological Perspective: Gaia Theory and the Problem of Co-operatives in Turn-of-the-Century Germany', *American Historical Review* 99.4 (Oct. 1994), pp. 1203–1239.

43. Pioneering work on 'moral economy' in practice was done by E. P. Thompson in *Customs in Common* (Harmondsworth: Penguin, 1993), particularly chapters 4 and 5. This work has not yet been sufficiently used as a way into understanding CMEs, although the concept of 'moral economy' is slowly creeping into the study of Friendly Societies and Co-operatives.

44. Gareth Stedman Jones, 'Engels and the Genesis of Marxism', *New Left Review* 106 (1977), pp. 79–104.
45. Stephen Yeo, 'Co-operative Association' and 'Working-class Movements' in Tom Bottomore (ed.), *A Dictionary of Marxist Thought* (Oxford: Blackwell, 1983), pp. 95–6, 528–531.
46. Max Weber, *The Protestant Ethic and the Spirit of Capitalism,* trans. Talcott Parsons, with a Foreword by R. H. Tawney (London: Unwin University Books, 1930).
47. H. H. Gerth and C. Wright Mills, *From Max Weber: Essays in Sociology* (London: Routledge, 1948). See Part 3, 'Religion', pp. 267–363, particularly 'Religious rejections of the world and their directions'; Max Weber, *The Sociology of Religion* (1922), trans. E. Fischoff (London: Methuen, 1963); R. Bendix, *Max Weber: An Intellectual Portrait* (London: Heinemann, 1960).
48. Giddens, *Durkheim,* pp. 1–2.
49. Giddens, *Durkheim,* p. 41.
50. The question is raised at the end of Weber's *The Protestant Ethic.*
51. Bryan Wilson, *Sects and Society: A Sociological Study of Three Religious Groups in Britain* (London: Heinemann, 1961), and many subsequent works on 'Patterns of Sectarianism'.
52. Giddens, *Durkheim,* p. 10.
53. Giddens, *Durkheim,* p. 45.
54. Giddens, *Durkheim,* p. 2.
55. Giddens, *Durkheim,* p. 10.
56. Giddens, *Durkheim,* p. 21.
57. Giddens, *Durkheim,* pp. 22–24.
58. Giddens, *Durkheim,* p. 21.
59. Giddens, *Durkheim,* pp. 20–21. Guild Socialism became attractive to G. D. H. Cole in Britain, a generation after Durkheim. As a committed academic and political advocate of co-operation in Britain, Cole will remain an important figure in Co-operative Studies. He wrote a great deal on co-operation, including *A Century of Co-operation* (Manchester: Co-operative Union, 1944) to mark the centenary of the Rochdale

Pioneers. A. W. Wright (a leading New Labour MP who stood down in 2010 to return to academia) published *G. D. H. Cole and Socialist Democracy* (Oxford: Clarendon Press, 1979) without an indexed reference to the Co-operative Movement.

60. Giddens, *Durkheim*, p. 9.
61. John Ruskin, *The Political Economy of Art* (London: Unwins, 1857).
62. Giddens, *Durkheim*, p. 7. The *Gemeinschaft* idea is mine, not Durkheim's. This may explain why Edgar Parnell is so definite in *Reinventing Co-operation* that Co-operation has nothing to do with the 'collective', but is all about maximising the 'individual'.
63. Giddens, *Durkheim*, p. 6.
64. Giddens, *Durkheim*, p. 12.
65. Johnston Birchall and Richard Simmons, 'Member Participation in Mutuals: A Theoretical Model', in Johnston Birchall (ed.), *The New Mutualism in Public Policy* (London: Routledge, 2001), pp. 202–225; Fairbairn, 'History from the Ecological Perspective', pp. 1203–1239; and Richard Simmons and Johnston Birchall, 'What Motivates Co-op Members to Participate?' (research carried out by Stirling University as part of 'Creating and Supporting Stakeholder Members in Social Enterprises', a draft report, June 2003, available from the Co-operative College UK).
66. J. Habermas, *The Structural Transformation of the Public Sphere: An Inquiry into a Category of Bourgeois Society*, trans. T. Burger and F. Lawrence (Cambridge Mass: Harvard University Press, 1989); Eileen Yeo (ed.), *Radical Femininity: Women's Self Representation in the Public Sphere* (Manchester: Manchester University Press, 1998).
67. E. Durkheim, *Professional Ethics and Civic Morals* (London and New York: Routledge, 1957), pp. 76–110, lectures on 'Civic Morals — Form of the State — Democracy'.
68. Giddens, *Durkheim*, pp. 20–21.
69. The best-known examples are Stephen Jay Gould, Richard Dawkins, and Steve Jones, and each has published voluminously. For Gould, see ten volumes of 'Reflections in Natural History', published between

1977 and 2002, beginning with *Ever Since Darwin* and ending with *I Have Landed* (London: Cape and Penguin, 1977-2002). For Dawkins, see volumes between *The Selfish Gene* (Oxford: Oxford University Press, 1976) and *A Devil's Chaplain* (London: Weidenfeld, 2003). For Jones, see, for example, *The Language of the Genes: Biology, History and the Evolutionary Future* (London: Harper Collins, 1994).

70. David Rogers, *New Mutualism and the Third Estate* (London: the Co-operative Party, January 1999).

71. Gould is strong on this in his essays cited above, but in all his work culminating in *The Structure of Evolutionary Theory* (Harvard: Belknap, 2002).

72. Most notably between Gould and Dawkins in the *New York Review of Books* and elsewhere. For Gould's polemic, see 'Darwinian Fundamentalism', Parts 1 and 2, in *New York Review of Books*, June 12th 1997, pp. 34-7 and June 26th 1997, pp. 47-52. For Dawkins' summation of the outstanding issues after Gould's early death, see *The Devil's Chaplain*. As a social historian, I am struck by the issues in common between these debates and those, for example, between E. P. Thompson and L. Althusser/Althusserians during the 1970s and early 1980s, for which see E. P. Thompson, *The Poverty of Theory and other essays* (London: Merlin, 1978). Gould and Thompson are equally fine polemicists.

73. Gurney, *Co-operative Culture*, ch. 5, 'The sense of the past' (pp. 111-143) is the first attempt at an overview of these histories which represent a singular cultural achievement. Co-operators' 'sense of the past' is closely connected to our sense of an available future, and it is an object for research and development in Co-operative Studies.

74. See R. G. Garnett, 'E. T. Craig, Communitarian, Educator, Phrenologist', *The Vocational Aspect of Secondary and Further Education* 30 (Spring 1963), pp. 135-150.

75. Logie Barrow, *Independent Spirits: Spiritualism and English Plebians 1850-1910* (London: Routledge, 1986), is one among many 'History Workshop' studies of plebeian intellectuals, many of whom were, of

course, CME members and activists.
76. Matt Ridley, *The Origins of Virtue* (London: Penguin, 1997), pp. 259–265, ends with a vivid section: 'Who stole the community?'. This is of great interest to Co-operators, coming as it does more from a Rightist than a Leftist, anti-State position.
77. Rogers, *New Mutualism and the Third Estate*, pp. 6–8.
78. Gould, *The Structure*, pp. 471–3.
79. Barry J. Nalebuff and Adam M. Brandenburger, *Co-opetition* (London: Harper Collins Business, 1997); for 'islands of meaning', see E. Zerubavel, *The Fine Line: Making Distinctions in Everyday Life* (New York: Free Press, 1991); for 'groupish', see Margaret Gilbert in a commentary on an article in *Behavioural and Brain Sciences*, cited in Matt Ridley, *The Origins*, p. 270 n. 5.
80. Mary Midgley, 'James Lovelock', *New Statesman* (14 July 2003), p. 21.
81. Fairbairn, 'History from an Ecological Perspective'.
82. Fairbairn, 'History from an Ecological Perspective', p. 1204.

Notes to Chapter 8

1. Gregory Claeys, *Citizens and Saints: Politics and Anti-politics in Early British Socialism* (Cambridge: Cambridge University Press, 1989), p. 7.
2. In the *London Co-operative Magazine*, Nov. 1827. The reference was to 'the Communionists or Socialists'. The word was not widely used by Owenites until the mid-1830s. In the 1820s they used phrases such as the 'new view of society', the '*social* system' [my emphasis] and 'co-operation'. See A. E. Bestor, 'The Evolution of the Socialist Vocabulary', *Journal of the History of Ideas* 9 (1948), pp. 259–302, and J. F. C. Harrison, *Quest for the New Moral World: Robert Owen and the Owenites in Britain and America* (New York: Scribner, 1969), p. 45. For earlier usages in Latin and Italian in the mid-eighteenth century, see Claeys, *Citizens and Saints*, p. 40.
3. Gregory Claeys, "'Individualism', "Socialism", and "Social Science":

Further Notes on a Process of Conceptual Formation 1800–50', *Journal of the History of Ideas* 47 (1986), pp. 81–93.

4. Ian MacPherson's keynote speech 'The Values of Co-operation' at the 'Co-operative Values' Manchester conference in July 2009, for which my chapter here was also first drafted, contained an interesting discussion of individualism and co-operation which generated a fruitful discussion, for and against allowing individualism into co-operation.

5. Divisions of labour between concepts as well as persons is a crucial, perhaps *the* crucial point of entry into the history and practice of different forms and periods of socialism. They are also a way of seeing a, or the, central concern of co-operatives and mutuals, and they need theorising and historicising as such. The index references in Claeys, *Citizens and Saints* to the 'division of labour', and to 'specialisation' and 'all-rounded development' are particularly helpful, as are the index references in Claeys, *Machinery, Moral Economy and the Millennium: From Moral Economy to Socialism, 1815–60* (Cambridge: Polity, 1987). See also Richard N. Hunt, *The Political Ideas of Marx and Engels, vol 2 Classical Marxism, 1850–1895* (London: Macmillan, 1984); Ali Rattansi, *Marx and the Division of Labour* (London: Macmillan, 1982); Hal Draper, *Karl Marx's Theory of Revolution,* 2 vols (New York: Monthly Review Press, 1977); Tom Bottomore, 'Socialism and the Division of Labour', in Bhiku Parekh (ed.), *The Concept of Socialism* (New York: Holmes and Meier, 1975), pp. 154–61.

6. Rob Hopkins, *The Transition Handbook: from Oil Dependency to Local Resistance* (Dartington: Green Books, 2008), p. 50.

7. See Chapter 7 above for what was first published as Stephen Yeo, 'Theorizing Co-operative Studies: Obstacles and Opportunities for Twenty-First Century Co-operative and Mutual Enterprises', in Ian MacPherson and Erin McLaughlin-Jenkins (eds), *Integrating Diversities within a Complex Heritage: Essays in the Field of Co-operative Studies* (University of Victoria, Canada: New Rochdale Press, 2008), pp. 345–391.

8. William Lovett, *The Life and Struggles of William Lovett in his Pursuit of Bread, Knowledge and Freedom* (1876; incomplete reprint, London: MacGibbon and Kee, 1967).
9. Hopkins, *Transition Handbook*.
10. Sidney and Beatrice Webb, *History of Trade Unionism* (London: Longmans, Green & Co., 1894).
11. Sidney and Beatrice Webb, *Industrial Democracy* (Longmans, Green & Co., 1897).
12. Royden Harrison, *The Life and Times of Sidney and Beatrice Webb, 1858–1905, The Formative Years* (London: Macmillan, 2000), p. 218.
13. John Dunn, *Political Obligations in their Historical Context* (Cambridge: Cambridge University Press, 1980); *The Politics of Socialism* (Cambridge: Cambridge University Press, 1984); *Democracy, a History* (London: Penguin, 2006).
14. And there is every indication that he has the stamina to continue: during 2009 he completed a 145,000-word book on the late-nineteenth to early-twentieth-century 'age of imperialism' phase of the story of socialism in Britain. A dozen articles in books and learned journals are listed in *Citizens and Saints*, pp. 348–9, and there have been many since then.
15. Stephen Yeo, 'Notes on Three Socialisms – Collectivism, Statism and Associationism – Mainly in Late-Nineteenth and Early-Twentieth-Century Britain', in Carl Levy (ed.) (1987), *Socialism and the Intelligentsia 1880–1914* (London: Routledge, 1987), pp. 219–270; also in 'Three Socialisms: Statism, Collectivism, Associationism', in William Outhwaite and Michael Mulkay (eds), *Social Criticism and Social Theory: Essays for Tom Bottomore* (Oxford: Basil Blackwell, 1987), pp. 83–113; 'Socialism, the State, and Some Oppositional Englishness', in R. Colls and P. Dodd, (eds), *Englishness, Politics and Culture 1880–1920* (London: Croom Helm, 1986), pp. 308–369. See also Vol. 2 of *A Useable Past* for these essays, lightly revised.
16. A. E. Bestor, *Backwoods Utopias: the Sectarian and Owenite Phases of Communitarian Socialism in America, 1663–1829* (Philadelphia, PA:

University of Pennsylvania Press, 1950), was important in identifying specifically 'communitarian' socialism and contrasting it with other socialisms. In a different discipline, 'communitarian' philosophers such as Alasdair Macintyre continue to point to small communities and co-operatives as cells for ethical transmission and growth against individualism in our times: see his *Selected Essays, Vol 1 Tasks of Philosophy* and *Vol 2 Ethics and Politics* (Cambridge: Cambridge University Press, 2006).

17. In his correspondence (Book X) with the Emperor Trajan, from Bithynia, where he had been sent as a Roman Senator, Pliny the Younger reported on a bad fire and asked Trajan to consider setting up a small fire company or guild, small enough to be easy to keep an eye on. Trajan's reply is a wonderful example of the fear of any more or less free-standing associations which might turn into 'hetaeriae', like political clubs/secret societies/factions etc. 'Give them the name we may and however good the reasons for organisation, such associations will soon degenerate …'. He refused the request. I owe this reference to Stirling Smith. Statists are always wary of free associational life, however un-political. Pliny the Younger's *Complete Letters* translated by P. G. Walsh are in a World's Classics edition (Oxford, OUP, 2006).

18. Stephen Yeo, 'Co-operation, Mutuality and the Democratic Deficit', in Ian MacPherson and Erin McLaughlin-Jenkins (eds), *Integrating Diversities within a Complex Heritage: Essays in the Field of Co-operative Studies* (University of Victoria, Canada: New Rochdale Press, 2008), pp. 223–279. Also in this book as Chapter 6.

19. For a defence of socialism against the Cold War assumption that it necessarily results in totalitarianism, see Claeys, *Citizens and Saints*, pp. 13–14; and, for Owen's democratic thought, the whole of chapter 2, 'Paternalism and democracy in the politics of Robert Owen', pp. 63–105, and chapter 3, 'Communitarianism and personal liberty', pp. 119–129.

20. Claeys, *Citizens and Saints*, p. 14.

21. Peter Brown, *Augustine of Hippo* (1967; new edn., Berkeley: University

of California Press, 2000), p. 314.

22. With the communist or socialist party or branch playing a similar role to the church as theorised by St Augustine: 'in waiting', representative of what *will* occur rather than as an active agent. There was something of this in the 'religion of socialism' which I described in Stephen Yeo, 'A New Life, the Religion of Socialism in Britain, 1883–1896', *History Workshop* 4 (Autumn 1977), pp 5–56 and which is revised in Volume 2 of my *A Useable Past*. Such *attentisme* clearly has the effect of making tactical and strategic planning and organisation seem less necessary.

23. Claeys, *Citizens and Saints*, p. 219.

24. 'It is now often conceded that the anti-political impulse in social and political thought after 1750 was much more extensive than was once believed and was built upon a widely circulated and powerfully articulated distinction between state and society', Claeys, *Citizens and Saints*, p. 15 at n. 17. Sheldon Wolin, *Politics and Vision* (Boston: Little Brown, 1969), pp. 286–434, is a key reference for this orientating, strategic observation by Claeys.

25. Claeys, *Citizens and Saints*, p. 313.

26. Claeys, *Citizens and Saints*, p. 162.

27. Claeys, *Citizens and Saints*, p. 66.

28. In chapter 27 of *Capital* vol. 3, for which, alongside other treatments of co-operatives by Marx, see Stephen Yeo, 'Co-operative Association', in Tom Bottomore (ed.), *A Dictionary of Marxist Thought* (Oxford: Blackwell, 1983), pp. 95–6.

29. Claeys, *Citizens and Saints*, pp. 192–3.

30. For which, see all of Part III of Claeys, *Citizens and Saints*, 'The Origins of Social Radicalism', pp. 167–326.

31. Claeys, *Citizens and Saints*, p. 220.

32. E. P. Thompson, *The Making of the English Working Class* (1963 and Harmondsworth: Penguin Books, 1977), p. 861.

33. E. J. Hobsbawm, *Primitive Rebels* (Manchester: Manchester University Press, 1959).

34. The Leeds Redemption Society (1845) formed the last strictly Owenite

community in Britain, in South Wales. It lasted from 1847 to 1855; see J. F. C. Harrison, *Social Reform in Victorian Leeds: the Work of James Hole, 1820–1895* (Leeds: Thoresby Society, 1954).

35. Claeys, *Citizens and Saints*, p. 267.
36. William Morris, 'The Policy of Abstention', in May Morris, *William Morris: Artist, Writer, Socialist: Vol 2 Morris as a Socialist* (1936; New York: Russell, 1966). The best modern exposition of this policy is in Perry Anderson, *Arguments Within English Marxism* (London: Verso (1980).
37. Raymond Williams, *Culture and Society* (London: Chatto and Windus, 1958), 'Conclusion', argues for association as class culture.
38. Claeys, *Citizens and Saints*, p. 14.
39. Claeys, *Citizens and Saints*, Chapter 5, 'Owenism and the emergence of social radicalism', pp. 169–207: 'the specifically Owenite contribution to the radicalism of these years … has never been detailed and categorised adequately', p. 170.
40. Claeys, *Citizens and Saints*, pp. 14–15.
41. Claeys, *Citizens and Saints*, p. 170.
42. Peter Gurney, 'Labour's Great Arch: Cooperation and Cultural Revolution in Britain, 1795-1926', in Ellen Furlough and Carl Strikwerda, *Consumers against Capitalism?: Consumer Co-operation in Europe, North America, and Japan, 1840-1990* (Lanham, MD and Oxford: Rowman and Littlefield, 1999), pp. 135–171. See also his *Co-operative Culture and the Politics of Consumption in England, 1870-1930* (Manchester: Manchester University Press, 1996), and 'George Jacob Holyoake: Socialism, Association and Co-operation in Nineteenth-Century England', in Stephen Yeo (ed.), *New Views of Co-operation* (London: Routledge, 1988), pp. 52–72. Philip Corrigan and Derek Sayer, *The Great Arch: English State Formation as Cultural Revolution* (Oxford: Blackwell, 1982), inspired much of this work by using Marx's 'Great Arch' trope for the long transition to capitalism.
43. *Man*, no. 14 (13 October 1833) p. 108, quoted in Claeys, *Citizens and Saints*, p. 197.

44. Claeys, *Citizens and Saints*, p. 197.
45. Claeys, *Citizens and Saints*, p. 199.
46. Claeys, *Citizens and Saints*, pp. 148–50 and 159–161, on exchange as a focus for early socialist thought, will be of interest to fair-trade and trade-justice activists. As with fraternity in *liberty, equality and* ..., so exchange in *production, distribution and* ... has been neglected in later socialist thinking.
47. Claeys, *Citizens and Saints*, p. 186: 'the Owenites, as well, were capable of changing their minds on both strategic issues and the ultimate value of Owen's views on property, commerce and other matters'.
48. Claeys, *Machinery, Moral Economy and the Millennium*, p. 111.
49. Claeys, *Machinery, Moral Economy and the Millennium*, p. 117.
50. The quotes from Mudie are in Claeys, *Machinery, Moral Economy and the Millennium*, pp. 86–87.
51. Percy Redfern, *New History of the CWS* (Manchester: Co-operative Wholesale Society, 1913); Stephen Yeo, *Who Was J. T. W. Mitchell?* (Manchester: Co-operative Wholesale Society Membership Services, 1995).
52. For the burying of 'education' in institutions during the nineteenth century, see Raymond Williams, *The Long Revolution* (London: Chatto and Windus, 1961); and Stephen Yeo, 'Education for association; Re-membering for a new moral world', in Jay Derrick and others, *Remaking Adult Learning: essays in adult education in honour of Alan Tuckett* (London: Institute of Education, 2010), pp. 128–146.
53. 'Liberty consists not in the *right* but in the *power* given to each individual in the community to develop his faculties ...': an editorial in *Labour League*, 16 Sept. 1848, quoted in Claeys, *Citizens and Saints*, p. 316.
54. See chapters 6 and 7 of Claeys, *Citizens and Saints*, 'Owenism and Chartism, 1836–45' and 'The legitimation of political socialism', pp. 208–273.
55. In chapter 4 of Claeys, *Citizens and Saints*, '"A mere trifle by comparison": social science, republicanism and political economy',

pp. 142-166 (with a useful summary on p. 145), he analyses 'the socialist notion of economic thought and development' in five ways, comparing it with the impact that classical political economy had on liberal political thought. He looks at 'the machinery question'; the emphasis on *exchange* as a central social activity and the 'displacement' of issues of justice and rights to the exchange process; the rejection of political radicalism's description of taxation as the principal cause of economic distress; the use by Owenites of the American model as the main example of the inadequacy of merely political institutions; and the re-emergence of enriched political ideals within Owenite economic theory and of 'quasi-political plans for future economic organisation'.

56. Eileen Yeo, 'Robert Owen and Radical Culture', in Sidney Pollard and John Salt (eds), *Robert Owen: Prophet of the Poor* (London: Macmillan, 1971), pp. 84-114.
57. These 'wings' were largely the creation of Sidney and Beatrice Webb.
58. Claeys, *Citizens and Saints*, p. 220.
59. Yeo, 'Co-operation, Mutuality and the Democratic Deficit'.
60. For surrounding mankind with circumstances, see Henry Hetherington's 'Last Will and Testament', as he was dying of cholera in 1849, in Claeys, *Citizens and Saints*, p. 229.
61. *New Harmony Gazette,* 12 July 1826, quoted in Harrison, *Quest for the New Moral World,* p. 82 n. 2.
62. Claeys, *Citizens and Saints*, p. 114.
63. Claeys, *Citizens and Saints*, p. 121.
64. Claeys, *Citizens and Saints*, p. 75.
65. J. F. C. Harrison (ed.), *Utopianism and Education: Robert Owen and the Owenites,* Classics in Education No. 31 (New York: Teachers College Press, 1968), is a useful collection of documents; see also Harold Silver, *English Education and the Radicals, 1780-1950* (London: Routledge, 1975).
66. Claeys, *Citizens and Saints*, p. 16.
67. Claeys, *Citizens and Saints*, p. 101: communities should contain no more than 3,000 people 'for very many important reasons respecting

education, training, occupation, wealth, amusements, and the general enjoyment of life; but especially because by this simple arrangement every one from birth to death will have his physical, intellectual, moral, practical and spiritual character well formed for him, and will be without difficulty well cared for through life by society'.

68. Claeys, *Citizens and Saints*, p. 81.
69. Claeys, *Citizens and Saints*, p. 77.
70. The now-classic sources for Robert Owen on education, morality, character, and the family are (for these and other Owenite writings which still speak directly to teachers): J. F. C. Harrison (ed.), *Utopianism & Education: Robert Owen and the Owenites*, cited in n. 65, and J. F. C Harrison, *Robert Owen and the Owenites in Britain and America; The Quest for the New Moral World* (London: Routledge, 1969).

Index

A
Accrington and Church Industrial Co-operative Society, 125
altruism, 275–276
apathy
  anti-politics, 285
  class, 18, 45
  human attribute, 36
  members, 40, 224–225
  politics, 87, 193, 194, 208, 285
Associate, The, 11
Association of Friendly Societies, 230
associations
  associationist socialism, 282–283
  autonomy and independence, 44, 45
  class, 27, 40–47
  class conflict, 37–38, 43
  collaboration, 230
  conflict over forms, 14–15
  definition, 10, 13
  democracy, 38, 40–47
  development, 28–29, 43, 48–49, 50–52, 281
  education, 39
  forms, 20–21, 23, 35–47, 51–52, 216, 227, 241
  funding, 39
  Guilds, 264, 265
  J.T.W. Mitchell, 126–133
  members, 38
  Owenite forms, 300–302
  power, 110–112
  registration, 42–43, 245–246
  religious, 258–261
  slogans, 11–13
  socialism, 84–85, 299–302
  specialisation, 217–218
  state involvement, 38, 39, 84–85, 86
  threats, 43
  voluntary, 14–15, 215–216, 222
  working class, 54, 113–114, 122, 123, 132–133, 190, 224
  (*see also* types of association)
Auden, W. H., 236
Augustine, St, 285–286
autonomy and independence, 44, 86–87, 163–164

B

Backstrom, Philip N., 113
Balfour, Gerald, 155
Belloc, Hilaire, 85
belonging, 218–219
Benjamin, Walter, 252
Bernstein, Eduard, 214
Beveridge, W. H., 65, 80, 216
Beveridge Report, 63
Birmingham, 84
Blake, William, 241, 242
Booth, General, 131
Braithwaite, William J., 46, 54, 55, 67–68, 71, 72, 74, 78, 82
Bray, John Francis, 295, 297
Brecht, Bertolt, 20, 33, 159
Briggs, Asa, 159, 174
Brighton, 12
British Association for the Promotion of Co-operative Knowledge, 293
British Medical Association, 71
Brown, Gordon, 164
Building Societies, 38, 225, 230, 245, 246
Bunbury, Sir Henry, 66
Bunyan, John, 147
Burke, Edmund, 184, 190, 224
Burt, Thomas, 132
Bury, 16
Butterworth, Thomas, 94, 100

C

Canada, 234
Capital, 29–30
capitalism
    class conflict, 26–27
    co-operation, 12, 13, 19
    growth of companies, 211–213
    history, 28–35
    and labour, 46–47
    production, 26–27
    social relations, 25
    use of term, 239
Carlyle, Thomas, 55
Carnegie, Andrew, 136
Chamberlain, Joseph, 45, 60, 73, 84
Charity Organization Society, 56
Chartism, 29, 45, 288, 294, 299
Christian Socialists
    Co-operative Wholesale Society, 114–115, 142
    correspondence, 114–115
    ideals, 108, 137
    productive co-operatives, 99–100, 113, 124, 140
    reactions to J. T. W. Mitchell, 107, 112, 130
civil society, 222, 227, 248, 262, 298, 302
Claeys, Gregory, 278, 280–282, 285, 292–295, 306

class, 25–26, 40–47, 137–151
(*see also* working class)
class conflict
  associations, 37–38, 43
  capitalism, 26–27
  change in social relations, 23–28, 34–35
  clubs, 38, 39, 69
  co-operatives, 10, 15, 69, 114, 133–137, 140, 256–257
  Marx, Karl, 255–257
clubs
  activities, 246
  class conflict, 38, 39, 69
  development, 37, 41–42
  finances, 102
  Leeds Club, 80
  study of, 245
Cobbett, William, 206
Cole, G. D. H., 170
collecting societies, 58, 69–70
Combine, 69–71
communism, 32, 50, 51, 236, 289
community, 13, 202, 218
companies, 21, 211–214, 215
Companies Acts, 41, 58, 228
competition
  business models, 217
  contrast with co-operation, 11, 296–297, 297–298
  co-operation, 12, 13, 19, 257
  struggle, 22–23
Conservatives, 151

consumers
  consumer or productive co-operation, 10, 13, 113–114, 122–123, 138–140, 146–148
  role, 222–223
co-operative and mutual organisations, *see* co-operatives; mutuals
Co-operative College
  activities, 169, 172, 175, 177, 181, 235
  formation, 160
  S. Yeo, 159
Co-operative Commission, 248
Co-operative Commonwealth, 37, 39, 48, 198, 269
Co-operative Congress
  Beatrice Webb, 116, 123
  Catherine Webb, 11
  descriptions, 273
  first series, 289, 300
  G. J. Holyoake, 118
  J. T. W. Mitchell, 99, 105, 116, 125, 128, 134, 137, 152–153
  presidents, 114, 134
co-operative education
  British Association for the Promotion of Co-operative Knowledge, 293
  development, 302–303
  funding, 14, 177
  organisation, 127, 169–170, 172, 176–177, 293

relevance of co-operation, 159
(*see also* co-operative studies)
Co-operative Futures, 247
Co-operative Group, 169, 223
Co-operative Heritage Trust, 159
Co-operative Insurance Society, 63
co-operative movement
  development, 17–18, 30, 44, 117–118
  ecology of enterprise, 247–248
  education, 14, 127
  Karl Marx, 30–31
  labour movement, 301
  missing from texts, 253–255
  practices, 46, 253
  radical experiment, 91, 92
  split between worker and retail, 247
  theory, 124–126
Co-operative News, The
  articles on Co-operative Wholesale Society, 108
  J. T. W. Mitchell, 99, 128
  letters, 142
  reports of Co-operative Wholesale Society meetings, 104
  title, 11
Co-operative Party, 283

co-operative politics
  aims, 279–280
  development, 283–284, 292
  neutrality, 284
  parliamentary representation, 162–163
  types, 283
co-operative principles, 163–167, 180, 181, 225–226
co-operative studies
  aims, 235–236
  definitions, 232–237
  focus, 248–249, 250, 253–261
  international comparisons, 245–246
  organic solidarity, 263–264
  social science, 271–277
  theories, 234, 237–244
  (*see also* co-operative education)
Co-operative Sundries Manufacturing Society, 147
Co-operative Union, 135, 153, 172, 176
Co-operative Wholesale Society
  bank, 109, 134
  bonus to labour, 100, 127
  brand names, 11
  Christian Socialists, 114–115, 142
  committees, 103–105, 115–116, 128–129, 146, 153, 155–156

competition, 111, 147
co-operative societies, 135, 143
  criticism, 140, 143, 146, 148
  descriptions, 115–116
  development, 12, 222–223
  director's fees, 102–105, 153
  employment, 146
  events, 103–104, 150
  governance, 143, 223–224
  growth of business, 110–111, 134, 148, 150, 298
  industrial disputes, 140–144
  leadership, 16–17
  members, 147
  membership of Manchester Chamber of Commerce, 106
  operations, 138, 139–141
  production, 15, 21, 139–142, 146–148, 150
  publications, 11, 12, 99, 108, 152
  publicity jigsaw, 90
  quarterly meetings, 99, 103–105, 106, 107, 110, 119, 123, 143, 155
  scale of business, 15, 91, 93, 225
  shipping, 110–111
  theory, 113
  threats, 230
  trade unions, 143

(*see also* Mitchell, J. T. W.)
co-operatives
  aims, 37, 243
  association not competition, 11
  attacks on, 130
  autonomy and independence, 45
  bonus to labour, 100, 127
  capital, 125
  capitalism, 141, 262
  class conflict, 10, 15, 69, 114, 133–137, 140, 256–257
  community, 202
  competition, 12, 13, 19, 257, 297–298
  concern of private capital, 15–16
  concern of state, 15–16
  conferences, 12
  consumer or productive co-operation, 10, 13, 113–114, 122–123, 138–140, 146–148
  criticism, 112–113, 121–122, 145
  definitions, 200, 252, 254
  democratic operations, 180–181, 183, 194–204
  democratic trends, 205, 207, 220–226
  development, 36, 99–100, 130–131, 134, 197–198, 202–203, 222

director's fees, 102–105
ecology, 229–230
elections, 98
employment for personal attributes, 142
forms, 232, 241
governance, 196, 198–200
ideals, 11
inequality, 230–231
large scale, 228–229
loyalty, 144–146
members, 37, 133, 135, 138, 196–197, 199–200, 230, 250–251, 268, 299–300
mutuality, 11, 203–204, 232, 248–252
neutrality, 284
ownership, 202–203, 205
parliamentary representation, 152–153
policies, 239–240
practices, 232
production, 15, 21, 49, 146–148, 296
profits, 13, 135, 138, 149–150, 150–151
reforming social order, 301–302
registration, 58, 215, 245–246
regulation, 214, 215, 216, 228–229
state support, 248
threats, 41–42, 229–230
universities, 158–159
working class, 16–18, 106, 109–110, 269
world-making project, 18
(*see also* associations)
Council for National Academic Awards, 163, 166
Crabtree, James, 106–108
Craig, E. T., 131
credit unions, 235, 245
Crosland, Anthony, 214

D
Dangerfield, George, 46
Darwin, Charles, 271, 272, 273, 275
democracy
  associations, 38, 40–47
  Chartism, 29, 45, 288, 294, 299
  Cold War, 192
  decision-making, 192, 208
  deficit, 206–208
  definition, 180, 187–193
  development, 206–208, 211
  forms, 190–191
  governance, 200–203
  mediation and democracy, 185–186, 190–191
  modern, 182–194
  move to private sector, 212
  participation, 182, 183, 184, 187, 188–189, 191–192, 193, 208–209

payment of members of parliament, 83
practice and project, 181–182, 226
traditional, 185
trends, 205
use of term by regimes, 211
(*see also* Co-operative Wholesale Society; co-operatives; members)
demutualisation, 250
Dicey, A. V., 53, 55, 56, 59–60, 67, 73, 77, 84–85
Dunn, John, 282, 284
Dunston-on-Tyne, 150
Durkheim, Emile
  Guilds, 265
  organic solidarity, 262–264, 266, 268
  religion, 295
  socialism, 84–85, 271
  writings, 161, 231, 254, 259–260, 270, 276

E
education
  adult, 174–175
  associations, 39
  J. T. W. Mitchell, 96, 136
  legislation, 56, 159, 177
  Owenite, 302–303
  relevance of co-operation, 159
  school boards, 47
  school co-operatives, 168, 169
  social history debates, 272–273
  transformative, 304–306
  working class, 49
  (*see also* co-operative education; universities)
Eldredge, Niles, 271
elections, 209
Elswick productive works, 139–140
Engels, Friedrich, 28, 31, 34, 257
Englander, David, 83
equality, 16, 219–221, 230–231, 242, 262, 304
equity, 202–203
eugenics, 81, 82
European Union, 213, 247

F
factories, 31
Fairbairn, Brett, 276, 277
families, 267–268, 270, 273, 298, 305
Federation of Worker Writers and Community Publishers, 160
fishing, 65–66
Ford, Boris, 158
Ford, Henry, 24
Foresters, 58, 60, 69
France, 161, 296, 301

Friendly Societies
　activities, 57–60, 71, 72, 75, 228
　affiliated orders, 58
　aims, 37
　Association of Friendly Societies, 230
　collaboration, 246
　democracy, 58
　governance, 54
　legislation, 228
　members, 68, 73, 198
　Registrar of Friendly Societies, 177
　Social Democratic Party disinterest, 83
　state control, 60, 84, 86
　state replacement of activities, 46, 49, 58, 72, 76
　state support, 41, 57–58
　study of, 245
　types, 57–60, 201
　use of registration, 245
　welfare state, 63, 65, 67–69
Fukayama, Francis, 192
funerals, 69, 93–95, 108

G
Gaia theory, 276–277
Gaia University, 171–172
Gandhi, Mahatma, 292
Germany, 276
Giddens, Anthony, 230, 254, 262, 264, 270
Gide, Charles, 242
Gilbert, Bentley, 68, 71–73
Gladstone, William Ewart, 190
Godin, Jean-Baptiste André, 141
Gosden, P. H. J. H., 58
Gould, Stephen Jay, 271
Gowers, Sir Ernest, 76
Grand National Consolidated Trade Union, 293–294, 298
Gray, John, 295–296
Gray, Kirkman, 80
Green, David, 289
Greening, Edward Owen, 107, 140, 141, 143, 153
Greenwood, Abraham, 124
Grundtvig, N. F. S., 170
Guilds, 264, 265
Gurney, Peter, 293

H
Halstead, Robert, 119
Hardie, Keir, 83
Harris, R. W., 75–76
Harrison, J. F. C., 306
Hayes, Thomas, 142
Healy, George, 127
Heckmondwike Co-operative Society, 107
Heckmondwike Manufacturing Company Ltd, 107
Hennock, E. P., 75

Hobhouse, L. T., 78, 85
Hobsbawm, E. J., 289
Hobson, J. A., 186
Hollowell, Hirst, 120
Holton, Bob, 85
Holyoake, George Jacob
  correspondence, 114–115
  temperance, 118
  writings, 18, 46, 130, 199, 203
  writings on Rochdale Pioneers, 12, 13, 109
Howard, Abraham, 94
Hughes, Thomas, 107, 114–115, 118, 124, 133, 148
human needs
  fundamental, 298
  material needs, 20–21, 23–24, 68–69
  membership, 195–196, 218–219
human rights, 63
Humboldt, Wilhelm von, 158
Huxley, T. H., 206, 271

I
Independent Labour Party, 70, 83, 151
individualism, 279, 298
Industrial and Provident Society Acts, 14, 41–42, 58, 228, 269, 291
inequality, 219–221, 230–231, 262, 270

insurance
  health insurance, 66–67
  National Insurance, 21
  providing organisations, 57–58, 59–60, 69–70
International Co-operative Alliance
  member of Ruskin College, 176
  Statement on the Co-operative Identity, 157, 158, 162, 169, 181, 196, 233, 234
International Labour Organization, 247
Ireland, 235

J
Jevons, W. S., 115
jigsaw, 90
Jones, Benjamin, 113, 142

K
Keeling, Ben, 79, 81, 86, 87
Khan Academy, 171–172
Knee, Mr, 82–83
Kropotkin, Peter, 273–274

L
labour
  association, 10–11
  bonus to labour, 100, 127
  capitalism, 29–35, 46–47

competition, 296–297
divisions of labour, 201, 217, 265, 266–267
Guilds, 264, 265
importance of class, 26, 27
potential of association, 18
strikes, 140–143
theories, 296
working conditions, 28, 70–71, 138, 140–143
(*see also* Royal Commission on Labour)
Labour Association, 140–141
labour movement, 192–193, 301
Labour Party
   development, 37, 38, 290
   Independent Labour Party, 70
   introduction of National Insurance, 83
   labour movement, 301
Lancashire and Yorkshire Productive Society, 97–98, 107, 108–109
Lancashire and Yorkshire Railway Company, 128
leadership, 258
Leeds Club, 80
Leeds Labour Exchange, 80
Leeds Redemption Society, 289
legislation
   associations, 42
   clubs, 41–42

Companies Acts, 41, 58, 228
education, 56, 159, 177
element of mutuality, 266
factories, 31
Friendly Societies, 228
Industrial and Provident Society Acts, 14, 41–42, 58, 228, 269, 291
National Health Service, 56
National Insurance, 49, 62, 67, 74
pensions, 56, 63
Poor Laws, 54, 61, 63
replacing democracy, 55–56
Ten Hours Act, 31
welfare, 64
Leicester Co-operative Boot Factory, 140, 142
Lever, W. H., 15, 49, 105, 151
Liberal Party, 206
liberalism, 45, 46, 151
liberty, 189, 242, 262
libraries, 96–97
Liebknecht, Karl, 48
Lincoln, 152, 171, 177
Lindqvist, Sven, 233
Lister Stead, J., 60
Lloyd George, David, 49, 54, 66, 67, 71, 74, 75, 76, 82, 83
locality, 233, 267, 305
London Co-operative Trading Association, 161
Lovelock, James, 276

Lovett, William, 161, 281, 296
loyalty to co-operatives,
144–146

M

MacPherson, Ian, 234
Malthus, Thomas Robert, 275
Manchester, 29, 91, 257
Manchester and Salford
Equitable Co-operative
Society, 106
Manchester Chamber of
Commerce, 106
Mann, Tom, 135, 148, 154
Mansbridge, Albert, 172
Margulis, Lynn, 276
Marshall, Professor, 116–117, 154, 155
Marx, Karl
class, 254, 255–257, 270
modernisation, 259, 262
social economy, 28–31
writings, 32, 33–34, 230–231, 288
Masterman, C. F. G., 74, 76, 77
Masterman, Lucy, 74
Mauss, Marcel, 161
Maxwell, William, 108, 109, 119, 120–121, 132
McKinsey Consultants, 173
Melmoth, Graham, 169
members
apathy, 40, 224–225

associations, 38
complexity of membership, 144–146
co-operative ownership, 198–200, 204–205, 230
definition, 194, 197–198
education co-operatives, 169–170
forms, 39
legislation, 269
limitations of membership, 207
loyalty, 144–146
needs, 195–196, 218–219
participation, 194–204, 208–209, 221–222, 224–226
universities, 160, 161, 168–170
value in co-operatives, 138, 250–251, 268, 299–300
voluntary membership, 196–197
working class in co-operatives, 37, 135
Mercer, T. W., 11
Michels, Roberto, 185, 217
Mill, John Stuart, 36, 185, 207, 241, 287
Millennium, 289
Miller, Miss, 94
Millgate Monthly, The, 11
Milton, John, 241, 242

Mitchell, J. T. W.
  accusations of corruption, 101–102
  attacks on, 104–105, 107–108, 110, 115, 120
  bonus to labour, 100, 127
  bringing consumers and producers together, 122–123
  business interests outside Co-operative Wholesale Society, 107, 128
  chairman of Co-operative Wholesale Society, 101, 103–104, 128–129
  childhood, 95–96
  Christian Socialist reactions, 107, 112, 130
  class, 133–137
  commitment to equality, 16
  Co-operative Congress, 99, 105, 116, 125, 128, 134, 137, 152–153
  death and funeral, 93–95, 104, 108, 133
  descriptions, 101, 112–114, 115–116, 119–121, 130
  education, 96, 136
  election to Co-operative Wholesale Society, 98
  ethic of association, 126–133
  friendships, 94
  gifts, 100
  human needs, 36
  humanity, 137–138
  humour, 118, 120
  importance of loyalty, 144
  importance of production, 147–149
  influence, 91–93, 99, 100
  Lancashire and Yorkshire Productive Society, 97–98, 107, 108–109
  membership of Mitchell Hey Society, 127
  membership of Rochdale Pioneers Society, 97, 98, 126–127
  personal attributes, 91–95
  politics, 151–156
  power of association, 110–112
  relationship with Co-operative Wholesale Society, 100, 101
  religion, 93, 95, 96–99, 118, 126, 128, 129, 137
  Royal Commission on Labour, 120, 125, 130, 133, 134, 138, 142, 146, 149, 154–156
  speeches and writings, 99, 124–126, 128, 134, 150, 152–153
  state control, 154–156
  strikes, 140–143

system, 137–151
teetotalism, 96–97, 118, 126, 129
tributes, 108
vision for co-operatives, 124–126, 137–139, 154–156, 234
working life, 97–98
Mitchell Hey Co-operative Manufacturing Society, 127
Mondragon, 178, 235
Morant, Robert, 72, 74
Morris, William, 31, 198, 291
Morrison, James, 288, 293
Mudie, George, 296–297
music, 164
mutuality
  co-operatives, 11, 203–204, 232, 248–252
  definitions, 249–250
  in legislation, 266
  members, 230
  new mutualism, 243, 271, 274–275
  as project, 248–252
  use of term, 247, 248–249
mutuals
  definitions, 203–204, 223–224, 254
  demutualisation, 250
  ownership, 200
  study, 242
  (*see also* co-operatives)

N
National Health Service, 56, 61
National Insurance
  aims, 85–86, 88
  funding, 81
  introduction, 63, 67–69, 71–78, 82–83
  legislation, 49, 62, 67, 74
  state control, 21
National Union of the Working Classes, 293
Neale, Edward Vansittart, 107, 108, 115, 124, 147, 150
Neil, John, 175
New Harmony, 203, 273, 289
new mutualism, 243, 271, 274–275
Newman, John Henry, 158
Newtown, 104
North East Music Co-operative, 164
Nuttall, William, 153

O
O'Brien, Bronterre, 288, 294–295
Oldham Equitable Co-operative Society, 136
Oliver, W. H., 294
Open College Network, 167, 172
Open University, 164, 165–166, 172
openness, 164–167

organic solidarity, 262–264, 267, 268
Owen, Robert
  associations, 300–302
  education, 302–303
  influence, 91–92, 126
  J. T. W. Mitchell as Owenite, 91–92, 134
  New Harmony, 203, 273, 289
  Owenite movement, 14, 123, 138, 155, 163, 296
  politics, 280–281, 286–289, 292, 293–295, 298
  Queenwood, 289
  social reform, 305–306
  social science, 186, 236
  socialism, 203–204, 278
  writings, 123
Oxford University, 170

P
Pagan, Mr, 96, 97
Paine, Thomas, 206
Parnell, Edgar, 199, 200
pensions
  Friendly Societies, 72–73
  funding, 62
  government subsidy, 59–60
  National Insurance, 71
  Pensions Act, 56, 63
People's Charter, 45
Pigstone, Mr, 106

Pitman, Henry, 104
policy studies, 239–240
politics
  anti-politics, 278, 285–286, 287–298
  apathy, 87, 193, 194, 208, 285
  associationism, 290, 291
  Chartism, 29, 45, 288, 294, 299
  co-operative, 279–284
  co-operative representation, 152–153
  development, 208, 209–211
  forms, 210
  J. T. W. Mitchell, 151–156
  mediation and democracy, 185–186, 190–191
  Owenite, 280–281, 286–289, 292, 293–295, 298
  social radicalism, 292–295
  society, 290–291
  support for co-operatives, 151
  (*see also* socialism)
Poor Laws, 54, 61, 63
Poor Man's Guardian, 157
Pratt, John Tidd, 14
pressure groups, 217
privatisation, 230
production
  Christian Socialists, 99–100, 113, 124, 140
  co-operative, 15, 21, 49,

146–148, 296
Co-operative Sundries
   Manufacturing, 147
Co-operative Wholesale
   Society, 15, 21, 139–142,
   146–148, 150
   Elswick works, 139–140
   Heckmondwike
      Manufacturing, 107
   Lancashire and Yorkshire
      Productive, 97–98, 107,
      108–109
   Leicester Co-operative Boot
      Factory, 140, 142
   Mitchell Hey Co-operative
      Manufacturing, 127
necessity, 25
ownership by workers or
   consumers, 10, 13, 113–114,
   147
Rochdale Flour Mill, 124
Rochdale Manufacturing, 98
profits
   bonus to labour, 100, 127
   in co-operatives, 13, 135, 138,
      149–150, 150–151, 202
Protestantism, 258–260
Prudential, 69–70
Pullman, Philip, 242
Putnam, Robert, 230

Q
Queenwood, 289

R
radicalism, 292–295
Radley, Bro, 59–60
Ralahine, 131
Reay, Lord, 114, 124
Redfern, Percy, 122, 149, 227
Reeves, Mrs Pember, 57
Registrar of Friendly Societies,
   177
religion
   anti-politics, 285
   capitalism, 27
   Christian Socialists, 99
   communities, 218
   J. T. W. Mitchell, 93, 95,
      96–99, 118, 126, 128, 129,
      137
   neutrality, 284
   Protestantism, 258–260
   purpose, 264
   religious studies, 251, 295
   support for bonus to labour,
      127
Reynolds, Stephen, 53, 66, 86,
   87–89
Ridley, Matt, 274
Rigby, Thomas, 16
Robinson, Eric, 157, 167
Rochdale, 93, 95, 156
Rochdale Corn Mill, 128
Rochdale Equitable Pioneers
   Society
   aims, 13, 240, 242, 299

development, 12, 13, 105
influence, 134, 245
loyalty, 144–145
membership of J. T. W.
 Mitchell, 97, 98, 126–127
Rochdale Flour Mill, 124
Rochdale Manufacturing
 Society, 98
Rogers, David, 274
Royal Commission on Health
 Insurance, 73
Royal Commission on Income
 Tax, 41
Royal Commission on Labour,
 120, 125, 130, 133, 134, 138,
 142, 146, 149, 154–156
Royal Commission on the Poor
 Laws, 54
Ruskin, John, 132, 186, 267
Ruskin College, 159, 160,
 166–167, 167, 175, 176–177
Russia, 274

S
school co-operatives, 169–170
Schools Co-operative Society,
 168
Schumpeter, J. A., 193
Scottish Co-operative
 Wholesale Society, 16–17,
 108, 132
self-help, 57
Shakespeare, William, 239

Shaw, George Bernard, 54
shipping, 110–111
Skinner, Quentin, 206
Smiles, Samuel, 130
Smith, Adam, 214
Smith, Elisha, 293
Smith, J. E., 288
Smith, William Hawkes, 302
soap, 15, 49
Social Democratic Party, 82, 83
social enterprises, 228, 248
social science, 203–204, 235–
 237, 252–255, 271–277
socialism
 associationist, 282–283
 associations, 84–85, 299–302
 class, 84
 class conflict, 85
 definitions, 278, 279–280
 development, 280–283,
  298–302
 social reform, 203, 305–306
 state, 45, 50, 252, 282–283
 transition, 242–244
society
 changes, 242–244, 262, 269
 history and struggle, 22–24
 human needs, 20–21, 298
 individuals, 298
 modernisation, 258–259,
  261–262
 organic solidarity, 262–264
 politics, 290–291

social relations, 24, 25–26
Society for the Study of Labour History, 83
Spencer, Herbert, 207
state
  appeals to, 286–287
  commercial transactions, 214
  control of Friendly Societies, 60, 84, 86
  co-operatives, 122
  definition, 189
  disconnect from society, 287
  funding, 47
  involvement in associations, 38, 84–85, 86
  regulation of organisations, 42–43, 213–217, 265–266
  relationship with individuals, 264
  socialism, 45, 50, 252, 282–283
  statism, 79–82
  support for associations, 39
  support for co-operatives, 248
  support for friendly societies, 41, 57–58
  welfare state, 60–65, 69, 74, 87–89
Statement on the Co-operative Identity, 157, 158, 162, 169, 181, 196, 233, 234
statism, 45, 46
Stedman Jones, Gareth, 78
suffrage, 31, 55–56
Sussex, University of, 159–160, 173
Sydney, Bernard, 79

T
Tawney, R. H., 172, 262
taxation, 41
teetotalism, 96–97, 118, 126, 129
Ten Hours Act, 31
Thatcher, Margaret, 298
Thompson, E. P., 173–174, 197, 205, 289
Thompson, William, 239, 295
Tillett, Ben, 55
Tit-Bits, 66, 75
Titmuss, Richard, 62
Tolpuddle Martyrs, 245
Tonnies, Ferdinand, 266
Totnes, 282
trade unions
  class conflict, 15
  and co-operatives, 134, 143
  development, 37, 72, 83, 246, 273
  education, 172, 176
  Grand National Consolidated, 293–294, 298
  labour movement, 301
  politics, 293–294
Tremenheere, H. S., 59
Tweddell, Thomas, 141, 142

U

United Kingdom Co-operative Council, 230
United Nations, 236
universities
  access to learning, 164, 165–166, 171–172, 172
  company universities, 175
  co-operative principles, 163–167
  co-operatives, 158–159, 167, 175–178
  definition, 158
  development, 158–160, 165–167, 170–173
  governance, 162, 165, 168, 169–170, 171–172, 176–177, 178
  members, 160, 161, 168–170
  research, 177–178
  transformation of higher education, 158
  (*see also* education)

V

values, 46–47
voluntary associations, 14–15, 215–216, 222
voluntary membership, 196–197

W

Wallace, Alfred Russel, 273
Watkins, W. P., 180
Watts, Dr John, 12, 126
Webb, Beatrice
  associations, 44, 122
  co-operation, 106, 116, 118, 121–122, 123
  descriptions, 54
  effect on co-operation, 191
  J. T. W. Mitchell, 93, 120, 121
  legacy, 123
  writings, 66, 72, 73, 282
Webb, Catherine, 11
Webb, Sydney
  associations, 44, 122
  co-operation, 106, 121–122, 191
  descriptions, 54
  legacy, 123
  writings, 66, 72, 73–74, 282
Weber, Max, 112, 230–231, 231, 254, 258–261, 270
welfare state, 60–65, 66, 74, 87–89
Wells, H. G., 54, 79
Wesley, John, 181
Wheatsheaf, The, 12
Wilby, Miss, 94
Williams, Raymond, 43, 168, 183, 241, 249
Williams, William Carlos, 22, 240
Wilson, Harold, 164

women, 11, 35, 75
Wood, Kingsley, 69, 71
Woolley, Bob and Tom, 53, 86, 87–89
Woolfenden, Thomas, 144–145
workers, *see* labour
Workers' Educational Association, 49, 168, 172, 198
working class
　associations, 54, 113–114, 122, 123, 132–133, 190, 224
　capacity to engage, 38, 40–41, 286–287, 299
　class conflict, 15–17
　concern of state, 18
　control of co-operatives, 16–18, 106, 109–110, 269
　criticism of statism, 45, 82
　education, 49
　involvement in associations, 40–47, 238–239
　involvement in elected bodies, 47
　movements, 30
　National Union of the Working Classes, 293
　potential for development, 15
　socialism, 281
working men's clubs, *see* clubs
Working Men's Clubs and Institute Union, 176
World Bank, 213
World Trade Organization, 212
Wright Mills, C., 186

Y

Yeo, Stephen, 159–160, 166, 175, 176–177, 233–234

www.ingramcontent.com/pod-product-compliance
Lightning Source LLC
Chambersburg PA
CBHW052129010526
44113CB00034B/1052